Margarete
Schütte-Lihotzky.
Architecture.
Politics. Gender.

NATIONAL **FUND**
OF THE REPUBLIC OF AUSTRIA FOR VICTIMS OF NATIONAL SOCIALISM

Edition Angewandte
Book Series of the University of Applied Arts Vienna
Edited by Gerald Bast, Rector

edition:'ʌngewʌndtə
Universität für angewandte Kunst Wien
University of Applied Arts Vienna

Margarete Schütte-Lihotzky. Architecture. Politics. Gender.

New Perspectives on Her Life and Work

Marcel Bois, Bernadette Reinhold (Eds.)

Birkhäuser
Basel

Contents

Encounters

The Political Margarete Schütte-Lihotzky

Kindergartens and Kitchens: Reflection and Reception

Appendix

Foreword

Juliet Kinchin

For a decade a photograph of Margarete Schütte-Lihotzky—indomitable, committed, cosmopolitan, and fun-loving—was pinned to the board above my desk in the Architecture and Design department of New York's Museum of Modern Art. Before going to university in the late 1970s I worked as an au pair in Frankfurt am Main, Germany, a city strongly identified with Schütte-Lihotzky's early career, and spent considerable time in kitchens and kindergartens, both typologies in which she excelled. Primed by this experience, I have found myself constantly returning to her work in my developing career as a design historian, university professor, and curator since the 1980s. While not blind to her flaws, I count myself as one of many women to have drawn inspiration from her professionalism, pragmatic idealism, and political engagement. What emerges strongly from discussions of the different dimensions of her life and work is a belief in community as well as a generosity in the way she continually sought to share knowledge and experience and to involve others, particularly women, making them aware of their potential to contribute to positive change and social transformation.

A century has now passed since Lihotzky and a small cohort of women studying at Vienna's Kunstgewerbeschule (today's University of Applied Arts Vienna) first broke into the male-dominated profession of architecture, a legacy celebrated by the recent opening of a center in the last apartment she occupied in Vienna's fifth district, which will focus on research into female pioneers of architecture. Now is a timely moment at which to revisit her contribution to affordable, socially driven design, not solely in relation to New Frankfurt, but also to her work further afield. At a time of "permacrisis" (a word chosen by Collins Dictionary to sum up the year 2022) and of a backlash against image-driven "starchitecture" and the sway of corporate culture, her star has continued to

Pinboard with a photo of Margarete Schütte-Lihotzky at a demonstration for women's rights and against nuclear weapons, Vienna 1961, in Juliet Kinchin's office, MoMA, New York, January 31, 2018.

rise. She is being discovered as a beacon of socially engaged architecture and collaborative, self-help practices by a new generation of artists, architects, and political activists. War in Europe, a cost-of-living crisis, growing social inequality, and the suppression of women's rights in many countries worldwide are all issues that Schütte-Lihotzky confronted directly through a combination of architectural practice and political activism. Her attempt to provide "warmed rooms" for Vienna's cold and hungry in 1945, for example, resonates with today's community-based warm banks.

Much of the German-language literature relating to Schütte-Lihotzky—including her 1985 memoir, *Erinnerungen aus dem Widerstand* (Memories of the Resistance), and her autobiography *Warum ich Architektin wurde* (Why I became an architect), published posthumously in 2002—has yet to be translated into English (other than selected passages from the latter). This fact accentuates the way in which her most famous project, the Frankfurt Kitchen, dominates the available English-language literature. The kitchens—some 10,000 examples of which were installed in Frankfurt in the late 1920s—also loom large in public perceptions of her material legacy. Since the 1970s, many have been dismantled, recycled, and presented in museums around the world. Indeed, the *afterlife* of the Frankfurt Kitchen as a museum object and basis for contemporary artworks has become a subject of intellectual inquiry in its own right. To the end of her life, Schütte-Lihotzky remained indignant that so little attention was accorded to her other activities: "If I had known that everyone would keep talking about nothing else, I would never have built that damned kitchen!" she said at the age of 101. Her significance certainly extends beyond a body of physical artifacts that can be reproduced, collected, or gathered in art galleries and museums from time to time, as emphasized by research in this volume drawing attention to the many immaterial dimensions of her life and work: some authors focus on her political formation, while others explore unrealized projects and the impact of pedagogical and social theory upon her working practices, or tackle her postwar conceptual work as an architectural adviser and commentator. New research is also deepening our understanding of her professional practice, whether in respect of the architectural training and opportunities open to women in Vienna or the nature of her contractual employment in Frankfurt and the Soviet Union.

Scholarship has developed apace since Schütte-Lihotzky's rediscovery in the wake of second-wave feminism in the late 1970s, and in recent years her life and work have been scrutinized from an increasingly diverse range of perspectives. In this volume of essays, architecture, politics, and gender—the themes that defined Margarete Schütte-Lihotzky's turbulent life story—are alternately teased apart and brought together across time and space in new and revelatory ways. Her life, work, and legacy are examined in all their multifaceted complexity through nuanced and amplified interpretations of her claims to fame—as a pioneering female architect, designer of the Frankfurt Kitchen, and a Resistance fighter.

The supportive intellectual and political climate of Frankfurt in the late 1920s was a far cry from Schütte-Lihotzky's experience of a "second exile" in her native Vienna during the Cold War. Her reputation has veered from international visibility in the late 1920s to a period of postwar obscurity before rediscovery in the last decades of her life, a process culminating in the recent spread of a posthumous hagiography. Schütte-Lihotzky lived long enough to assemble the extensive archive now lodged with her alma mater, the Kunstgewerbeschule, and to craft her life narrative in autobiographical writings and interviews. Her role in shaping her own critical reputation is now coming under scrutiny, pointing to telling omissions, errors, and elisions in her narration. She consciously guarded from public view the details of certain close relationships, such as that with her husband Wilhelm Schütte, who is markedly absent from her autobiographical writings. Ironically, his recent rehabilitation as a significant figure in architectural discourse and investigation of his contribution to projects undertaken jointly with Margarete have suffered the inverse of moves to uncover women's professional reputations that have so often been overshadowed by those of their more famous male partners. Excavations of her relationships with Otto Neurath and Herbert Eichholzer reveal how her political outlook ricocheted into her personal and professional life. The complex nature of collaboration and the intersection between politics and architectural practice are recurrent themes. Given the length of her career and the varied cultural contexts and political regimes in which she worked, it comes as no surprise to find that her dual roles as party activist and female architect were often fraught with tension and contradiction.

New lines of transnational enquiry elucidate the formation of her political outlook as well as the impact of her international networks upon architectural discourse on both sides of the Iron Curtain, despite limited opportunities for the practical implementation of her expertise in reconstruction projects. Schütte-Lihotzky spent many years living and working outside of Germany and Austria. The inclusion in this book of new perspectives relating to her time spent in the Soviet Union, Turkey, and China testify to the local and global reach of her legacy and her openness to foreign cultures and building traditions. Wherever she found herself she attempted to understand the local cultural context, resources, and needs of those she was working for, applying a lifelong principle based on helping others to help themselves. New research detailing her work in these different national contexts more precisely than ever, and examination of the complex localized reception of her ideas and projects, is beginning to adjust our overall sense of Schütte-Lihotzky, and opens up exciting lines of enquiry for the future.

November 2022
Scotland, UK

More than Just "That Damned Kitchen." New Perspectives on the Life and Work of Margarete Schütte-Lihotzky

Marcel Bois and Bernadette Reinhold

To the end, it was reduced to 1.9 by 3.4 meters: blue fronts, short distances, and an affordable price. The Frankfurt Kitchen was undoubtedly Margarete Schütte-Lihotzky's most revolutionary work. This, the first built-in kitchen in the world, was designed for the confined living conditions in the new social housing of the 1920s. Tasks in this room were subjected to time-motion studies. This invention catapulted the Austrian architect to international fame and is now found in design collections and museums worldwide, including the Museum of Modern Art in New York.[1] Nonetheless, she was loath to accept being reduced to it in public, as she often was: "If I had known that everyone would keep talking about nothing else, I would never have built that damned kitchen!"[2] In actual fact, Margarete Schütte-Lihotzky's life was much too multifaceted to be discussed only in terms of her famous kitchen space. As an architect, she aspired to shape society with the buildings she created. To achieve this goal, she worked with the giants in her profession, such as Adolf Loos, Ernst May, and Bruno Taut,

1 http://www.moma.org/collection/object.php?object_id=126451, accessed December 22, 2022. The reader is also referred here to an art project by the photographer Laura J Gerlach, *Die Bibliothek der Frankfurter Küchen* (the Frankfurt Kitchen library), which documents the worldwide locations of Frankfurt Kitchens.

2 Wojciech Czaja, "Besuch bei keiner Köchin," in Patrick Werkner (ed.), *Ich bin keine Küche. Gegenwartsgeschichten aus dem Nachlass von Margarete Schütte-Lihotzky* (Vienna: University of Applied Arts Vienna, 2008), 21–24, here 23.

Exhibition model of the "Frankfurt Kitchen," Frankfurt, 1927, photo: Hermann Traugott Collischonn.

designing municipal housing complexes in Red Vienna, village schools in Anatolia, and children's furniture in the Soviet Union. She drew up guidelines for the construction of kindergartens for the Chinese Ministry of Education and exhibited her projects at the World's Fair in Chicago. As a woman, she determined the course of her own life and forged a successful career in a male-dominated profession. In general, she had little interest in conventional notions of morality. In the conservatively Catholic Austria of the

1950s, she divorced her husband Wilhelm Schütte with no qualms at all and then lived alone for an extended period of time.

Aside from architecture, the biggest constant in her life was politics. Margarete Schütte-Lihotzky was an anti-Fascist, a Communist, and an activist on women's issues. For more than 60 years, she was a member of the Communist Party of Austria (KPÖ). For two decades, she chaired the League of Democratic Women of Austria (Bund demokratischer Frauen Österreichs, BDFÖ), an organization closely affiliated with the KPÖ. Eric Hobsbawn called his book on the period 1914–91 *The Age of Extremes*, and many of the extremes he discussed were reflected in her long life to an extent scarcely found in any other biography.[3] She not only lived in several European countries but also fought for her ideas in different political systems. These efforts were by no means beneficial to her career.

3 Eric Hobsbawm, *The Age of Extremes. A History of the World, 1914–1991* (New York: Pantheon Books, 1994).

From the mid-1950s onward, she received almost no public contracts from her home city of Vienna and also played virtually no role in the public discourse. Her architectural ability was beyond doubt. However, her being a Communist, an anti-Fascist Resistance fighter, and also a woman doomed her to social oblivion in the postwar era when the focus was on restoring the old order of an earlier age. Moreover, the networks that had supported her professional advancement in the interwar years had collapsed. She became a persona non grata, as she herself once said in later years.

That changed in the mid-1970s when she was rediscovered first by young architects and ultimately also by the broader public. The long-forgotten native daughter was now showered with honors and awards. It was as if Austria wanted to make amends for the wrongs done to her. She received the Austrian Decoration for Science and Art (*Österreichisches Ehrenzeichen für Wissenschaft und Kunst*) and the Grand Decoration of Honor in Gold with Star for Services to the Republic of Austria (*Grosses Goldenes Ehrenzeichen mit Stern für Verdienste um die Republik Österreich*). In addition, she was awarded a number of honorary doctorates. Exhibitions on her life's work were staged in Vienna and Milan.

The architect, who had spent more than four years in Nazi prisons because of her active involvement in the Resistance, increasingly appeared as a "contemporary voice of warning." In 1985, she attracted quite a bit of public attention when she published her Resistance memoirs *Erinnerungen aus dem Widerstand*. A decade later, she joined four other fellow victims of the Nazi terror to sue Jörg Haider, the chairman of the right-wing Freedom Party of Austria (FPÖ), for statements he had made that trivialized the Nazi extermination camps.[4] Schütte-Lihotzky observed with great concern the rise of Haider's party and right-wing populist tendencies in general. She was no longer alive to witness the swearing-in of the first coalition government between the FPÖ and the centrist-right Austrian People's Party (ÖVP). She had died just days before, on January 18, 2000, at the age of nearly 103.

4 "'Ein Hohn für alle Opfer der Nazis.' Fünf NS-Opfer klagen Haider wegen 'Straflager'-Aussage," *Wiener Zeitung* (July 14, 1995).

Even after her death, Schütte-Lihotzky continued to be present in the Austrian media. Yet the coverage focused mainly on only a few aspects of her life, so she is still considered today to be an "undisputed legend in the history of 20th century architecture." Reference works praise her as "Austria's first female architect," "a pioneer of social architecture," "the inventor of the Frankfurt Kitchen," "an activist in the women's movements," and "a heroine in the Resistance against the Nazi dictatorship."[5] Her rich body of architectural and interior design work is usually reduced to the Frankfurt Kitchen, as mentioned above. In short, the picture the public has of Schütte-Lihotzky is anything but nuanced and is restricted to a certain image. Many narratives are repeated constantly.

5 Wojciech Czaja, "Margarete Schütte-Lihotzky: Diese verdammte Küche!," *Der Standard* (January 20, 2017).

At the same time, researchers have recently intensified their efforts to explore Schütte-Lihotzky's life and work, which led to a small publication boom around the 20th anniversary of her death. For instance, Karin Zogmayer shepherded the reissuing of Schütte-Lihotzky's memoirs up to 1939, *Warum ich Architektin wurde* (Why I became an architect), which had long been out of print. Thomas Flierl published the heretofore unknown prison correspondence between Margarete and Wilhelm Schütte from the years 1941 to 1945. Christine Zwingl explored the mark that Schütte-

Lihotzky had made on Vienna. Mona Horstcastle presented the first biography of her that is aimed at a general audience, and Wilhelm Schütte has also become the subject of initial research work.[6]

Further publications are expected in the near future. Of special note are the efforts of the Margarete Schütte-Lihotzky Club in Vienna, which actively seeks to keep its namesake's memory alive with exhibitions, events, and publications. S. E. Eisterer is preparing an English translation of Schütte-Lihotzky's *Erinnerungen aus dem Widerstand* (Memories from the Resistance). The American author Helen Young Chang is taking a literary approach to Schütte-Lihotzky's biography. And Marcel Bois is conducting a historical and biographical research project to show the transnational political and professional networks in which the Communist and architect moved.

All this research is based on the estate of Schütte-Lihotzky located in the University Archive of the University of Applied Arts Vienna ("die Angewandte"), where it is the most frequently requested set of archival holdings. New questions and perspectives from a variety of disciplines have given rise to a more differentiated view of Schütte-Lihotzky and led to the idea of staging an academic conference to focus on all of these research trends. It took place at the Angewandte in Vienna on October 9 and 10, 2018 and set off a productive exchange, as evidenced by the conference proceedings released in 2019.[7] We are pleased that this publication is now available in English, giving an international audience their first comprehensive overview of the life and work of Margarete Schütte-Lihotzky.

A broad interdisciplinary approach was applied throughout the book. The essays are divided into five main sections. The first, Biographical and Gender-Historical Perspectives, begins with Karin Zogmayer exploring Schütte-Lihotzky's "One Hundred Years Lively and Alert," her personality, and the myth surrounding her. In the next chapter, Christine Zwingl traces the path the artist took in her life and work, always true to the motto "Planning and Building—These Things Matter to You Women." Zwingl is a member of the Schütte-Lihotzky Research Group and helped to compile

6 See the selected bibliography in the annex.

7 Marcel Bois and Bernadette Reinhold (eds.), *Margarete Schütte-Lihotzky. Architektur. Politik. Geschlecht. Neue Perspektiven auf Leben und Werk* (Basel: Birkhäuser, 2019); also see the conference reports: Sebastian Engelmann, "Architektur. Politik. Geschlecht. Neue Perspektiven auf Leben und Werk Margarete Schütte-Lihotzkys. Konferenz in Wien," *Arbeit. Bewegung. Geschichte. Zeitschrift für historische Studien* 18, no. 1 (2019): 142–45; Anna Stuhlpfarrer, "Architektur. Politik. Geschlecht. Neue Perspektiven auf Leben und Werk Margarete Schütte-Lihotzkys," *H-Soz-Kult* (March 13, 2019), accessed December 8, 2022, http://www.hsozkult.de/conferencereport/id/tagungsberichte-8162, printed in *Zeitgeschichte in Hamburg 2018* (Hamburg: Forschungsstelle für Zeitgeschichte in Hamburg, 2019), 109–16.

the oeuvre catalog around 1990, which remains valid today. Sabine Plakolm-Forsthuber then examines the dictum of Schütte-Lihotzky being "the first female architect" by outlining the education and work situation of the earliest female architects and putting Schütte-Lihotzky's own career into context. Finally, Bernadette Reinhold considers the interface of reception and (auto)biographical narrations but also examines the omissions in Schütte-Lihotzky's own memoirs.

The section entitled Stations in the Life of a Transnational Female Architect covers a large span in terms of both time and place. S. E. Eisterer analyzes Lihotzky's active involvement in the early Viennese settlement movement in a collation applying contemporary theory and practice. In her chapter, Claudia Quiring demonstrates just how pervasive political and gender-specific aspects are in Schütte-Lihotzky's work by describing the broad range of projects from her time in Frankfurt am Main (1926–30). Until now the architect's years in the Soviet Union (1930–37) have barely been illuminated for many reasons. Drawing on heretofore unknown sources, Thomas Flierl offers a critical and nuanced overview of the architect's projects but especially of her work situation and of the way in which she positioned herself politically. Her projects in Turkey (1938–40) also clearly show that a young state generates new construction tasks. Burcu Dogramaci delves into, among other things, the development of standard-type village schools that could be modified to meet local conditions. Tapping into forgotten architectural discourses in postwar Vienna, Monika Platzer investigates Schütte-Lihotzky's (non)participation in the building sector in the context of the Cold War. The architect also had important transnational experiences on her travels to China in 1934 and 1956. Helen Young Chang shows how stimulating the architectural and urban tradition of this country became for Schütte-Lihotzky and how ambivalently she articulated her attitude toward its political system. Little is known about the architect's engagement in Socialist countries after 1945. Carla Aßmann describes examples of how surprisingly uncompromising Schütte-Lihotzky was in her judgment of construction policies in the GDR despite her political convictions.

The next section, Encounters, revolves around significant yet scarcely explored relationships. They were selected in part based not on their duration but their intensity. An inspiring friendship was the bond connecting Schütte-Lihotzky to Otto Neurath, for instance, one of the least conventional protagonists in Red Vienna. In his essay, Günther Sandner delineates how this friendship came about and ultimately ended in a politically motivated alienation between the two of them. In Turkey, the architect Herbert Eichholzer became Schütte-Lihotzky's crucial link to the Communist Resistance in Austria, as Antje Senarclens de Grancy explains in her contribution. Amazingly enough, Schütte-Lihotzky's autobiographical writings make little or no mention of her husband Wilhelm Schütte. This was one reason that Wilhelm, the focal point of David Baum's essay, long stood in the shadow of his prominent wife and architectural colleague.

The title of the section The Political Margarete Schütte-Lihotzky actually applies to the entire publication. Nonetheless, a separate section is devoted to the architect's explicitly political work. Marcel Bois leads off by outlining Schütte-Lihotzky's decades-long commitment as an activist that spans from her politicization in 1920s Red Vienna to her self-critical coming to terms with Stalinism after 1990.[8] Next is a chapter by Elisabeth Boeckl-Klamper, who puts Resistance activity and imprisonment in context on the solid basis of source material. After 1945, a change could be observed in Austrian society from a general anti-Fascist consensus to anti-Communist hegemony, as Manfred Mugrauer vividly depicts in his essay. Schütte-Lihotzky was affected by this change in several ways. It is why she shifted her professional focus and became politically engaged in the League of Democratic Women of Austria, as Karin Schneider so clearly explains.

It would be amiss if a scholarly compendium of writings about Margarete Schütte-Lihotzky failed to examine her best-known areas of work. The section Kindergartens and Kitchens: Reflection and Reception starts with Sebastian Engelmann's pedagogical look at the planning of buildings for children. Christoph Freyer then presents the evolution of Schütte-Lihotzky's kindergarten buildings and explains

8 This text is a slightly revised version of the following article: Marcel Bois, "'Bis zum Tod einer falschen Ideologie gefolgt.' Margarete Schütte-Lihotzky als kommunistische Intellektuelle," in *Zeitgeschichte in Hamburg 2017* (Hamburg: Forschungsstelle für Zeitgeschichte in Hamburg, 2018), 66–88. This contribution was not in the German version of this book. In exchange, we refrained from including an English translation of Bois's text "Soziale Beziehungen und kommunistische Netzwerke. Annäherungen an Hans Wetzler (1095–1983)" (Social Relationships and Communist Networks. Pondering Hans Wetzler (1905–1983)) that was originally found in the Encounters chapter.

their significance. And, last but not least, there are two essays that focus on the Frankfurt Kitchen and its reception. Änne Söll's analysis covers, inter alia, the gender-specific aspects that are included in as well as those that are omitted from presentations and stagings of the kitchen in a museum context. Finally, Marie-Theres Deutsch describes how the famous kitchen has taken on a life of its own, one manifestation of which is a "facadism" in international art trade and contemporary art production.

Besides a brief biography and an overview of key literature by and about Margarete Schütte-Lihotzky, the appendix contains a word of thanks to everyone who assisted with this publication. We would like to mention several of them at this juncture. Along with the authors, we want to express our thanks in particular to Gerald Bast, Rector of the University of Applied Arts Vienna, who has supported this project from the outset with keen interest and the necessary resources. Our appreciation also goes out to our collaborator for the 2018 conference, the Research Center for Contemporary History in Hamburg (FZH), particularly to Deputy Director Kirsten Heinsohn. In addition, we extend our thanks to Juliet Kinchin. We are delighted that she agreed to write the preface to the English edition of this book.

The entire endeavor would have been completely inconceivable without the tireless support we received from the University Archive of the University of Applied Arts Vienna. A special thanks goes to Archive Director Silvia Herkt and to Nathalie Feitsch, who was responsible for providing a large part of the reproductions. The wonderful translation of this book was carried out by Mark Wilch. Along with the authors' essays, he translated the numerous quotations in the text with tact and sensitivity. All of them were originally in German unless explicitly stated otherwise. Belinda Zauner copyedited and proofread the volume with the greatest of care, patience, and flexibility. Our warm thanks to both of them and to Olga Wukounig and Anja Seipenbusch-Hufschmied from the University of Applied Arts Vienna for the smooth project management on the part of Edition Angewandte and Katharina Holas from Birkhäuser Verlag. Not least, we would like to thank the Stransky family, who accompanied this project with warm goodwill. From their attitude, it was always clear that they were so much more than just Margarete Schütte-Lihotzky's legal successors.

In this collection of writings, the research coalesces and interconnects at many points yet also reveals areas in which desiderata may lie. The book will have met a main objective if it not only opens up new perspectives on Margarete Schütte-Lihotzky's life and work to an international readership but also provides fresh impetus above and beyond that.

Vienna and Hamburg, spring of 2023

Biographical and Gender-Historical Perspectives

One Hundred Years Lively and Alert. On the Vitality of Margarete Schütte-Lihotzky

Karin Zogmayer

How does a person observe his or her 100th birthday? What is a fitting way to mark a century of life? Margarete Schütte-Lihotzky had a convincing answer to this question: she celebrated with a large and festive birthday gathering at MAK—Austrian Museum of Applied Arts, Vienna, where she danced a waltz with the then mayor of Vienna to one of Johann Strauss's best-known works: *Künstlerleben (Artist's Life)*.

It was foreseeable that her Viennese waltz on January 23, 1997 would quickly make the rounds as an anecdote and contribute to the late stylization of her personality. This image of the waltzing centenarian is as inseparably linked to Schütte-Lihotzky today as is the image of her as the inventor of the Frankfurt Kitchen.

What may appear to be simplistic codifications at first glance become more than superficial clichés on closer examination. In fact, they can be read as pointed and apt characterizations.

The Misunderstanding about the Kitchen

Let's look first at this identification of Schütte-Lihotzky with the kitchen she co-designed while working for the Hochbauamt (central building authority) in Frankfurt.

Well into old age, Schütte-Lihotzky expressed intense indignation that the Frankfurt Kitchen had been declared her most important work and she argued for decades against this view. Yet she did devote two chapters to this project in *Erinnerungen und Betrachtungen* (Memories and reflections), the working title of her autobiographical manuscript. In doing so, she conceded its significance in her architectural oeuvre.[1]

1 Margarete Schütte-Lihotzky, *Warum ich Architektin wurde*, ed. Karin Zogmayer, 1st ed. (Salzburg: Residenz, 2004), 145–63. A second edition was published by Residenz in 2019; however, the quotations below are taken from the first edition.

In a move typical of her, she made the best of this attribution by shifting the matter to a rational, objective level, where she could check it off as a marketing message by the Hochbauamt and as naïveté in the public reception of the kitchen: "It fed into the notions among the bourgeoisie and petite bourgeoisie at the time that women essentially work in the home at the kitchen stove. That is why—so this logic continues—a female architect would know best what is important for cooking."[2] As with all her planning tasks, Schütte-Lihotzky approached this one systematically—and did not build on any personal skills in kitchen matters. On this subject, she always felt it important to point out that she herself had never run a household prior to helping develop the Frankfurt Kitchen nor had she had any cooking experience.

2 Ibid., 150.

She always sought to accurately grasp the situation at hand, then come up with and clarify possibilities for improving it. That is clear from her highly precise and conscientious use of language and terms of art. For instance, she said the very name "Frankfurt Kitchen" was "misleading," because the project involved but was not solely confined to "designing a kitchen—with a more or less practical layout, fitted with more or less practical elements."[3] To her mind, the revolutionary aspect lay in the project's "technical and financial merging of housing construction with a fully appointed kitchen" that spared "so many people work and effort for two to three decades."[4]

3 Ibid., 148.

4 Ibid., 152

On its inception in the mid-1920s, the Frankfurt Kitchen represented a huge advance in at least two respects. First, the meticulously designed layout of all the elements that were used in such carefully considered ways saved time that occupants could spend in other ways. Schütte-Lihotzky saw the rationalization of housework as a very concrete chance for women running a household to pursue a career and to lessen their economic dependence on their husband, while freeing up time for their own education—although she did somewhat idealize the time actually freed up. In a word: it represented emancipatory progress. Second, the Frankfurt Kitchen consisted of built-in furniture designed for the space and rented out as a fixed part of the apartment. This innovation allowed for a much smaller kitchen floor plan and thus lower costs that could, in turn, be invested in other kitchen features. It also saved renters time and money they would otherwise have had to spend on these items.

The Frankfurt Kitchen can therefore definitely serve as a prototypical work in Schütte-Lihotzky's oeuvre. However, it should not be seen in the simplified way it usually is—namely, as a practical kitchen design still attractive to today's eyes—but rather viewed as historically embedded and in its totality.

Living the "Artist's Life" for a Century

The waltz on her 100th birthday sprang not from the spry centenarian's spontaneous desire for exercise; it was a set item on the program for this celebration. Its inclusion was not a clever idea cooked up by a PR agency either. Very simply, it suited Margarete Schütte-Lihotzky to celebrate festive occasions whenever the opportunity arose. That same year she also opened the traditional dress ball of the Communist Party of Austria (KPÖ), the "Left Dance," by dancing a short waltz.

Celebrate festive occasions, celebrate life. That may well have been the secret to her long life, which she lived as she saw fit, lively and alert to the very end—until dying of influenza on January 18, 2000, just days before her 103rd birthday. She reached this mythical age despite or perhaps because of the many adversities she faced—illnesses, the sudden loss of her parents, involuntary childlessness, betrayal, four years of imprisonment during World War II, painful separations, professional disappointments, her partner's suicide ...

Frail Child, Tuberculosis as the Family Disease

No one would probably have prophesied that the teenage Grete Lihotzky would have such a long and healthy life. She

5 Margarete Schütte-Lihotzky, *Erinnerungen aus dem Widerstand 1938–1945*, ed. Chup Friemert (Hamburg: Konkret Literatur Verlag, 1985), 11.

6 University Archive of the University of Applied Arts Vienna, Nachlass Margarete Schütte-Lihotzky (UAUAK, NL MSL), TXT/587, 18.

7 Ibid.

described herself several times as "very delicate of health,"[5] as "of frail health from childhood on"[6] and cites this as the reason her parents made her take a "year of rest"[7] at the less demanding Graphische Lehr- und Versuchsanstalt (Graphic Teaching and Research Institute) before transferring to the Kunstgewerbeschule (School of Arts and Crafts; today's University of Applied Arts Vienna). There she completed her architectural studies in 1919, becoming one of the first women to do so.

Lihotzky's father died in 1923 of acute tuberculosis, followed just a year later by her mother, who also succumbed to *morbus viennensis* or the Viennese disease. That same year Margarete Lihotzky came down with this raging public disease herself and had to spend several months at the tuberculosis sanatorium in Grimmenstein to recover from it. This by no means meant that the young architect, who had already gained a firm foothold professionally, took a rest from her work. During her stay, she did an in-depth study of the spaces surrounding her and devised a project called "Tuberculosis Sanatorium," which was shown at the Hygiene Exhibition in the Vienna Messepalast in the spring of 1925.

Although physical vitality was perhaps not a trait genetically passed on to her, the stories Schütte-Lihotzky told do indicate that her parents created a home environment very conducive to good mental health.

Wartime, Death Sentence, Communal Living

In January 1941, it certainly looked as if her last hour had come. To work in the anti-Nazi Resistance, she had left Turkey after an extended stay and returned to her hometown of Vienna. An informer betrayed her as an activist one day before her 44th birthday, and she was arrested by the Gestapo. A death sentence was certain. But thanks to an employment contract her husband Wilhelm Schütte had falsified in Ankara and other fortunate circumstances and coincidences, she was merely sentenced to 15 years in prison.

During the years she spent there until liberation in the spring of 1945, Margarete Schütte-Lihotzky was subject to the more severe physical and psychological conditions of incarceration in times of war—a challenge she accepted

Margarete Schütte-Lihotzky, age 94, at the University of Fine Arts Hamburg receiving honorary membership of that institution, June 1991.

and overcame. Two documents bear testimony to this: her prison correspondence with her husband and sister,[8] which was published by Thomas Flierl in 2021, and her incredibly powerful and sometimes astonishing *Erinnerungen aus dem Widerstand* (Memories from the Resistance). In the latter she gives impressive, and sometimes humorous, accounts of communal life among the (political) prisoners, despite their

8 Margarete Schütte-Lihotzky and Wilhelm Schütte, *"Mach den Weg um Prinkipo, meine Gedanken werden Dich dabei begleiten!" Der Gefängnis-Briefwechsel 1941–1945*, ed. Thomas Flierl (Berlin: Lukas Verlag, 2021).

being in solitary confinement at times. For instance, she did not miss the opportunity to celebrate International Workers' Day on May 1, 1942—using her toilet and the train of pipes leading from it as a means of communication. As a keynote speaker, Schütte Lihotzky once held a short address about the position of women in the Soviet Union. And shared an anecdote that had to be included in this context: "We ended by all singing 'The Internationale.' Prison was the only place in Austria 'The Internationale' could still be sung on International Workers' Day, May 1, 1942. An unforgettable celebration."[9]

Besides her own life-affirming disposition, the strong social cohesion among the comrades was certainly a crucial factor in Schütte-Lihotzky living through this period so relatively unscathed: "I never had the feeling at the time of being excluded from human society, despite the locked door, despite the iron bars between the sky and my cell. Only my physical life was restricted; my intellectual life was livelier than ever and far-ranging [...].[10] True life unfolds on the inside: "The everyday external adversities to which you become accustomed after such a long time played no role to speak of [...] even being screamed at and the diatribes, insults, and humiliations, you simply did not feel them as such, they bounced off you [...]."[11] Later, from a distance, Schütte-Lihotzky herself expressed surprise that "not a single one of the women who expected death sentences for themselves or for close family members broke down," and emphasized the "extraordinary self-discipline" each and every one of them displayed for the good of all: "Because if a single prisoner had broken down, it would have set off a chain reaction and caused others to break down, too."[12]

In his numerous publications and lectures, the American author and longevity expert Dan Buettner cites certain principles as reasons for a healthy, century-long life. Besides natural exercise and nutritional habits, they include having a purpose in life, belonging to a group or a faith, and living life in an environment that is sustaining and supportive. These last three factors are part of Schütte-Lihotzky's vita even in what appear from the outside to be her darkest days—namely, her time in prison during World War II.

9 Margarete Schütte-Lihotzky, *Erinnerungen aus dem Widerstand. Das kämpferische Leben einer Architektin von 1938–1945*, ed. Irene Nierhaus, new ed. (Vienna: Promedia, 1998), 92.

10 Ibid., 108–9.

11 Ibid., 178.

12 Ibid., 103.

Of course, these extreme years did leave their debilitating marks on her. Among them was a new tuberculous focus that forced Margarete Schütte-Lihotzky first to move into a TB cell in the infirmary at Aichach Prison and, after liberation in the spring of 1945, to spend nearly half a year in the tuberculosis sanatorium in Hochzirl in the Austrian province of Tyrol as a stopover point before finally being able to move about at will in the fall of 1945. In a taped conversation with Chup Friemert, she also cited the war years as the reason for her and her husband's divorce in 1951. They had spent those years in such different ways that it made reconciliation impossible, as was the case for so many other couples during this period.[13] Schütte-Lihotzky concluded her anti-Nazi Resistance memoirs with a quote from Pablo Neruda: "One minute of darkness does not make us blind"[14]—these words are the elderly author's summation of the war years she spent in prison. She had checked off this chapter of her life and now turned to a new page. And given her long life, these four years that she reduces to a minute lose quantitative significance, also when viewed from the outside. The fact that she escaped the execution planned for her in 1941 and went on to live in peace and good health for another 60 years was also a form of redress for what she had suffered at the hands of the Nazis.

13 See Schütte-Lihotzky, *Erinnerungen* (1985), 39.

14 Schütte-Lihotzky, *Erinnerungen* (1994), 185.

The major significance of the KPÖ in Margarete Schütte-Lihotzky's life and her unshakable, even unreflecting, commitment to it certainly had much to do with the powerful experiences of community she had had while incarcerated. The security that political prisoners felt among themselves served as a kind of life insurance, and their solidarity as something they could implicitly rely upon. Along with her general view of the world, this experience was also one reason she remained a loyal party member to the very end.

Party Life, Family Life

The significance of political comrades in her life could well have had something to do with the vacuum created by her not having a family of her own: the party took over this function, and Schütte-Lihotzky never questioned her clear and public commitment to it despite serious disadvantages for her career.

Margarete Schütte-Lihotzky and Wilhelm Schütte remained friends even after their divorce and carried out projects together. But their marriage was in ruins. They had no children. This unfulfilled wish diminished neither her buoyant enjoyment of life nor her professional preoccupation with kindergartens and day nurseries, which became a focal point, perhaps the main focal point, of her work. With keen interest and dedication, she devoted herself to researching the lifeworld of children and to creating environments full of suitable, nurturing spaces for them.

Her adult life prior to World War II revolved around her career. She met her future husband Wilhelm Schütte as an architectural colleague at the Hochbauamt in Frankfurt. Their relationship was shaped by their shared interests and their work together.

After the war, the center of Schütte-Lihotzky's life shifted from architecture to politics, so it is only logical that her second life partner would also come from this realm and from her political networks. Unlike her marriage to Wilhelm Schütte, she declared her 30-year friendship and relationship with Hans Wetzler to be an absolutely private matter. Through papers and photos contained in two boxes in her estate labeled "Hans," Schütte-Lihotzky unveiled him to the public for the first time posthumously as the second important man in her life.[15]

15 On Hans Wetzler, see Marcel Bois, "Soziale Beziehungen und kommunistische Netzwerke. Annäherungen an Hans Wetzler (1905–1983)," in *Margarete Schütte-Lihotzky. Architektur. Politik. Geschlecht. Neue Perspektiven auf Leben und Werk*, ed. Marcel Bois and Bernadette Reinhold (Basel: Birkhäuser, 2019), 224–36.

When Hans Wetzler, already ravaged by disease, committed suicide in 1983, the then 86-year-old Schütte-Lihotzky lost her most trusted friend. She saved the farewell letter from her soul mate, a man eight years her junior. And she carried on with her life.

"Banned from Her Profession"

Although Schütte-Lihotzky initially received several public contracts in the early postwar years, she was boycotted as an architect by the Stadtbauamt, the central building authority in Vienna, from the late 1940s on. The suspicion of a formal municipal decision to this effect was confirmed when Roland Rainer sought to hire her as an employee and the Stadtbauamt denied his request. Whether this happened because she had left the Social Democratic Workers' Party in 1927 owing to the events surrounding the Vienna Palace of Justice fire or, as is commonly assumed, because of her membership in the Communist Party, the reason was in any case political.

On his radio show *Im Gespräch*, Peter Huemer asked his guest Schütte-Lihotzky whether she had ever considered leaving the KPÖ in order to land contracts again. The energetic talker became audibly irritated: "No, I have never considered that; the thought never entered my mind."[16] To deny the party, her own family, in order to get back on her feet professionally was not even a conceivable option for Schütte-Lihotzky. She lived an upright life and made the best out of the situation. Contracts from abroad kept her afloat.

16 Peter Huemer in conversation with Margarete Schütte-Lihotzky, Radio Ö1, first broadcast June 1994.

Nonetheless, she naturally thought the boycott by liberated Austria was unjust—especially considering that former National Socialists were landing major public construction contracts. What bothered her more about the boycott was that it prevented her from doing something beneficial for her country and city. She commented on this aspect in a 1994 interview: "I am clearly not given to bitterness; I do not feel at all hopeless."[17] In other words, no great lament from her even in this context; instead, the simple regret of not being allowed to bring her decades of skills to bear in rebuilding her hometown.

17 Ibid.

The situation did not change until around 1980 when she began being singled out for special honors and tributes. But at that point she was already too old to work as an architect anyway.

A Century Lived in Full Awareness

Margarete Schütte-Lihotzky is probably one of the few individuals who consciously experienced the entire 20th century—and not just in her hometown of Vienna. She lived abroad for more than 20 years: several months in Rotterdam after completing her studies, later in Frankfurt am Main, in the Soviet Union, in Paris, in Istanbul and after World War II, for a short time also in Cuba and East Berlin. Her extensive travels took her, inter alia, on trips throughout China and Japan and to the most important cities of Europe.

Her affirmation of the present also always extended to places and people that were different from herself. This is shown by her openness and her unbiased interest in foreign cultures and her matter-of-factness in the way she approached them. Margarete Schütte-Lihotzky viewed herself as a socially responsible human being acting within society and on behalf of society. And for her, society was always greater than her immediate surroundings: "Humankind—A Family" were three words she wrote down as a possible title for her autobiographical memoir.[18]

18 UAUAK, NL MSL, TXT 554.

Margarete Schütte-Lihotzky not only saw more than most people of her generation, she also probably experienced much more. The hand of fate by no means spared her; life showed itself to her in all its manifold complexity. She approached life with keen interest, always alert and present, for more than a century.

Of course, the music program at Schütte-Lihotzky's large 100th birthday party did not confine itself to a single Strauss waltz. The organizers wanted to give the doyenne of Austrian architecture a fitting musical tribute as well. After a polonaise by Schubert, Webern's op. 5, *Five Movements for String Quartet*, was played. In this piece the composer freed himself from rigid tonality and from established forms to create a work that stood for a whole new way of experiencing time.

"Planning and Building—These Things Matter to You Women." Margarete Schütte-Lihotzky's Lifelong Democratic Commitment on Behalf of Women

Christine Zwingl

> It is so very important for all aspects of our life—that things are built and how they are built—so important for our work in the household, factory, or office—so important for our health, for the health and education of our children and young people—so important for overall happiness in our families and in our lives! And practically everything is important for us women—starting with overall regional planning to urban planning, from housing construction to apartment appointments, to furniture and even to the way we can store our cooking spoon in the kitchen, all these things are interdependent.

The architect Grete Schütte-Lihotzky was addressing women with this article entitled "Planen und Bauen, Euch Frauen geht es an" (Planning and building—these things matter to you women). She spoke directly to them, conveying a message about architecture and a position that we would refer to today as feminist and highly political.

> And it is important for us women to recognize that every mistake made in planning and building—regardless of whether it is in regional planning or in the features of a kitchen [...] has important consequences for public health and for the way we live our entire life. That is why we women must be able to have a say in planning and in building [...]. We women need to have a say in all these issues, in public bodies, in Parliament, and in the municipalities.[1]

Margarete Schütte-Lihotzky wrote this article in 1953, age 56, as a politically minded woman and architect active in the women's movement and the peace movement. For six years, she had been living in Vienna again, in postwar Vienna. In her article, she talked about issues surrounding housing and democratic consciousness, housing for single working women and for the elderly, and about the need for childcare facilities. She stated clearly that women were taxpayers and made up the majority of the population.

Writing about her conception of architecture, Friedrich Achleitner noted that it consisted "of improving all conditions of life by means of construction [...] even more, of an architecture that reflects all the forces and principles capable of creating a brighter future. [...] The actual message of her work seems to me to lie in the indivisibility of her efforts and in the inseparability of theory and practice, of thoughts and actions."[2]

These words of recognition draw attention to Schütte-Lihotzky's high level of professional and moral integrity. Yet above and beyond that, it seems important to me to consider more closely the special social component of the architect's oeuvre. From her earliest works onward, she perceived the contexts in which women lived their lives and from there, she defined tasks and imbued them with meaning. She placed these tasks right alongside and on an equal footing with all the other aspects of construction and did so self-confidently and as a matter of course. This approach was not a matter of course at the time nor is it today.

1 Grete Schütte-Lihotzky, "Planen und Bauen. Euch Frauen geht es an," *Stimme der Frau* 6 (February 7, 1953): 5 and 11.

2 Friedrich Achleitner, "Bauen, für eine bessere Welt," in *Margarete Schütte-Lihotzky. Soziale Architektur. Zeitzeugin eines Jahrhunderts*, exhibition catalog, MAK—Austrian Museum of Applied Arts, Vienna, ed. Peter Noever (Vienna: Böhlau, 1993), 9–11.

In this text, I want to explore the question of where this motivation originated and how she developed these abilities. I will attempt to answer this question by elaborating on several examples and key biographical stages in her life.

Beginnings in Vienna

Grete Lihotzky was one of the first women to become a professional architect. Her initial years as a young architect in Vienna coincided with the beginning of the First Republic, which saw women be given the right to vote and hold political office as well as the right to study at higher education institutions. At the same time, there were major social problems in the city because of widespread destitution in the population. Even during her architectural studies at the Kunstgewerbeschule (School of Arts and Crafts) in Vienna (today's University of Applied Arts Vienna) from 1915 to 1919, Grete Lihotzky was confronted with poverty and horrific living conditions in parts of the city. After she expressed interest in taking part in a competition for the construction of housing for workers, her teacher Oskar Strnad recommended that she first go to the workers' districts in the city to find out what housing and living conditions there were actually like.[3] This experience touched her and she would refer to it repeatedly thereafter.[4] Housing construction and the social dimension of construction became her topic.

For Grete Lihotzky's father, a civil servant in the Urban Renewal Fund (Stadterneuerungsfonds), the proclamation of the First Republic in 1918 meant retirement. It was through him that she became familiar with the offices in the top floor of the Neue Burg, a section of the Hofburg palace in central Vienna. The building was empty, and the young architect was able to use one of the rooms as a work space. Thus it came to be that a room in one of the last imperialistic structures built by the Austro-Hungarian Monarchy was occupied by a young woman working on aspects of housing and settlement construction and on ways of easing women's housekeeping burdens.

From early 1921 on, Grete Lihotzky was busy planning the Friedensstadt Settlement near Lainzer Tiergarten. Her employer was the First Non-Profit Settlement Cooperative

3 Project 3 in *Margarete Schütte-Lihotzky. Soziale Architektur*, 34 and 281; competition for "A kitchen-cum-living room in the outer suburbs"—she won the competition and received the Max Mauthner Award from the Chamber of Commerce and Industry (Handels- und Gewerbekammer), Vienna I, on July 21, 1917.

4 See Margarete Schütte-Lihotzky, *Erinnerungen aus dem Widerstand 1938–1945* (Hamburg: Konkret Literatur Verlag, 1985), 13–14; Margarete Schütte-Lihotzky, *Warum ich Architektin wurde*, ed. Karin Zogmayer (Salzburg: Residenz, 2004), 26.

PLANEN UND BAUEN

Euch Frauen geht es an

ARCHITEKTIN GRETE SCHÜTTE-LIHOTZKY

Wie wichtig ist es doch für unser ganzes Leben — daß gebaut wird und wie gebaut wird — wie wichtig für unsere Arbeit in Haushalt, Fabrik oder Büro — wie wichtig für unsere Gesundheit, für die Gesundheit und Erziehung unserer Kinder und Jugend — wie wichtig für unser ganzes Familien- und Lebensglück!

Und wichtig für uns Frauen ist faktisch alles — angefangen mit der Gesamtplanung unseres Landes bis über die Planung der Städte zum Wohnungsbau, zur Wohnungseinrichtung, den Möbeln und sogar bis zur Art und Weise, wie wir unsern Kochlöffel in der Küche aufbewahren können, sind voneinander abhängig.

Von der Landesplanung hängt es ab, wo die Industrien und wo die Wohngebiete liegen, und davon hängt es ab, ob der Rauch oder schädliche Gase der Fabriken in die Wohnungen dringen, davon hängt es ab, ob unsere Kinder krank werden oder nicht. Und von der Stadtplanung ist abhängig, wie unsere Straßen und Plätze angelegt werden, ob wir durch Grünanlagen zu unserer Arbeit gehen oder nicht, ob die Kinder und Jugend genügend Spiel- und Sportplätze erhalten können, wie weit sie zur Schule oder in den Kindergarten haben, ob sie über verkehrsreiche Straßen gehen müssen oder nicht, und schließlich, wie unsere Wohnungen gelegen sind, ob sie eine Nordfassade haben, durch die nie ein Sonnenstrahl in unsere Zimmer dringt und unsere Kinder tuberkulös werden oder nicht — das alles ist von der Stadtplanung abhängig, geht uns Frauen also wesentlich an.

Architektin Grete Schütte-Lihotzky, Präsidentin des Bundes Demokratischer Frauen Österreichs, ist Kandidatin der VO. Ihr Beruf, dem sie voll Liebe ergeben ist, führte sie von Wien nach Deutschland, von dort in die Sowjetunion, nach Frankreich und China und in die Türkei. Eine Reihe sehr guter Bauten, auch in Österreich, stammen von ihr. Selten hat eine Frau für ihre Leistungen so viel Anerkennung erhalten wie sie.

Grete Schütte-Lihotzky ist seit frühester Jugend mit den Menschen, für die sie ihre Pläne entwirft, tief verbunden. Ihnen zu helfen, in Frieden und Glück zu leben, ist der innerste Wunsch dieser Frau.

Und von der Stadtplanung ist wieder die ganze Grundrißgestaltung der Wohnungen abhängig, von der Grundrißgestaltung die Lage der Zimmer und ihre Größe, ob die Hausarbeit viele Griffe und Schritte erfordert oder wenige, wo die Küche liegt, wie sie eingerichtet werden kann, ob der Kochlöffel praktisch oder unpraktisch, hygienisch oder unhygienisch aufbewahrt werden kann, mit einem Wort, ob wir durch die Wohnung eine Arbeitsersparnis im Haushalt erzielen können, oder ob dieser Haushalt wie ein Bleigewicht an uns Frauen hängt.

Und es ist wichtig für uns Frauen, zu erkennen, daß jeder Fehler, der beim Planen und Bauen gemacht wird — einerlei, ob bei der Landesplanung oder bei der Kücheneinrichtung und Unterbringung des Kochlöffels, wichtige Konsequenzen für die Volksgesundheit und unsere ganze Lebensführung hat.

Deshalb müssen wir Frauen beim Planen und Bauen mitsprechen können und Einfluß auf die Produktion von Möbeln und andern Einrichtungs- und Haushaltgegenständen nehmen. Wir sind ja in der Hauptsache der leidende Teil der Bevölkerung, wir haben zum großen Teil die Last des Wohnungselends, der Hausarbeit, der Pflege kranker Familienmitglieder zu tragen. Wir sind außerdem heute der größere Teil der Bevölkerung, die Verbraucher der Wohnungen, die Käufer aller Dinge für die Wohnung und deren Einrichtung, mehr als die Hälfte des Volksvermögens geht durch die Hände der Frauen. Schon allein dadurch könnten wir weit größeren Einfluß gewinnen, als wir ihn heute haben — wir müßten uns zuerst nur der Stärke bewußt werden.

Grete Schütte-Lihotzky, "Planen und Bauen. Euch Frauen geht es an," *Stimme der Frau* 6 (February 7, 1953): 5 (excerpt).

for Austrian War Invalids (Erste gemeinnützige Siedlungsgenossenschaft der Kriegsinvaliden Österreichs). She worked together with Adolf Loos from February to early May 1921 at the site office on Hermesstrasse. Here was what Loos wrote in the letter of reference he gave to her: "I can most earnestly recommend Miss Lihotzky to one and all; she outshone many of her male colleagues, also with her diligence and precision."[5] She was receiving her first acknowledgment as a woman in this field.

In the spring of 1921, the architect Ernst May arrived in Vienna from Breslau (the German name for today's Polish city of Wrocław) to tour the new Vienna settlements (*Siedlungen*). Lihotzky was asked to serve as the visitor's guide and also presented her own work to him, including her first reflections on how to rationalize housekeeping. Ernst May was impressed and invited her to write about this topic for *Schlesisches Heim*, a journal he published in Breslau. Grete Lihotzky thus penned her first article, which was published in August 1921.[6] In it, she wrote extensively about the subject of households and how they work. She presented an intelligent and critical analysis of the tasks, needs, roles, and housework itself. She wrote about carefully planned, economical furnishings and considered the health of the occupants. She noted that floor plans had to be systematically designed, pointing to Frederick Winslow Taylor and how his theories had been applied to factories and agriculture. She added that no such application existed for housekeeping, let alone a book. She called for the first time for precise studies to be conducted on work processes. Basically, her article covered all the principles on which she based her work, and which led to successes in Vienna and later in Frankfurt.

From February 1922 on, she worked as an employee at the site office of the Austrian Settlement and Allotment Garden Association (Österreichischer Verband für Siedlungs- und Kleingartenwesen, ÖVSK).[7] She advised settlers and held lectures at the Settlement School; her topic: "Furnishing a Settlement House." She planned settler huts and settler houses, the system of the core-house (*Kernhaus*), a growing expandable house, and above all, the scullery as the optimum addition to the live-in kitchen in the settler house.[8]

For her successful work at the settlement exhibitions at Rathausplatz in 1922 and in 1923, she received honorary medals from the City of Vienna.

She was working in a male domain where a progressive climate prevailed. The secretary-general of the association

5 Letter of reference issued by architect Adolf Loos on May 1, 1921, University Archive of the University of Applied Arts Vienna, Nachlass Margarete Schütte-Lihotzky (UAUAK, NL MSL), Q/10.

6 Grete Lihotzky, "Einiges über die Einrichtung österreichischer Häuser unter besonderer Berücksichtigung der Siedlungsbauten," *Schlesisches Heim* 8 (1921): 217–22.

7 The ÖVSK was created by the merger of the Main Association of Settlements and the Central Association of Allotment Gardeners and Settlement Cooperatives; see Zwingl, "Die ersten Jahre in Wien," in *Margarete Schütte-Lihotzky. Soziale Architektur*, 17–29, here 24–26; letter of employment of the ÖVSK, February 15, 1922, UAUAK, NL MSL, Q/16.

8 See project 28 in *Margarete Schütte-Lihotzky. Soziale Architektur*, 52–53 and 280–81.

was Otto Neurath, who was close to her, and she often worked for the architect Adolf Loos. The contract for the Winarskyhof public housing complex brought her together with the architects Peter Behrens and Josef Frank and with her former teacher Oskar Strnad.

She identified as a Socialist and joined the Social Democratic Party. In *Die Neue Wirtschaft*, she published an article entitled "Beratungsstelle für Wohnungseinrichtung" (Advice center for furnishing an apartment). In it, she called on the Warentreuhand (merchandise trust), her initiative within the ÖVSK, "to raise the general standard of living [Wohnniveau] of the working class."[9] In her article entitled "Vergangenheit und Zukunft im Wiener Wohnungsbau" (Past and future in Viennese housing construction), she took a stand against speculative transactions with apartment buildings and against their decor and emphasized the special connection the settlers had to their apartments and houses. "People would have more from a sink in the home than from an angel on the roof."[10]

Her work attracted attention, especially from the journalist and activist Gisela Urban, who repeatedly wrote articles about Lihotzky.[11] In her initial years, the ambitious young architect experienced recognition and encouragement in an intellectual and politically engaged environment and developed a markedly social attitude toward her profession.

9 Grete Lihotzky, "Beratungsstelle für Wohnungseinrichtung," *Die Neue Wirtschaft* (January 31, 1924): 12; see also the chapter "The New Dwelling: 'The Gemeinde-Wien-Type,'" in Eve Blau, *The Architecture of Red Vienna*, 1919–1934 (Cambridge, MA: MIT Press, 1999), 174–215, here 189.

10 Grete Lihotzky, "Vergangenheit und Zukunft im Wiener Wohnungsbau," *Die Neue Wirtschaft* (February 21, 1924): 11.

11 Gisela Urban, "Das Schaffen einer modernen Architektin" (Vienna, 1926); ibid., "Die Frau als Architektin" (Vienna, 1929), UAUAK, NL MSL, TXT/177.

Frankfurt am Main

In early 1926, Ernst May invited Grete Lihotzky to come to Frankfurt am Main, where he had since become head of the central building authority (Stadtbaurat und Leiter des Hochbauamtes). With modern methods incorporating standardization and typification, the staff there developed large urban-development settlements featuring low-rise buildings. Grete Lihotzky was in the typification department of the central building authority where she worked on housing construction concepts and on floor plans for different house types, always with an eye to rationalizing housekeeping. It was there that she decided in favor of a working kitchen, taking into account labor-saving and energy-saving aspects and the use of modern technical equipment. She developed the kitchen in different versions and sizes for all housing units in the settlements.

The newly established magazine *Das neue Frankfurt* reported on the progress being made with the new advances and with construction. Above and beyond that, extensive information was provided in exhibitions and numerous lectures for the target audience, for instance women's organizations.

Lihotzky wrote as follows: "Every thinking woman must sense how backward housekeeping has been up until now and recognize this as the most serious impediment to her own development and thus also to the development of her family."[12] In her texts, she expressed the attitudes of a progressive woman. She embraced a modern lifestyle and criticized the backwardness of women and in the trades, industry, and planning.[13]

At the central building authority she met an architect colleague named Wilhelm Schütte, who worked in the large buildings department. In general, she described the Frankfurt colleagues and society as politically disinterested,[14] but Schütte may well have shared her political convictions from the outset. The two of them married in 1927. She took the name Schütte but continued to call herself Schütte-Lihotzky because she was well known and had already published extensively. She was the only woman at the Frankfurt central building authority and was soon noticed by the public. The response to her work was appreciative, on the one hand, but also skeptical and mockingly derogatory.

She did not join the German Social Democratic Party—on the contrary: in 1927 she announced she was leaving the Austrian Social Democratic Party.[15]

The housing situation for single working women was an acute problem. Most of them had to resort to sublet rooms or were housed in homes for single women. Schütte-Lihotzky rejected this approach, advocating instead mixed housing construction and affordable apartments corresponding to the women's income. She developed a concept she called *Wohnungen für berufstätige Frauen* (Apartments for working women). It consisted of different types of small apartments on the top floor of regular multistory apartment buildings. The housing units of varying sizes were designed to offer

12 Grete Lihotzky, "Rationalisierung im Haushalt," *Das Neue Frankfurt* (May 1927): 120–23.

13 See Grete Schütte-Lihotzky, "Wie kann durch richtigen Wohnungsbau die Hausfrauenarbeit erleichtert werden," *Mitteilungen der Österr. Gesellschaft für Technik im Haushalt* 1, no. 9 (August 1927).

14 Schütte-Lihotzky, *Warum ich Architektin wurde*, 118.

15 In Frankfurt she came into contact with Carl Grünberg, the director of the Institute for Social Research, with whom she was soon on friendly terms. It was through his influence that she left the Austrian Social Democratic Party in 1927. After the events in Vienna in July 1927 related to the Palace of Justice fire, she informed the party leadership of her decision "with a somewhat dramatic letter." See Schütte-Lihotzky, *Warum ich Architektin wurde*, 120.

women independence but also the opportunity for community, neighborly assistance, and central services.

After her marriage to Wilhelm Schütte, Margarete Schütte-Lihotzky's employment contract at the central building authority was extended only on a fixed-term basis by way of special exemptions. According to a decision by the municipal authorities, the city was not allowed to employ both members of a married couple. At the end of 1928, she left her position as a city employee for good. After that, she received fee-based fixed-term contracts from the city, even though the central building authority was greatly interested in her continuing to be employed "as a specialist for planning further projects for Frankfurt residential buildings."[16]

She was working on her own projects and was often invited to hold lectures, also in Austria. At the 15th general meeting of the National Council of Women Austria (Bund Österreichischer Frauenvereine, BÖFV) in Vienna in April 1929, the speakers included Schütte-Lihotzky on the subject *Wohnung der berufstätigen Frau* (The working woman's apartment) and Gisela Urban on *Frau und Wohnung* (Woman and apartment).[17]

That same year she drew up the design for the Praunheim kindergarten—a building task that would become her main focus during the years she subsequently spent in the Soviet Union and also in her later years in Vienna.

In her professionally successful years in Frankfurt am Main, Margarete Schütte-Lihotzky belonged to a community of modern architects who stood up for and fought for their own conceptions of architecture. This also included demanding equal rights for women and the consequence—namely, making women's lives easier by implementing labor-saving ideas.[18]

16 See Jutta Zwilling's research in municipal department files: "'Ich würde es genossen haben, ein Haus für einen reichen Mann zu entwerfen' – Margarete Schütte-Lihotzky: Architektin – Widerstandskämpferin – Kommunistin," in *Frankfurter Frauengeschichte(n), Band 77*, Archiv für Frankfurts Geschichte und Kunst, ed. Evelyn Brockhoff and Ursula Kern (Frankfurt am Main: Societäts-Verlag, 2017), 190–205, here 200–1.

17 "Die 15. Generalversammlung des B.Ö.F.V.," *Die Österreicherin* 2, no. 5 (May 1, 1929): 1–2.

18 Schütte-Lihotzky, *Warum ich Architektin wurde*, 202–3.

Soviet Union

In 1930, Ernst May received an appointment to go to the Soviet Union to build new residential towns in connection with the industrial development program. He was accompanied by a group of 17 experts, among them Margarete Schütte-Lihotzky as the only female expert. She was entrusted with heading up the department for kindergartens and day nurseries while Wilhelm Schütte was put in charge of school buildings. The brigade lived together and worked jointly on the huge task they were given. Life in this "other world" was impressive. Schütte-Lihotzky described the important experience of becoming familiar with a different culture, having respect for it, and overcoming prejudices. She was not a member of any political party during those years.

The couple took numerous trips to various parts of the huge country. In 1934 they set off for China and Japan. She was becoming an open-minded citizen of the world. She took photographs on her travels and wrote letters to her sister in Vienna on a regular basis.

In 1937 Margarete and Wilhelm Schütte left the Soviet Union and traveled to Paris and London in search of a place of exile.

Exile—Istanbul—Resistance

In the summer of 1938, Bruno Taut arranged for the couple to move to Istanbul, where Margarete Schütte-Lihotzky worked at the Academy of Fine Arts, which was under the Education Ministry.

In Istanbul, Schütte-Lihotzky joined an Austrian Communist Resistance group against National Socialism that had formed around the architect Herbert Eichholzer. In the winter of 1940, she traveled to Vienna to take an active part in the Resistance. She was arrested in Vienna and a motion was filed for her to be sentenced to death. At the trial, she ended up being given a 15-year prison sentence, which sent her to Aichach Prison in Bavaria, where she remained until the end of the war in May 1945. She survived more than four years of imprisonment. During this time, she was together with many women who had also put their lives on the line and who encouraged each other with their strength, cunning, courage, will to live, and solidarity.[19] These were decisive years and experiences for her, and they left an indelible mark.

Her Second Life

From 1947 on, Margarete and Wilhelm Schütte lived in Vienna. They contacted the municipal administration in Vienna. In the fall, Schütte-Lihotzky presented her design

19 She wrote the following book about these years: Margarete Schütte-Lihotzky, *Erinnerungen aus dem Widerstand. 1938–1945*, ed. Chup Friemert (Hamburg: Konkret Literatur Verlag, 1985); latest edition: Margarete Schütte-Lihotzky, *Erinnerungen aus dem Widerstand. Das kämpferische Leben einer Architektin von 1938–1945* (Vienna: Promedia, 2014).

for a construction and urban planning department in the exhibition *Wien baut auf* (Vienna builds) at the Vienna City Hall. Her proposal for a housing construction exhibition entitled *Wie sollen neue Wohnungen aussehen?* (What should new apartments look like?) was turned down. In liberated Austria, in war-ravaged Vienna, the architect had hoped to take an active part in the reconstruction with her special knowledge of social housing construction. This proved to be an illusion, however, for the Communist Resistance fighter.

Margarete Schütte-Lihotzky drew up the Neues Wiener Wohnbauprogramm (New Viennese housing construction program) for the Communist Party of Austria (KPÖ) and wrote about the program in an article entitled "Licht, Luft, Sonne" (Light, air, sun), which appeared in *Stimme der Frau*, a magazine published by the League of Democratic Women of Austria (Bund demokratischer Frauen Österreichs, BDFÖ). At the founding of the BDFÖ in 1948, Margarete Schütte-Lihotzky was elected in absentia as the organization's first president, an office she would hold until 1969.[20] Back in the 1940s the architect had written a series of articles for *Stimme der Frau* containing practical tips, such as "Hubers bekommen ein Kind" (The Hubers are expecting a baby).[21]

In November 1949, the Austrian Peace Council (Österreichischer Friedensrat) was founded, with Margarete Schütte-Lihotzky as one of the participants. The peace movement was the second focal point of her activism.

In 1949, Margarete and Wilhelm Schütte landed an initial contract from the City of Vienna for a public housing project on Barthgasse in Vienna's third district.[22] The couple separated in 1951, but still worked together on later contracts such as the office building of the Globus publishing company.

In 1952 she landed a contract for a public housing project on Schüttelstrasse and for a kindergarten at Kapaunplatz in Vienna's 20th district.

Reconstruction set the economy back in motion, and men took back their positions and, in the process, their earning opportunities. Women were pushed into the background. Against this backdrop, Eva Ottillinger wrote about kitchen design in the postwar era: "Whereas Margarete Schütte-Lihotzky wanted to free women from the needless

20 At the time of her election the architect was residing in Paris, where she designed the Austrian section of a large women's exhibition staged by the Women's International Democratic Federation (WIDF).

21 Grete Schütte-Lihotzky, "Hubers bekommen ein Kind," *Stimme der Frau* 51 (December 17, 1949).

22 In 1949 she received her license to practice as a civil engineer and worked as a self-employed architect until 1967.

burden of housework with her optimally planned Frankfurt Kitchen, the Viennese Built-in Kitchen of the postwar era was a place of assimilation to assigned roles. It is no surprise that these kitchens after 1945 were largely designed by men."[23]

Parts of the Austrian population experienced the end of the war not only as liberation but also as the beginning of a time of occupation. The KPÖ was isolated because of deeply rooted anti-Communism in the country and the party's close relationship with and uncritical attitude toward the Soviet Union. In the 1950s, the impact of the Cold War became palpable. What this meant for KPÖ member Margarete Schütte-Lihotzky was that her professional activity was limited, and she was excluded from public contracts for years.

It was not until the early 1960s that she received another contract from the City of Vienna for a children's daycare center—a major project whose main features corresponded to the modular system she had developed and to elements of her design theory for kindergartens.[24]

She was an independent, self-confident woman who was pursuing her profession, traveling, still politically active, and still a KPÖ member.[25] As president of the BDFÖ, and from 1969 onward honorary president for life, she saw the inclusion of women as a central societal concern and viewed solidarity among women as a significant strength.

In response to the reemergence of anti-Semitic rioting in Vienna in 1960, she joined like-minded women to establish a nonpartisan women's committee, which showed antiwar and anti-Fascist films at the Urania, a public educational institute (and observatory) in central Vienna. These events featuring speeches and film screenings took place regularly until 1994. Having women from all classes of society, across party and ideological lines, collaborate and work together was of paramount importance to her.

In 1980 Margarete Schütte-Lihotzky was awarded the City of Vienna Prize for Architecture. She held lectures about her life at the Austrian Society of Architecture (Österreichische Gesellschaft für Architektur, ÖGFA) and the Technical University of Vienna (TU Wien). The 1980s saw the emergence of a new societal awareness that made it possible for people to take a critical look back at their history.

23 Eva B. Ottillinger, "Küchenmöbel – Kochräume. Von der Feuerstelle zur Designerküche," in *Küchen/Möbel. Design und Geschichte*, exhibition catalog (Vienna: Hofmobiliendepot, 2015), 29–80, here 68.

24 Städtisches Kindertagesheim 1110 Wien, Rinnböckstrasse, 1961–63. She first wrote her design theory for kindergartens and day nurseries in Bulgaria in 1946 and later revised it for East Germany and Cuba. See projects 148, 189, 196, and project 198, the modular system for childcare centers, in *Margarete Schütte-Lihotzky. Soziale Architektur*, "Werkverzeichnis," 283–91.

25 The fight against Fascism, the victory, and liberation by the Red Army remained of central importance to her.

The architect was working on her memoirs at the time.[26] In 1990, at the age of 93, she wrote the text "'Begrünte Wohnberge'—Eine städtebauliche Utopie für künftiges Wohnen" (Green housing mountains—an urban planning utopia for future housing), where she laid out her view of the 20th century and the development of the task of "Social Building" (*Soziales Bauen*).[27] She said the most important change was the employment of women in general. In 1994, Vienna announced a competition for female architects called Frauen–Werk–Stadt (Women–work–city). Its aim was to implement criteria for residential construction that met the needs of everyday life and of women—Schütte-Lihotzky happily served as the honorary chair of the jury. During this period, she received numerous prizes, honors, and honorary doctorates. She experienced this late acclaim and recognition because she had lived so long.

26 Schütte-Lihotzky, *Erinnerungen* (1985); Schütte-Lihotzky, *Warum ich Architektin wurde* was published after her death.

27 Margarete Schütte-Lihotzky, "'Begrünte Wohnberge.' Eine städtebauliche Utopie für künftiges Wohnen" (manuscript, December 1990), UAUAK, NL MSL, 204/1/TXT.

In her life, Margarete Schütte-Lihotzky exhibited many abilities, especially the ability to look back and ahead at the same time and to think in a forward-looking way. She also had the ability to perceive the problems of life and daily routines, not disqualifying or pushing them aside as unimportant but rather, if necessary, examining them with professional scientific precision. For her, the demands of different occupations and everyday tasks were on an equal footing. Margarete Schütte-Lihotzky lived a life of equality, remained unbroken and self-confident, and displayed her unequivocally social and democratic attitudes as a woman and as an architect.

From 2014 to 2021, the Margarete Schütte-Lihotzky Room in Vienna was an exhibition and information space where this important figure was remembered. After Margarete Schütte-Lihotzky's last apartment in Vienna's fifth district had been placed under a preservation order in 2021, the Margarete Schütte-Lihotzky Club was able to rent it. The Margarete Schütte-Lihotzky Center subsequently opened to visitors in the fall of 2022 and is establishing itself as a center of research on female pioneers of architecture in Vienna.[28] After all, planning and building—these things matter to us women!

28 See https://www.schuette-lihotzky.at. The Margarete Schütte-Lihotzky Club has been running the Margarete Schütte-Lihotzky Center in Franzensgasse 16/40, 1050 Vienna since July 2021. From 2014 to 2021, it was the Margarete Schütte-Lihotzky Room, Untere Weissgerberstrasse 41, 1030 Vienna.

Profession: "Frau Architekt." On the Training of Vienna's First Female Architects

Sabine Plakolm-Forsthuber

Compared to other European countries, Austria was relatively late in admitting women to architectural studies. This is confirmed by a look at Germany, where the Technische Hochschulen (THs)[1] had already opened their doors to female students between 1903 and 1908.[2] It was not until the First Republic was proclaimed and women were given the right to vote and hold office in 1918 that the continued exclusion of women from technical studies in Austria became untenable as a social and educational policy. In Vienna, women were allowed to study at the Technical University (today's TU Wien) starting in 1919 and at the Academy of Fine Arts starting in 1920. Women who wanted to pursue architectural studies before 1919 went abroad or opted to study in Vienna at the Kunstgewerbeschule (School of Arts and Crafts; today's University of Applied Arts Vienna).

The Kunstgewerbeschule, which was not granted university status until 1941, was open to artistically ambitious women from its founding in 1867. To be admitted, students had to pass an entrance exam but did not need to have the Matura secondary school diploma required for university studies. Equal access to all study programs was soon restricted, however, and not fully reinstated until around 1900. Among the architecture class programs, the ones led by Josef

1 These higher education technical institutions in Germany and Austria were all originally colleges but some had received full university status (i.e., the right to confer doctorates) by the period covered in this essay—for example, the THs Vienna, Munich, and Graz. I therefore refer to "Technische Hochschule Wien" as "Technical University" in English in this essay and the other THs as either college or university depending on their status.

2 Ute Maasberg and Regina Prinz, *Die Neuen kommen! Weibliche Avantgarde in der Architektur der zwanziger Jahre* (Hamburg: Junius, 2004); Despina Stratigakos, "'I Myself Want to Build': Women, Architectural Education and the Integration

of Germany's Technical Colleges," *Paedagogica Historica* 43, no. 6 (2007): 727–56; https://architekturpionierinnen.at/ (accessed October 3, 2022); Ingrid Holzschuh, Sabine Plakolm-Forsthuber, and Zentralvereinigung der ArchitektInnen, *Pionierinnen der Wiener Architektur* (Basel: Birkhäuser, 2022)

3 Siegfried Theiss was still complaining in 1935 that the "professional title of architect" was "extremely commonplace" and "always incorrectly used." Siegfried Theiss, "Was wollen die Architekten," in *Festschrift*

Hoffmann, Heinrich Tessenow, and Oskar Strnad between 1899 and 1936 were the most significant. The diploma bestowed on graduation attested to the acquired qualifications, but the professional title of "Architect" was not formally granted. In practice, however, the graduates (male and female) designated themselves as architects, a practice not all of their professional colleagues approved of.[3] Civil engineers insisted on a clear distinction being made between themselves on the one hand and the building trades and graduates of the Kunstgewerbeschule on the other. The demand for binding criteria regarding training, licensing, and rights was first raised in 1913 but not set down in law until the 2nd Civil Engineer Ordinance of 1937.[4]

However, in everyday life, professional experience counted more than having a title or license legitimized by a diploma. Margarete Schütte-Lihotzky naturally referred to herself as an architect, although she did not acquire her official license until 1948 (fig. 1).[5] Another example is Liane

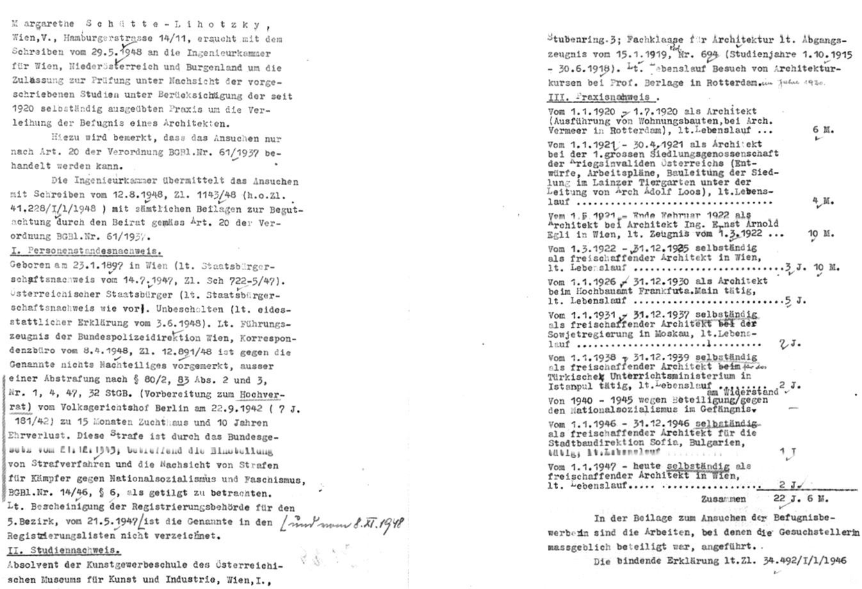

Margarethe S c h ü t t e - L i h o t z k y , Wien,V., Hamburgerstrasse 14/11, ersucht mit dem Schreiben vom 29.5.1948 an die Ingenieurkammer für Wien, Niederösterreich und Burgenland um die Zulassung zur Prüfung unter Nachsicht der vorgeschriebenen Studien unter Berücksichtigung der seit 1920 selbständig ausgeübten Praxis um die Verleihung der Befugnis eines Architekten.

Hiezu wird bemerkt, dass das Ansuchen nur nach Art. 20 der Verordnung BGBl.Nr. 61/1937 behandelt werden kann.

Die Ingenieurkammer übermittelt das Ansuchen mit Schreiben vom 12.8.1948, Zl. 1143/48 (h.o.Zl. 41.228/I/1/1948) mit sämtlichen Beilagen zur Begutachtung durch den Beirat gemäss Art. 20 der Verordnung BGBl.Nr. 61/1937.

I. Personenstandesnachweis.

Geboren am 23.1.1897 in Wien (lt. Staatsbürgerschaftsnachweis vom 14.7.1947, Zl. Sch 722-5/47). Österreichischer Staatsbürger (lt. Staatsbürgerschaftsnachweis wie vor). Unbescholten (lt. eidesstattlicher Erklärung vom 3.6.1948). Lt. Führungszeugnis der Bundespolizeidirektion Wien, Korrespondenzbüro vom 8.4.1948, Zl. 12.891/48 ist gegen die Genannte nichts Nachteiliges vorgemerkt, ausser einer Abstrafung nach § 80/2, 83 Abs. 2 und 3, Nr. 1, 4, 47, 32 StGB. (Vorbereitung zum Hochverrat) vom Volksgerichtshof Berlin am 22.9.1942 (7 J. 181/42) zu 15 Monaten Zuchthaus und 10 Jahren Ehrverlust. Diese Strafe ist durch das Bundesgesetz vom [illegible], betreffend die Einstellung von Strafverfahren und die Nachsicht von Strafen für Kämpfer gegen Nationalsozialismus und Faschismus, BGBl.Nr. 14/46, § 6, als getilgt zu betrachten.
Lt. Bescheinigung der Registrierungsbehörde für den 5.Bezirk, vom 21.5.1947 ist die Genannte in den Registrierungslisten nicht verzeichnet.

II. Studiennachweis.

Absolvent der Kunstgewerbeschule des Österreichischen Museums für Kunst und Industrie, Wien,I., Stubenring.3; Fachklasse für Architektur lt. Abgangszeugnis vom 15.1.1919, Nr. 694 (Studienjahre 1.10.1915 - 30.6.1918). Lt. Lebenslauf Besuch von Architekturkursen bei Prof. Berlage in Rotterdam.

III. Praxisnachweis .

Vom 1.1.1920 - 1.7.1920 als Architekt (Ausführung von Wohnungsbauten,bei Arch. Vermeer in Rotterdam), lt.Lebenslauf ...	6 M.
Vom 1.1.1921 - 30.4.1921 als Architekt bei der 1.grossen Siedlungsgenossenschaft der Kriegsinvaliden Österreichs (Entwürfe, Arbeitspläne, Bauleitung der Siedlung im Lainzer Tiergarten unter der Leitung von Arch Adolf Loos), lt.Lebenslauf	4 M.
Vom 1.5.1921 - Ende Februar 1922 als Architekt bei Architekt Ing. Ernst Arnold Egli in Wien, lt. Zeugnis vom 1.3.1922 ...	10 M.
Vom 1.3.1922 - 31.12.1925 selbständig als freischaffender Architekt in Wien, lt. Lebenslauf	3 J. 10 M.
Vom 1.1.1926 - 31.12.1930 als Architekt beim Hochbauamt Frankfurt a.Main tätig, lt. Lebenslauf	5 J.
Vom 1.1.1931 - 31.12.1937 selbständig als freischaffender Architekt bei der Sowjetregierung in Moskau, lt.Lebenslauf	2 J.
Vom 1.1.1938 - 31.12.1939 selbständig als freischaffender Architekt beim Türkischen Unterrichtsministerium in Istanpul tätig, lt.Lebenslauf	2 J.
Von 1940 - 1945 wegen Beteiligung am Widerstand gegen den Nationalsozialismus im Gefängnis.	—
Vom 1.1.1946 - 31.12.1946 selbständig als freischaffender Architekt für die Stadtbaudirektion Sofia, Bulgarien, tätig, lt.Lebenslauf	1 J.
Vom 1.1.1947 - heute selbständig als freischaffender Architekt in Wien, lt. Lebenslauf.....	2 J.
Zusammen	22 J. 6 M.

In der Beilage zum Ansuchen der Befugnisbewerberin sind die Arbeiten, bei denen die Gesuchstellerin massgeblich beteiligt war, angeführt.

Die bindende Erklärung lt.Zl. 34.492/I/1/1946

Fig. 1. Margarete Schütte-Lihotzky, application for a license to practice as a civil engineer, 1948.

Fig. 2. Friedl Dicker-Brandeis and Franz Singer, axonometric plan view of the Dr. Heller one-room apartment, Wallnerstrasse, Vienna, 1927/28, tempera on paper.

Zimbler (1892–1987), who presumably had no professional degree to show either, yet from 1918 onward, carried out planning and construction projects for a bourgeois clientele who were largely Jewish. She was savvy about writing extensive articles on her buildings and apartment conversions and about becoming better known through lectures and club activities. She too signed her plans "Liane Zimbler, Architect." On presenting evidence of her extensive architectural experience, she was allowed to take the civil engineer examination

anläßlich des 75jährigen Bestandes der Ziviltechniker, ed. Vienna Chamber of Civil Engineers (Vienna: Wiener Ingenieurkammer, 1935), 56.

4 *Reichsgesetzblatt* dated May 7, 1913, accessed April 22, 2022, http://alex.onb.ac.at/cgi-content/alex?aid=rgb&datum=19130004&seite=00000288 and *Bundesgesetzblatt* (*BGBl.*) dated March 2, 1937, accessed April 22, 2022, http://alex.onb.ac.at/cgi-content/alex?aid=bgl&datum=19370004&seite=00000297.

5 Austrian State Archives/Archiv der Republik, Vienna (ÖStA/AdR), HBbBuT BMfHuW Titel ZivTech S–Z 9343, Schütte-Lihotzky Margarethe [sic], GZl. 220.091-I/1-48.

6 Sabine Plakolm-Forsthuber, "Ein Leben, zwei Karrieren. Die Architektin Liane Zimbler," in *Visionäre & Vertriebene. Österreichische Spuren in der modernen amerikanischen Architektur*, ed. Matthias Boeckl (Berlin: Ernst & Sohn, 1995), 295–309.

7 Katharina Hövelmann, *Bauhaus in Wien? Möbeldesign, Innenraumgestaltung und Architektur der Wiener Ateliergemeinschaft von Friedl Dicker und Franz Singer* (Vienna: Böhlau, 2021); Franz Singer and Friedl Dicker,

2x Bauhaus in Wien, exhibition catalog, University of Applied Arts Vienna, ed. Georg Schrom (Vienna: Hochschule für angewandte Kunst, 1988); Stefanie Kitzberger, Cosima Rainer, and Linda Schädler (eds.), *Friedl Dicker-Brandeis. Werke aus der Sammlung der Universität für angewandte Kunst Wien* (Berlin/Boston: De Gruyter, 2022); Brigitte Reutner-Doneus and Hemma Schmutz (eds.), *Friedl Dicker-Brandeis – Bauhaus-Schülerin, Avantgarde-Malerin, Kunstpädagogin / Friedl Dicker-Brandeis – Bauhaus Student, Avant-Garde Painter, Art Teacher*, exhibition catalog, Lentos Kunstmuseum Linz (Munich: Hirmer, 2022); Katharina Hövelmann, Andreas Nierhaus, and Georg Schrom (eds.), *Atelier Bauhaus, Wien – Friedl Dicker und Franz Singer*, exhibition catalog, Wien Museum (Salzburg: Müry Salzmann, 2022).

8 Sabine Plakolm-Forsthuber, "'ZV-Frauen bauen mit!' Wege und Irrwege der ersten Architektinnen der ZV (1925–1959)," in *BauKultur in Wien 1938–1959*, ed. Ingrid Holzschuh in cooperation with Zentralvereinigung der Architekten Österreichs (Basel: Birkhäuser, 2019), 56–77; Ingrid Holzschuh and Sabine Plakolm-Forsthuber, *Auf Linie. NS-Kunstpolitik in Wien. Die Reichskammer der bildenden Künste* (Basel: Birkhäuser, 2021).

in 1938 and emigrated shortly thereafter to the United States.[6] Friedl Dicker-Brandeis (1898–1944) enjoyed similar success. After her initial artistic training in Vienna, she followed Johannes Itten to the Bauhaus in Weimar. On returning to Vienna as a designer and as Franz Singer's studio partner, she designed the interiors of some 50 residential and commercial buildings.[7] The hallmark of her interiors was the utmost in spatial economy, convertibility, individuality, and a rich variety of materials and colors (fig. 2). Alongside Zimbler's elegant bourgeois style, Dicker-Brandeis added a more objective, functional facet to Viennese interior design in the years between the world wars. The third style, a proletarian-functional approach—to continue the pigeonholing—was represented by Schütte-Lihotzky, whose works are described in other essays in this volume.

I want to focus below on the little-researched first female graduates of these three Viennese higher education institutions: the Kunstgewerbeschule, the Technical University, and the Academy of Fine Arts. What qualifications did they acquire and what professional fields were open to them? How did they manage to prevail in this male-dominated profession? The period examined here extends from 1918 to 1938. These two decades beginning with women's admission to academic architectural studies and ending with the year of Nazi Germany's *Anschluss* (annexation) of Austria allow us to trace the initial steps the female graduates took in their careers. Among those first female architects were a number of women of Jewish heritage. For them, the year 1938 was a turning point that threatened their very existence. In 1938 the architectural profession was placed under the Reichskulturkammer (Reich Chamber of Fine Arts). Membership required a person to present proof of belonging to the "Aryan race" (*Ariernachweis*) under Nazi racial laws and was a prerequisite for engaging in any professional activity; a license was not required. So, for more than a few of these women, their first years in the profession coincided with the Nazi period. Many were forced to serve on behalf of the Nazi Party apparatus or worked in the planning offices of the war and armaments industry, some perforce, others as enthusiastic party members.[8]

Kunstgewerbeschule

Not all students who attended a master class program for architecture at the Kunstgewerbeschule were aspiring to graduate in that discipline. This may seem surprising, but it had to do with the very open, progressive teaching approach taken by Hoffmann and Strnad. They viewed architecture and the applied arts, the major area of study for most students, as design approaches of equal value. Men and women who wanted to qualify for architecture also had to take subjects involving technical drafting and structural design theory. They concentrated mainly on furniture designs, interior designs, and simple houses, and prepared work drawings.

The first female graduate was not Schütte-Lihotzky, but rather Elisabeth Niessen (born 1884) from Bielitz, the German name for today's Bielsko, Poland. She attended the school from 1913 to 1917. In his overall evaluation of her work, her professor Heinrich Tessenow noted that she created "initial design plans and precise final plans for petite bourgeois and more lavish pieces of furniture [...] interior designs and residential buildings." He went on to say that she "had a great gift for architectural work."[9] The evaluation was quite typical of the time and showed two things: first, that interior design was a priority subject at the Kunstgewerbeschule and second, that technical training in building construction, statics, and urban planning tended to be subordinate subjects. Nonetheless, Niessen's qualifications were sufficient for her to be hired by the Stadtbauamt (central building authority) in Vienna in 1918 in the "status of a male civil servant."[10]

Friederike Domnosil met with a typical woman's fate. She was able to develop her promising talent to only a limited extent because she married and started a family. Domnosil (1904–2000) entered the school in 1922 with the intention of becoming an architect and attended Strnad's class until 1925. He attested to her "very fine talent," noting that she was able "to give concrete form to her poetic sensibility" and was "highly adept at creating [all manner of] abstract forms."[11] She made her mark with several charming and elegant interior designs and a beach house. Her works appeared in international trade journals and were awarded prizes. In 1928, she married the architect Otto Niedermoser, who was

9 University Archive of the University of Applied Arts Vienna (UAUAK), Abgangszeugnis für (diploma for) Elisabeth Niessen, no. 658, evaluation by Heinrich Tessenow, June 30, 1917.

10 E.T., "Wiens erste Architektin," *Neues Wiener Tagblatt* (May 31, 1918): 3–4. She was hired at a time when Heinrich Goldemund headed up the central building authority. One of her tasks was to plan housing for returning soldiers (settlements in Aspern and apartments on the Schmelz). No information was found about completed projects or her fate after 1932 when Niessen was declared legally incapable "on account of mental illness (alcoholism)." See Wiener Stadt- und Landesarchiv (WStLA), Meldeauskunft (registration information) 1932, Beschluss des Bezirksgerichts VIII dated January 16, 1932, Zl. 3L47/31/8.

11 UAUAK, Abgangszeugnis für (diploma for) Friederike Domnosil, no. 893, May 12, 1925, evaluation by Oskar Strnad.

successful as a stage designer and teacher at the Kunstgewerbeschule. After that, Domnosil worked in his studio and also headed up their joint furniture company.[12] The career of Margarete Fingerlos (born 1906) developed along similar lines. She attended Hoffmann's class from 1925 to 1929 as a holder of the Matura. Hoffmann gave her "top marks as an interior designer." From the late 1920s on, she collaborated with her husband Gerhard Lohner in designing micro-apartments and furniture and conducted applied art courses at Landesausschuss Linz (1930). She apparently stopped working as a self-employed designer after that.[13]

So, the majority of the women who graduated from the school in those years were active as interior designers. The career of Rosa Weiser (1897–1982) from the Austrian province of Salzburg can be traced over an extended period. In 1925 Strnad assessed that she had mastered "the building trade completely and for all these reasons is highly recommended."[14] Her model of a country house received special recognition at the 1924 Viennese Architecture Exhibition organized by Oswald Haerdtl.[15] The further stages of her career are well documented. She worked at Siedlungsverband xv Moeringgasse (Settlement association for Moeringgasse in Vienna's 15th district) and set up exhibition structures for the Gesellschafts- und Wirtschaftsmuseum (Museum for Social and Economic Affairs). In 1927 she was hired by the company Haus & Garten, founded and run by Josef Frank and Oskar Wlach. From then on, she worked as a self-employed architect in Vienna and Salzburg, participating in competitions and undertaking projects involving apartment interior furnishings, renovations, and summer houses. After World War II, she erected residential buildings in Vienna and Salzburg.[16]

The other schools were suspicious of the competition from the architects educated at the Kunstgewerbeschule and of their insufficient technical training. Time for action came after the success that Hoffmann and his school had at the Paris Applied Arts Exhibition in 1925, when he was vehemently attacked in the local press and by some of his professional colleagues. The tenor of the criticism was "that the Austrian applied arts have recently ended up all too often

12 Annemarie Bönsch, *Wiener Bühnen- und Filmausstattung. Otto Niedermoser 1903–1976* (Vienna: Böhlau, 2003), 14.

13 See UAUAK, Abgangszeugnis für (diploma for) Margarete Fingerlos, no. 1116, June 30, 1929, evaluation by Josef Hoffmann, *Tagblatt* (November 19, 1930): 6; *Tagblatt* (September 23, 1930): 11. *Der Baumeister* 27, no. 12 (1929): 410–13.

14 See UAUAK, Abgangszeugnis für (diploma for) Rosa Weiser, no. 1088, June 30, 1928, evaluation by Oskar Strnad.

15 See Dr. Loenström, "Eine Architektur-Ausstellung im Wiener Österreichischen Museum für Kunst und Industrie," *Deutsche Kunst und Dekoration* 54 (1924): 332–40.

16 See ÖSTA/AdR, UBbBuT, BMfHuV, Allg. Reihe PTech, Weiser Rosa, GZl. 68800/1937.

in women's hands and could do with more earnestness, power, and masculinity." There was a call to return to "material authenticity and practicality."[17] With the simmering conflict threatening to reach a boil, the Kunstgewerbeschule went on the offensive and stepped up its instruction in technical subjects; from 1925/26 on, it introduced courses in structural mechanics and statics. It met the accusation of an overly feminine touch by offering physical training courses on subjects such as fencing from 1928/29 on, which women attended in great numbers.

Of course, these innovations no longer helped at all because the statutory study requirements for obtaining a license to practice as an architect had already been amended in 1924. These studies could only be completed at the Technical University or the Academy of Fine Arts. The requirements called for "[...] the successful completion of a master class program for architecture or the art historical seminar at the Technical University or the master class program at the Academy of Fine Arts."[18] The graduates of the Kunstgewerbeschule were therefore at a definite disadvantage in pursuing their careers. As a result, several of them subsequently tagged on further studies at one of the other two institutions.[19] As the rector of and a professor at the Academy of Fine Arts, Clemens Holzmeister ultimately succeeded in 1937 in having this institution be granted the sole right of representation for artistic architectural training. Architectural training at the Kunstgewerbeschule was temporarily interrupted in 1936, with only a reduced program being offered for interior design.[20]

Among the women not content with graduating from just the Kunstgewerbeschule, one worth noting is Hilda Döring-Kuras (1910–96). In 1932, she completed the master class program conducted by Strnad, who described her as a "superb talent." After working for Lois Welzenbacher in Innsbruck and Munich until 1936, she returned to school to earn the Matura. She then registered at the technical university in Graz (today's TU Graz) and completed her architectural studies there in 1938. In 1941 she was hired by the Hochbauamt (central building authority) in Wels, where she worked as a licensed architect (1949) for the rest of her life,

17 Hans Ankwicz-Kleehoven, "Österreich auf der Internationalen Kunstgewerbeausstellung Paris 1925," *Wiener Zeitung* (September 12, 1925): 1–3.

18 See *BGBl.* no. 21 issued on January 13, 1925, Ordinance of December 27, 1924: Amendment of the Civil Engineer Ordinance, accessed April 22, 2022, http://alex.onb.ac.at/cgi-contentalex?aid=bgb&datum=1925&page=181&size=45.

19 For example, Elisabeth Glück, née Porges, Pongracz by marriage (1909–74), or Erna Grigkar, née Kapinus (1909–2001), studied at the Technical University.

20 Gabriele Koller, "Die verlorene Moderne. Von der Kunstgewerbeschule zur (Reichs-)Hochschule für angewandte Kunst, Wien," in *Im Reich der Kunst. Die Wiener Akademie der bildenden Künste und die faschistische Kunstpolitik*, ed. Hans Seiger, Michael Lunardi, and Peter J. Populorum (Vienna: Verlag für Gesellschaftskritik, 1990), 196.

erecting numerous buildings, schools, and kindergartens in the historicist architectural style known as *Heimatstil*.[21]

Three Jewish female graduates—Margarete Zak, née Hoffmann (1891–1977), Charlotte Zenter (born 1905), and Judith Zweig, Katinka by marriage (1915–2003)—subsequently studied at the Academy of Fine Arts. Zak managed to complete her professional degree in June 1938 before emigrating first to England in 1939 and from there to New York in 1940, whereas the other two were forced to break off their studies. Although Haerdtl predicted in 1936 that Zweig would have a successful career,[22] the trend of the times precluded her from practicing her profession. As the daughter of Egon Zweig, a famous Zionist and cousin of the renowned Austrian writer Stefan Zweig, she emigrated to Jerusalem in 1937 and did not practice as an architect thereafter.[23]

Technical University

There were massive reservations at the Technical University about women engaging in academic studies. As long as women did not have the Matura, the Technical University could reject them on the basis of statutory requirements. However, women were becoming ever more qualified and education for girls ever more advanced. For example, in 1892 the first university-track secondary school for girls was founded in Vienna (Mädchen-Gymnasium des Vereins für höhere Frauenbildung). As a result, the Technical University was increasingly running out of arguments. Leonie Pilewski, Karlsson by marriage (1897–1992), is a case in point. The admission applications she submitted from 1915 onward were regularly denied even though she had a Matura. The various reasons given for rejecting her applications are interesting. In 1915, for instance, the young woman was accused of trying to exploit the war in order to have her unreasonable request granted: at a time when men "faced enemies in battle," her application was especially "inappropriate" because the admission of women would create a "new group" of "competitors in the profession."[24] Besides these arguments about competition or lack of space, the Technical University also expressed fundamental biases, casting doubt on women's mathematical skills or their spatial visualization ability.

21 Stadtarchiv Wels, Nachlass Hilda Döring-Kuras.

22 "Her completed studies will show her the road to becoming an architect." See UAUAK, Abgangszeugnis für (diploma for) Judith Zweig, no. 1531, June 30, 1936, evaluation by Oswald Haerdtl.

23 Israel State Archive, Judith Zweig, www.archives.gov.il/en/archives/#/Archive/0b07170680034dc1/File/0b0717068098ec5f, accessed August 28, 2018. Information kindly provided by Sigal Davidi. Sigal Davidi, *Building a New Land: Women Architects and Women's Organizations in Mandatory Palestine* (Ra'anana: Lamda, Open University Publishing House, 2020) [published in Hebrew].

24 Juliane Mikoletzky et al. (eds.), *"Dem Zuge der Zeit entsprechend ….". Zur Geschichte des Frauenstudiums in Österreich am Beispiel der Technischen Universität Wien* (Vienna: WUV-Universitätsverlag, 1997), 54.

Because of her tenacity, Pilewski succeeded in at least auditing classes in certain subjects before going on to earn her architectural degree at what is today's Technical University Darmstadt (TU Darmstadt) in 1922. She designed apartments in Vienna and wrote articles for trade journals about modern construction projects in Czechoslovakia and the Soviet Union from 1928 until emigrating to Sweden in 1938.[25]

A similarly circuitous route was taken by Ella Briggs-Baumfeld (1880–1977), who studied painting at the Kunstgewerbeschule from 1901 to 1906.[26] After 1907 she undertook her first architectural assignments in New York.[27] Like Pilewski before her, Briggs-Baumfeld managed to audit courses in individual subjects at the Technical University between 1916 and 1918 but was never formally admitted as a regular student. In 1919 she was awarded the Matura by the State Trade School (Staatsgewerbeschule) in Salzburg and in 1920 earned a professional degree at the technical university in Munich (today's TU München or TUM). After further years working in the profession in New York, she spent two years (1925–27) planning the Pestalozzi-Hof, a public housing complex prominently situated in Vienna's 19th district, as well as the neighboring Ledigenheim, an apartment building for singles. Apart from Schütte-Lihotzky, Briggs-Baumfeld was the only female architect to receive a contract under Red Vienna's housing construction program. After carrying out building projects in Berlin in 1927/28, she emigrated to Great Britain in 1936. From 1945 onward, she played an active role in a participative urban renewal project initiated by Otto and Marie Neurath for a section of Wolverhampton called Bilston (today Stowlawn) that had become very run down because of local coal mining activities, and designed a number of houses for this project.

The types of reservations about women varied among the professors, who included Siegfried Theiss, Karl Holey, Erwin Ilz, and Alfred Keller. Lisl Close (1912–2011) cited the misogynous climate as one of the reasons she broke off her studies in 1932 after two years and went to Boston, where she completed her master's degree at Massachusetts Institute of Technology (MIT) in 1935. She was the daughter of the Social Democratic councilman Gustav Scheu and author Helene

25 Maasberg and Prinz, *Die Neuen kommen!* 72–73. ÖStA/AdR E-uReang AHF K Karlsson Leonie. Pilewski designed interiors for the Werkbundsiedlung in Vienna in 1932—a public housing project of model single-family homes—as did colleagues of hers such as Rosa Weiser, Adele Gomperz, and Ilse Bernheimer. Other women interested in studying did not even attempt studying in Vienna but registered straight away at a German technical college, such as the Viennese-born Lilia Skala, née Sofer (1896–1994), who went to Dresden in 1916 and completed her professional degree there in 1920. On returning to Vienna, she worked as an architect and then discovered her talent for acting at the Reinhardt Seminar. In 1931–37 she appeared in various feature movies before emigrating in 1939 with her Jewish husband Erik Skala and their children to the United States, where she proceeded to forge a career as an actress of stage and screen. See International Archive of Women in Architecture, Virginia Tech, Special Collections (IAWA), MS 2003-015.

26 Katrin Stingl, "Ella Briggs(-Baumfeld). Wohnbauten in Wien (1925/26) und in Berlin (1929/30)" (master's thesis, University of Vienna, 2008); Robert Schmid, Ella Briggs (1880–1977): *Beiträge der*

Scheu-Riesz, who lived in the villa that Adolf Loos had built for them in Vienna's 13th district in 1913. Lisl Close and her husband, the architect Winston Close, ran a successful architectural firm in Minneapolis and St. Paul, Minnesota. Their extensive oeuvre includes public buildings and more than a hundred private homes, most of them cubic flat-roofed modernist houses with open floor plans nestled in the countryside.[28]

Karola Bloch, née Piotrkowska (1905–94), was born in Łódź and grew up in Moscow and Berlin. She must have had similar feelings about everyday life as a female student at the Technical University between 1929 and 1931. "We had to draw many building components from Antiquity and the Gothic and Baroque periods" and had "an ancient, fossilized professor in statics, who could not get used to the fact that women studied architecture." The overall assessment of the Communist and women's activist was clear: "Discrimination of the female gender in this subject area was visible."[29] In 1931 she transferred her studies to Berlin, where she encountered teachers such as Bruno Taut and Hans Poelzig; she completed her studies in Zurich in 1934 and then married the philosopher Ernst Bloch in Vienna. She spent the next two years

Fig. 3. Dora Gad, villa in Caesarea, Israel, 1974.

österreichischen Architektin zum Bauen in einer Zeit der gesellschaftlichen Umwälzung, des politischen Umbruchs und der wirtschaftlichen Not (master's thesis, Technical University of Vienna, 2019). New insights into Ella Briggs's life and work were presented at the international workshop "Rediscovering Ella Briggs—The Challenge of Writing Inclusive Architectural Histories for Women Who Broke the Mold," organized by Elana Shapira, Despina Stratigakos, and Monika Platzer at the Architekturzentrum Wien on June 6, 2022. The following accompanying publication is planned: Elana Shapira and Despina Stratigakos (eds.), *Ella Briggs: An Unconventional Architect* (Princeton: Princeton University Press, 2024).

27 The contracts presumably came about with the help of her brother Maurice (Moritz) Baumfeld, the head of the German-speaking Irving Place Theatre in New York (lounges in the German theater, in the New York Press Club, etc.). E.F., "Aus dem Reiche der Frau," *Fremden-Blatt* (May 5, 1914): 17.

28 Christine Kanzler, "Scheu Close, Elizabeth, geb. Scheu," in *Wissenschafterinnen in Österreich. Leben – Werk – Wirken*, ed. Brigitta Keintzel and Ilse Korotin (Vienna: Böhlau, 2002),

living in Prague, where she worked with Friedl Dicker-Brandeis before emigrating with her own family to the United States in 1937. After returning to Leipzig in 1949, she planned kindergartens and day nurseries at the Deutsche Bauakademie (German Building Academy) in East Berlin. After being expelled from the Socialist Unity Party of Germany (East German Communist Party, ruling party of the GDR) as an anti-Stalinist, she fled with her husband to Tübingen in 1961.

Interestingly enough, there was a group of Zionists among the female students at the Technical University, among them the first female graduate Helene Roth (1904–95), followed by Dora Siegel (1912–2003) and Anna Klapholz (born 1909). Between 1934 and 1936, they emigrated to Palestine, where there was great demand for specialists from Europe who were willing and able to help build the society and modern cities such as Tel Aviv or Haifa. All three found initial positions as interior designers in offices run by German emigrant architects (Alfred Abraham, Oskar Kaufmann).[30] Dora Siegel had an unparalleled career. She studied at the

645–46. Judith Eiblmayr is currently conducting research on Lisl Close's oeuvre. Jane King Hession, *Elizabeth Scheu Close: A Life in Modern Architecture* (Minneapolis: University of Minnesota Press, 2020).

29 Karola Bloch, *Aus meinem Leben* (Tübingen: Neske, 1981), 61–62; Claudia Lenz, "Karola Bloch und das Kinderwochenheim 'Zukunft der Nation,'" in *Frau Architekt. Seit mehr als 100 Jahren: Frauen im Architekturberuf*, exhibition catalog, Deutsches Architekturmuseum (DAM), Frankfurt am Main, ed. Mary Pepchinski et al. (Berlin: Wasmuth, 2017), 153–57.

Fig. 4. Edith Lassmann, Kaprun-Oberstufe, powerhouse at the foot of the Limberg Dam during construction, 1950.

30 Sigal Davidi, "Architektinnen aus Deutschland und Österreich im Mandatsgebiet Palästina," in *Frau Architekt*, 49–57.

31 Ran Shechori, *Dora Gad. The Israeli Presence in Interior Design* (Tel Aviv: The Architecture of Israel, 1997).

32 IAWA, the Melita Rodeck Architectural Collection, MS 1992-028.

33 Ute Georgeacopol-Winischhofer, "Sich-bewähren am Objektiven," in Mikoletzky, *"Dem Zuge der Zeit entsprechend …,"* 185–254.

Technical University from 1930–34 and married her colleague Yehezkel Goldberg in 1936. Working under the name Dora Gad, she became one of Israel's most renowned architects and designers in the 1950s and 1960s. She had had a solid Viennese education that was rooted in traditional principles and knew how to combine it with a unique feel for material and color. She was also adept at working productively with artists. Her airy rooms with their open layouts must be viewed as a response to the local climate. The work she did for the State of Israel and its highest representatives such as the prime minister (in Jerusalem in 1950) include the interior design of the Israeli National Library (in Jerusalem in 1956), the Knesset (in 1966), and the Israel Museum (with Al Mansfeld in 1965). Her most remarkable project is probably the sculptural house in Caesarea in 1974; she was responsible for its planning, construction, and interior design (fig. 3).[31]

Among the Technical University female graduates who emigrated to the United States, mention should be made of the former Zimbler collaborator Melita Rodeck (1914–2011). From the 1950s on, she busied herself with restoration concepts for historical city buildings or entire sections of Washington D.C., displaying a keen interest in urban planning and sociology, which she supported with numerous studies. Later she built for the US Army (1968–73) and for the Catholic Church. In 1960, she founded the Regina Institute of Sacred Art to help with the design of the Catholic building projects.[32]

Although two-thirds of the women who had initially enrolled broke off their studies at the Technical University, most of the 32 graduates from 1919 to 1938 did gain a foothold in the profession, working in architectural firms, in public administration, in the preservation of historical monuments, or in higher education.[33] Three women had even earned doctorate degrees by 1938, and after 1945 many of them obtained a license to practice architecture. The technical training they received at the Technical University enabled them to undertake building assignments that had clearly been associated with men up to that point. Brigitte Kundl, Muthwill by marriage (1906–92), earned a doctorate in 1935 with her design of a city airport for Vienna, and Edith Lassmann, née Jurecka (1920–2007), made a name for herself in the 1950s in power plant construction (fig. 4).[34] After 1945, women were represented as pioneers in all areas, especially social housing construction. Mention should be made of Adelheid Gnaiger, née Spiegel (1916–91),[35] the first female architect in the Austrian province of Vorarlberg, who gained a reputation as a planner of government buildings, and Helene Koller-Buchwieser (1912–2008), who had a successful career building sacred structures and housing.[36]

Academy of Fine Arts

The Academy of Fine Arts had the fewest female graduates. Of the approximately 25 women who enrolled between 1920 and 1945, only 10 completed their studies. As already mentioned, many of them had already completed their studies at the Kunstgewerbeschule, such as Josefine Kraus, Eisler by marriage (born 1914); Isabella Hartl; Irene Hittaller, Kutzbach by marriage (1903–87); and Margarete Zak. Admission criteria included completion of studies at the Kunstgewerbeschule as well as the first state examination at the Technical University or completion of comparable studies abroad. Although Peter Behrens was a professor at the Academy of Fine Arts from 1921 to 1936, no female students completed his master class program. In the words of Ernst Plischke, that school did not attract "chirping birds" as the Strnad class did, "but rather officers returning from the World War, young, self-confident men."[37] Virtually all female students passed through the master class program run by Holzmeister until his emigration to Turkey in 1938, when it was taken over by Alexander Popp. The first female graduate was Martha Bolldorf-Reitstätter (1912–2001). Holzmeister encouraged her during her studies and employed her after her successful diploma examination in 1934 as one of his "best supports."[38] She directed the construction of the interior of the Broadcasting Center for him from 1936 to 1940. As a member of the Nazi Party, her activities included working for a paramilitary engineering group known as Organisation Todt.[39] Another woman with no reservations about associating with the Nazi environment was Isabella Hartl, Ploberger by marriage (1913–2002). After graduating in 1938, she debuted in Berlin as a set designer for Leni Riefenstahl's movie adaptation of

34 Alexandra Kraus, "Zum Leben und Werk der Architektin Edith Lassmann (1920–2007)" (master's thesis, TU Wien, 2018).

35 Ingrid Holzschuh (ed.), *Adelheid Gnaiger (1916–1991). Die erste Architektin Vorarlbergs* (Zurich: Park Books, 2014).

36 IAWA, the Helene Koller-Buchwieser Architectural Papers, MS 1995-020.

37 Ernst A. Plischke, *Ein Leben mit Architektur* (Vienna: Löcker, 1989), 55.

38 UAUAK, Personalakt (personnel file of) Martha Reitstätter (Bolldorf by marriage), no. 1213.

39 Ute Georgeacopol-Winischhofer, "Martha Bolldorf-Reitstätter," in Keintzel and Korotin, *Wissenschafterinnen*, 85–88.

40 "The movie came under suspicion and became the subject matter

the opera Tiefland (1940–44).[40] Even after World War II, she and her second husband Werner Schlichting were much-sought-after movie set designers for well-known German, Austrian, and American productions.

Holzmeister's master class program was likely a gathering place for students with greatly diverging political views. They included a female Resistance fighter from Chile named Ines Victoria Maier, Gonzalez by marriage (1914–2004), who graduated in 1939 and heeded her teacher's call in September of that same year and followed him to Istanbul. In Turkey, she joined the Communist Resistance group that had formed around architects such as Herbert Eichholzer and the married couple Margarete and Wilhelm Schütte, who were working in proximity to Holzmeister.[41] Maier (alias Wera) took an active part in setting up the foreign section of the Communist Party and made several trips as a courier. On January 22, 1941, she was arrested, interrogated by the Gestapo, and—like Schütte-Lihotzky—put in prison in Vienna.[42] With help from the Chilean consulate, her family brought about her release and removal to the "Old Reich" (i.e., Germany). From there she was deported to Chile, where she lived and worked as an architect until her death in 2004.[43] The multifaceted careers of these first female architects illustrate that it was not easy for them to enter professional life because of their social, political, or personal circumstances. They shared this experience with many women in other academic and artistic professions. Mainly, they became employees in architectural firms; only a few of them ventured to become self-employed architects, mostly doing so after 1945. Jewish female architects who succeeded in fleeing abroad forged amazing careers in their countries of exile. I think it is also worthy of note that these female architects were in contact with each other in various ways and also institutionalized these connections after World War II. For instance, 1963 saw the founding of the International Union of Women Architects, an organization in which the former Technical University student Judith Roque-Gourary (1915–2010) was actively involved.[44] As a Jew, she had decided to flee to Brussels in 1938 and completed her studies there at the renowned visual arts school La Cambre in 1941. In 1978 she

of a […] trial because of the alleged mistreatment of gypsies who were intermittently let out of the concentration camps to participate in the film and whom Leni Riefenstahl did not champion despite her promises to do so." See Kay Weniger, *Das große Personenlexikon des Films, Band 6* (Berlin: Schwarzkopf & Schwarzkopf, 2001), 532.

41 https://www.univie.ac.at/biografiA/projekt/Widerstandskaempferinnen/Maier_Victoria.htm, accessed April 22, 2022. See also the essay by Antje Senarclens de Grancy in this volume.

42 Margarete Schütte-Lihotzky, *Erinnerungen aus dem Widerstand, 1938–1945*, ed. Chup Friemert (Hamburg: Konkret Literatur Verlag, 1985), 92–98 and 120.

43 See Sophie Hochhäusl, "Spatial Histories of Dissidence: Imagination, Memory, and Resistance in Istanbul, Vienna, and Santiago de Chile, 1938–1945," *Ediciones* ARQ, no. 105 (2020): 40–61, accessed April 22, 2022, https://archives.cl/en/spatial-histories-of-dissidence-imagination-memory-and-resistance-in-istanbul-vienna-and-santiago-de-chile-1938-1945/.

44 IAWA, the Judith (Dita) Roque-Gourary Architectural Collection, MS 2011-074.

helped to set up the Union of Women Architects in Belgium. These and other networks of female architects were instrumental in the establishment in 1985 of the International Archive of Women in Architecture at Virginia Tech in Blacksburg, Virginia, USA, an archive in which the estates of several Austrian female architects await researchers.

Life Number Three. Reflections on Margarete Schütte-Lihotzky's Autobiographical Work

Bernadette Reinhold

> Dear Ms. Architect,
> You should definitely consider committing all your memories to paper! [...]
> Letter from Friedrich Achleitner (1977)[1]

1 Friedrich Achleitner to Margarete Schütte-Lihotzky, Vienna, April 26, 1977, University Archive of the University of Applied Arts Vienna, Nachlass Margarete Schütte-Lihotzky (UAUAK, NL MSL), Korrespondenz Inland [underlining in the original].

The Austrian writer Karl-Markus Gauss is known for his literary explorations of remote regions in Europe. In his 2019 novel *Abenteuerliche Reise durch mein Wohnzimmer* (Adventurous journey through my living room), he turns his focus on territory familiar to him: his own living room and study. On closer examination and with the author as the point of departure, the furniture, pictures, and objects start telling their own stories, which extend far beyond the author yet ultimately return to him, to his living room. The idea of making a person's world of concrete things the narrator is not unusual and opens up new perspectives (also as a possible autobiographical vehicle). In the crypto-portrait genre—van Gogh's 1886 painting *Shoes* comes to mind—objects and room depictions can represent the individuals with whom they are associated and can become a likeness in a broader interpretive framework. Pictures of artists' studios or writers' studies, rendered by them or by someone else, lead to places of origin and suggest the possibility of discovering—as in a hidden-objects drawing—biographical traces on the cusp between work and life.

This essay revolves around Margarete Schütte-Lihotzky's autobiographical work. It was articulated in various courses of action and reflected in different media and formats. To this day, they all remain part of a complex reception process, primarily academic yet also artistic. Two of her published texts serve as the starting points: *Erinnerungen aus dem Widerstand. Das kämpferische Leben einer Architektin von 1938–1945* (Memories from the Resistance. The combative life of a female architect 1938–1945),[2] first published in 1985, and *Warum ich Architektin wurde* (Why I became an architect), released posthumously in 2004. Schütte-Lihotzky's motivation and the complicated genesis of her autobiographical publications will be described here, and questions raised about these life narratives:[3] What does the author remember, what does she hide—what is her motivation for speaking out (or for remaining silent)? From the perspective of gender, it is also relevant to consider the places and time periods she evokes and how her memories became etched into her physical being. Since the autobiographical self also etches itself into the material space it inhabits, I would like to start my reflections by sharing a photograph of Margarete Schütte-Lihotzky's bedroom-cum-workspace. It was taken in July 2000, six months after her death, by the architectural photographer Margherita Spiluttini. This room is in an apartment on Franzensgasse in Vienna, whose floor plan and interior design she began planning in 1967 (fig. 1).[4] In the strict central perspective, the long, narrow room seems stretched widthwise, balancing out the contrast between the packed bookshelves on the left-hand wall and the row of light-flooded windows opposite them. The space ends in the diffuse shadows of the sleeping alcove—a reference to the multipurpose *Schlafraum einer Dame* (Bedroom for a Lady) she designed in 1925.[5] The room looks tidy, with a few items put down here and there, a small reading lamp switched on. A viewer aware that the room's occupant was no longer alive

2 An English translation is planned in S. E. Eisterer's ongoing publication project *Margarete Schütte-Lihotzky and the Architecture of Collective Dissidence, 1919–1989.*

3 See Sidonie Smith and Julia Watson, *Reading Autobiography. A Guide for Interpreting Life Narratives*, 2nd ed. (Minneapolis: University of Minnesota Press, 2010).

4 Ulrike Jenni, "Margaretes Wohnungen in Wien," in *Margarete Schütte-Lihotzky. Spuren in Wien*, ed. Christine Zwingl (Vienna: Promedia, 2021), 25–33.

5 Original in the MAK Permanent Collection, Vienna.

Fig. 1. Margarete Schütte-Lihotzky's bedroom-cum-workspace in her apartment on Franzensgasse in Vienna in July 2000, photo by Margherita Spiluttini.

at the time the photograph was taken might feel a sense of stillness and absence setting in. Schütte-Lihotzky, a major figure of the 20th century (*Jahrhundertgestalt*),[6] had passed away shortly before her 103rd birthday. It is not a place steeped in sentimentality but rather a room faithful to her lifelong professional creed, a functional and eminently comfortable living space.

Three adjacent areas for different uses are lined up here with fluid transitions from one to the next, creating an atmosphere of inspiration, concentration, and refuge. The desk, illuminated from the left for the right-hander, was a place of communication. A phone and a second stool (which is visible in other photos) are silent witnesses to the many conversations Schütte-Lihotzky had and interviews she gave here up to just weeks before her death. In her later years, her political

6 Anja Kramer, "Margarete Schütte-Lihotzky. Jahrhundertgestalt," *Architektur. Im Strom der Zeit. Von Coop Himmelb(l)au über Margarete Schütte-Lihotzky bis Pilgram – diese Architekten haben Österreich geformt*, *Kurier Trendo* 3 (2019): 62–66.

convictions and her career as an architect had turned into an obligation for her to pass on knowledge but warnings as well. The aim of her autobiographical work was to textualize her life story but also to directly narrate, repeat, and tailor it to the given addressee. I will elaborate below on these aspects, which play an essential part in how her life narratives developed.

Schütte-Lihotzky was a prolific writer. For a long time, the desk was an ideal place for her to write, surrounded by books, plans, sketches, and documents, some of which were kept in an adjoining closet. She wrote down and typed her own texts herself, even as her eyesight began to fail, until the day came when she had to leave this task to others. That explains why her much-used typewriter no longer garnered a spot here toward the end of her life. Lying on and even under her desk are folders that are now preserved in the estate, among them extensive autobiographical manuscripts. Others are on the small tables grouped around the armchair —a place for her to read, listen to the radio, or collect her thoughts. At the end of the room is a sofa bed and above it an Uzbek suzani, a richly embroidered wall hanging traditionally made by brides as part of their dowry. Virtually all her memorabilia are pragmatically integrated into the scheme of daily life and work in this apartment. So too this textile, a memento of her years in the Soviet Union (1930–37). It becomes an element that informs and shapes this space. The same is true of furniture in the living-dining area: the Biedermeier chairs, presumably family pieces, and the massive Canadian armchairs, designed by Wilhelm Schütte for the apartment they shared in Istanbul (1938–40).[7]

7 David Baum, "Wilhelm Schütte – Soziale Architektur" (MA thesis, University of Art and Design Linz, 2016), 210.

Life Number Three

Margarete Schütte-Lihotzky's move to Franzensgasse marked the start of what I posit to be her life number three, a thesis that also serves as the title of this essay. She herself divided her own life story into two parts. The first comprised her time in Vienna (till 1925), in Frankfurt (1926–30), in the Soviet Union (1930–37), and then mostly in Turkey (1938–40) with brief stays in London and Paris. This was followed by her return from Turkey to Vienna in late 1940 where she was arrested in January 1941 after putting in 25 days of Resistance work against the Nazi regime. She narrowly escaped execution but was sentenced to 15 years of the most severe form of incarceration (*schwerer Kerker*) involving forced confinement and wretched conditions. In the spring of 1945, she was freed from Aichach Prison in Bavaria. She soon returned to Vienna to do her part in building the new Austria: "My life after 1945—following liberation, the horrors of death—felt like life number two to me."[8] After the general anti-Fascist consensus had shifted to anti-Communist hegemony,[9] Schütte-Lihotzky, as a staunch Communist, saw no public contracts come her way with a few rare exceptions. She became someone who "in time-honored Viennese fashion [was] *not even worth ignoring.*"[10] Her expertise lay fallow in the country for which she had risked her life. Marcel Bois talks about a form of "political and social isolation" that became a "second exile" for many of the returning Communist intellectuals.[11] But Schütte-Lihotzky turned her energies to new tasks: setting up memorial sites for victims of Nazi terror, carrying out construction contracts for the Communist Party of Austria (KPÖ), serving as an expert consultant in East Germany and in Cuba, but most of all, becoming deeply involved in politics as an activist in the League of Democratic Women, in the peace movement, and elsewhere. She published extensively throughout this "life number two." The period also coincides with her divorce from her husband Wilhelm Schütte, with whom she remained on friendly terms until his death in 1968, even sharing an office with him for a time. Around her 70th birthday, she was working on her final building projects: a modular system for kindergartens that was never realized, the planning of her own apartment, and a construction/renovation project involving a vacation home her sister had in Radstadt in the Austrian province of Salzburg. She ended her active career as an architect in 1975 after designing a four-story residential building where the ground-floor apartments had gardens and the upper ones, terraces.

After an impressive career of nearly 20 years as "Frau Architekt," she disappeared from the collective consciousness for decades because of her political convictions and other factors.[12] Her canonization in architectural, contemporary,

8 UAUAK, NL MSL, Interviews Radio/TV, Mappe TV-Interview, ORF—Harald Sterk, May 1, 1985, "Abschluss II Alternativ" concept.

9 See Manfred Mugrauer's essay in this publication.

10 Friedrich Achleitner, "Bauen, für eine bessere Welt," in *Margarete Schütte-Lihotzky. Soziale Architektur. Zeitzeugin eines Jahrhunderts*, exhibition catalog, MAK—Austrian Museum of Applied Arts, Vienna, ed. Peter Noever (Vienna: Böhlau, 1993), 10 [italics in the original].

11 See Marcel Bois's essay in this publication.

12 Ibid.

and design history may be undisputed today; back then it was inconceivable. She had been all but forgotten. Yet that changed in the mid-1970s. Viennese modernism after 1900, the settlement movement, Red Vienna[13] and New Frankfurt[14] became research topics for a young, politically charged generation that was eagerly delving into the recent past and its protagonists. In times of the "economic miracle" in Germany and Austria after World War II, the *Gemeindebauten*—the exemplary public housing complexes in Vienna built in the 1920s and early 1930s—had long since lost their sheen and the Frankfurt Kitchen had become an unloved relict of prewar times.[15] Society was spoiled by progress. Then came the protests of 1968 and the oil crisis of 1973. It was their aftereffects, inter alia, that shifted attention to earlier days of prosperity and crisis and created a desire to break the silence of the parents' generation with regard to the still-virulent shadows cast by Nazism. In the late 1980s but especially from the 1990s on, interest was sparked in Schütte-Lihotzky as a female architect, a perception reflecting a public sensitized to the issue of gender.[16] The third life of Margarete Schütte-Lihotzky had begun.

The Complicated Genesis of an Indivisible, Divided Autobiography

Schütte-Lihotzky was able to report firsthand on major developments in the history of modern architecture and urban planning and on encounters with renowned protagonists ranging from Adolf Loos to Ernst May. She was a contemporary witness par excellence, with a superb memory and a gift for presenting even complex matters in a clearly delineated and precisely formulated manner. Moreover, she had a large archive in which she kept her own work as well as materials bearing witness to her professional and political environment. As the questions sent to her multiplied, so too did the requests for her to write her memoirs. In her 80s by this time, she proved to be fertile ground for this idea. Margarete Schütte-Lihotzky said repeatedly that she "never really enjoyed writing and only wanted to build,"[17] but she did pen a steady stream of articles about architecture from 1921 on and about explicitly political issues after 1945. In

13 On the history of the reception of Red Vienna, see Werner Michael Schwarz, Georg Spitaler, and Elke Wikidal, "Einleitung," in *Das Rote Wien 1919–1934. Ideen, Debatten, Praxis*, ed. idem, exhibition catalog, Wien Museum (Basel: Birkhäuser, 2018), 12–15.

14 On the history of the reception of New Frankfurt, see Jörg Schilling, "Begriff und Rezeption: Fragen an und um das 'Neue Frankfurt,'" in *Akteure des Neuen Frankfurt. Archiv für Frankfurts Geschichte und Kunst*, Band 75, ed. Evelyn Brockhoff et al. (Frankfurt am Main: Societäts-Verlag, 2016), 13–22; Claudia Quiring et al., "Vorwort," in *Ernst May. 1886–1970*, ed. idem, exhibition catalog, Deutsches Architekturmuseum (DAM), Frankfurt am Main (Munich: Prestel, 2001), 9–13.

15 See Marie-Theres Deutsch's essay in this publication.

16 Particular reference should be made here to the Schütte-Lihotzky research group with Renate Allmayer-Beck, Susanne Baumgartner-Haindl, Marion Lindner, and Christine Zwingl.

17 Conversation with Margarete Schütte-Lihotzky, in *Margarete Schütte-Lihotzky. Soziale Architektur*, 15.

keeping with her oft-cited motto "Every millimeter makes sense," she also revised her autobiographical manuscripts time and time again. In an effort to communicate her views unequivocally, she altered text structures, content, even individual sentences and words over and over to perfect them and render them more precise. She was also always well prepared for interviews, often formulating certain statements in advance.[18] Her interviewers could count on her being open and curious, but she left nothing to chance.

18 See UAUAK, NL MSL, Interviews Radio/TV.

Although often plagued by eye problems, Schütte-Lihotzky worked intensively on her autobiography, which she never would have designated as such. Her parents had attached great importance to the education of their daughters and had instilled a sense of self-confidence in them. So, her intention decades later was to portray herself in a way that was self-confident but never conceited or egotistical. She viewed herself as a significant witness of the times. In writing her memoirs, she wanted to pass on knowledge that would otherwise have been lost. She knew what and why she was remembering and for whom. In one of her early correspondences with publishers, she noted: "This is the situation: for some time now, I have been urged to write my memoirs by various architects and others, as well as by institutions, including the Documentation Centre of Austrian Resistance and similar institutes that have a purely historical interest in the period 1938–45. I am the only one still able to recount my time working in the Resistance and all the ensuing events because everyone else I was involved with during the Nazi era was killed. That is why I began with this period. [...] It never occurred to me to simply exclude those years and their contexts from my memoirs as a professional architect."[19]

19 Schütte-Lihotzky to Ulrich Conrads, Radstadt, August 20, 1979, UAUAK, NL MSL, Erinnerungen und Betrachtungen/ Verlagskorrespondenz/ Bauwelt, TXT/588.

Her goal was originally to write *one* book, arranged chronologically. In the 1993 exhibition and work catalog of the MAK—Museum of Applied Arts, Vienna, Friedrich Achleitner wrote as follows: "'The actual message of her work seems to me to lie in the indivisibility of her efforts and in the inseparability of theory and practice, of thoughts and actions. Grete Schütte-Lihotzky never divided herself into three separate persons: professional, political, and private. Nor did she consider architecture a separate system only about skills and bids, nor her political activism a mere sideline confined to Austria."[20] That would change: the German-language publishing scene, inter alia, posed a dilemma for her indivisible memoirs, *Erinnerungen*.[21] She made initial plans in 1979 with Ulrich Conrads to publish these memoirs in *Bauwelt Fundamente*, a now legendary book series he had initiated. It featured monographs on notables such as Le Corbusier, Frank Lloyd Wright, and Bruno Taut as well as manifestos on modern and contemporary architecture. But even in his first letter, Conrads made it clear that the "more professionally oriented yet diverse readership" of this series would "not be a forum for the political part of your memoirs" and suggested observing reasonable limits in integrating the Resistance years.[22] He does not appear to have been fully persuaded by the project anyway, as it failed after about three years. The author was in contact with various German and also Austrian publishers at that same time.

Also significant from 1981 on was the German designer and design theoretician Chup Friemert, who was conducting research on the Frankfurt Kitchen at the time. He helped "Comrade Grete" establish her ties with Konkret Literatur Verlag in Hamburg and constantly encouraged her to work on what he coined her "architectural history/life story."[23] In the spring of 1983, she had apparently completed the first two chapters. The first covered her "Architectural Studies and Practical Experience in the Vienna Settlement Movement up to 1926;" the second, "The Frankfurt Period (1926–1930)." She was still working on the third chapter about her years in the Soviet Union (1930–37).[24]

Her account of her Communist Resistance work already existed in around 1980 and by then had taken on a life of its own, a parallel life, as the subject matter for a movie. A new protagonist in this turn of events was the Austrian playwright Peter Turrini, who also wrote the screenplay for *Alpensaga* (Alpine saga), a highly controversial TV series at the time. After reading her Resistance memoirs with great admiration, he helped her establish further contacts with publishers and Austrian Broadcasting Corporation (Österreichischer Rundfunk, ORF).[25] The goal was to produce a TV movie by 1985, the 40th anniversary of the end of World War II. But a

20 Friedrich Achleitner, "Bauen, für eine bessere Welt," 10.

21 On the complex history of the genesis and publication history of her Resistance memoirs *Erinnerungen aus dem Widerstand*, see also Margarete Schütte-Lihotzky and Wilhelm Schütte, *"Mach den Weg um Prinkipo, meine Gedanken werden Dich dabei begleiten!" Der Gefängnis-Briefwechsel 1941–1945*, ed. Thomas Flierl (Berlin: Lukas Verlag, 2021).

22 Ulrich Conrads to Schütte-Lihotzky, Berlin, August 15, 1979, UAUAK, NL MSL, Erinnerungen und Betrachtungen/Verlagskorrespondenz/Bauwelt, TXT/588.

23 Chup Friemert to Schütte-Lihotzky, Hamburg, November 19, 1981, UAUAK, NL MSL, Buch *Erinnerungen III*, Briefverkehr, Presse, Abbildungslisten, Korrespondenz Jup [sic] Friemert & andere.

24 Schütte-Lihotzky to Rainer Nitsche, Vienna, June 29, 1983, UAUAK, NL MSL, Erinnerungen und Betrachtungen/Verlagskorrespondenz/Transit, TXT/589.

25 Peter Turrini to Schütte-Lihotzky, Vienna, June 6, 1981, UAUAK, NL MSL, Buch *Erinnerungen III*, Briefverkehr, Presse, Abbildungslisten.

documentary by Harald Sterk was broadcast on ORF first, on May 1, 1985; its title: *Der Architektur kann keiner entrinnen. Die Architektin und Widerstandskämpferin Margarete Schütte-Lihotzky* (No one can escape from architecture. The architect and Resistance fighter Margarete Schütte-Lihotzky). It was not until the next year that the planned ORF production *Eine Minute Dunkel macht uns nicht blind* (One minute of darkness does not blind us) was filmed and not until January 1987 that it was broadcast on ORF in honor of Schütte-Lihotzky's 90th birthday. This feature film was based on a screenplay by Susanne Zanke, who also directed it.

It was clear by the fall of 1981 that Chup Friemert would publish not Schütte-Lihotzky's "architectural history/life story" but instead her Resistance memoirs *Erinnerungen aus dem Widerstand*. They were published in 1985 by Konkret Verlag and concurrently in a licensed edition by Volk und Welt, a publisher in East Berlin.[26] The existing text was edited and a lengthy interview by Friemert was added to it. He and the publisher were well aware that these were the memoirs of a figure largely unknown, both as an architect and as a political activist. The subject was comparatively new from the perspective of West German *Vergangenheitspolitik*, its policies and politics concerning its (Nazi) past. In East Germany, the Communist Resistance was part of the country's political and national self-image whereas in West Germany, it was long viewed as treason against the fatherland and counterbalanced by westward orientation, the Cold War, and hegemonic anti-Communism. This situation changed in the course of the 1970s and 1980s. However, the role women played in the Resistance would still not be a subject of research for some time to come. In Germany, about 15 percent of the Communist Party members were women. From that, one can estimate the percentage share of female Resistance fighters (a group which, in itself, must be considered with discernment).[27] In its reception, the Resistance against the Nazi regime long connoted masculinity or heroism while the prevailing role model for women depicted them as largely apolitical. Oftentimes, women's Resistance work took on other forms and was invisible—for example, carrying out acts of sabotage in everyday settings or hiding victims

26 Margarete Schütte-Lihotzky, *Erinnerungen aus dem Widerstand. Das kämpferische Leben einer Architektin von 1938–1945* (Hamburg: Konkret Literatur Verlag, 1985 and Berlin: Volk und Welt, 1985; Vienna: Promedia, 1994 and 2014). In this essay, I quote from the second edition published in 1994.

27 Christl Wickert, "Widerstand und Dissens von Frauen – ein Überblick," in *Frauen gegen die Diktatur – Widerstand und Verfolgung im nationalsozialistischen Deutschland*, ed. Christl Wickert (Berlin: Edition Hentrich, 1995), 18–31, here 18.

of persecution. Women were stereotypically deemed to be above suspicion. Although this perception soon faded, attempts were made to exploit it following an initial phase in which large numbers of male Resistance fighters were arrested, deported to concentration camps, or executed. Nonetheless, a broad historical awareness of female Resistance fighters emerged very late, in some cases not until the 1990s.[28] In 1985 one was still in virtually uncharted territory with Schütte-Lihotzky's Resistance memoirs.[29]

In his interview, Friemert ranged far beyond the narrower topic at hand, covering the entire sweep of Schütte-Lihotzky's life, her work as an architect, and her political activism, from childhood up into the postwar era. He was attempting to contextualize her and linguistically to create "a vivid portrayal"[30] of her as a person. The author, for her part, wanted a succinct biographical summary as an appendix to her text as well as a preface by Turrini. Shortly before the book was to go to press, the conflict came to a head because no provisions had been made for the preface. Moreover, Schütte-Lihotzky felt that "[...] what the interview conveyed was the exact opposite of why this book is being written: today's neo-Fascist threat."[31] With this comment, she explicitly stated one of her main motivations for her autobiographical work: remembrance as a present-day political act.

Biographical Labels—Auto/biographical Constructs

Today Margarete Schütte-Lihotzky is deemed a moral authority, a female architect who was always politically minded, always dogged about social responsibility, *and* a woman who was politically active to the very end. In a nutshell, her claim to fame is twofold: as the inventor of the Frankfurt Kitchen and as probably the most prominent (Austrian) female Resistance fighter. She is mostly viewed simplistically as the former, a fact she criticized during her lifetime: "I have done much more in my life than just that. If I had known that everyone would keep talking about nothing else, I would never have built that damned kitchen!"[32] Yet her magnum opus does in fact invite polylateral associations as an icon of modernism, as a solution for making housekeeping more efficient, and as an emancipatory act[33] or it becomes a political

28 See inter alia Wickert, *Frauen gegen Diktatur*; Inge Hansen-Schaberg and Beate Schmeichel-Falkenberg (eds.), *Frauen erinnern. Widerstand – Verfolgung – Exil 1933–1945* (Berlin: Weidler, 2000).

29 Regarded as a pioneering achievement in this respect: Karin Berger (ed.), *Der Himmel ist blau. Kann sein. Frauen im Widerstand, Österreich 1938–1945* (Vienna: Promedia, 1985).

30 Chup Friemert to Schütte-Lihotzky, n.p., n.d. [1984?], UAUAK, NL MSL, Buch *Erinnerungen III*, Briefverkehr, Presse, Abbildungslisten, Korrespondenz Jup [sic] Friemert & andere.

31 Schütte-Lihotzky to Konkret Literatur Verlag, n.p., July 30, 1984, UAUAK, NL MSL, Buch *Erinnerungen III*, Briefverkehr, Presse, Abbildungslisten, Korrespondenz Konkret Verlag.

32 Wojciech Czaja, "Besuch bei keiner Köchin," in *Ich bin keine Küche. Gegenwarts geschichten aus dem Nachlass von Margarete Schütte-Lihotzky*, exhibition catalog, University of Applied Arts Vienna, ed. Patrick Werkner and exhibition and cultural communication management (ecm) (Vienna: University of Applied Arts Vienna, 2008), 21–24, here 23.

statement when referenced in an artwork. The latter is exactly what transpired in 2009 at the Biennale in Venice, where the English artist Liam Gillick engaged in institutional critique with his installation in the German pavilion. The Frankfurt Kitchen had been installed tens of thousands of times in New Frankfurt and was itself a manifestation of emancipation and democracy. Now, Gillick's extensive installation inspired by and alluding to this kitchen spread its way throughout the very exhibition hall that Fascist Germany had built in 1937.

Not least, the labels attached to Schütte-Lihotzky involve associated pictorial form(ula)s, *icons*, that are readily conveyable and apt for multimedia use. As such, they open the way to her popularization or auratization. Few examples could better demonstrate this than the 2008 song "My Tribute to the Frankfurt Kitchen" and the accompanying music video. Both were created by Robert Rotifer, an Austrian musician living in England.[34] In the video's animation consisting of Rotifer's black-and-white brush drawings, the eponymous kitchen features audibly and visibly in the refrain (fig. 2). In between, different buildings and sketches appear along with a well-known portrait photo of Schütte-Lihotzky from the 1920s in many variations. The video pays tribute to her as a female architect but also as a female Communist Resistance fighter by including two icons: a beret with a Soviet star and the cover of her Resistance memoirs *Erinnerungen aus dem Widerstand*. Rotifer undoubtedly had an affinity to the subject because of his grandmother, Irma Schwager (1920–2015), a well-known female Resistance fighter and one of the unifying figures in the Communist women's movement alongside Schütte-Lihotzky. Through the use of playful dissolves, a pictorial identification arises between the musician and his "idol": Grete Lihotzky goes pop.

Schütte-Lihotzky offered multiple possibilities for others to identify with her, and her autobiographical writings, although published in fragmentary form, were a major reason for that. Rotifer's music video, Spiluttini's photo of Schütte-Lihotzky's workspace, Susanne Zanke's feature film, and Liam Gillick's installation all show that biography can manifest itself in different media. Nevertheless, biography is

33 Even the accusation of "redomestication" in the feminist critique of the Frankfurt Kitchen does not undermine Schütte-Lihotzky's emancipatory aspirations; see Susan R. Henderson, "A Revolution in the Woman's Sphere: Grete Lihotzky and the Frankfurt Kitchen," in *Architecture and Feminism*, ed. Debra Coleman, Elizabeth Danze, and Carol Henderson (New York: Princeton Architectural Press, 1996), 221–53.

34 Rotifer, "The Frankfurt Kitchen," music video, 3:42, accessed May 7, 2022, https://interactive.wohnzimmer.com/video-rotifer-the-frankfurt-kitchen.html.

Fig. 2. "My Tribute to the Frankfurt Kitchen," a still from Robert Rotifer's music video, 2008 (00:53).

difficult "to imagine beyond the concept of text," especially since other forms of expression are ultimately also understood via the "circuitous route of commentary."[35]

Based on theoretical approaches to biography, especially those of Sidonie Smith and Julia Watson, several obvious questions arise about Schütte-Lihotzky's life narratives.[36] Generally—and specifically in this case—autobiography is deemed to be more authentic in character and to have the more compelling claim to truth. Without digressing here about Roland Barthes's post-structural *The Death of the Author* postulate and the complex issue of identity, one must figure in the factors of subjectivity and simply the "difference between the two timeframes involved: the time at which an act or mental state occurs and the time at which an account of it is written down."[37] From brain research, we know that human memory works selectively. As mentioned above, Schütte-Lihotzky deemed herself a key witness of the times. This claim is indisputable but does beg a question: Which narratives are in play, what did she very consciously decide to include or to omit? Tied to this is the question of how she narrated, how she employed language. For a woman and

35 Bernhard Fetz, "Die vielen Leben der Biographie. Interdisziplinäre Aspekte einer Theorie der Biographie," in *Die Biographie – Zur Grundlegung ihrer Theorie*, ed. Bernhard Fetz (Berlin/Boston: De Gruyter, 2009), 3–66, here 4–5.

36 Smith and Watson, *Reading Autobiography*.

37 Manfred Mittermayer, "Die Autobiographie im Kontext der 'Life-Writing'-Genres," in Fetz, *Biographie*, 69–101, here 89.

38 Christina Altenstraßer, Gabriella Hauch, and Hermann Kepplinger (eds.), *gender housing. geschlechtergerechtes bauen, wohnen, leben* (Innsbruck: StudienVerlag, 2007).

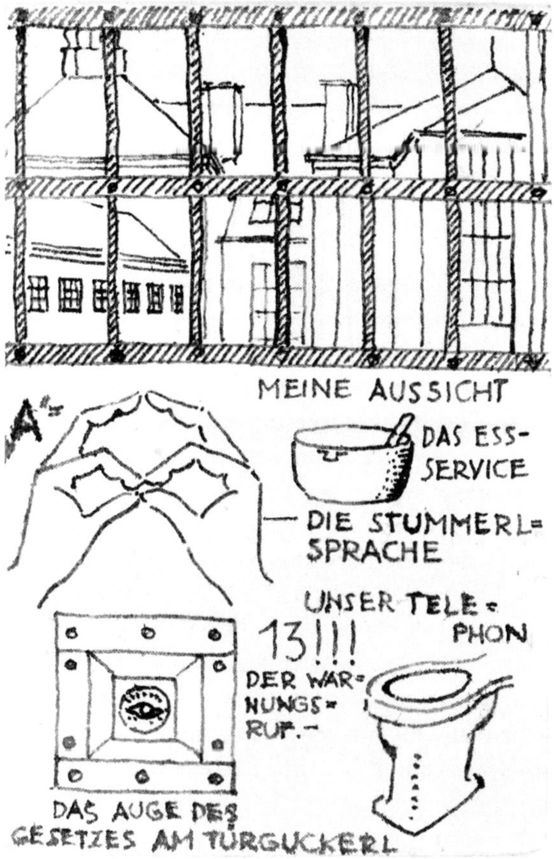

Fig. 3. Page of drawings from Margarete Schütte-Lihotzky's prison notebook, undated.

39 See Meike Penkwitt, "Erinnern und Geschlecht," *Erinnern und Geschlecht, Freiburger FrauenStudien* 19 (*Zeitschrift für interdisziplinäre Frauenforschung* 12, no. 19): 1–26; on relational biography, see inter alia Caitríona Ní Dhúill, "Biographie von 'er' bis 'sie.' Möglichkeiten und Grenzen relationaler Biographik," in Fetz, *Biographie*, 199–226.

female architect so often referred to as a "pioneer,"[38] how does recollection along gender-specific lines manifest itself —especially since women's autobiographical writing is often relational and oriented toward a more prominent man?[39] Specific spaces and sites also play a role in remembering, not least when the person engaged in auto/biographical reflection is a female architect. In a broader context, these can be realms of memory (*lieux de mémoire*), as defined by Pierre Nora, which allow for a collective memory. It is evident from Gillick's project that the Frankfurt Kitchen is suitable as a realm of memory. But the cell in the prison on Schiffamtsgasse in Vienna (1941) also has the potential to serve as a realm of memory for the anti-Nazi Resistance (fig. 3). This raises a host of questions about the settings of the scenes that are portrayed: Are they safe places or places of fear, places in the public or the private sphere, places with codifications that are clearly gender-specific? The body is also an essential factor as a source and site of autobiographical manifestations.[40]

40 "Reading for the Body," in "Autobiographical Subjects" chapter, in Smith and Watson, *Reading Autobiography*, 54.

Warum ich Architektin wurde (2004, 2019) (Why I became an architect)

Schütte-Lihotzky's memoirs were published posthumously in 2004 (2nd edition in 2019) under the title *Warum ich Architektin wurde* (Why I became an architect). The working title had been *Erinnerungen und Betrachtungen* (Memories and reflections). Karin Zogmayer is to thank for publishing the parts of her life narratives that were largely in final form and for making them available to a broad readership. They extend from Schütte-Lihotzky's childhood, her education and years of study to her work in the Vienna settlement movement from 1920 on and her time in Frankfurt from 1926 on, all the way up to her departure for the Soviet Union in 1930.[41] She had already been writing, taking notes, and compiling materials about her time in the Soviet Union and beyond into the postwar years. Before his death in 1983, Hans Wetzler, her confidant late in life, had still been encouraging her to continue this work, which she did in fact do into the early 1990s.[42] Nonetheless, the autobiography remained a torso. The published part followed a clear, chronological structure corresponding to a bildungsroman in terms of literary equivalent and embedded in sometimes detailed historical contexts.

Schütte-Lihotzky speaks with three different voices: In the first chapter, it is mainly the voice of a self-confident female subject. The reader can experience a girl growing up in a middle-class family that values education and see her succeed in a male preserve with her choice of profession. Next is the voice of the female architect giving detailed explanations of the Frankfurt Kitchen or her modular system for kindergartens. And third comes the voice of an unmistakably political person.

41 Margarete Schütte-Lihotzky, *Warum ich Architektin wurde*, ed. Karin Zogmayer (Salzburg: Residenz, 2004; Vienna: Residenz, 2019). In this essay, I refer to the first edition published in 2004.

42 See Marcel Bois, "Soziale Beziehungen und kommunistische Netzwerke. Annäherungen an Hans Wetzler (1905–1983)," in *Margarete Schütte-Lihotzky. Architektur. Politik. Geschlecht. Neue Perspektiven auf Leben und Werk,* Edition Angewandte, ed. Marcel Bois and Bernadette Reinhold (Basel: Birkhäuser, 2019), 224–36; see excerpts on Mikhail Gorbachev, *Peristroika, die zweite russische Revolution. Eine neue Politik für Europa und die Welt* (Munich: Droemer Knaur, 1987 (1989)), UAUAK, NL MSL, Erinnerungen SU Manuskripte.

Yet the narrative flow is interrupted at many points by digressions, for instance when she characterizes important, exclusively male contemporaries and describes her encounters with them. These men include her teachers Oskar Strnad and Heinrich Tessenow as well as figures from her early years in Vienna such as Max Ermers, Adolf Loos, Ernst Egli, Josef Frank, or Otto Neurath; and Ernst May later in Frankfurt. She looks back at them in part with fascination or gratitude, but at no point does she employ narrative structures that reference a dominant male subject.[43] Nor do strong female (identification) figures appear, because she herself became the role model. It seems that Schütte-Lihotzky proceeded almost effortlessly to shed traditional identity patterns of a woman born around 1900 and to penetrate realms defined by patriarchy such as the Kunstgewerbeschule (School of Arts and Crafts; today's University of Applied Arts Vienna). Women were allowed to study there from the outset (1867), albeit only in the decorative arts and crafts—for instance in Josef Hoffmann's architecture class. Her desire to become an architect met with initial resistance, which she obviously soon overcame. Other male-connoted realms were the coffee houses, which she used as external study spaces, or the smoke-filled taverns of the settlement movement in Vienna, where she held lectures as a young woman in the early 1920s. The reader encounters not a single word about discriminatory incidents at construction sites. Schütte-Lihotzky was obviously trying to strike a straightforward and unemotional tone on such matters and in the process sometimes ignored instances of real discrimination. From her interview with Friemert in 1985 and from other sources, it is clear that she never received longer-term work contracts in the Soviet Union, unlike her husband, and was paid a substantially lower salary. She mentions only that she was affected by a double-earner clause in Frankfurt when the 1929 global economic crisis hit and only Wilhelm retained his position.

43 See the double biography by Edith Friedl, *Nie erlag ich seiner Persönlichkeit … Margarete Lihotzky und Adolf Loos. Ein sozial- und kulturgeschichtlicher Vergleich* (Vienna: Milena, 2005).

Erinnerungen aus dem Widerstand (1985, 1994, 2014) (Memories from the Resistance)

Today this book by Schütte-Lihotzky is a standard work and a much-quoted source on the subject of the Resistance. In

1981, prior to its publication, Peter Turrini characterized it as follows: "Your book absolutely fascinated me and did so in two respects. It is a historical document of an accuracy and precision unmatched by any other I know of, and I am glad you had the energy to write it all down. I admire your ability to remember; after all, these things occurred 30 years ago. Second is the extent of unsentimental rationality with which you describe your memories. It is almost shyness the way you avoid becoming all too personal and that is precisely what makes the whole thing all the more impressive and powerful, because one never has the feeling here that a person is trying to take center stage with her experiences and woes. I would like to say it again: I find this book harrowing and brilliant."[44]

The language in Schütte-Lihotzky's book is lucid, free of pathos or bitterness. At no point is there even a hint of victimization, on the contrary: "I did not feel like a suffering, innocent victim of the Nazis. I had fought them and their regime, so they had to arrest me as soon as they could get their hands on me. The interrogations were the continuation of the fight under different conditions. That is why I felt little personal hatred toward the Gestapo men as individuals. As a result, I was able to give my answers free of emotion, guided only by a sense of political obligation and clear reasoning."[45] The settings in which these events occurred appear to be extremely confined and hermetic. They contrast with her transnational experiences and travels. The prison cell becomes a microcosm of horror presumably under perpetual guard (fig. 3). There is almost no distance between self and body. She does not leave out borderline situations, such as a tremor lasting for days on end, interrupted only by hours-long Gestapo interrogations or an infestation with scabies because of the catastrophic hygienic conditions.

Outside relationships play almost no role. Wilhelm Schütte is scarcely mentioned, as was already the case in the other publication. This is striking, especially since it was precisely her husband, still living in Turkey at the time, who had kept her alive emotionally and intellectually, a fact documented in their mutual correspondence published by Thomas Flierl.[46] Unlike Primo Levi, who ascribed his (emotional) survival in Auschwitz mainly to his friend and fellow

44 Peter Turrini to Schütte-Lihotzky, Vienna, June 6, 1981, UAUAK, NL MSL, Buch *Erinnerungen III*, Briefverkehr, Presse, Abbildungslisten.

45 Schütte-Lihotzky, *Erinnerungen* (1994), 66. It is jarring that Susanne Zanke's black-and-white feature film (1986), which is otherwise very faithful to the original text, repeatedly shows the figure of Schütte-Lihotzky crying in close-ups.

46 See Flierl, *Gefängnis-Briefwechsel 1941–1945*.

47 Primo Levi, *If This Is a Man*, trans. Stuart Woolf (New York: The Orion Press, 1959).

48 Schütte-Lihotzky, *Erinnerungen* (1994), 7.

prisoner Leonardo De Benedetti,[47] Schütte-Lihotzky does not focus on individuals but rather on the collective of political prisoners and the solidarity among them. It is all about maintaining inner resolve and self-esteem, bolstered by the conviction of doing the right thing politically. As an author, three decades later, she is prepared to accept covering up or hiding certain things in order to use more powerful rhetorical devices in her writing. Her objective is to captivate the public, as she writes time and again. Her creed is already revealed by the Brecht quote she chose as the epigraph to the book: "I recount it because it's old—that is to say, because it will be forgotten and could be considered true only for the past. Aren't there myriads of people to whom it's completely new?"[48]

Also of interest are the other paratexts in her autobiography because they are closely connected to what directly motivates her in the political present. In 1994 the second edition of Schütte-Lihotzky's Resistance memoirs *Erinnerungen* was published by an Austrian publisher; sales of the first edition had already been mainly in Austria. Schütte-Lihotzky added words of introduction to preface the text and, unsurprisingly, addressed them to these three target groups: historians, the young upcoming generation, and as the third group, artists, writers, and filmmakers.

The book subsequently became a key-witness account of the anti-Nazi Resistance in its specifically Austrian form. Between the first and second editions, a paradigm shift with a broad impact had occurred in Austria's *Vergangenheitspolitik*, its policies and politics concerning its (Nazi) past. The notion of Austria being the first country to fall victim to Nazi Germany had been eroded by the complicity of large numbers of Austrians in advancing Nazism. The 1985/86 presidential election campaign of former SA officer Kurt Waldheim fueled this change and Schütte-Lihotzky was one of the figures representing the "other Austria." At the same time a new political minefield turned virulent, as the Freedom Party of Austria (FPÖ) under Jörg Haider swung to the right from 1986 on. 1994 saw the staging of the "Austria First" referendum, generally known as the "Anti-Foreigner Referendum." Before that, in January 1993, civil society had made a political show of opposition to these trends by organizing the non-partisan *Lichtermeer* (sea of lights) demonstration on Heldenplatz, a large central square in Vienna with relevant Nazi connotations since 1938. The preface to the second edition of Schütte-Lihotzky's Resistance memoirs *Erinnerungen* was written by Peter Huemer, co-initiator of the Republican Club—New Austria (from 1986 on)[49] and co-organizer of SOS-Mitmensch, the association that had organized the *Lichtermeer* demonstration. In the preface, he wrote about the anachronistic concept of the hero or heroine and about Austria's literally shameful treatment of those who had opposed injustice. Austria was late, very late, in bestowing on its "famed native daughter" the honors she had so long been denied.

49 See http://www.repclub.at/

Stations in the Life of a Transnational Female Architect

On Settler Huts and Core-Houses. Margarete Lihotzky's Contribution to Cooperative Labor in the Vienna Settlement Movement[1]

S. E. Eisterer

Prologue

In 1922 Margarete Lihotzky wrote an article for the German architectural journal *Schlesisches Heim* that put the concerns of inhabitants at the forefront of her considerations about architectural design (fig. 1).[2] "It does not matter whether the house is large or small," wrote the then 25-year-old Lihotzky, "housekeeping and the inhabitants' everyday habits are always at its core."[3] At the time, she had already been collaborating for more than a year with the architect Adolf Loos on the development of small yet spacious houses for the Vienna settlement movement that followed a strict row-house typology.[4] Lihotzky's independent work as an architect that year was also devoted to the settlement movement but instead of row-house designs, it focused on *Siedlerhütten* (settler huts) and what were referred to as *Kernhäuser* (core-houses). These were minimal houses which could be enlarged outward in phases.[5] Drawing on her professional experience in the settlement movement, Lihotzky wrote in *Schlesisches Heim* that a

1 This article has been slightly revised and adapted from the original German. Short passages from this article have been published previously; Sophie Hochhäusl, "From Garden Settlement to Cooperative Economy: Housing, Labor, and Socialization Theory in Vienna and Berlin, 1920–1925," in *Landscapes of Housing. Design and Planning in the History of Environmental Thought*, ed. Jeanne Haffner (New York: Routledge, 2022), 77–99.

2 Since I will be discussing Margarete Lihotzky's early working

years, I have decided to use her maiden name "Lihotzky" throughout this essay with the exception of the conclusion, which discusses a time when she was already married. I would like to thank Mary McLeod for her advice on the politics of naming, especially in regard to female architects.

3 Margarete Lihotzky, "Die Siedlerhütte," *Schlesisches Heim* 3 (1922): 33–35, here 35.

4 *Margarete Schütte-Lihotzky, Soziale Architektur. Zeitzeugin eines Jahrhunderts*, exhibition catalog, MAK—Austrian Museum of Applied Arts, Vienna, ed. Peter Noever, 2nd ed. (Vienna: Böhlau, 1996), 21.

5 For a detailed analysis of Margarete Schütte-Lihotzky's core-houses, see Sophie Hochhäusl, "From Vienna to Frankfurt inside Core-House Type 7. A History of Scarcity through the Modern Kitchen," *Architectural Histories* 1, no. 1 (2013): 1–19, accessed May 11, 2022, http://dx.doi.org/10.5334/ah.aq.

6 Lihotzky, "Siedlerhütte," 35.

7 See Eve Blau, "Learning How to Live," in *The Architecture of Red Vienna, 1919–1934* (Cambridge, MA: MIT Press, 1999), 88–133; Susan Henderson, "Housing the Single Woman: The Frankfurt

Fig. 1. Grete Lihotzky, sketch of the alcove seating area in the settler hut, Vienna, 1922, from *Schlesisches Heim* 3, no. 2 (1922).

"house must grow out of this innermost core until it reaches its final limits, the façade—not the other way around!"[6]

With her core-house designs and ideas about the architecture of small dwellings in times of crisis, Lihotzky contributed to the Vienna settlement movement and to the resolution of the acute housing and food shortages after World War I. In her planning work, she incorporated modern ideas on settlements that were widespread in international architectural circles. However, she also formulated an early critique of normative housing models, in which she drew attention to the contradictory nature of modern life. In this essay, I will illuminate a possible interpretation of Lihotzky's core-houses and settler huts as critiques of modern architecture and explain how they enriched the settlement discourse.[7] In doing so, I will indicate Lihotzky's place in a history of architectural ideas in Vienna and show how she created alternatives to common housing typologies. Of paramount importance to her were design concepts that strengthened the social fabric of settlement clubs through cooperative work and organization. In addition, at a time of an immense scarcity of resources, Lihotzky paid attention to varied ways of life, especially when it came to people who lived in non-nuclear families.

"Utilizing Garden and Kitchen Waste": The Vienna Settlement Movement after World War I

The Vienna settlement movement arose in the years after World War I from the allotment garden movement. Impoverished Viennese combated the postwar food shortage by creating vegetable and allotment gardens.[8] The lack of available housing led to the founding of settlement cooperatives on the outskirts of the city that called for the construction of small dwellings. Based on the efforts of the Social Democratic politicians Gustav Scheu and Max Ermers, a *Siedlungsamt* (settlement office) was established in 1920. Loos was the director of this office and was soon joined there by a representative from the German garden city movement, Hans Kampffmeyer.[9] The settlement office was tasked with handling the planning and implementation of row houses for thousands of families and with advising settlement cooperatives on the construction of facilities, including communal services, roads, and pathways. In 1921, Lihotzky was hired as an employee in the settlement office's first provisional building bureau, located at Lainzer Tiergarten. Before World War I, this wildlife preserve had been part of the imperial hunting grounds in a section of Vienna's affluent 13th district. Once on site, Lihotzky supported the early collaboration with a cooperative, the First Non-Profit Settlement Cooperative for Austrian War Invalids in Lainz, for which she and Loos designed settlement houses based on *Typen*, or types.[10] In the months prior, the cooperative had illegally occupied Lainzer Tiergarten to utilize it permanently for inhabitation in settlements.[11]

An economic plan for the facility, likely written by Loos and Kampffmeyer, spelled out ample vegetable cultivation and small buildings for 2,000 families, based on the princi-

Experiment," *Journal of the Society of Architectural Historians* 68, no. 3 (2009): 358–77; Nader Vossoughian, *Otto Neurath: The Language of the Global Polis* (Rotterdam: NAI, 2008), 46–87; Günther Sandner, *Otto Neurath. Eine politische Biographie* (Vienna: Zsolnay, 2014), 156–89.

8 See Maureen Healy, *Vienna and the Fall of the Habsburg Empire. Total War and Everyday Life in World War I* (Cambridge: Cambridge University Press, 2004), 31–86; Maureen Healy, "Vom Ende des Durchhaltens," in *Im Epizentrum des Zusammenbruchs. Wien im Ersten Weltkrieg*, exhibition catalog, Wiener Stadt- und Landesarchiv, ed. Andreas Weigl and Alfred Pfoser (Vienna: Metroverlag, 2013), 132–240; Siegfried Mattl, "Lob des Gärtners. Der Krieg und die Krise der Urbanität," in ibid., 470–75.

9 On Max Ermers, Hans Kampffmeyer, and the early years of the Vienna settlement movement, see Blau, *Red Vienna*, 90–94.

10 On the beginnings of the Austrian settlement movement, see Klaus Novy, Wolfgang Förster, and Verein für Moderne Kommunalpolitik, *Einfach Bauen. Genossenschaftliche Selbsthilfe nach der Jahrhundertwende. Zur Rekonstruktion der Wiener Siedlerbewegung* (Vienna: Picus, 1991);

ples of cooperative agriculture.[12] Apart from several agricultural settlers who were to work in planned large-scale farming operations on site, the plan called for hundreds of plots for so-called *Kleinsiedler* (small settlers), who were to till small vegetable gardens. The plan further specified that settlers in the facility overall would control their own food production and that part of the yields would benefit the population of Vienna. Finally, the scheme described the extent of productive land areas and the number of animals each settler was to keep on a small plot.

With these parameters, the economic plan held strictly to the ideas of Leberecht Migge, a German landscape architect who wrote a manual in 1918 on settlement construction and national food autarky entitled *Jedermann Selbstversorger! Eine Lösung der Siedlungsfrage durch neuen Gartenbau* (Everybody self-sufficient! Solving the settlement issue with a new approach to gardening).[13] The manual was widely read in Germany and Austria in the years after World War I because it contained simple instructions for city dwellers on how to make productive use of garden plots. In the publication, Migge took the position that it was imperative to establish cooperatives to achieve regulated settlement construction with agricultural production. Moreover, he linked agricultural production to reproductive issues, an argument Loos incorporated in the planning of row houses. For instance, Migge envisaged that the size of the family would be directly linked to the number of animals to be kept and subsequently to the size of the productive land to be cultivated.

Science historian Jimena Canales and architectural historian Andrew Herscher have shown how racialized ideas underpinned Loos's writings from the prewar period, and landscape historian David Haney characterizes Migge's late works as potentially eco-Fascist.[14] A related but still overlooked aspect in both men's activities in settlements was their advocacy for a reactionary communal ideology centered not only on food autarky in a nationalist context, but also on a biological determinism that strongly favored families with multiple children as main constituents of the movement. In Loos and Kampffmeyer's plan, a plot's capacity to produce food and sustain small animals, for example, was principal

Ulrike Zimmerl, *Kübeldörfer. Siedlung und Siedlerbewegung im Wien der Zwischenkriegszeit* (Vienna: Österreichischer Kunst und Kulturverlag, 2002); Robert Hoffmann, "Proletarisches Siedeln. Otto Neuraths Engagement für die Wiener Siedlungsbewegung und den Gildensozialismus 1920 bis 1925," in *Arbeiterbildung in der Zwischenkriegszeit. Otto Neurath – Gerd Arntz*, ed. Friedrich Stadler (Vienna: Löcker, 1982), 140–48; Wilfried Posch, "Die Gartenstadtbewegung in Wien. Persönlichkeiten, Ziele, Erfolge und Misserfolge," *Bauforum. Fachzeitschrift für Architektur, Bau, Energie* 77/78 (1998): 9–24.

11 *Lainzer Tiergarten: Gedenkschrift 1920–1930* (Vienna: Erste Gemeinnützige Genossenschaft der Kriegsbeschädigten Österreichs, 1930), 10.

12 *Wirtschaftsplan für die Siedlung der Kriegsbeschädigten im Lainzer Tiergarten*, October 28, 1920, Adolf Loos Archiv, The Albertina Museum, Vienna, ALA47 (B6).

13 The publication was in such demand that it was reprinted in 1919. Leberecht Migge, *Jedermann Selbstversorger! Eine Lösung der Siedlungsfrage durch neuen Gartenbau* (Jena: Diederichs, 1918).

14 See Jimena Canales and Andrew Herscher,

for reasons of population calculation and planning. These calculations turned systems of counting calories during wartime into a managerial logic of bureaucracy projecting biological reproduction in the context of national food autarky.

"Criminal Skins: Tattoos and Modern Architecture in the Work of Adolf Loos," *Architectural History* 48 (2005): 235–56; David Haney, "The Biological Garden: c. 1930–1935," and "Conclusion," *When Modern Was Green. Life and Work of Landscape Architect Leberecht Migge* (London: Routledge, 2010), 225-67.

Reactionary ideas regarding labor, the distribution of resources, and their relationship to family life underpinned architectural considerations in other writings by Loos on settlements. In the essay "Die Moderne Siedlung" (The modern settlement), Loos asserted that daily functions in row houses—activity and rest—were to be strictly separated on two floors and that buildings overall should be able to be adapted to the size of the family—and this meant families with multiple children.[15] This functionalism, praised by some architectural historians, inscribed uniformity into the rowhouse typology and gave childbearing and the nuclear family absolute priority in the social structure of the settlement movement. While Migge, Loos, and Kampffmeyer sought to ameliorate the fate of disabled soldiers, they saw the role of women as limited to household labor and childbearing. As

15 Adolf Loos, "Die Moderne Siedlung," in *Sämtliche Schriften in zwei Bänden. Erster Band*, ed. Franz Glück (Vienna: Herold, 1962), 418.

Fig. 2. Three women with a boy and dog in front of an allotment hut in Lainz, ca. mid-1920s.

such, Siedlung Friedensstadt in Vienna's 13th district became an atavistic test case for the restructuring of the economy in the Austrian settlement movement during the prolonged state of emergency.

Lihotzky, for her part, viewed the settlement not as a reproductive unit but as a diverse community in which the focus of cooperative life should be on coexistence and on the practical value of furniture and material objects. She developed this emphasis in her initial tasks at the settlement office's building bureau: dedicated to working through the technical, formal, and economic aspects of row houses, she based them on typified and variable floor plans. This meant houses featured standardized building elements and recurring but differently sized layouts, but none of these components were industrially prefabricated.[16] Creating these conditions enabled settlers to acquire construction materials and building elements at favorable prices. Furthermore, this approach allowed construction elements to be processed manually on site. This possibility was particularly crucial considering that many settlers in the cooperative of war veterans were unskilled in construction and suffered from debilitating physical and sometimes mental disabilities.

Although Lihotzky was entrusted with the typification of floor plans and building components, the initial row houses of the settlement movement in Lainz bore the definite stamp of other Loos principles—for example, the strict division of daily activities in the house on two floors as well as the strong dedication of urban agriculture. Despite the opening and completion of one row of houses in 1921, the City of Vienna rejected further development of the planned Siedlung Friedensstadt on formal grounds.[17] The situation in Lainz was further exacerbated by the fact that Vienna was elevated to the status of federal province at the end of 1920, putting the settlement at the Tiergarten outside city limits. As a result, the cooperative lost its claim to subsidies from the City of Vienna. Loans from the Federal Housing and Settlement Fund (BWSF) also quickly dried up.[18] Although an additional 46 houses and seven foundations were finished between 1921 and 1922, cooperative work almost ground to a halt. Since there was no binding master plan, settlers had no

16 Lihotzky was one of the first within the settlement movement to think about industrial prefabrication processes. See Grete Lihotzky, "Wiener Kleingarten- und Siedlerhüttenaktion," *Schlesisches Heim* 4, no. 4 (1923): 83–85.

17 Burkhardt Rukschcio and Roland L. Schachel, *Adolf Loos. Leben und Werk* (Salzburg: Residenz, 1982), 255.

18 Gedenkschrift 1920–1930, 12–16.

choice but to build houses themselves.[19] These structures were rarely planned by architects and resembled the small garden huts already widely found in Vienna during World War I (fig. 2).

19 Ibid., 26.

"New Occupations and Organizational Forms for People": Cooperative Work in the Austrian Settlement and Allotment Garden Association (ÖVSK)

Essential to the overall development of the settlement movement in the early 1920s and certainly to an analysis of Lihotzky's work within it were the economic theories of the philosopher and economist Otto Neurath (1882–1945). As early as 1917, Neurath had published the article "The Converse Taylor System" in which he presented a theory on the essence of labor that called for work tasks to be adjusted to people's abilities.[20] Neither technology nor increased productivity should take center stage, but rather the mental and physical capacities of individuals and their opportunity to engage in different professional pursuits. Neurath considered age and psychological factors central to this theory and proposed that certain laborers could work, say, four-hour or five-hour days. After analyzing the negative ramifications of the current work system, he wrote:

> But all this is avoided if we also use the 'converse Taylor system,' which, unlike the hitherto usual Taylor system, does not seek to regard the professions as something given, but puts men [*Menschen*] themselves in the foreground, and then examines the possible professions and forms of organization as to how far they correspond to men as we find them. Perhaps existing professions and forms of organizations are inadequate; perhaps in order to achieve full humanity and the best use of all energies towards each envisaged goal, we must create new forms of profession and organization.[21]

Given the persistent unemployment at the time, one of Neurath's responsibilities in the settlement movement was to formulate forms of organization and cooperative work that were adapted to these conditions. Among other issues, Neurath conceptualized construction processes that did not rely on advanced industries, but rather on manual, at times

20 Otto Neurath, "The Converse Taylor System. Reflections on the Selection of the Fittest," in *Otto Neurath. Empiricism and Sociology. With a Selection of Biographical and Autobiographical Sketches*, ed. Marie Neurath and Robert S. Cohen (Boston: D. Reidel, 1973), translations from the German by Paul Foulkes and Marie Neurath, 130–34.

21 Ibid., 131–2.

labor-intensive fabrication and building methods. If this system were further deployed on a larger scale, Neurath held, it could result in wide-ranging job creation programs. The decision to construct buildings out of wood and not out of bricks, as was common in Vienna at the time, was later summarized by Loos as follows: "I have come up with a system that requires no other skill than the ability to hammer in a nail, something any gardener has to understand."[22] This formulation can only be interpreted as derogatory shorthand for the complex problems related to labor theory and social policy in Vienna in the early 1920s that also disregarded the attainments of disabled settlers. Neurath, by contrast, was intent on implementing a system of organizing labor in which the desires and capabilities of the individual were not only respected but considered and celebrated.

Cooperative work and self-help were two of the instruments for transforming construction and, by extension, labor processes in Vienna in the context of the settlement movement. In early 1921, Neurath helped merge the Central Association of Allotment Gardeners and the Main Association of Settlers to create the Austrian Settlement and Allotment Garden Association (Österreichischer Verband für Siedlungs- und Kleingartenwesen, ÖVSK).[23] At the end of that same year, the ÖVSK was incorporated into the larger Settlement, Housing, and Construction Guild of Austria, thereby uniting consumers and producers of housing under one umbrella organization. As ÖVSK secretary, Neurath also had a hand in founding the Cooperative Settlement and Building Material Association (Gemeinwirtschaftliche Siedlungs- und Baustoffanstalt, GESIBA). The GESIBA was henceforth tasked with acquiring materials and machinery and with handling settlement construction.[24]

Moreover, in the years that followed, new building methods with alternative materials and fabrication processes were tested throughout the city, some of which had been considered for use at Lainz. The architect Josef Frank had already experimented with residential building materials, including cast concrete.[25] In the early 1920s, many settlement cooperatives, such as the one in Altmannsdorf-Hetzendorf, fired manually produced hollow bricks known as *Pax-Ziegel*

22 Adolf Loos, "Regeln für die Siedlung" (1920), *Wiener Zeitung*, supplement (December 8, 1934): 1; reprinted in Adolf Loos, *Die Potemkinsche Stadt. Verschollene Schriften, 1897–1933*, ed. Adolf Opel (Vienna: Prachner, 1983), 178–79.

23 Otto Neurath, "Entstehung des österreichischen Verbandes für Siedlungs- und Kleingartenwesen," in *Österreichs Kleingärtner- und Siedlerorganisation* (Vienna: Wiener Volksbuchh., 1923), 16.

24 On GESIBA, see Renate Banik-Schweitzer, "Der staatlich geförderte, der kommunale und der gemeinnützige Wohnungs- und Siedlungsbau in Österreich bis 1945" (PhD thesis, University of Vienna, 1972); Barbara Feller, *75 Jahre Bauen für Wien. Die Geschichte der GESIBA* (Vienna: GESIBA, 1996).

25 Josef Frank, Hugo Fuchs, and Franz Zetting, "Wohnhäuser aus Gußbeton," *Der Architekt* 2, no. 1/2 (1919): 33; Josef Frank, "Die Wiener Siedlung," *Der Neubau* 6, no. 3 (1924): 25–29.

(hollow bricks) that could be "harvested" on site.[26] In collaboration with Frank, the Altmannsdorf-Hetzendorf cooperative utilized these bricks to transform an existing allotment garden facility into a modern residential settlement including communal and social amenities for 270 families.[27] In the resulting settlement, called Siedlung Hoffingergasse, each settler initially contributed 1,000 and later up to 1,600 hours of labor to the overall cooperative construction process.[28] The work of young people and women was credited to the family at a rate 25 percent less than the work of adult male settlers.[29] With an abundance of communal facilities, Siedlung Hoffingergasse became an example of cooperative work and construction the City of Vienna had subsidized.

"Enabling Many People to Obtain a Small House": The Core-House Campaign of the City of Vienna

The establishment of the ÖVSK and the GESIBA allowed Lihotzky to address a problem she had become familiar with during her work at Lainz, but which had never been resolved. With settlers championing the cooperative approach of contributing hours to the overall construction process, she had observed that many new members did not have the time to steadily work on site, or even to help build row houses in one go. She understood that several allotment gardeners had erected only makeshift huts because the city was unable to extend municipal loans. Yet she believed it was precisely the poor settlers and allotment gardeners who should benefit from cooperative work, including the services performed by designated architects. Lihotzky wrote:

> There are about 40,000 allotment gardeners in Vienna whose plots generally do not exceed 400 square meters in size. A majority of these allotment gardeners have taken matters into their own hands and built rudimentary pergolas and huts in self-help endeavors. Individually they bought bricks, posts, boards, cardboard wherever they could get their hands on them; many roofed their huts with the tin from old cans of condensed milk or bought an old car from an electric tramway to live in. We must not complain too much about this type of self-help, although it did not particularly

26 See "Bei den Siedlern am Rosenhügel," *Arbeiter-Zeitung* (July 31, 1921), 6–7; also see Klaus Novy, "Die Pioniere vom Rosenhügel," *UmBau* 4 (1981): 43–60, here 51; Blau, *Red Vienna*, 112; Novy and Förster, *Einfach Bauen*, 62–64.

27 On Josef Frank in the Austrian settlement movement, see Christopher Long, *Josef Frank. Life and Work* (Chicago: University of Chicago Press, 2002), 52–64; Leon Botstein, "The Consequence of Catastrophe," in *Josef Frank, Architect and Designer. An Alternative Vision of the Modern Home*, ed. Nina Stritzler-Levine (New Haven: Yale University Press, 1996), 30–44; Maria Welzig, *Josef Frank (1885–1967). Das architektonische Werk* (Salzburg: Böhlau, 1998), 90–105; Iris Meder (ed.), *Josef Frank 1885–1967. Eine Moderne der Unordnung* (Salzburg: Pustet, 2008), 31–51.

28 Hans Kampffmeyer, *Siedlung und Kleingarten* (Vienna: Springer, 1926), 25.

29 Ibid., 28–29.

Fig. 3. Margarete Lihotzky, design for a "Type A" settler hut, front and side view, 1922, drawing in ink on architectural tracing paper, watercolored.

> beautify Vienna's environment; without these makeshift measures and self-help, many of these [organized cooperative] efforts would not have come to fruition; and the movement would not have become so strong that it finally enables the centralized fabrication of huts.[30]

Recognizing the immense precarity in which people lived, Lihotzky set herself the task of designing the aforementioned *Siedlerhütten* (settler huts) in 1922. They offered minimal comfort and convenience, yet could be enlarged in phases to create fully completed homes (fig. 3). In the following months and working with the ÖVSK building bureau, she developed 20 further versions and variations. They ranged from a minimal 10 m² settler hut to a fully completed core-house 57.2 m² in size.[31] In addition, the building bureau provided settlers with individual planning advice during office hours and recorded data on their needs drawing on questionnaires.[32] "Due to the cessation of government loans, the settlement cooperatives, which in Austria rely on the settlers contributing their own labor, have been forced to fully restructure their building program," Lihotzky explained. "With the minimal municipal funding they receive, they are no longer able to produce houses with a live-in kitchen, scullery, and three bedrooms and are therefore

30 Lihotzky, "Wiener Kleingarten- und Siedlerhüttenaktion," 83.

31 "Wer Hütten bauen will," *Kleingärtner und Siedler* 1, no. 3 (1923): 2.

32 Lihotzky, "Wiener Siedlerhüttenaktion," 85.

resorting to the logical idea of the so-called core construction (the settler hut), which later forms part of the [enlarged] settler house."[33] The settler huts alone, she conceded at another point, were certainly "emergency homes" and should "by no means be presented as ideal housing."[34] Without having to undergo major modifications, settler huts could be transformed into full-fledged houses over the long term. Thus, the ultimate goal was attained, Lihotzky noted, to create "full-fledged settler houses as finished types grown from an allotment garden hut."[35]

33 Ibid., 83.

34 Lihotzky, "Die Siedlerhütte," 35.

35 Lihotzky, " Wiener Kleingarten- und Siedlerhüttenaktion," 84.

Once buildings were finalized, providing good and durable furniture produced specifically for these small homes was an additional goal of architects working within the settlement movement. Like other modern architects at the time, Lihotzky believed that the most important furniture should be incorporated in the interior design of the house as a way of defining the space.[36] Other furniture, however, was interchangeable and settlers would make their own choices of heirlooms and material objects they held dear to furnish their homes. These specific considerations led to the found-

36 See Grete Lihotzky, "Einiges über die Einrichtung österreichischer Häuser unter besonderer Berücksichtigung der Siedlungsbauten," *Schlesisches Heim* 2 (1921): 217–22; Loos, "Moderne Siedlung," 197.

Fig. 4. Margarete Lihotzky, core-house "Type 4," built on a 1:1 scale for the Fifth Allotment Garden, Settlement, and Housing Exhibition on Rathausplatz in Vienna, September 1923.

37 Grete Lihotzky, "Beratungsstelle für Wohnungseinrichtung," *Die Neue Wirtschaft* (January 31, 1924): 12.

ing of an independent department within the ÖVSK. It was known as the Warentreuhand and produced sturdy furniture at reasonable prices for those settlers in need of acquiring new furniture. Warentreuhand also offered services to Viennese workers at large—among them a consultation center for furnishings. Lihotzky served as its chief designer.[37] These efforts and those of hundreds of other clubs and cooperatives were put on display at the Allotment Garden, Settlement, and Housing Exhibition staged at the City Hall in Vienna in the fall of 1923.[38] Its highlight exhibits were seven model homes built to scale at Rathausplatz in front of City Hall. Four of the model homes were core-houses designed by Lihotzky (fig. 4), which were conceived to be built in four phases. Typified by Lihotzky, the building elements themselves could be purchased through the GESIBA at reduced prices.[39] One house contained a fully prefabricated kitchen with type furniture—in other words, sturdy standard furniture which could be bought at the Warentreuhand.[40]

The press was enthusiastic about the exhibited designs and the products and services available through Warentreuhand and the GESIBA. Neurath wrote several articles about the core-house campaign for a variety of newspapers, praising Lihotzky's work in particular. "Just think, all dead corners are eliminated, the entire space can be fully utilized thanks to the cupboards! Up there, winter clothes can be stored in the summer and summer clothes in the winter; canning jars and supplies of all kinds find a safe and orderly shelter," he noted euphorically about the built-in furniture.[41] The workers' newspaper *Arbeiter-Zeitung* reported on the advantages of the enlargeable settler houses for the working class: "The core-house campaign of the City of Vienna will enable many who perhaps do not even have their own apartment right now to obtain a small house."[42] The journalist Elisabeth Janstein even asserted that the triumph of rational efficiency had rarely been so compelling and cozy as in the core-houses:

> So, there they are, these magic houses with their "Tables, Set Yourself!;" with their lively colors, the low roof, and the beams, they are somewhat reminiscent of the alpine kitchen hut in "Hansel and Gretel." But they just pretend

38 Max Ermers, *Führer durch die Wiener Kleingarten-, Siedlungs- und Wohnbauausstellung, Rathaus, 2.–9.9.1923* (Vienna: Ausstellungsleitung; Wien I, Rathaus, 1923); Otto Neurath, "Entstehung des österreichischen Verbandes für Siedlungs- und Kleingartenwesen," in Otto Neurath, *Österreichs Kleingärtner- und Siedlerorganisation* (Vienna: Wiener Volksbuchh., 1923).

39 Otto Neurath, "Kernhausaktion der Gemeinde Wien," *Österreichische Städte Zeitung* (July 7, 1923): 1–8.

40 The prefabricated kitchen of core-house "Type 7" had already been exhibited and won a prize in 1922. In 1923, the kitchen was shown in a fully completed core-house for the first time. See text documents in the University Archive of the University of Applied Arts Vienna, Nachlass Margarete Schütte-Lihotzky (UAUAK, NL MSL), PRNR 28.

41 Otto Neurath, "Die Vorbereitung der Kleingarten-, Siedlungs- und Wohnbauausstellung, 1923," *Österreichische Städtezeitung* (September 9, 1923): 132–33.

42 "Neues Leben – Zur Kleingarten-, Siedlungs- und Wohnbauausstellung im Rathaus," *Arbeiter-Zeitung, Morgenblatt* (September 2, 1923): 2.

> to be so fairy-tale-like and impractical; in reality they are serious adult dwellings, offering a level of comfort and convenience that people with a three-story house might envy. It is really true—in each of these wonderfully laid out rooms, artistically furnished with the simplest means, you have the feeling you want to set down your hat and umbrella and say: "This is the place for me!" The triumph of reason and expediency has rarely been so compellingly designed as here; you feel: "It is the way it is and cannot be otherwise;" every chair, every book is in the spot it really demands, following a deeper law than pedantic order could ever create.[43]

Francesca Wilson was one of the few international journalists to devote a long article to Lihotzky's core-houses. In it, she emphasized their functionality, comfort, and convenience. The arduous household chores, she wrote, were considered in the design of the cooking niche and kitchen—zones that struck one as "amazingly convenient."[44] This positive contemporary reception accorded to the houses was mainly attributable to Lihotzky's idea that housekeeping and everyday habits of the inhabitants must always be the focal point for the way the house is organized.[45]

The core-houses continued to resonate even in the months after the Allotment Garden, Settlement, and Housing Exhibition of 1923. For instance, Neurath hoped they would be able to alleviate the housing shortage in times of enormous crisis, especially in cases where no federal or municipal subsidies were available. "It is possible to continue small dwelling construction as scheduled, with the ÖVSK and the GESIBA serving as centers in this difficult time of crisis. A number of construction cooperatives whose major projects cannot be continued have already begun erecting core-houses," he wrote as early as July prior to the exhibition.[46]

Embedded in the greater cooperative work, several core-houses were in fact built over the following years in the Vienna settlements, although they did not achieve the expected commercial success because of the substantial financial resources the inhabitants had to raise on their own.[47] Nonetheless, about 200 core-houses still did provide about 1,000 people with a new home. And although in Lainz

43 Elisabeth Janstein, "Die Wohnbau- und Siedlungsausstellung der Gemeinde Wien. Tiere, Blumen und Obst im Rathaushof," *Der Tag* (September 2, 1923): 4.

44 Francesca Wilson, "The Resurrection of Vienna, Houses on the Land Settlement," *The Manchester Guardian* (October 26, 1923): 6.

45 Irene Witte to Margarete Lihotzky, January 2, 1923, UAUAK, NL MSL, PR 28/10/TXT.

46 Neurath, "Kernhausaktion der Gemeinde Wien," 8.

47 *Gedenkschrift 1920–1930*, 27.

there were no further row houses erected after 1921, settlers began to build 34 core-houses in 1922 in the area.

"First the Core, then the Facade": Organization, Variability, and Modern Life

In the article "A Revolution in the Woman's Sphere," architectural historian Susan Henderson points out that Schütte-Lihotzky's Frankfurt Kitchen—contrary to her own claims and intentions—contributed to a redomestication of women in the Weimar Republic in the late 1920s.[48] Because core-houses focused on similar objectives, such as rationalization in housekeeping, they could be viewed through a similar lens. Indeed, the settlement movement overall came under intense scrutiny within Viennese working class organizations from the mid-1920s onward for its petit bourgeois character and its use of outdated technology, which bound women more closely to the home.[49] Settlements on the fringes of the city seemed to be an outmoded individualistic typology to many, especially once Vienna's large communal dwellings, the *Höfe*, had been erected, complete with fully functioning laundries, parks, and health services. Yet core-houses specifically were a criticism of some of the dominant atavistic aspects of the settlement movement as well as modern architecture at large at the time. For example, Lihotzky's postulate "First the core, then the facade" points to a fundamental criticism of modern architecture—namely, its failure to prioritize social questions and its focus on formal practices and theories.[50] Her focus on promoting general welfare, especially for women, can be seen as a direct contradiction of the ideas in the settlement movement advanced by Migge and Loos, where the garden, production, and reproductive logic determined row-house typologies. By contrast, Lihotzky placed not just a functional kitchen at the heart of architectural debates, but the live-in kitchen—in other words, life and living together in a house. This notion of strengthening community through organization was further exemplified in the efforts in and by the Warentreuhand. Offering solid furniture and design advice at low prices, Warentreuhand gave a wider portion of the Viennese population access to cooperative services and achievements.[51] With her designs, Lihotzky tried to meet the

48 Susan Henderson, "A Revolution in the Woman's Sphere. Grete Lihotzky and the Frankfurt Kitchen," in *Architecture and Feminism*, ed. Debra Coleman, Elizabeth Danze, and Carol Henderson (New York: Princeton Architectural Press, 1996), 221–53.

49 See Herda Müller, "Die Werkbundausstellung und Wir," *Arbeiter-Zeitung* (July 18, 1932): 3.

50 Nicholas Bullock ascribes the aphorism "First the Kitchen—Then the Façade" to German home economist Marie Elisabeth Lüders. It is likely Lüders was familiar with Lihotzky's writing. See Nicholas Bullock, "First the Kitchen—Then the Façade," *Journal of Design History* 1, no. 3/4 (1988): 177–92.

51 See Grete Lihotzky, "Neues Wohnen. Der Kampf gegen den Möbelschund," *Arbeiter-Zeitung* (September 8, 1923): 9.

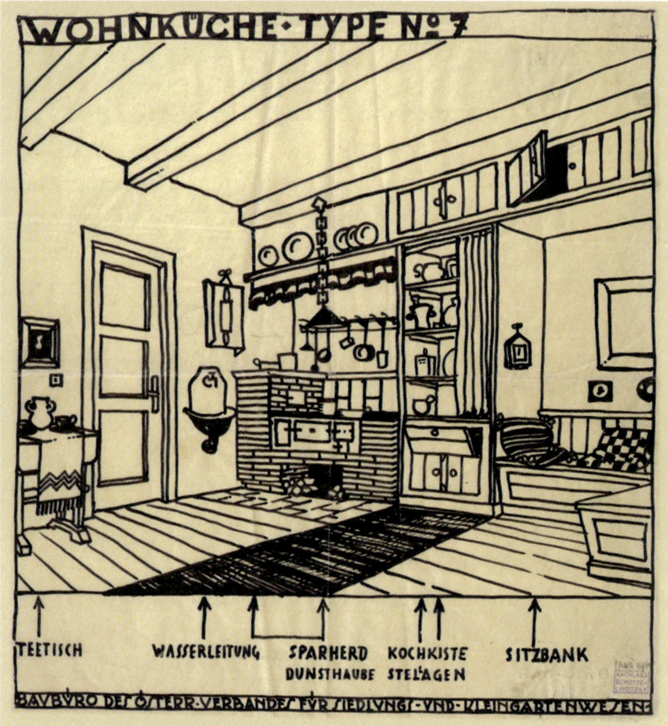

Fig. 5. Margarete Lihotzky, core-house "Type 7," live-in kitchen with oven and bench seat, 1923, pen-and-ink drawing.

needs of a varied population who inhabited settlements, allotment gardens, as well as small and large dwellings.

Indeed, in the very first article she wrote in 1921 she had insisted: "A dwelling is the tangible organization of our everyday habits." She urged that precise studies be conducted about housework, about enjoyment, and rest.[52] In Vienna, unlike in Frankfurt later on, she introduced resource-saving household goods and furniture into the settlement movement that were made of easily obtainable materials such as brick or wood and produced in a combination of manual and industrial fabrication processes (fig. 5). By pointing out the central importance of inhabitants' everyday habits and having introduced the expandable core-houses, Lihotzky promoted one idea in particular: that settlement houses had

52 Lihotzky, "Einiges über die Einrichtung österreichischer Häuser," 217.

to offer greater opportunities for a variety of family relations and constellations of kin within a cooperative framework. This included single people, young couples, and non-nuclear families—for instance, long-term relationships between women after the war, including sisters, cousins, or women who raised other people's children—all of which received little attention in the male-dominated settlement movement.

Settler huts and core-houses designed for the Vienna settlement movement are thus useful in analyzing Lihotzky's early concerns about architecture, but they also speak to a tumultuous political period in Vienna after World War I. Among other issues, core-houses and settler huts reflected complex questions about labor, resource, and material shortages at the time and how modern architects responded to them. Finally, they illuminate Lihotzky's early emphasis on the social aspects of design and her intensive dialog with other planners and economists about cooperative work and cooperative construction. She conducted this dialog primarily with Neurath and Frank, with whom she also shared similar political outlooks in the 1920s. Her efforts to design core-houses reveal a multifaceted and independent approach within that framework and to the question of settlement as well. While many architects attempted to achieve variability within housing types, Lihotzky indeed sought solutions for diverse life circumstances. With this agenda, she distanced herself from the atavistic productive and reproductive logic of a Migge and in part also from Loos.

* I would like to thank Bernadette Reinhold and Marcel Bois for organizing the symposium *Architecture, Politics, Gender* in October 2018. I would also like to express my sincere gratitude to Silvia Herkt and Natalie Feitsch (Collection and Archive at the University of Applied Arts Vienna), who through our many years of collaboration on the estate of Margarete Schütte-Lihotzky have always assisted me with patience and a great willingness to help.

Designed by a Woman with Women. Margarete Schütte-Lihotzky and New Frankfurt

Claudia Quiring

Margarete Schütte-Lihotzky's work at the Frankfurt Hochbauamt (central building authority) is associated almost exclusively with the development of the Frankfurt Kitchen: the Frankfurt Kitchen is equated with Margarete Schütte-Lihotzky, and Margarete Schütte-Lihotzky with the Frankfurt Kitchen. This epitome of a built-in kitchen designed for practicality and functionality has been described and analyzed in detail many times,[1] so we will dispense with that here. Instead, this essay will describe the setting in which the developer found herself and the place and opportunities she encountered as well as her network and the reactions to her work. For this task, I draw on the research that numerous authors conducted from 2013 to 2016 for the biographical dictionary *Akteure des Neuen Frankfurt*[2] (Actors in New Frankfurt) that ultimately yielded a volume containing some 150 biographies. The focus was not confined to those most closely associated with the Frankfurt Hochbauamt, because the editors were interested in broadening the range of actors beyond the "usual suspects" to include, for example, the business community or more conservative figures, in some cases even opponents. Biographies that had been fragmentary up to that point were to be fleshed out with an eye to obtaining

1 See, for example, Joachim Krausse, "Die Frankfurter Küche," in *Oikos. Von der Feuerstelle zur Mikrowelle. Haushalt und Wohnen im Wandel*, exhibition catalog, Design-Center Stuttgart and Museum für Gestaltung Zürich (Giessen: Anabas, 1992), 96–113; Renate Allmayer-Beck, "Projekte in Frankfurt 1926–1930," in *Margarete Schütte-Lihotzky. Soziale Architektur. Zeitzeugin eines Jahrhunderts*, exhibition catalog, MAK—Austrian Museum of Applied Arts, Vienna, ed. Peter Noever (Vienna: Böhlau, 1993), 83–124; Sophie Hochhäusl, "From Vienna to Frankfurt Inside Core-House Type 7: A History of Scarcity through the Modern Kitchen," *Architectural Histories* 1, no. 1 (2013), accessed June 26,

2022, https://journal.eahn.org/article/id/7455/.

a fuller picture of what happened. Two major aspects for all biographies came in the form of these questions: How did the person come to be involved with the Frankfurt Hochbauamt? What impact did this involvement have on the subsequent stages of his/her work?

Schütte-Lihotzky's Work at the Frankfurt Hochbauamt

Schütte-Lihotzky described the first aspect many times: Ernst May discovered her in Vienna when she stepped in for Adolf Loos to guide May through the construction projects of the Siedlungsamt (settlement office) there.[3] A loose collaboration ensued, with her writing articles for May's magazine *Schlesisches Heim* on "her" topics: living in cramped quarters and interior design, especially for kitchens. This soon led to him giving her a concrete job offer. It came in the nick of time because by around 1925 Lihotzky's work situation in Vienna had become very difficult for her, if not precarious, due to her employer's economic straits and advocates of hers leaving the office or Vienna altogether. In Frankfurt she was to continue her previous work for the Hochbauamt in the typification department, which had been newly set up to handle the typification and standardization of construction elements (fig. 1). The precise terms and conditions of her contract are unknown for this initial period at the Hochbauamt from February 1926 on. All that has been found is a handwritten summary of her work for the Hochbauamt dated February 1, 1926 and an employment contract dated February 23 (!), 1926, which was evidently concluded for a term of one year.[4] In March 1927, May then attempted to hire her for a three-year term as head of a newly established "Construction advice center for housekeeping matters in apartments, especially kitchens," emphasizing that she "can be considered, artistically and technically, to be a top expert in her specialty area in Germany and neighboring countries."[5] In other words, her fields of work were to differ very little from her activities in Vienna for the Austrian Settlement and Allotment Garden Association (Österreichischer Verband für Siedlungs- und Kleingartenwesen, ÖVSK). There she founded an office (Warentreuhand), where she also provided advice on apartment furnishings. With her health impaired by tuberculosis,

2 Evelyn Brockhoff et al. (eds.), *Akteure des Neuen Frankfurt. Biografien aus Architektur, Politik und Kultur* (*Archiv für Frankfurts Geschichte und Kunst* 76) (Frankfurt am Main: Societäts-Verlag, 2016).

3 Margarete Schütte-Lihotzky, *Warum ich Architektin wurde*, ed. Karin Zogmayer, 1st ed. (Salzburg: Residenz, 2004), 105–6. A second edition was published by Residenz in 2019; however, the quotations below are taken from the first edition.

4 The summary was prepared on January 25, 1930. Institute for the History of Frankfurt (ISG), Magistratsakte T 639.

5 Ernst May to the personnel officer, March 17, 1927, ISG, Magistratsakte T 650, vol. 10.

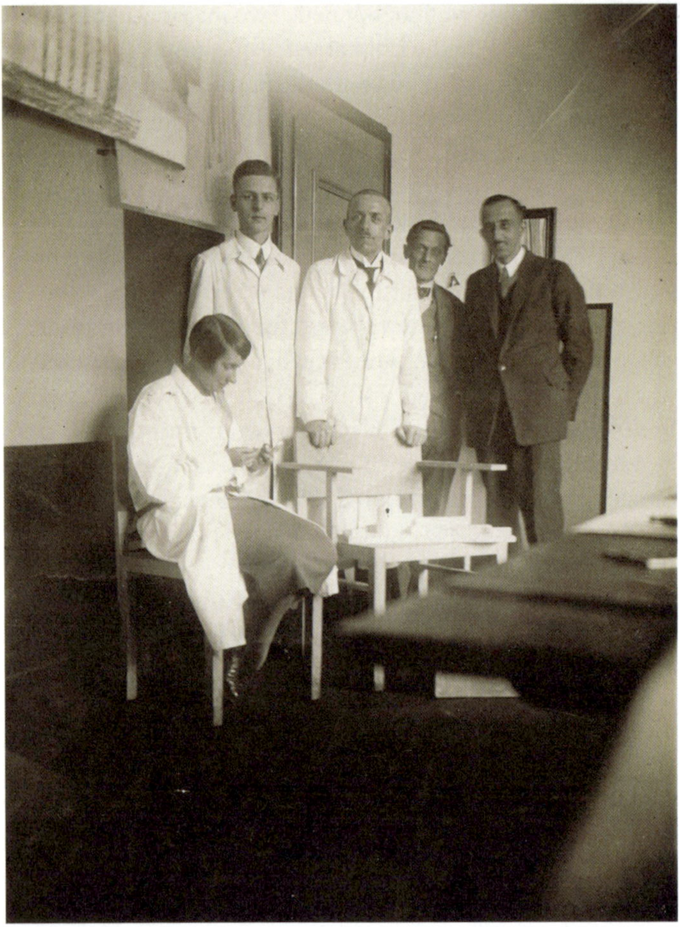

Fig. 1. Margarete Schütte-Lihotzky with colleagues from the Frankfurt Hochbauamt, 1928.

she was only able to be hired as a technical employee and not as a supernumerary employee, as many other colleagues had been.

From 1928 on, she was once again hired for one year on a fixed-term basis under a contract for work and services. Her job duties included designing and handling overall artistic management in connection with producing the kitchens, school kitchens, and laundries for New Frankfurt and providing advice to private architects working in this area for the Hochbauamt. She was obligated to have at least two consultation hours per week.[6] A work schedule for the typification department from July 1928 gives us more concrete information about her role in projects. She is listed there under "Settlement construction and associated individual buildings" together with August Menges and Anton Brenner for Siedlung Praunheim (Praunheim Settlement, i.e., a public housing development). In the column "Design department, main person in charge," her name is the only one that appears for Rödelheim, where 500 tiny apartments were to be built; for the laundry and kindergarten in Praunheim; for small structures in allotment garden colonies; and for furniture in school kitchens and other training kitchens, specifically at the Berufspädagogisches Institut (vocational training institute).[7] The Praunheim kindergarten was never completed but the innovative pavilion system she developed at the time is a concept she would use in her later designs.

6 ISG, Magistratsakte T 639, Arbeitsvertrag (contract for works and services) dated December 22, 1928.

7 ISG, Magistratsakte T 650, vol. 10.

Frankfurt Work Covered in the Viennese Estate

Schütte-Lihotzky's estate in Vienna contains further information about her work on individual projects in Frankfurt. In fact, it has an astounding amount of material considering her turbulent biography. The estate materials are surprising not just for their large quantity, however, but also for their quality. Even while she was working—in this case in Frankfurt, but this insight pertains to subsequent chapters in her career, too—she must have very intentionally collected material and passed it along to relatives, for example, for safekeeping. This implies clear reflection on her own significance, indeed almost a foresighted historiography to which she could later turn, especially from the 1980s on, as inquiries began coming her way. Nonetheless, what remains is presumably a selection—other materials were probably not included in the collection, consciously or unconsciously. The estate in Vienna contains abundant material featuring photos and plans that bear official stamps and cover a variety of tasks such as precast-concrete and metal kitchens. Material on an apartment for single working women included not just sketches but also tables covering income and rent; material on model furnishings for accessory dwelling units included stills from films. Other material, especially photographic documentation, can be found on her weekend house, on her ZWOFA duplex comprising two tiny apartments, on her 1928 training kitchen where women were taught to cook on a gas stove, and on her Wohnung für das Existenzminimum (i.e., dwelling for minimal existence, a concept in German public housing at the time). In addition, there are various texts and plans providing evidence of several designs of allotment garden houses by Schütte-Lihotzky and of her collaboration on an exhibition (fig. 2). Schütte-Lihotzky also developed industrial products such as kitchen appliances and modular furniture designed to be assembled "without the help of a carpenter"—documents on these items include photo documentation and a comprehensive "list for a sales catalog for modular furniture," along with all the dimensions and a brief description.[8] Most of this material probably came directly from the work process or served as documentation of her own contributions at the time, but there was noticeably more of it in her estate than in the estates of other Frankfurt colleagues. The list of modular furniture bearing the stamp of the typification department of the Hochbauamt, for instance, was a six-page typewritten document that Schütte-Lihotzky submitted to her superior Eugen Kaufmann, who then returned it with the comment "Duly noted, back to Ms. Schu-Lih with many thanks." Documents such as these actually tend to be found in company estates of private architects and cannot necessarily be explained by her status as a fee-based worker at the Hochbauamt. These materials and the collection of Schütte-Lihotzky's publications also contained in the estate are a great help today when it comes to evaluating her work and her spheres of activity.

8 University Archive of the University of Applied Arts Vienna, Nachlass Margarete Schütte-Lihotzky (UAUAK, NL MSL), PRNR 87 [underlining in the original].

Material in Frankfurt Covering Her Work There

The situation with source material in Frankfurt itself is totally different, mostly due to the impact of war. Besides the above city material passed down mostly in municipal authority files and also individual property files (sometimes with plans) at the Institute for the History of Frankfurt (ISG), holdings from the Parks Department at ISG also contain several sets of documentation of Schütte-Lihotzky's work. They consist mainly of a rather large collection of glass nega-

Fig. 2. Model of an allotment garden house type II, around 1927.

tives documenting official projects.[9] When all these holdings are combined with the material from Vienna, a fairly comprehensive picture emerges of her allotment garden house designs. Most of these houses were standard types ingeniously reduced to a minimum, and some of them still stand today. However, not all types have been able to meet the requirements of the plot holders in terms of practical use. This has been true for several years now, for instance, of a show garden of Ernst-May-Gesellschaft e.V. Additions were soon built because the possible storage spaces for tools and equipment were too small and further limited by the planned space for bicycles.

9 ISG, inventory of the Parks Department.

The Involvement of Women

Just as Schütte-Lihotzky did not enter the annals of history as a passionate gardener, neither was she well versed as a cook and housekeeper: "I had nothing to do with kitchens and cooking. But the men around me just pressured me to take on this task," she once admitted quite frankly.[10] Besides the colleagues in the typification department, the main figure to keep in mind here was May himself. In his eyes, Schütte-Lihotzky was perfectly cast for the role, also and

10 Quoted in Tanja Scheffler, "Margarete Schütte-Lihotzky. Küche, Kinder, Kommunismus," in *Frau Architekt. Seit mehr als 100 Jahren: Frauen im Architekturberuf*, exhibition catalog, Deutsches Architekturmuseum (DAM), Frankfurt am Main, ed. Mary Pepchinski et al. (Tübingen: Wasmuth, 2017), 122–29, here 126.

especially for the purpose of external advertising. In his 1930 activities report on five years of housing construction,[11] he touted the Frankfurt Kitchen with the slogan: "Designed by a woman [...] with women." This was a unique selling point compared to all other institutions dedicated to modernism and could be promoted as the best possible way of addressing modern needs, the New Human Being, the New Woman. The additional phrase "with women" was a declaration of support for grassroots participation, as one might describe it today. It is largely unclear exactly what concrete form this participation took beyond possible follow-up discussions after the extensive lectures Schütte-Lihotzky gave. An article in *Stadt-Blatt der Frankfurter Zeitung* had this to say on the matter: "The modern mode of construction, in some cases with the advice and support of female architects and housewifely building commissions, has got off to a remarkable start in eliminating long-standing shortcomings in the layout and equipping of kitchens."[12] No sources for these building commissions have yet been identified. The exhibition staged by the Hochbauamt *Die neue Wohnung und ihr Innenausbau* (The new apartment and its interior finishings) featured a special show by the Frankfurter Hausfrauenverein (Frankfurt Housewives' Association) called *Der neuzeitliche Haushalt* (The modern household), which presented five types of kitchens by Schütte-Lihotzky. This fact presupposes some kind of exchange between her and the association.[13] A direct exchange probably also took place for a presentation of her design *Die Wohnung der berufstätigen Frau* (Apartment for a working woman) in Essen at the general meeting of the Federal Housewives' Association in 1927.[14] No independent sources on the matter have been found, however. These activities are vividly described only in Schütte-Lihotzky's own publications where she talks about lectures in "large, smoke-filled halls" and the like.[15]

Nonetheless, a variety of practical difficulties arose, especially concerning the use of the Frankfurt Kitchen, as she herself stated in a report for the Reichsforschungsgesellschaft (RFG), a prominent national research association at the time focusing on cost-efficiency in construction and housing.[16] The Frankfurt Kitchen therefore underwent con-

11 Ernst May, "Fünf Jahre Wohnungsbautätigkeit in Frankfurt am Main," *Das neue Frankfurt* 4, no. 2/3 (1930): 21–70, here 38.

12 "Die Küche und Kochen im neuzeitlichen Haushalt," *Stadt-Blatt der Frankfurter Zeitung* (August 30, 1930).

13 Documents in Vienna primarily attest to extensive lecturing and publishing activities. More in-depth research into the building commissions would require very time-consuming source studies, which would not necessarily be successful due to the great losses suffered during the war. This could not be done as part of the dictionary project. It should also be noted that even more of Schütte-Lihotzky's work was on display at the exhibition: a weekend house designed with her husband and an allotment garden house as well as the 1:1 model of her *Plattenhaus*, a prefabricated building made of concrete slabs.

14 See Margarete Schütte-Lihotzky, *Soziale Architektur*, 104 f.

15 See Schütte-Lihotzky, *Warum ich Architektin wurde*, 191.

16 See *Bauliche Anlagen von Küchen in neuen Siedlungswohnungen (Mitteilungen der Reichsforschungsgesellschaft, Bericht Nr. 2)* (Berlin: Reichsforschungsgesellschaft, 1929).

STÄDTISCHE BERATUNGSSTELLE FÜR ARBEIT-SPARENDE KÜCHEN IN FRANKFURT AM MAIN

Die Frankfurter Küche ist in den Jahren 1926 1927 in verschiedenen Abwandlungen rund 3000 mal hergestellt worden und von allen Frauen-Organisationen, vor allem auch vom Reichskuratorium für Wirtschaftlichkeit als großer Fortschritt auf dem Gebiete der Rationalisierung des Haushaltes bezeichnet worden.

ZWECK DER ARBEITSPARENDEN KÜCHE IST:

1. Der Hausfrau alle unnötigen Wege und Handgriffe zu ersparen.
2. Den in der Küche gesparten Raum den Wohnräumen zugute kommen zu lassen.

Diese Ziele werden dadurch erreicht, dass alle erforderlichen Einrichtungsgegenstände dem Raum vollkommen angepasst sind und eingebaut werden. Auf einer Grundfläche von 6½ qm enthalten diese Küchen folgende

EINRICHTUNGSGEGENSTÄNDE:

Topf-, Vorrats- und Geschirrschrank, zweiteiliges Spülbecken, Abtropfbrett, Abtropfgestell, Speiseschrank, Tisch mit Rinne für Küchenabfälle, Kochkiste, Gewürzgestell, 9 Schubladen, 2 Behälter für Mehl und Salz, herabklappbares Bügelbrett, Schiene für eine Schiebe-Lampe, Müll- und Besenschrank, vom Flur zugänglich.

Durch Massenherstellung der Küchen war es möglich, den Preis so niedrig zu halten, daß der Einbau einer solchen Küche auch für Wohnungen der Minderbemittelten in Frage kommt.

Da sowohl von auswärtigen Hochbauämtern u. Siedlungsgenossenschaften als auch von Architekten und Privaten in steigendem Maße Anfragen wegen Lieferung der Frankfurter Küche eingehen, wurde dem Hochbauamt der Stadt Frankfurt eine Beratungsstelle f. arbeitsparende Küchen angegliedert, die Aufträge für Planung, Kosten-Anschläge und Ausführung übernimmt.

ANFRAGEN SIND ZU RICHTEN AN DIE

STÄDTISCHE BERATUNGSSTELLE F. ARBEIT-SPARENDE KÜCHEN, FRANKFURT-M, RATHAUS

3000. 3. 27. (V. St. 2048/26) A. 8.

Fig. 3. Information sheet issued by the city advice center for "labor-saving kitchens" in Frankfurt am Main, 1927.

stant further development in response to user feedback. One would have to envisage a similar situation regarding the original development process with colleagues in the typification department and the exchange with the companies working at the same time in Frankfurt and beyond on the further development of the kitchens, such as Haarer, for example.[17] Otherwise, a variety of information events were held to help teach users about the kitchens (fig. 3).

17 See Schütte-Lihotzky, *Warum ich Architektin wurde*, 159, and Ulrike May, "Haarer, Anni und Haarer, Otto," in Brockhoff, *Akteure*, 112.

It is not possible to clarify Schütte-Lihotzky's personal involvement in the model apartments furnished in each settlement (public housing development) to illustrate and "elevate the culture of household goods in a planned manner" or in the city-financed promotional films, in which enthusiastic occupants appeared as amateur actors to demonstrate the benefits of this new approach to housing. Reports in the daily press indicate that in this context, too, construction by a woman for women was viewed as a guarantee of success—even where technical concerns were involved: "The resourceful Hochbauamt can certainly be trusted to overcome the technical difficulties; after all, it does have a woman on the staff."[18]

18 Special apartments for working women, quoted in Schütte-Lihotzky, "Die Wohnung der alleinstehenden berufstätigen Frau," 34–35, quoted in Margarete Schütte-Lihotzky, *Soziale Architektur*, 106.

Frankfurt Colleagues

Do we find out anything about other instances of teamwork? The official sources cannot be expected to yield much at all. Ernst May's estate material at the Deutsches Kunstarchiv (German art archive) in Nuremberg covers his work in Frankfurt but its items on Schütte-Lihotzky's activities are confined almost exclusively to photo documentation. In published texts, he described the work at the Hochbauamt in only very general terms. By contrast, Eugen Kaufmann, Schütte-Lihotzky's boss in the typification department, left extensive memoirs behind, which also reveal interpersonal relations.[19] In his memoirs from around 1977, Kaufmann wrote enthusiastically about the wonderful collaboration at the Hochbauamt and at Siedlung Fuchshohl (Fuchshohl Settlement, a public housing development), where he and many other employees of the authority lived—but not Schütte-Lihotzky. He referred to his work in Frankfurt as the high point of his career. His comments on the female architect's work are disappointingly brief. For instance, he said this about her commencing work in Frankfurt in 1926: "[…] then there arrived a lady architect from Vienna, Grete Lihotzky, who had studied there under Strnad […]."[20] Later, he elaborated on the activities of the department but said only this: "The experiments initiated by May for furthering new constructional ideas, such as building with large building blocks, instead of with bricks, were tried out, mainly at

19 Other work materials smuggled out of the Soviet Union later fell victim to vandalism.

20 Memories of Eugen Kent [Eugen Kaufmann], London, Royal Institute of British Architects (RIBA) Collection, KEE/1, around 1977, 169.

Praunheim, [...] then still under construction under my supervision and guidance."[21] In the report on his activity in the Soviet Union, he briefly touched on his personal relationship with his female colleague and on her political engagement: "Frau Schutte-Lihotzky, our close friend from our joint Frankfurt time and now here in Russia, was one of the most active."[22] But we hear no word about the division of labor within the typification department. Besides prefabricated buildings made of concrete slabs (*Plattenbauten*), the department developed floor plans and had a subdepartment on household goods.

Schütte-Lihotzky's colleagues here were Ferdinand Kramer, Franz Schuster, and Anton Brenner, the latter two from Vienna. Kramer won a competition staged by Städtische Hausrat GmbH in 1925 on the development of standardized furniture (*Typenmöbel*) and, like Franz Schuster, later designed household goods and furnishings for kindergartens, among other places. He also worked on standardized floor plans. Städtische Hausrat GmbH carried Kramer's and Schuster's furniture along with Schuster's publication *Ein Möbelbuch* (A furniture book). The company's product range does not appear to have included designs by Schütte-Lihotzky, even though their inclusion would have seemed obvious.

Documents on court proceedings from 1930 provide insights into exchanges and procedures within the typification department. Anton Brenner had filed a suit against Eugen Kaufmann, claiming that Kaufmann had published plans under his own name that Brenner had played a large part in producing. Brenner viewed himself as being at a disadvantage as a private architect but was unable to win the case. He also saw himself cheated out of the fame he was due for developing the Frankfurt Kitchen, as later publications suggest.[23] Brenner and Schütte-Lihotzky did in fact work on very similar design issues. Memoirs are not always the most reliable sources to clarify such questions. For instance, Schütte-Lihotzky herself never commented on these disputes. Instead, she described the collaboration in retrospect as follows: "Once again I was part of a community, the then sworn community of modern architects [...]."[24]

21 Ibid., 178.

22 Ibid., 215.

23 The title of his memoirs, which were published posthumously by his son and refer to Anton Brenner as "an unrecognized genius" and "the true inventor of the 'Frankfurt Kitchen,'" shows that this perspective was passed down in the family: *Mit Ach und Krach durchs Leben. Autobiographie eines verkannten Genies. Aus dem Leben des Wiener Architekten Professor Anton Brenner, dem wahren Erfinder der "Frankfurter Küche,"* edited and published by his son Tonio Brenner, three volumes (Vienna: Edition Brento, 2005–07).

24 Quoted in Margarete Schütte-Lihotzky, *Soziale Architektur*, 82.

One task for the biographical dictionary was to find comments from occupants of the houses built at the time and the kitchens in them. And a secondary teacher who had transferred to a Frankfurt school in 1927 did in fact share his memories about his apartment: "The best thing about the house was the kitchen, a design by Ms. Leistikow. The Leistikows went on to Russia later [...]. They also lived in Fuchshohl. Everything in the kitchen was built in. The only personal possession I had there was a stool. All doors [were] sliding doors; a cooking niche [was] next to the gas stove. The entire room was 2 by 3 meters in size, a cooking lab.

Fig. 4. Margarete Schütte-Lihotzky in front of the *Plattenbau* (prefabricated building made of concrete slabs) at the exhibition staged by the Werkbund in Stuttgart, 1927.

A serving hatch to the dining room [...] doubled there as a serving table. If I had built myself a house, I would have built this kitchen."[25] This description was from Fritz Malsch, who wrote his memoirs after 1945. He moved into an apartment in the Ginnheimer Siedlung (public housing development) in Frankfurt, where a number of employees from the Hochbauamt lived. We know that Schütte-Lihotzky was not among them. She lived at the other end of the city in Sachsenhausen, in a house built by Ernst Balser. So even if the similarity in names obviously caused a mix-up with Grete Leistikow, the photographer of New Frankfurt, the source clearly indicates that the Frankfurt Kitchen was fondly remembered and, for example, that the cooking box (*Kochkiste*) there was still in place. It would have been nice to know whether the cooking box was still being used instead of being quickly repurposed as it was in many other households, but the source is silent on this matter.

25 Fritz Malsch, *Lebenserinnerungen*, ISG, S5/Bl, 121.

A Variety of Work Activities in Frankfurt

The sources and publications paid much more attention to the Frankfurt Kitchen than to the standardized types of prefabricated row houses made of concrete slabs (*Plattenbau-Reihenhaustypen*) that Schütte-Lihotzky developed for Praunheim. They too were deemed a central prestige project of New Frankfurt and were presented accordingly in the following year at the exhibition staged by the Werkbund in Stuttgart. Schütte-Lihotzky poses proudly in a photo in front of them (fig. 4). In 1928, apartment furnishings of hers could be viewed at exhibitions such as Heim und Siedlung (Home and settlement) in Munich. A joint design with her husband for a *Wohnung für das Existenzminimum* (dwelling for minimal existence) was also displayed in 1929 at an exhibition of the same name staged by CIAM (Congrès internationaux d'architecture moderne, or International Congresses of Modern Architecture) and she was represented with works at many other exhibitions as well.

Despite these successes that helped make her known internationally, there were other more prestigious projects she was not able to realize. Representational single-family houses (e.g., for Prof. Strasburger in Frankfurt or Haus

Chabot in Rotterdam) did not get past the paper stage, nor did larger-scale projects such as beach hotels or clinics. Her name was closely associated at the time with small to tiny apartments and with interior furnishings, especially for kitchens. Her biggest success, the Frankfurt Kitchen, was at the same time her biggest obstacle.

End of Her Work in Frankfurt

Schütte-Lihotzky's time at the Hochbauamt ended in 1930. In February of that year, the extension of her contract was first delayed by suspended negotiations on personnel cuts at the Hochbauamt. A law against double earners—that is, hiring both members of a married couple—unfavorably impacted her, too, because she was married to Wilhelm Schütte.[26] Then her contract was extended by just six months subject to the explicit exclusion of extension "in any form."[27] Confusion persisted until April 1930. It was not until May that her January (!) 1930 contract for work and services was approved for six months. At the end of July 1930, an inquiry elicited the response that "the wife of Government Master Builder Schütte also works, but after relinquishing her part-time employment at the Hochbauamt on June 30, 1930, no longer has a permanent position."[28] In the press, the number of employees terminated "to rationalize" the public administration was estimated to amount to 34 staff members hired under special contracts and conditions. Things would not improve again for some time to come. But Schütte-Lihotzky was more fortunate: she was offered a new employment prospect through Ernst May and set off for the Soviet Union.

26 ISG, Magistratsakte T 639, note of February 2, 1930.

27 ISG, Magistratsakte T 639, Beschluss der Magistrats-Personal-Kommission (decision of the municipal authorities' staff committee) of February 19, 1930.

28 ISG, Magistratsakte T 650, Hochbauamt to the Magistrats-Personal-dezernenten, letter of July 28, 1930.

Margarete Schütte-Lihotzky's Soviet Years (1930–37)

Thomas Flierl

In her publications, Margarete Schütte-Lihotzky unfortunately provided very little information about the time she spent in the Soviet Union. In her two books *Erinnerungen aus dem Widerstand 1938–1945* (Memories from the Resistance 1938–1945), published in 1985, and *Warum ich Architektin wurde* (Why I became an architect), published posthumously in 2004, she touched on her Soviet years but only in a brief look back and forward, respectively.[1] During those years, she worked intensively as an architect and designer and acquired her political orientation as a Communist, which would be so crucial to her subsequent life. Unlike China, to which she devoted a separate book manuscript based on the dual vantage point of her trips in 1934 and in 1956,[2] she left behind no memoirs specifically on the Soviet Union. She brought the topic up in just two published texts. First, on the occasion of Ernst May's 100th birthday, she wrote an article for *Bauwelt* about her collaboration with her former boss in Frankfurt am Main and in Moscow.[3] Second, the Soviet Union was the sole topic of the interview she did with Günter Höhne, editor-in-chief of the GDR design journal *form + zweck*, one day after her 90th birthday.[4] In the long, recorded version of this interview, she started by classifying the contents of her collection of materials. She had obviously planned to add a chapter on the Soviet Union to the chapters she had already written about her years in Vienna and Frankfurt.[5]

1 Margarete Schütte-Lihotzky, *Erinnerungen aus dem Widerstand 1938–1945*, ed. Chup Friemert (Hamburg: Konkret Literatur Verlag, 1985; in parallel also Berlin/GDR: Volk und Welt, 1985); Margarete Schütte-Lihotzky, *Warum ich Architektin wurde*, ed. Karin Zogmayer (Salzburg: Residenz, 2004). A new edition was published in 2019. However, the quotations below are taken from the 2004 edition.

2 Margarete Schütte-Lihotzky, *Millionenstädte Chinas. Bilder- und Reisetagebuch einer Architektin (1958)*, ed. Karin Zogmayer (Vienna: Springer, 2007). See also Helen Young Chang's essay in this volume.

3 Margarete Schütte-Lihotzky, "Meine Arbeit mit Ernst May in Frankfurt a. M. und Moskau," *Bauwelt* 28 (1986): 1051–54.

It is not known whether Margarete Schütte-Lihotzky had talked with others about her Soviet years prior to this. In any event, at the time of the interview, her memories flowed out in carefully crafted statements, a practice she always followed in her later years. Scarcely any detail, any reflection interrupted the coherence of her narrative—with one exception, which will be discussed later. The transcription of the interview helped her to formulate her own written texts; many passages from the interview can be found in the final chapter of her *Architektin* book. Unfortunately, no further in-depth interviews followed and thus her memoirs project that was to have extended into the postwar era[6] remained unfinished.

This may be attributable to age but beyond that also to structural reasons intrinsic to memory itself. In all her accounts of her Soviet years, it is striking that she concentrates on experiences she had in her very first years after moving from Frankfurt am Main to Moscow in October 1930. One could almost conclude that in Schütte-Lihotzky's memory, her enthusiasm about moving to Moscow and starting her work there as a specialist for children's facilities in the project planning office of Cekom Bank headed by Ernst May and later at SGP (the Standardized Town Planning Institute within the Standardized Union Housing Construction Trust, referred to below as "Trust SGP") culminated directly in anti-Fascist Resistance—that is to say, she simply "bypassed" the dramatic social upheavals in the Soviet Union between 1932/33 and 1937. However, if we take the documents associated with her work biography, the Moscow letters she sent to her sister Adele Hanakam,[7] and other documents from Moscow and Vienna archives and read them *collectively*, we arrive at a more nuanced picture of her Soviet experiences. Not only do these sources reveal a number of interesting details about her work and life in the Soviet Union, but they also help us understand the things she did not touch upon in her later memoirs.

The Matter of the Employment Contract

The crux of this "bypassing" is her repeated assertion that shortly before her departure she, along with her husband

However, while they do not produce a consistent text, notes and preliminary work about her time in the Soviet Union can be found in the University Archive of the University of Applied Arts Vienna, Nachlass Margarete Schütte-Lihotzky (UAUAK, NL MSL), Erinnerungen SU Manuskripte.

4 "Damals in der Sowjetunion. Gespräch mit Margarete Schütte Lihotzky, Teil 1: Aufbruch und Ankunft," *form + zweck* 4 (1987): 11–14, "Teil 2: Aufbaujahre," *form + zweck* 5 (1987): 8–15.

5 In addition to a collection of monographs about individuals (including Taut), she created folders on the following items for her memoirs (later published as *Warum ich Architektin wurde*): 1. Preface, 2. Politics, general development, industrialization/culture/agriculture, 3. Architecture: "How it came to the turrets and then back again," 4. Our tasks: urban planning, housing construction, children's buildings, children's furniture, organization of planning, 5. Architects' association, 6. Personalities, 7. Travels (through the Soviet Union, Japan/China), 8. Personal life (housing situation, transport), 9. Conclusion, appendix with photos and figures. See tape recording in the possession of Günter Höhne (Berlin).

Wilhelm Schütte and other leading employees of Ernst May, signed a five-year contract at the Soviet embassy in Berlin. Asked in 1987 about the duration of her stay in the Soviet Union, she replied laconically: "So, those seven years—we had committed ourselves to five years from the outset and for me it simply became two additional ones..."[8] At another juncture, she wrote: "An exciting time followed. The contracts had to be signed. May, we [Schütte and Schütte-Lihotzky] and most of the others signed them for a term of five years. Those who did not want to commit to such a long period received a contract with a shorter term."[9]

However, the signed employment contracts now held in the Archive of the University of Applied Arts Vienna reveal otherwise—namely that the draft of Margarete Schütte-Lihotzky's contract was initially issued for a term of two years and was then reduced to one year by way of handwritten revisions apparently made during the final negotiations and signing (with an option to extend one further year), whereas Wilhelm Schütte (like May, Hebebrand et al.) actually did receive a five-year contract.[10]

This extension of the term of her employment contract served three functions in Margarete Schütte-Lihotzky's later recall of these events: 1. It hid the actual hierarchies among the German specialists as well as the difference between her situation and her husband's. 2. It suppressed the 1932 crisis when the Soviets illegally terminated the employment contracts and imposed shorter terms and lower foreign currency exchange rates. 3. Lastly, it omitted the conditions in the Soviet Union from her work biography.

In his negotiations in Moscow, Ernst May obtained permission to hire a further 23 foreign employees. May's contract of July 15, 1930 reads as follows:

> The foreign specialists whom Dr. May hired to serve in the office are concluding special contracts with the bank. The salaries of the six following assistants of Dr. May from the group of foreign specialists are not allowed to exceed an average of $400 and RUB 800 per month. Two specialists receive a salary of $200 and RUB 500. Other foreign specialists, no more than 15 in total, receive a salary of $50 and RUB 400 on average per month.[11]

6 See her dedication in the *Architektin* book: "In terms of time, the material covers 50 years of practice as an architect. In terms of place, it is wide ranging. It extends from Europe to Japan, from China to Cuba." Schütte-Lihotzky, *Warum ich Architektin wurde*, 12.

7 In addition to the letters in UAUAK, NL MSL, I had the family papers at my disposal, to which Michael Stransky kindly granted me access. They have since been transferred to UAUAK.

8 "Damals in der Sowjetunion, Teil 1," 11.

9 Schütte-Lihotzky, *Warum ich Architektin wurde*, 208.

10 Wilhelm Schütte's employment contract has not been located to date. However, Schütte cited his five-year contract when he registered in Magnitogorsk; see Evgenija Konyševa and Mark Meerovič, *Linkes Ufer, rechtes Ufer. Ernst May und die Planungsgeschichte von Magnitogorsk*, ed. Thomas Flierl (Berlin: Theater der Zeit, 2014), 74.

11 Employment contract with Cekom Bank dated July 15, 1930; see Thomas Flierl (ed.), *Standardstädte. Ernst May in der Sowjetunion 1930–1933. Texte und Dokumente* (Berlin: Suhrkamp, 2012),

So, on departing for Moscow in early October 1930, the Schüttes had their signed employment contracts in their pockets with the following terms and conditions: Wilhelm: term of five years, monthly salary of RUB 500 plus USD 200; Margarete: term of one year, monthly salary of RUB 350 plus USD 50. According to the employee categories specified in the agreement with Ernst May, they belonged to the second and third categories, respectively.

Margarete Schütte-Lihotzky thus saw her situation in Frankfurt repeat itself: she may have directed project planning for children's facilities for the All-Union authority (Trust SGP), with up to 30 employees by her account,[12] but her contract had much worse terms and conditions than that of her husband, who was in charge of school construction, and than those of the other senior colleagues.

She made the following pragmatic comments to her sister Adele in January 1931:

> Besides the office, there is actually a lot of interesting work to be had; I am supposed to make standardized types of furniture now for a big new store (government-run, of course) but I don't want to overburden myself. If the office does become too much for me after a year, I see that there are also good types of work like this to be had.[13]

In fact, her contract with Trust SGP was extended in 1931 for one further year to 1932. To complete their buildings in Magnitogorsk, Schütte and Schütte-Lihotzky received separate contracts that lasted until 1933. "I signed a new one-year contract starting April 7 [1932]."[14]

Neither her *Erinnerungen* nor her correspondence (which was certainly monitored) made any mention of the dramatic conflicts that arose in late 1931/early 1932 when the Soviets breached and ultimately terminated the foreign specialists' contracts as part of a comprehensive reorganization of the administrative apparatus and in response to acute foreign currency problems. Of course, these actions had the biggest impact on the specialists with multiyear contracts. In early 1932, it was only through the intervention of the Deputy People's Commissar for Foreign Affairs, Nikolaĭ Krestinskiĭ, that Ernst May managed to avert the termination of his contract and convert it to a two-year follow-up contract with

422. The original can be found in the Ernst May estate in the Deutsches Kunstarchiv at the Germanisches Nationalmuseum, Nuremberg.

12 See "Damals in der Sowjetunion, Teil 2," 13.

13 Margarete Schütte-Lihotzky to Adele Hanakam, Moscow, n.d. [between January 23 and February 7, 1931], UAUAK, NL MSL, MSL, n.d./6.

14 Margarete Schütte-Lihotzky to Adele Hanakam, Moscow, April 12, 1932, UAUAK, NL MSL, MSL 1932/4/12.

15 See Flierl, *Standardstädte*, 104–10. (For the sake of consistency with the other essays in this book, the author has refrained from using the scientific transliteration from Russian that he otherwise favors.)

16 See Thomas Flierl, "Wilhelm Schütte als Schulbauexperte in der Sowjetunion (1930–1937)," in *Wilhelm Schütte. Architekt. Frankfurt – Moskau – Istanbul – Wien*, ed. ÖGFA and Ute Waditschatka (Zurich: Park Books, 2019), 24–47 and 165.

17 Margarete Schütte-Lihotzky's employment contract was published in

Evgeniia Konysheva, *Evropeĭskie arkhitektory v sovetskom gradostroitel'stve ėpokhi pervykh piatiletok: dokumenty i materialy* (European architects in Soviet urban development in the era of the first five-year plans. Documents and materials) (Moscow: BooksMArt, 2017), 121–24. NKTP—People's Commissariat of Heavy Industry, the supervisory body for the Standartgorproekt.

18 Walther Schulz, "Wie arbeitet die Gruppe May in Moskau," *Die neue Stadt* 3 (1932): 66–67, and Walther Schulz, "Planmäßiger Städtebau in der UdSSR in Theorie – und Praxis," *Bauwelt* 26 (1932): 633–35.

19 "Echo aus Moskau. Brief an die Bauwelt," and Walther Schulz, "Zuschrift zum Brief aus Moskau," *Bauwelt* 31 (1932): 764–65. Schulz replied temperately: "Despite the Russian breach of contract, which was the cause—and despite my temper at the time, which was the reason for the immediate termination of my contract[—]I have no reason to be ungrateful to the Soviet Union for one and a half valuable years of my life. But that is why I will not shy away from describing the conditions as I have seen them with open eyes, even at the risk of offending personal or societal vanity." (ibid.).

lower foreign currency pay.[15] Wilhelm Schütte protested the illegal termination of his contract both at the Central Control Commission with the People's Commissar of the Workers' and Peasants' Inspectorate (NK RKI, Rabkrin), Ian Rudzutak (Latvian: Jānis Rudzutaks), and with the Office for Foreign Specialists of the Federation of Labor Unions—but to no avail.[16] Like Ernst May, he and the other foreign employees were offered follow-up contracts by Trust SGP with shorter terms and lower foreign currency pay.

Margarete Schütte-Lihotzky also signed her own 1932 contract with the handwritten addendum: "The signature is only valid if the supplementary letter [...] to the contract about foreign currency pay for the period from October 7, 1931 to March 31, 1932 is confirmed by the NKTP."[17] In other words, Schütte-Lihotzky also faced problems with her foreign currency pay and used the signing of the new contract to enforce her claim on the outstanding foreign currency retrospectively.

Walther Schulz—the Schüttes shared the four-room apartment in the apartment building at Bol'shoĭ Karetnyĭ Pereulok 17 with him and his wife—lost his patience in the disputes with the trust management and was not reinstated. He and his family left the Soviet Union. Schulz reported in *Bauwelt* about difficulties in urban construction in the USSR[18] and held lectures in Germany that were picked up by right-wing daily newspapers. In response, an open letter was sent from Moscow in which "the members of the Plan(ning) Office for Socialist Cities with Heavy Industry (Standartgorproekt)," among them Wilhelm Schütte and Margarete Schütte-Lihotzky, condemned the activity of those colleagues "who, unmoved by the facts of Soviet Russian development, took the knowledge they acquired here about the inevitable growth difficulties and put it at the service of the opponents of the Soviet Union—consciously or unconsciously—at a politically crucial moment." The letter was printed in *Bauwelt* together with a rebuttal by Schulz.[19]

The work situation in 1932/33 had now taken the following form: Wilhelm Schütte with a term of one year, monthly salary of RUB 750 plus USD 100; Margarete Schütte-Lihotzky with one year, RUB 500 plus USD 25. The letter of reference Ernst May issued for Schütte-Lihotzky was dated April 15, 1933.[20]

After the contracts with Trust SGP expired in April 1933, the situation for both Schüttes was very tense: "Our situation here is still very uncertain for the time being. I expect we will certainly stay here another half a year at least, but it cannot be ruled out that we might have to send several things back." Their biggest concern was losing the apartment. "Wilhelm is not working right now either, but we hope the matter will get straightened out soon."[21] In her next letter she voiced welcome relief: "W's matter appears to be resolved favorably, so we will definitely stay here. All essential things, in particular the apartment, are settled, so we can stay at Karetnyĭ."[22]

After working for a year at the Institute of Health Protection for Children and Adolescents at the People's Commissariat for Health, Wilhelm Schütte received a permanent position as a high-level scientific employee, which he held uninterrupted from the beginning of June 1933 until his departure from the Soviet Union in 1937.[23] As in Frankfurt, he was given preference again in Moscow over his wife. Margarete Schütte-Lihotzky's work biography continued to be characterized by alternating project tasks, including private contracts.[24]

Besides her ten standard types of buildings (*Typenbauten*) for day nurseries and kindergartens for Magnitogorsk and the cities in Kuzbass from 1931, she made mention in 1932 of her project in Briansk[25] and her "Children's Club for Magnitogorsk"[26] (figs. 1, 2). In April 1932 she reported as follows: "At the moment, I am working on lightweight children's buildings for summertime for Sokolniki Park [...]."[27] The kindergartens in Kuznetsk in Western Siberia and in Kashira south of Moscow have been preserved. In October 1932 she wrote that she had designed a day nursery for Karaganda.[28] Finally, in March 1933 the Schüttes were both living in Magnitogorsk. Of their children's facilities at the time, "a kindergarten and a nursery school [were] under construction."[29]

She described her situation after leaving Trust SGP as follows:

> I am working a good deal right now, but very cozily and pleasantly at home. I am participating in a paid compe-

20 See Ernst May, Zeugnis (Moscow, April 15, 1933), UAUAK, NL MSL, Zeugnisse SU 1930–37, Q/23.

21 Margarete Schütte-Lihotzky to Josef Hanakam, Moscow, June 9, 1933, UAUAK, NL MSL, MSL 1933/6/9.

22 Margarete Schütte-Lihotzky to Adele Hanakam, July 12, 1933, UAUAK, NL MSL, MSL 1932/7/12.

23 See Auskunft des Zentralen Wissenschaftlichen Forschungs instituts für den Gesundheitsschutz der Kinder und Jugendlichen des Volkskommissariats für Gesundheit der RSFSR dated July 21, 1937, UAUAK, WS 0235/Q.

24 "I have a nice private job, which I can do well here at the dacha." Margarete Schütte-Lihotzky to Adele Hanakam, Moscow, July 12, 1933, UAUAK, NL MSL, MSL 1933/7/12.

25 Margarete Schütte-Lihotzky to Adele Hanakam, Moscow, March 6, 1932, UAUAK, NL MSL, MSL 1932/3/6.

26 Margarete Schütte-Lihotzky to Adele Hanakam, Moscow, January 21, 1932, UAUAK, NL MSL, MSL 1932/1/21.

27 Margarete Schütte-Lihotzky to Adele Hanakam, Moscow, April 12, 1932,

UAUAK, NL MSL, MSL 1932/4/12.

28 Margarete Schütte-Lihotzky to Adele Hanakam, Moscow, October 12, 1932, UAUAK, NL MSL, MSL 1932/10/12.

29 Margarete Schütte-Lihotzky to Adele Hanakam, Magnitogorsk, March 17, 1933, UAUAK, NL MSL, MSL 1933/3/17.

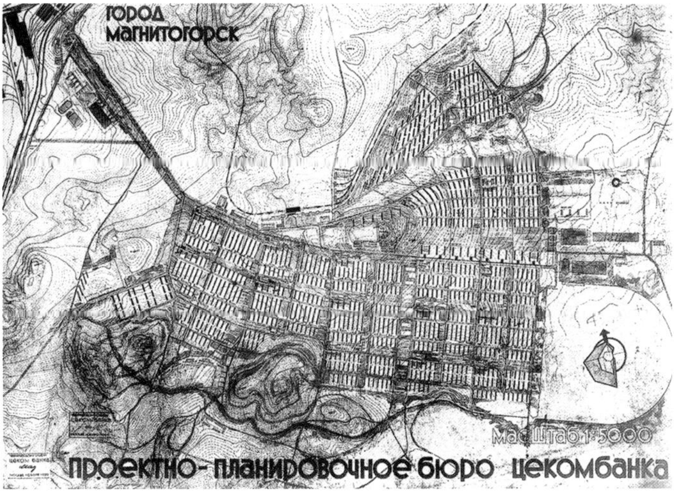

Fig. 1. Ernst May and Walter Schwagenscheidt, general plan for Magnitogorsk, November 1930.

> tition (besides me, there are two Russian competitors) for a children's home (100 day nursery children and 140 kindergartners) for the children of War Academy engineers, which is supposed to be built this summer in Moscow. It is a wonderful task but unfortunately at a less than ideal building site in the middle of the city. November 25 is my deadline, so I have a good deal of work to do because the project has to be presented just so. The person who wins the prize also receives a monetary bonus, so for me that could mean either a fur coat or the round trip to Vladivostok [here she was already anticipating her trip to Japan to visit Bruno Taut; author's comment]. For afterwards, I have work on two books, one about kindergartens and one about nursery schools.[30]

30 Margarete Schütte-Lihotzky to Adele Hanakam, [Moscow], October 30, 1933, UAUAK, NL MSL, MSL 1933/10/30.

Two and a half months later, she wrote:

> A few days ago the jury declared our child combine project for the Engineer Academy in Moscow (100 nursery school children, 140 kindergartners) to be the winner and we very much hope to land the contract to carry out

its construction. [The trip to Vladivostok—that is, to Japan—was therefore funded; author's comment.]
Today we were in Mostorg, the big state department store in Moscow, and negotiated on setting up a childcare department for approximately 100–150 children a day (1–3 hours per child while the mother [sic] shops.[31]

In 1934 prior to taking off on their three-month trip to Japan and China, the Schüttes took on the contract from Trust SGP to design school projects for Makiivka (fig. 3). But what were their work tasks and living conditions in the period *after* this trip—that is, during the time about which Schütte-Lihotzky said so little?

31 Wilhelm Schütte to Adele Hanakam, [Moscow], January 12, 1934, UAUAK, NL MSL, MSL 1934/1/12.

Apartment Worries Once Again

The concern about losing the apartment after leaving Trust SGP arose again in 1935. Actually, the Schüttes were supposed to move out on December 1 "because it belonged to an enterprise for which we no longer worked. But fortunately, we were able to settle the matter because we would have really hated to move out of that building."[32]

The Schüttes lived in apartment no. 81, initially with the Schulz family and then in 1932/33 with Fred Forbat.[33] Later

32 Margarete Schütte-Lihotzky to Adele Hanakam, [Moscow], December 18, 1935, UAUAK, NL MSL, Q/118.

33 "The Forbats will probably be traveling to Constantinople and Athens this month; we hope to get the Schmidts into the apartment." Margarete Schütte-Lihotzky to Adele Hanakam, [Moscow], February 6, 1933, UAUAK, NL MSL, MSL 1933/2/6. The apartment number changed to 89.

Fig. 2. Margarete Schütte-Lihotzky, children's club in 2nd Quarter of Magnitogorsk, photograph, 1932/33.

they shared the four-room apartment with Hans Schmidt, his wife Lilly Schmidt-Imboden, and their daughter Madleen. After most foreign specialists returned home in 1932/33, Werner Hebebrand, Hans Leistikow, Hans Schmidt, Mart Stam (till 1935), and the Schüttes were the only members of the original team left at Karetnyĭ Pereulok.[34] Living and interacting with each other was definitely a fundamental part of this remaining core group's life in the Soviet Union that one should not underestimate.

After most of the specialists had left the Soviet Union in 1932/33, other tenants moved in. They must have also included the earlier head of Trust SGP, Jakov Pavlovich Shmidt, who was registered as living in apartment no. 88. On August 10, 1937, just days after Hans Schmidt and family and the Schüttes had departed together from Moscow, he was arrested, sentenced, and ultimately executed by firing squad in October 1938.[35]

34 See the biographies in *Akteure des Neuen Frankfurt*, ed. Evelyn Brockhoff (Frankfurt am Main: Societäts-Verlag, 2016).

35 See *Zhertvy politicheskogo terrora v SSSR* (The victims of the political terror in the USSR), Memorial, Moscow, 2007, accessed April 10, 2022, http://lists.memo.ru.

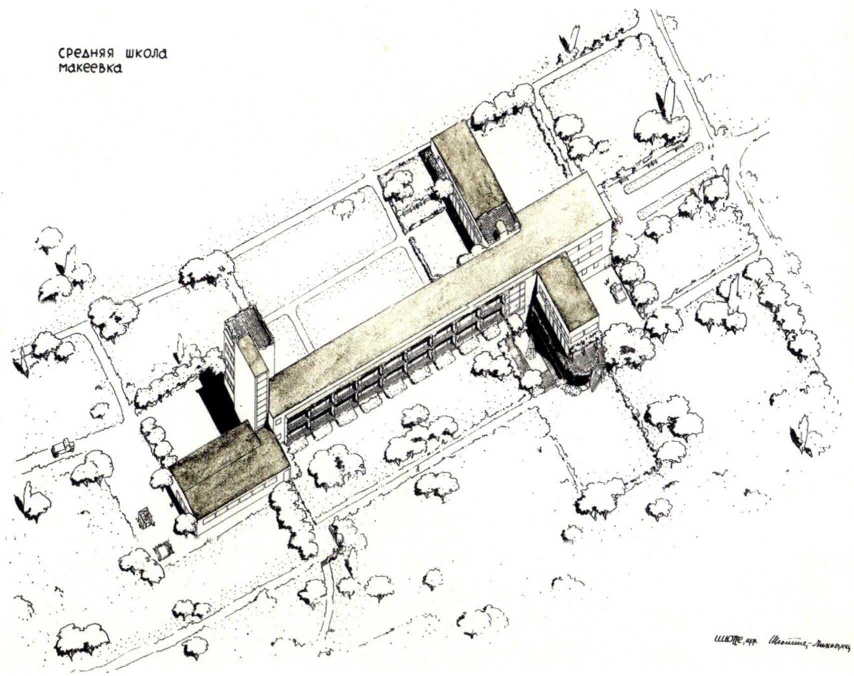

Fig. 3. Margarete Schütte-Lihotzky and Wilhelm Schütte, design for a middle school for 590 pupils in Makiivka, Donbas, 1934, photo on cardboard.

Relative Stabilization in the Years When State Terror Was On the Rise

In late 1933, Margarete Schütte-Lihotzky was already describing the general improvement in living conditions after the exaggerated objectives of the First Five Year Plan had been dropped:

> Now, you can buy all kinds of things here. You would be amazed how much Moscow has changed in the one and a quarter years since you stayed here. There are a lot of cafés and restaurants, many shop windows full of goods, all of which you can purchase. Our store has less and less but people can buy everything in the other stores, including food of all kinds. Of course, there is still not the quality and choice of goods available as in foreign, Western European countries, but the goods are there and many of them are certainly no worse than ours. A fundamental change has also taken place outdoors on the streets of the city. Many people are much better dressed than they used to be, many are wearing fine shoes and hats, etc. Of course you also still see the dirty Russian peasant alongside them wearing his old bast shoes with rags wrapped around his feet. Many new buildings have also been completed and new stories added to other buildings. A lot of it is actually well executed technically, with facades rendered in fine plaster; much of it already looks quite good.[36]

36 Margarete Schütte-Lihotzky to Adele Hanakam, Moscow, October 30, 1933, UAUAK, NL MSL, MSL 1933/10/30.

In 1934 she wrote: "[...] life in general has also become so much better and easier this last year for the Russians. We feel more at home here than ever and above all, have had a lot of contact with so many nice and fine people."[37] She talked about concerts with German conductors, about a concert with Shostakovich, about American movies—both kitschy feature-length color films as well as her favorites: Mickey Mouse and Chaplin movies. They were better integrated than ever before: "There is more work for us than ever right now; overall conditions for us are also much more pleasant since all but a handful of Germans remain; many of them behaved so badly and that naturally hurt everybody else."[38]

37 Margarete Schütte-Lihotzky to Adele Hanakam, Moscow, July 21, 1934, UAUAK, NL MSL, MSL 1934/7/21.

38 Ibid.

On October 1, 1936, food prices dropped, food stamps were eliminated, and the stores for foreigners (*Insnab*) were closed.[39] In her New Year's Eve/New Year's Day letter to her sister in 1936/37, Schütte-Lihotzky wrote as follows:

39 See Margarete Schütte-Lihotzky to Adele Hanakam, Moscow, October 27, 1936, UAUAK, NL MSL, Q/117.

> We had four guests (Tandler's niece, two Russians, and [Asja] Lacis, a theater director, half Latvian and half Tatar). It was so pleasant; later the Hebebrands and Leistikows [came] up with their guests (actors), the Schmidts came at six o'clock in the morning from a party and at around 8:30 a.m. we finally managed, with some effort, to get them all out the door. But it was so charming, everyone had such a good time! […] The first [of January] was spent sleeping and enjoying a good meal with the Schmidts at a Caucasian restaurant; that evening we went into the city where charming decorations had been put up for the children, [a] Christmas tree, Chinese lanterns, animals, dolls, stands, all set up very artistically in holiday fair style; dancing in the squares to loudspeakers, a truly merry hustle and bustle, a festival for the people. Yesterday on the second the festivities continued; we were invited by a stage director—her husband was also a director, had just come from the Volga, where he had been rehearsing plays with a Volga German theater troupe. So, we didn't get home until about three o'clock in the morning today either and your brother-in-law was in such good spirits, you probably have never seen him like that. It happens with him sometimes, with some alcohol and pretty women at a party. In short, our New Year got off to a very fun but somewhat dissolute start.[40]

40 Margarete Schütte-Lihotzky to Adele Hanakam, Moscow, January 3, 1937, UAUAK, NL MSL, Q/129.

In February 1937, she wrote: "I received a beautiful Persian lamb coat for my birthday. Am quite fine and elegant now!"[41]

41 Margarete Schütte-Lihotzky to Adele Hanakam, Moscow, February 4, 1937, UAUAK, NL MSL, Q/132.

"My Career Is Truly on the Rise Right Now"

The Schüttes's circumstances consolidated and became discernibly bourgeois. There was no longer any mention of Socialist development or egalitarian perspectives. In fact, the social differences began growing again and were clearly expressed. As all this was happening, Schütte-Lihotzky began receiving more professional recognition than her husband. As she wrote to her sister, he had been "celebrated [in China] as the 'greatest school builder in the world' so

Fig. 4. Margarete Schütte-Lihotzky, design for a kindergarten for 100 children, 1935/36, photo on cardboard.

to speak."[42] Now her career was "truly on the rise,"[43] which manifested itself in copious requests to take over projects and certainly also in decent pay. "Wilhelm now has more time than I do"[44]—in other words, he has less to do.

In 1934/35, Margarete Schütte-Lihotzky worked at the Academy of Architecture for the Cabinet for Residential Housing, Interior Construction, and Public Buildings, a small exhibition and demonstration room run by Hannes Meyer; her topics: housing units and furniture. On July 15, 1935, the People's Commissariat of Education of the Russian Federal Soviet Republic confirmed three of her kindergarten designs as standard-type projects (*Typenprojekte*) for 1936[45] concessions to the anti-modern tastes of the time are obvious (fig. 4). And in the fall of 1935 she wrote: "I have ample and lovely work[:] 'children's furniture for apartments' on a large scale for production in Moscow"[46] (fig. 5). She had sought out Moscow party head Nikita Khrushchev and succeeded in winning him over for the project. In 1936: "I am creating children's furniture for nursery schools right now; besides that, site supervision for the construction of my kindergartens. My project is now being built nine times; unfortunately, just two of those are in Moscow."[47] The director

42 Margarete Schütte-Lihotzky to Adele Hanakam, Nanjing, May 29, 1934, UAUAK, NL MSL, MSL 1934/5/29.

43 Margarete Schütte-Lihotzky to Adele Hanakam, Moscow, April 12, 1936, UAUAK, NL MSL, Q/122.

44 Margarete Schütte-Lihotzky to Adele Hanakam, Sukhanovo, September 28, 1936, UAUAK, NL MSL, Q/126.

45 Certificate dated September 22, 1936, UAUAK, NL MSL, Zeugnisse SU 1930–37, Q/28.

46 Margarete Schütte-Lihotzky to Adele Hanakam, postcard, Moscow, September 13, 1935, UAUAK, NL MSL, Q/116.

47 Margarete Schütte-Lihotzky to Adele Hanakam, Moscow, March 2/3, 1936, UAUAK, NL MSL, Q/120.

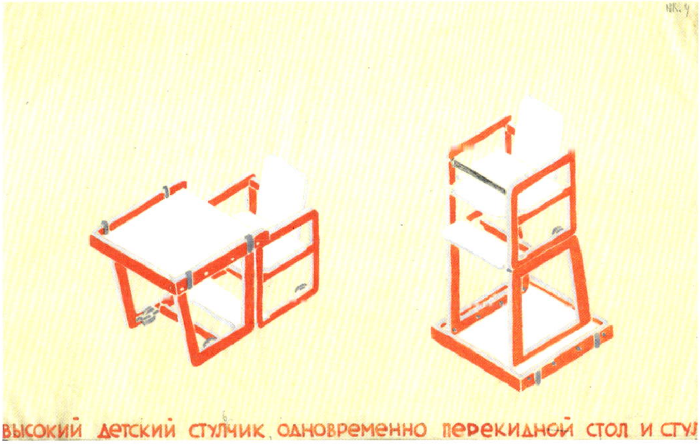

Fig. 5. Margarete Schütte-Lihotzky, design for a table and small chair for children up to age three (highchair) for the Academy of Architecture, Moscow, around 1935, gouache on paper.

of the museum exhibition on the protection of motherhood and babyhood asked Schütte-Lihotzky to submit designs and working drawings for furnishing infant units in day nurseries as a scholarly research project. She was allowed to set the fees and deadlines for the project herself.[48] Lovely color sketches from this project are preserved in the Archive of the University of Applied Arts Vienna (fig. 6).

She also talks about a store interior and a porcelain archive, which she is designing:

> […] and then a big job, creating standard types of furniture for the children's departments of department stores, and the overall design of these children's departments, for the time being for a new department store in Novosibirsk and one in Stalingrad; after that come eight new department stores over the course of 1937. This is a job for the People's Commissariat for Domestic Trade, which is in charge of all department stores throughout the Soviet Union. Moreover, my children's furniture for apartments is now being produced, so I am going to factories a lot right now; then I also have to create standard types of furniture for kindergartens.[49]

In early 1937 she reported: "Of my own projects, from what I could find out, there are now eight kindergartens under

48 See contract dated February 28, 1937.

49 Margarete Schütte-Lihotzky to Adele Hanakam, Moscow, May 30, 1936, UAUAK, NL MSL, Q/124.

construction, two of which are in Moscow. On the 29th [of December 1936] I spent the whole day at the building site; they are already building the second story."[50] Researchers have not yet identified all of these at least partially completed buildings. Finally, in the spring of 1937, she was "preparing an exhibition about apartment interiors together with [Hans] Schmidt and several Russian architects."[51]

50 Margarete Schütte-Lihotzky to Adele Hanakam, Moscow, January 3, 1937, UAUAK, NL MSL, Q/129.

51 Margarete Schütte-Lihotzky to Adele Hanakam, Moscow, April 6, 1937, UAUAK, NL MSL, Q/133.

Unlike her male colleagues, who had to experience their being pushed out of urban planning and construction tasks as a loss, Schütte-Lihotzky was now able to bring her multiple qualifications as an architect and furniture designer fully to bear.

Fig. 6. Margarete Schütte-Lihotzky, design for furniture in a nursery school, 1937, gouache, opaque white, pencil on tracing paper.

The Matter Involving Franz Weitz

In her 1987 interview with Günter Höhne, Margarete Schütte-Lihotzky initially gave a very general answer when asked how the 1933 transfer of power to the Nazis in Germany affected the specialists in the Soviet Union. She said Soviet citizens knew the specialists were opposed to the Nazis, and the specialists were no longer in close contact with the German embassy in Moscow. Surprisingly, she suddenly remembered Franz Weitz in this context, a German engineer who had worked at Trust SGP in 1931/32:

> Among the many who came afterward was a man who was obviously a Nazi, but that fact was not generally known. He worked a year in our trust—namely in urban planning. He was from Cologne; he was here with a woman and did not live in our building but sometimes visited us there and passed himself off as a Communist, and as such, attended the meetings of the party cell at the company. And after a year he then came and said he had envisaged things differently and was disappointed and was going back. And then we heard on the radio, Soviet radio, that he was a man in service to the Nazis. They were not yet at the helm, but he was in the SS. And then we got confirmation of this because I was on leave, [spending] a few days in Germany for a medical treatment, and I saw Mrs. Kratz there, [the wife] of our colleague Kratz, who had also returned to Germany, and she confirmed to me that this Weitz really had been in the SS. She had just happened to run into him in Berlin; he was wearing an SS uniform, that's what she told me.[52]

Of course, Günter Höhne had no idea who Franz Weitz was; the passage was not included in the printed interview. In the first Moscow trial in 1936, this Franz Weitz played a crucial role in constructing the prosecution's "Case of the Trotskyite-Zinov'evite Terrorist Center." The trial resulted in Grigoriĭ Zinov'ev and Lev Kamenev being sentenced to death and executed along with 14 other defendants. A passage in the report on the proceedings reads as follows:

> The preliminary investigation also revealed that the terrorist group led by Moisseĭ Lurye, whom L. Trotsky had sent abroad as a Trotsky agent, was in fact organized by

52 See recording of the interview with Margarete Schütte-Lihotzky on January 24, 1987, Archiv Günter Höhne. Schütte-Lihotzky also mentioned this man in her interview with Chup Friemert, although only in connection with the fact that there had been no Communists among the first 17 foreign specialists. "We were non-party specialists, so to speak. Many more came along later, technicians and younger architects. One of these was a Communist who had already been a Communist in Germany. There was a party cell in the company, of course; as a foreigner, he naturally took part in the party cell meetings at the company just like a Soviet Communist. But we didn't notice at all whether or not someone was a party member." Schütte-Lihotzky, *Erinnerungen* (1985), 31–32.

the active German Fascist Franz Weiz [sic], a representative of Himmler, who was head of the Fascist SS and is currently head of the German secret police (Gestapo).[53]

The Moscow Comintern Archive contains a file on Franz Weitz as a member of the Communist Party of Germany (KPD). He left the Soviet Union in 1932. If it were true that he had become a Nazi in Germany in the meantime, the opportunity would have presented itself to label him a Fascist agent and thereby "prove" the alleged merger of Trotsky and Zinov'ev followers with the German National Socialists. In the circles of architects and urban planners, the direct victim of these investigations against Franz Weitz was the Cologne architect and Communist Kurt Meyer. He had been instrumental in drawing up the Moscow General Plan of 1935, had known Weitz from Cologne, and had vouched for him in connection with an (unsuccessful) application for membership in the Communist Party of the Soviet Union (CPSU). He was arrested in 1936 and sentenced to eight years' detention in a prison camp in 1937, which he did not survive.[54]

An interesting aspect of Schütte-Lihotzky's reminiscences was that she now talked about finding out about Weitz's political turn on Soviet radio and having received confirmation for it in the accidental encounter that Mrs. Kratz had had with Weitz. However, according to her letters to her sister, Schütte-Lihotzky was in Germany in April 1936. She had medical consultations in Berlin with a specific physician recommended to her by Mrs. Taut. After that she traveled to Frankfurt am Main and visited her sister-in-law near Karlsruhe and her mother-in-law in Allgäu. She had planned to possibly make a side trip to Switzerland and then after that, on April 23, to begin her treatment in Berlin, which she intended to continue in the Soviet Union.[55] The meeting with Mrs. Kratz in Germany—wherever it may have occurred—at which she claimed to have found out about Weitz being in the SS would therefore have had to have taken place *before* the trial and the public announcements about it, because it is hardly likely that Soviet radio would have reported on a German engineer who had already left the country in 1932 long before the trial and outside the scope of the incredible conspiracy story.

53 *Prozessbericht über die Strafsache des trotzkistisch-sinowjewistischen terroristischen Zentrums, verhandelt vor dem Militärkollegium des Obersten Gerichtshofes der UdSSR vom 19.–24.8.1936* (Moscow: Volkskommissariat für Justizwesen der UdSSR, 1936), 16 (German edition). The "t" was lost when the German surname "Weitz" was transliterated into Russian and back.

54 See Harald Bodenschatz and Thomas Flierl (eds.), *Von Adenauer zu Stalin. Der Einfluss des traditionellen deutschen Städtebaus in der Sowjetunion um 1935* (Berlin: Theater der Zeit, 2016), in particular the editors' introduction ("Die Tätigkeit Kurt Meyers in Moskau und die sowjetische Rezeption des städtebaugeschichtlichen Hauptwerks von Albert Erich Brinckmann," 7–35), Hannes Meyer's explanation (126–30), and Tatiana Efrussi's comments on this matter (131–38).

55 See Margarete Schütte-Lihotzky to Adele Hanakam, Berlin, April 8, 1936, UAUAK, NL MSL, MSL 1936/4/8.

The bad news that the former Communist and Moscow colleague Franz Weitz had in the meantime become a member of the SS is something that Schütte-Lihotzky certainly would not have kept to herself. And it is also highly likely that the investigating authorities would have asked about this allegedly key figure in the conspiracy among his former colleagues at Trust SGP prior to the trial and would have gratefully accepted any information. Hannes Meyer also issued a statement in Switzerland about the "Gestapo Agent Franz Waitz" on August 29, 1936, albeit *after* the trial.[56]

If one reconstructs the memories shared by Schütte-Lihotzky, the radio actually appears to have confirmed this fact that she already knew. At the same time, it put the operation in the overarching context of the "Great Conspiracy."[57] The Schüttes may have been connected with Franz Weitz for another reason. Schütte had been renting a property from Weitz in Germany since 1931, probably for his family in the Rhineland.[58] In addition, Weitz had been among the vocal critics of "foreign currency pigs" at Trust SGP and wanted to get into trust director Gasparian's good graces, a man he supposedly lived with for a period of time.[59]

There is no intention whatsoever here to allege any kind of involvement by Schütte-Lihotzky in devising the adventurous and felonious criminal story of the first Moscow trial. She was apparently horrified about her former Moscow colleague later becoming a Nazi or, even worse, being unmasked as a Nazi. Fifty years later her horror about her own earlier closeness to Weitz still appears to be overshadowed by any reflection on his apparently construed role in the first Moscow trial and on the criminal dimension of Stalin's state terror.

Thus far, I have found only one instance in which Schütte-Lihotzky answered the question about how she experienced Stalinism in everyday life in the Soviet Union. In 1997 she gave this account to Günter Höhne:

> So, in plain language, under Stalinism people understood arrests. Of course, the people who were working there, like we were, knew about the arrests. It is nonsense if anyone says he didn't know about them. The first arrests we found out about—as you know it all started in

56 Hannes Meyer, Erklärung über den Gestapo-Agenten Franz Waitz vom 29. August 1936 (typescript), Russian State Archive of Sociopolitical History (RGASPI), Moscow, f. 495, op. 274, d. 82, sheet 20–22.

57 See the Stalinist hagiography: Michael Sayers and Albert E. Kahn, *The Great Conspiracy Against Russia* (New York: Boni & Gaer, 1947).

58 "It is known that we own latifundia as a sideline. Since the start of this year, we have been receiving a modest rent from Schütte (without accumulation)." Franz Weitz (Essen) to Kurt and Gertrud Meyer (Moscow), May 26, 1931, RGASPI, f. 495, op. 205, d. 5088, Franz Weitz, sheet 24.

59 Bert Niehues, "Bericht über eine Begegnung mit Franz Waitz in Moskau vom 11.10.1936," RGASPI, f. 495, op. 205, d. 5088, Franz Weitz, sheet 30–31.

1934, we had been there about four years already—engineers were involved. I think there were four at the time who were arrested. Well, you said to yourself at the time maybe they did do something. They were people you didn't know, who worked somewhere or other. Now from '34 to '37, until we left, the arrests really increased. As far as I know, they almost always involved arrests among Communists, Soviet nationals, and foreigners. But I personally never felt or noticed anything about it at all or any greater reserve shown toward myself or that I was frightened that I would be arrested; there was no talk of that. Incidentally, among the foreigners who were arrested, most of them were party members. And I was not a party member.[60]

Here once again one discerns in Schütte-Lihotzky a strange absence of any memory of the great political upheavals, the liquidation of Lenin's comrades-in-arms in the Revolution of 1917 and Stalin's approaching reign of mass terror—especially since she mentioned at other times that she and her husband already felt drawn to the Communists, but she "would have considered [an application for membership] to be the vilest kind of opportunism."[61]

60 Margarete Schütte-Lihotzky in an interview with Günter Höhne in 1997, "Margarete Schütte-Lihotzky," radio portrait to mark her 100th birthday, broadcast on Radio Brandenburg on March 8, 1997.

61 Schütte-Lihotzky, *Erinnerungen* (1985), 47.

A Love Affair

On May 28, 1937, Margarete Schütte-Lihotzky wrote a detailed letter to her sister from Tskaltubo, a health resort in the Caucasus to which she was sent for 14 days:

I am here in Tskaltubo, [...] a resort town with radioactive springs, which are supposed to work wonders. The town is on the southern slopes of the Caucasus, near the Black Sea coast. This is really my last attempt at having children. You take baths here mornings and evenings, you are also given lavages with the water, so you are occupied all the time. After the bath, you feel splendid.

After giving a detailed account of the health resort and the women she was sharing a room with, she mentioned that she looked very good again in the meantime:

[...] which I did not on departure. I had quite a bit of excitement recently because of a love affair (which involved me and another man but not W.). You really

62 Margarete Schütte-Lihotzky to Adele Hanakam, May 28, 1937, UAUAK, NL MSL, Q/135.

63 Gustav von Wangenheim (1895–1975), actor and director, studied acting under Max Reinhardt,

> should not start anything at such an advanced age! But it is an unbelievable story; you do not really have to read novels! Yes, life is not always so easy in those regards! On the 18th, I departed from M. [Moscow], leaving behind two loving men in a state of great excitement. And I have not heard a word from there since; it makes me feel somewhat uneasy.[62]

Unfortunately there are no further letters of hers preserved that clearly indicate who that other man was. But the following story dovetails with the account all too well. The personnel file of Wilhelm and Margarete Schütte in the Comintern Archive contains a report of the German Communist, actor, and director Gustav von Wangenheim[63] (the Russian version is dated August 19, 1941—that is, after Schütte-Lihotzky's arrest in Vienna). Unlike the majority of the members of Ernst May's group who had left the Soviet Union by 1933—Wangenheim called them the "whiners-in-chief"—the Schüttes had remained and continued to work:

> Apparently she was the more successful, as a specialist for the construction of children's homes. / I met both of them around '34. I found her exceptionally appealing. Industrious, talented, enthusiastic—Soviet through and through. He was less clear-cut. Smart, maybe less than open, maybe a bit angry because of work ... but [had] a library with the typical books of a qualified, anti-Fascist intellectual and in general: a somewhat reserved man but probably positively inclined. In '37 or '38 he wanted to take a trip outside the country because he was afraid that if he took on Soviet citizenship he would lose residual assets worth a few thousand marks that he had in Switzerland. She, Lisotskaia [sic] did not want to leave. For many reasons. I also mention the fact that L. was in love with me—I do so because it is perhaps important in this context and for the sake of completeness. There were certainly political reasons involved because she loved me for being an artist-Communist in contrast to her husband. My wife, who regarded L. as highly as I did, had been informed. But our relations remained strictly platonic, quite casual, because I was opposed in principle (maybe also for other reasons but

theatrical engagements in Vienna, Darmstadt, and Berlin, UFA film star, acted in Friedrich Wilhelm Murnau's *Nosferatu* in 1922, and in films by Fritz Lang and Ernst Lubitsch. Active on the left as an author after 1917, Independent Social Democratic Party of Germany (USPD) in 1918, Communist Party of Germany (KPD) in 1922, founded the Barbusse-Truppe—a workers' traveling theater group—in 1925. Between 1928 and 1933 director of the Truppe 1931, which was formed by KPD members of the artists' colony in the Friedenau area of Berlin. In 1933 he emigrated via Paris to the Soviet Union, where he undertook work in the movies (*Der Kämpfer*, about Georgi Dimitrov in the Reichstag fire trial) and in theater (*Kolonne Links*, with Arthur Pieck), wrote for publishing houses and Moscow radio, and was a member of the writers' association. Condemned to death by the Nazis in absentia, he took Soviet citizenship in 1940 and worked for the Red Army after war broke out. Evacuation to Tashkent in 1941–43; co-founder of the National Committee for a Free Germany and a departmental head at the radio station Freies Deutschland after 1943; was one of the first emigrants to return to Berlin, where he was director of Deutsches Theater for several months.

> certainly for political ones) to dalliances between married German Communists. It may have been this attitude that won me the special trust of, and I emphasize, Comrade L. —what I heard from her was strictly deep devotion to our cause and to the Soviet Union. Lisotskaia [sic] let herself be persuaded to leave by her husband and by the mounting difficulties with work. Both of them wrote to me from abroad. First from France, then from England, and finally from Turkey, where they both (probably he in particular) had very favorable governmental and teaching contracts (according to the letters).[64]

64 RGASPI, f. 495, op. 205, d. 5616, Wilhelm Schütte, sheet 19 [underlining in the original].

The months leading up to their departure from the Soviet Union in August 1937 were apparently turbulent—personally and politically. The plan to leave came as a surprise and was probably Wilhelm Schütte's idea, if one can trust Wangenheim's account. Margarete Schütte-Lihotzky had written to her sister at the end of May, saying that she was still hoping for a "reunion here in the fall" (in the Soviet Union).[65] The letter sent in mid-June indicated that the Schüttes wanted to go to Paris to attend the World's Fair. At the same time, Schütte-Lihotzky reported to her sister about the Congress of Soviet Architects that had just ended, calling it "extraordinarily interesting and also important for when I do further work here."[66] In her letter to her sister dated June 17, 1937, Schütte-Lihotzky informed her about the dates and the route of their planned trip to Paris, pointing out that she would "also have professional business" in Paris "because I am supposed to collect an abundance of materials for here, for all kinds of furniture and furnishings." She had received a French entry visa for one month to visit the exposition in Paris. The certificate concerning Wilhelm Schütte's departure from his institute is dated July 21, 1937.[67] It appears the decision to leave the Soviet Union permanently was not finalized until that point. Drawing on her fabulous organizational talent, Schütte-Lihotzky transported their Moscow household belongings (furniture, books, etc.) to Amsterdam with the help of a Dutch architect, probably Johan Niegemann.

65 Margarete Schütte-Lihotzky to Adele Hanakam, May 28, 1937, UAUAK, NL MSL, Q/135.

66 Margarete Schütte-Lihotzky to Adele Hanakam, Moscow, n.d. [after June 12, 1937], UAUAK, NL MSL, Q/137.

67 See Auskunft des Zentralen Wissenschaftlichen Forschungsinstituts dated July 21, 1937, UAUAK, NL MSL, WS.

It was not until August 14, 1937, that she wrote her sister a postcard from Athens informing her that they would receive new passports in Paris and did not know how long that would take.[68] And on August 28, 1937, she reported from Paris as follows: "We are not returning (that is to say, hopefully sometime down the road); all else on this matter to follow orally. The departure was very difficult. But for the moment our decision was probably the right one [...]."[69]

The Letters from Moscow

As demonstrated by the handful of quotes from letters cited here, the convolute of more than 140 letters, postcards, and telegrams from Margarete Schütte-Lihotzky to her sister about the Soviet years are an invaluable source and one that has hardly been explored and researched. The work biographies of Margarete Schütte-Lihotzky and Wilhelm Schütte can be reconstructed more precisely than ever, along with an understanding of their daily lives, their arrival in Moscow, their shared living arrangement at Bol'shoĭ Karetnyĭ Pereulok 17 with specialists accompanying May to the Soviet Union, and the evolving view of the Soviet Union undergoing societal development and upheaval. It would exceed the scope of this essay to elaborate on these aspects here. Pars pro toto, the fascinating letter dated November 12, 1930, is provided in full below. These holdings should definitely be transcribed, annotated, and published in their entirety.

68 Margarete Schütte-Lihotzky to Adele Hanakam, from Athens, August 14, 1937, UAUAK, NL MSL, Q/131.

69 Margarete Schütte-Lihotzky to Adele Hanakam, Paris, August 28, 1937, UAUAK, NL MSL, Q/140. A warning may have been one of the reasons for the rapid departure from the country: it was the last moment to escape from the "German operation" of the People's Commissariat of Internal Affairs (NKVD), which led to the arrest of all Germans in the armaments and transport industries on the basis of the secret order that the Politburo, on Stalin's initiative, agreed on July 20, 1937 and enacted on July 25. See Nikita Ochotin and Arseni Roginski, "Zur Geschichte der 'Deutschen Operation' des NKWD 1937–1938," in *Jahrbuch für Historische Kommunismusforschung 2000/2001* (Berlin: Aufbau-Verlag, 2001), 89–125. The repressions went far beyond these sectors and also included Soviet citizens of German origin and German-speaking political emigrants. Some 55,000 people had already been convicted by 1938, of whom around 42,000 were shot. See Aleksandr Vatlin, *"Was für ein Teufelspack." Die Deutsche Operation des NKWD in Moskau und im Moskauer Gebiet 1936 bis 1941* (Berlin: Metropol, 2012).

Margarete Schütte-Lihotzky to Adele Hanakam, letter dated November 12, 1930 from Moscow, typewritten manuscript, UAUAK, NL MSL, MSL 1930/11/12

November 12, 1930
Copy

Dear DELE,

The detailed letter I promised to send has certainly been a long time coming but you have probably heard from us indirectly via the NEURATS in the meantime, at least. My excuse is that we really have been extremely busy. Work at the office, learning Russian, and unpacking and moving. Off to the office in the morning, home at 4:30 p.m., finished eating by 5:30 p.m. at the latest, at six o'clock again till eight o'clock Russian lessons, but just every other day. I spend the rest of my free time doing Russian homework, setting up the apartment, buying food, occasionally going to the movies or getting together with someone we know. I still have not been to the theater, also we have seen very little of Moscow as yet. Once we are settled in the apartment, we will probably have more time and peace of mind.

Work has been absolutely fantastic. Nearly three weeks ago, MAY dropped by one day with a huge plan. He and three of us had to leave immediately for Magnitogorsk (south of the Urals, already in Asia), where a completely new city of 120,000 people is to be built in two years. A fantastic task!! There is a large scale iron industry there. Two years ago, there wasn't a single telegraph pole there, [it was a] complete wilderness; today all the factories are up and running, and 20,000 workers live in barracks there. For this city (imagine, the population is about as big as Wiesbaden or Innsbruck), we are supposed to build apartments, schools of all kinds, laundries, childcare centers, hospitals, post offices, department stores, clubs, etc. MAY, STAM, LEHMANN (road builders), and Burghardt (city planner) were traveling for 14 days, 10 days on the train and four [?] days in Magnitogorsk.

During this time, three new cities came in, one in Novosibirsk, a second one also in Siberia and one 200 km from here in the Moscow coal basin. Needless to say, we are not in a position to handle all this and must first concentrate on the one huge task. On the first day, when we were in the office and we were all sort of standing around not knowing how to start, HEBEBRAND said in his dry witty way: "Hand me a city." But the reality is that we were handed a new city to plan every few days.

I personally have had wonderful work—namely, to plan laundry centers, bathing facilities, nurseries, and kindergartens and specifically, to create standard types for variously sized groupings of residential buildings, so-called city quarters. For instance, for 1,000, 2,000, 5,000, and 7,000 inhabitants.

On the whole, everything in this country is gigantic; 1,000 people are nothing. Everything you hear and see, literally everything, is in huge dimensions for us and to grasp that, you must keep reminding yourself that you are in the capital of a country made up of 200 different nationalities and 146 million inhabitants, in the capital and in the intellectual center of a people that occupies one-sixth of the Earth's land surface.

Wilhelm works on schools (we had a fascinating lecture about the structure of and instruction at Russian schools) and clubs, also a department store. Just think, compulsory national education was not introduced until 1930. In general, from our Western European standpoint, there is still a primitiveness here that would have been almost unimaginable to us before. You have the impression that everything that was done and will be done here must be built completely new from the ground up and a large part of the population must first be woken up out of their unbelievable primitiveness, like from a sleep. (Of course this applies less to Moscow than to the countryside.) It is understandable that this type of awakening for a country cannot happen in 10 or 20 years. Housing construction will therefore probably be the most important task of all, because there can be no control there. All buildings do have a management that can see to the proper use of things, cleanliness, etc.

How many people living here in Moscow have probably never slept in a bed! The population has grown tremendously here, and most of those who have arrived are farmers and from all parts of Russia. And the way the peasants live in the more primitive areas here is said to be indescribable. Especially in Siberia, very crude pit dwellings or mud huts without windows and ventilation and without beds, etc. This first-ever pioneer work that must be performed in all areas, it is unbelievably impressive in itself. Transforming Russia from a primitive agricultural state, where people often live like primitive animals and of course continue to live that way today, to a modern industrial state, to a state that utilizes the enormous mineral resources that have lain fallow till recently.

If outer life here seems to be simpler, and to our minds, also, first and foremost dirtier and less civilized, more Eastern as it were, this situation is offset again by the gigantic tasks and truly grand line that runs through everything here.

We may have seen little of buildings, museums, etc. from the inside as yet, but we have taken in the whole atmosphere of the city out on the streets. There is nothing more interesting than walking around the streets here. You see, above all, extraordinary numbers of Mongolian types and also the widest variety of races otherwise, especially in the widest variety of getups. In general, you can walk around here however you like, in rags or the most stylish of clothes and with lipstick on your lips. In other words, everything is in such chaos that no one attracts attention. Of course, out in the streets you do have the feeling that the proletarians rule the city. For a moment, you think all the people are "vagrants," as we always call them. After a while, you realize that behind that vagrant appearance is a person just as cultivated as any you might find at home. Nothing is evident in terms of class; everything is a single class as it were, in which there are simply more educated and less educated people.

We were recently accepted into the Workers' Club of the National Economy; more on the interior and our interaction with clients some other time.

Please try to send me a can of sardines, medium size. I will see if it can be sent duty-free. They aren't available here and I am so fond of eating them. Letters up to now have all arrived safe and sound, from Vienna and from Cologne, five days.

If your phone rings one day and Moscow is on the other end, don't think that an accident has happened; we just found out that a three-minute call to Berlin costs only RUB 3.50; that is very affordable.

A call directly from the desk in our hotel room to your front room; how strange is that?!! I heard, though, that it is difficult to understand each other.

Till now, it was still warm here. Today, November 13, the first snowfall!

My warmest wishes to all

GRETL signed

Intermezzo in Istanbul. Margarete Schütte-Lihotzky's Projects in Turkish Exile

Burcu Dogramaci

How does a body of architectural work develop in emigration if the stay is limited to a few months or years? What continuity or transformational ability does such an oeuvre exhibit and how do emigrants respond to the specific challenges they face in their countries of destination? These questions will guide this examination of the architect Margarete Schütte-Lihotzky in Turkish exile.

Schütte-Lihotzky lived in Turkey for a little more than two years. During her stay, the architect was productive: she was active in school construction and also completed designs for private homes.[1] She was one of the few women to be invited by the Turkish Ministry of Education and to receive an employment contract. Schütte-Lihotzky's position in the history of emigration to Turkey is therefore already unique simply because of her gender. Beyond that, Schütte-Lihotzky is a revealing example of just how crucial networks were for (professional) survival in exile and of how new networks were often established.

Margarete Schütte-Lihotzky and her husband Wilhelm Schütte came to be in Turkey through their contacts with the architect Bruno Taut. Prior to that, the couple had lived in the Soviet Union for several years. When this period at

1 There are still relatively few studies on Schütte-Lihotzky's work in Turkey. The following are of note: Salih Birtan Karain, "Margarete Schütte-Lihotzky ve Türkiye'deki yapıları," *Mimarlık* 270 (1996): 8–13; Bernd Nicolai, *Moderne und Exil. Deutschsprachige Architekten in der Türkei 1925–1955* (Berlin: Verlag für Bauwesen, 1998), 154–56. This essay updates the findings of the author's habilitation thesis: Burcu Dogramaci, *Kulturtransfer und nationale Identität. Deutschsprachige Architekten, Stadtplaner und Bildhauer in der Türkei nach 1927* (Berlin: Gebr. Mann, 2008).

2 See Margarete Schütte-Lihotzky, "Ansprache für Istanbul" (manuscript, June 1978),

University Archive of the University of Applied Arts Vienna, Nachlass Margarete Schütte-Lihotzky (UAUAK, NL MSL), TXT/274, 3. In this text, Schütte-Lihotzky also reports on previous stays in Turkey: in 1932, she and Wilhelm Schütte visited Taut's predecessor, Ernst Egli, at the Academy of Fine Arts in Istanbul. Schütte traveled on to Ankara, where he met the sculptor Anton Hanak. They traveled across the country together to look for stones for the Security Monument. In 1937, after leaving the Soviet Union, Schütte-Lihotzky and Schütte paid a visit to Bruno Taut at the Academy in Istanbul.

3 See Jan Cremer and Horst Przytulla, *Exil Türkei. Deutschsprachige Emigranten in der Türkei 1933 1945*, 2nd ed. (Munich: Lipp, 1991); *Haymatloz – Exil in der Türkei 1933–1945*, exhibition catalog, Akademie der Künste (Berlin: Verein Aktives Museum, 2000); Kemal Bozay, *Exil Türkei. Ein Forschungsbeitrag zur deutschsprachigen Emigration in die Türkei (1933–1945)* (Münster: LIT, 2001).

4 Agreement between Türkiye Cumhuriyeti Kültür Bakanlığı (Turkish Ministry of Culture) and Margarete Schütte-Lihotzky, June 30, 1938, reproduced in Ataman Demir, *Arşivdeki belgeler ışığında. Güzel*

the side of the architect Ernst May came to an end, it was impossible for either of them to return to Nazi Germany because of their political views. During their stay in Paris in 1937, the couple received a letter with job offers from the architect Bruno Taut, who was in exile in Turkey.[2]

Founded in 1923, the Republic of Turkey had already been "importing" architects, artists, academics, and scientists since 1927 to advance the country's efforts to build up the fields of education and culture. After 1933, Turkey benefited from the persecution of prominent figures on the cultural and intellectual scene in Germany and their expulsion from that country.[3] For instance, the urban planners Martin Wagner and Gustav Oelsner and also the architect Bruno Taut went to Istanbul, where they were put in key positions. These émigrés, in turn, sought to bring former colleagues of theirs to Turkey, among them Margarete Schütte-Lihotzky and Wilhelm Schütte. As head of the architectural department at the Academy of Fine Arts and as the man responsible for school and university construction in Turkey, Bruno Taut was looking for capable colleagues. Schütte-Lihotzky and Schütte had already gained extensive experience in school and kindergarten construction during their time in Germany but also in the Soviet Union. This knowledge and experience was in high demand in Turkey. The contract with Margarete Schütte-Lihotzky was dated June 30, 1938 and obligated her to work for three years as an architect in the school construction office at the Academy of Fine Arts in Istanbul.[4]

First Construction Tasks in Turkey

On August 24, 1938, the couple arrived in Istanbul on a ship from Brindisi.[5] On September 16, 1938, Taut confirmed in writing that Margarete Schütte-Lihotzky commenced work on that day.[6] One day after her arrival she wrote as follows: "Overall, Istanbul seems much, much more Eastern and Oriental to us this time compared to the last times, where we were not coming from the West [but from the Soviet Union]."[7]All Turkish exiles faced the challenges of coming to grips with a culture that was foreign to them, with unknown customs and practices, and of resuming their professional careers after a profound and life-changing turning point.

One of the first tasks given to Schütte and Lihotzky was to design temporary architecture for ceremonies marking the 15th anniversary of the Republic of Turkey on October 29, 1938, for the Karaköy ferry terminal on the Anatolian side of Istanbul. The design (fig. 1) with the vertically projecting tower exhibits, for one thing, references to modern architecture in Turkey—for example Şevki Balmumcu's exhibition center for Ankara or the central train station in Ankara.[8] The couple were presumably familiar with these buildings, as they had been in Ankara on an educational tour in September 1938. The design is also reminiscent of temporary Soviet ceremonial architecture and grandstands, as shown by daytime and nighttime photos.[9] The couple was certainly familiar with these structures from their years of living in the Soviet Union.[10] Propaganda was formulated in quotations and inscriptions; grandstands and kiosks were employed as means

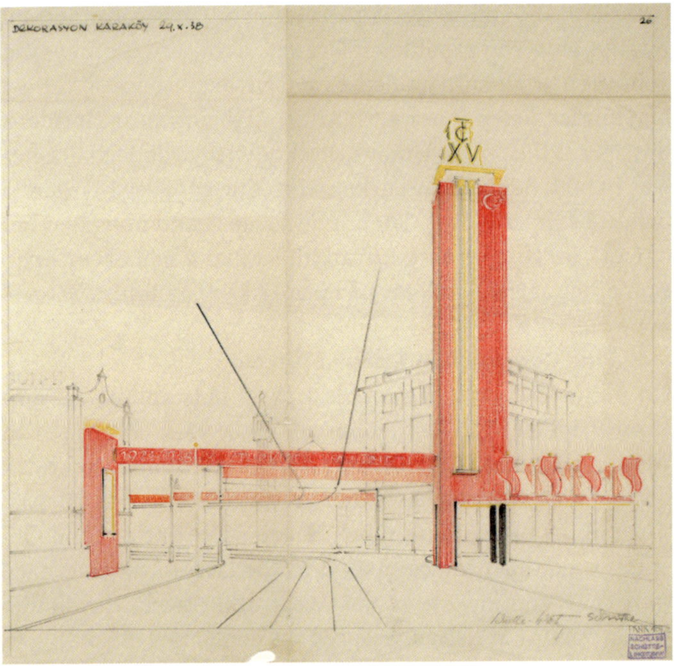

Fig. 1. Margarete Schütte-Lihotzky and Wilhelm Schütte, festival tower, festive decoration for the 15th anniversary of the Turkish Republic, beginning of Galata Bridge, Istanbul Karaköy, October 29, 1938, draft drawing.

Sanatlar Akademisi'nde yabancı hocalar. Philipp Günther'den (1929)–(1958) Kurt Erdmann'a kadar (Istanbul: Mimar Sinan Güzel Sanatlar Üniversitesi, 2008), 327–28. Also see Margarete Schütte-Lihotzky to Adele Hanakam, June 28, 1938, UAUAK, NL MSL, Korrespondenz von MSL (30er Jahre), Q/151.

5 Margarete Schütte-Lihotzky to Adele Hanakam, August 25, 1938, UAUAK, NL MSL, Korrespondenz von MSL (30er-Jahre), Q/160.

6 Bruno Taut, confirmation of Margarete Schütte-Lihotzky starting work, September 16, 1938, reproduced in Demir, *Arşivdeki belgeler ışığında*, 328.

7 Margarete Schütte-Lihotzky to Adele Hanakam, August 25, 1938, UAUAK, NL MSL, Korrespondenz von MSL (30er Jahre), Q/160.

8 Both buildings are depicted in Sibel Bozdoğan, *Modernism and Nation Building. Turkish Architectural Culture in the Early Republic* (Seattle: University of Washington Press, 2001), 180.

9 Photographs reproduced in Burcu Dogramaci, *Fotografieren und Forschen. Wissenschaftliche Expeditionen mit der Kamera im türkischen Exil nach 1933* (Marburg: Jonas, 2013), 63.

of media communication. Letters and symbols conveyed political messages. The Roman numerals "XV" and the initials "TC," which stand for Türkiye Cumhuriyeti (Republic of Turkey), can be seen on the tower and on the banners hanging over the street. The crescent and the star are well-known symbols of Turkey. The red flags are a reference to ceremonial street decorations of the kind the brothers Vesnin and Ivan Alexeyev used for holidays marking the Russian Revolution. A special relationship can be seen especially with the work of Boris Iofan. For the pavilion at the 1937 World's Fair in Paris, which Schütte-Lihotzky may well have seen during her stay in the city, Iofan set the horizontal element of the exhibition center in contrast to the tower-like facade of the entrance. Margarete Schütte-Lihotzky and Wilhelm Schütte also combined the verticality of cross-street elements with the horizontality of the tower, which was visible from afar and also at night because the letter signs were illuminated.[11]

School Construction under Kemalism

Teaching literacy skills to and educating the rural population was one of the big reform programs of the Turkish government. The construction of village schools was therefore an important concern, and specialists were hired to build elementary and village schools.[12] The intention was to raise compulsory schooling from three to five years and to improve the health care system in order to reduce child mortality. Providing schools for more than 34,000 villages involved tough economic and organizational demands. Prototypical designs were to be used as a way to guarantee implementation at the most reasonable cost. In a brochure from 1936, the Ministry of Education presented basic constellations for country schools and housing options for village teachers.[13] The size was set according to the number of pupils and varied from one to three classrooms. Various local building materials were suggested. Architects in the construction office of the Ministry of Education put special effort into the implementation of these village projects.

In Margarete Schütte-Lihotzky and Wilhelm Schütte, the Turkish Ministry of Education found employees who

10 On Agitprop, see Anatoli Strigaljov, "Agitprop – die Kunst extremer politischer Situationen," in *Berlin – Moskau 1900–1950*, exhibition catalog, Martin-Gropius-Bau, Berlin (Munich: Prestel, 1995), 111–17. Also see Alexander and Viktor Alexandrovich Vesnin, "Gestaltung des Moskauer Kremls und Roten Platzes zum 1. Mai 1918," in *Mit voller Kraft. Russische Avantgarde 1910–1934*, exhibition catalog (Hamburg: Museum für Kunst und Gewerbe, 2001), 110.

11 See also Burcu Dogramaci, "Festive Architecture for the 15th Anniversary of the Turkish Republic," METROMOD Archive, 2021, https://archive.metromod.net/viewer.p/69/2949/object/5140-10990319, last modified: September 18, 2021.

12 "In the 1938/39 school year, there were 7,862 elementary schools in Turkey compared with 4,894 in 1923/24." Friedrich Karl Kienitz, *Türkei. Anschluß an die moderne Wirtschaft unter Kemal Atatürk* (Schriften des Hamburgischen Welt-Wirtschafts-Archivs, vol. 10) (Hamburg: Weltarchiv, 1959), 62.

13 *Köy okulları müfredat programı taslağı* (Draft curriculum for village schools), ed. Turkish Ministry of Culture (Ankara:

came with years of previous international experience in school construction. The two architects, in turn, were being given the opportunity in Turkish exile to further their own reform aspirations in school construction. Soon after arriving in August 1938, they visited village schools within a large radius of Ankara and Istanbul.[14] The object of the trip was to gain an impression of local modes of construction and of climatic and topographical conditions. In addition, they had discussions with educators, physicians, and school directors to find out about the specific situation and needs in Turkey. Schütte-Lihotzky's task was to design expandable village schools to be built out of mud and air-dried bricks, which the villagers themselves could erect under the guidance of specialists.[15]

On behalf of the Ministry of Education, Schütte-Lihotzky developed concepts for building typified village schools, which she published in a brochure in 1939. The architect designed seven basic types of schools, which varied according to the number of pupils. These typologies extended from a small school with 30 children and accommodation for the village teacher to a maximum size of three classrooms for 180 pupils and two apartments for teachers (fig. 2). A school enlargement option was incorporated from the start since the number of pupils was expected to grow steadily.

This modular system is one that Schütte-Lihotzky had also employed in earlier periods of her career.[16] In the Soviet Union in the 1930s, Schütte-Lihotzky had already planned facilities for children for four different climate zones, taking into account climatic requirements and regional building materials.[17] The objective in Turkey, too, was to have the schools be visually integrated into the region and to build them from regional materials for financial and practical reasons. In her typified village schools, the architect considered the climatic, topographical, and economic circumstances and planned a traditional, flexible mode of construction in wood, mud, brick, or quarry stone. In her memoir, Schütte-Lihotzky wrote as follows: "The types of village schools will have to be very different from each other, depending on the part of the country in which they are built, depending on the climate, the landscape, the local building material and finally,

Turkish Ministry of Culture, 1936).

14 Schütte-Lihotzky, "Ansprache für Istanbul," 4. Also see a photograph of the excursion, reproduced in Dogramaci, *Kulturtransfer und nationale Identität*, 107.

15 Schütte-Lihotzky, "Ansprache für Istanbul," 4.

16 As in the conversion of a settlers' cabin into a settlers' house in 1922 and the type designs for Soviet kindergartens. See *Margarete Schütte-Lihotzky. Soziale Architektur. Zeitzeugin eines Jahrhunderts*, exhibition catalog, MAK—Austrian Museum of Applied Arts, Vienna, ed. Peter Noever, 2nd ed. (Vienna: Böhlau, 1996), 48–49 and 138–47.

17 See Mona Müry-Leitner, "Rationaler als die männlichen Kollegen. Ein Gespräch mit Margarete Schütte-Lihotzky," in Anita Zieher, *Auf Frauen bauen. Architektur aus weiblicher Sicht* (Salzburg: Anton Pustet, 1999), 15–16.

18 Margarete Schütte-Lihotzky, "Yeni köy okulları bina tipleri üzerinde bir deneme" (Experiment on typified village schools) (Ankara, manuscript, 1939, n.p.), UAUAK, NL MSL, PRNR 136/15/TXT.

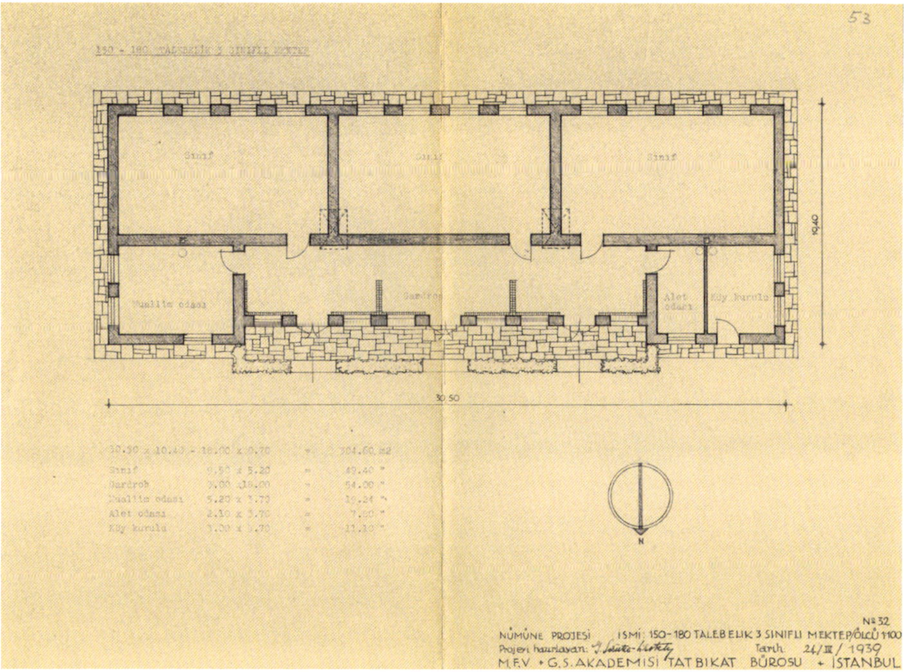

Fig. 2. Margarete Schütte-Lihotzky, typified village schools, type with three classrooms, 150–180 students, March 24, 1939.

depending on the size of the village or rural town."[18] The architect also designed furniture that could be produced by carpenters on site. In this approach of helping people help themselves, the villagers were to build these simple structures themselves under appropriate guidance.[19]

19 Ibid., n.p.

Many detailed features of the village schools are the result of considerations about school reform: for instance, Schütte-Lihotzky planned rooms that were as well lit as possible, group work areas, large sports facilities and playgrounds, along with plants, aquariums, and hutches for small animals to be cared for by the pupils. In a drawing (fig. 3), Schütte-Lihotzky visualized bucolic village life with the school. The educational institution was supposed to enjoy a prominent position as the community's social and cultural nucleus but was also supposed to be integrated aesthetically into the built environment of the region. She paid special attention to the color scheme, which was thought to be a significant factor

Fig. 3. Margarete Schütte-Lihotzky, village schools in the interior of Turkey, April 5, 1939, color reproduction.

for establishing mood and atmosphere: "But, in general, you can say that the village schools should be painted in bright, friendly colors, wooden elements should be colorful as well, so that the schools make a cheerful and happy impression from the outside."[20]

It is not possible to reconstruct if village schools were actually built according to this concept of Schütte-Lihotzky and if so how many other experts were also involved in building and expanding the village schools prior to her arrival in and after her departure from Turkey. For instance Thomas Flierl writes that Schütte-Lihotzky's designs for villages schools were not carried out, because by 1939 she no longer worked at Tatbikat Bürosü. In fact, Asım Mutlu and Ahsen Yapanar emerged as winners of a competition. Flierl notes that their school construction projects were carried out all over Turkey.[21] This categorical negation of Schütte-Lihotzky's work in practical village school construction

20 Ibid., n.p.

21 See Margarete Schütte-Lihotzky and Wilhelm Schütte, *"Mache den Weg um Prinkipo, meine Gedanken werden Dich dabei begleiten!" Der Gefängnis-Briefwechsel 1941–1945*, ed. Thomas Flierl (Berlin: Lukas Verlag, 2021), 441–43.

should be questioned in my opinion, perhaps even relativized. Asım Mutlu worked closely with Bruno Taut and after his death, played an instrumental role in completing Taut's school buildings.[22] This suggests that Asım Mutlu was familiar with Schütte-Lihotzky's work and that he may well have incorporated ideas from his female colleague in his work and in his design for the competition.[23]

Nonetheless, it can be said that Schütte-Lihotzky's plans continued to have an impact—and not least, also found resonance in contemporary Turkish art: the installation *Modernity Unveiled/Interweaving Histories* (fig. 4) created by the artist Gülsün Karamustafa for the *Tanzimat* exhibition at Belvedere Augarten Contemporary, Vienna, makes reference

22 See Bernd Nicolai, "Bruno Tauts Revision der Moderne. Stratigraphien aus dem türkischen Exil 1936–38," in *Symposion Bruno Taut. Werk und Lebensstadien. Würdigung und kritische Betrachtung*, ed. Landeshauptstadt Magdeburg (Magdeburg: Stadtplanungsamt, 1995), 90–98, here 91.

23 On the competition for village schools, see Fatma Nurşen Kul, "Cumhuriyet Dönemi Mimarlığı. Erken Cumhuriyet Dönemi Ilkokul Binaları," *Mimarlık* 360 (July/August 2011): 66–71, accessed August 18, 2022, http://www.mimarlikdergisi.com/index.

Fig. 4. Gülsün Karamustafa, *Modernity Unveiled/Interweaving Histories*, 2010.

to the Kemalist education reforms and the flows of exiles to Turkey. Karamustafa's large work is a wooden structure consisting of interlinked cubes, to which historical black-and-white archive and magazine photos are affixed.[24] So, Karamustafa made existing materials about the Kemalist education reforms her own using means of appropriation: the alphabet reform involving a change from Arabic to Latin script, the improvement of literacy within the population, and the building of village schools in Turkey in the 1930s. The point of departure for this installation was Margarete Schütte-Lihotzky's own work. The piece makes formal references to the school prototypes developed by Schütte-Lihotzky in that it incorporates methods of construction and extension using a basic form and size. The construction work depicted in the photos in *Modernity Unveiled* is reflected in the wooden structure of the installation. Karamustafa in her own words: "The wooden structure for *Modernity Unveiled* was built at a ratio of 1:4 based on the original floor plan [of the school for 30 pupils]. Its purpose is to hold photographs of pupils from that time, who are busy building their own school."[25]

Although it cannot be verified whether the construction work shown in the photos is actually being done according to Schütte-Lihotzky's design, Karamustafa's work does transport the architect's fundamental ideas for her village schools into the present day: building work is taken literally here and translated into the physis of the installation. Karamustafa also makes the simple construction methods depicted in the photos physically tangible by putting them into sculptural form. This experience would otherwise have been limited to the documentary description. Here, the fundamental principle in Schütte-Lihotzky's work becomes evident, a principle based on helping others to help themselves: learn how to do it yourself. The building was able to be erected by the local population and by graduates of the village institutes[26] without outside help and to become reality using regional building materials. These facts in themselves mark an emancipation from the architect's authority.

Nonetheless, Karamustafa's work also contains a latent reference to a Turkish criticism of imported modernism that was already being articulated in Schütte-Lihotzky's day.

24 See *Chronographia, Gülsün Karamustafa*, ed. Melanie Roumiguière and Övul Ö. Durmuşoğlu, exhibition catalog, Hamburger Bahnhof – Museum für Gegenwart – Berlin (Vienna: Verlag für moderne Kunst, 2016), 96–97; on *Modernity Unveiled/Interweaving Histories*, also see the project description in Turkish, accessed August 18, 2022, at http://saltonline.org/media/files/628.pdf.

25 "Über neuere Arbeiten. Ein Interview von November Paynter mit Gülsün Karamustafa," in *Solo für … Gülsün Karamustafa. ETIQUETTE*, exhibition catalog, ifa Galerie Stuttgart (Nuremberg: Verlag für moderne Kunst, 2011), 51–55, here 47.

26 The village institutes (*Köy Enstitütleri*) resulted from the educational reforms of the Kemalists and were used to train village schoolteachers. The aim was for these teachers to return to their villages after the training and promote the schooling of the population and the opening of new schools. Also see Karamustafa in ibid., 47.

Fig. 5. Model of the girls' secondary school by Ernst Egli and the extension by Margarete Schütte-Lihotzky, 1938, photo.

Architecture being built in Turkey by foreign architects such as Ernst Egli or Clemens Holzmeister had already been a subject of discussion since the late 1920s. For instance, the modernist architectural style with flat roofs and facades free of ornamentation was judged to be *kübik* (i.e., cubic) and thus negatively connoted as insensitive and dogmatic because this style ignored the regional building traditions and led to buildings perceived to be alien.[27] And in fact, one could imagine that the modules developed by Schütte-Lihotzky for the village schools could also stand in places other than Turkey. Karamustafa takes no position in her work for or against modernism as a project, but opens the critical view for a discourse that could otherwise remain hidden behind the historical photos, behind the buildings and construction achievements of the Kemalist leadership and their architects. Although the various village schools were relatively small projects, they contributed fundamentally to an ambitious national education and reform program that specifically included the education of girls and young women as well.

27 See Bozdoğan, *Modernism and Nation Building*, 234–39.

In another recourse to school reform approaches from the 1920s, Margarete Schütte-Lihotzky designed the extension of a girls' secondary school in Ankara (fig. 5). The school was designed by Ernst Egli and was located above the prominent arts and crafts school known as İsmet Paşa Girls' Institute (İsmet Paşa Kız Enstitüsü), also designed by Egli. The extension was planned for the area between the secondary school and the arts and crafts school with an eye to creating a larger complex for the education and training of girls and young women. That is why it can rightfully be called a prestigious project within gender equality policy. In Turkey, Schütte-Lihotzky's design is still interpreted accordingly—namely, as an expression of a new type of building for a new target group.[28]

Schütte-Lihotzky planned an extension of the existing structure that would add a two-story pavilion with an auditorium, library, and music room as well as a wing of classrooms. The laterally attached classrooms had double-leaf doors opening onto the park. Schütte-Lihotzky responded to the site topography in that she planned the extension as a substantially lower structure than the existing one, thereby leaving the view from the upper building unobstructed. In addition, pergolas, balconies, and terraces were intended to enable a smooth transition between outdoors and indoors. In response to the climatic conditions, Schütte-Lihotzky planned a garden with minimal lawn area because of the hot summers but in exchange, included trees and bushes to provide extensive shade.[29] Here, the architect integrated major components of the school construction reforms of the Weimar Republic, which were synthesized in Turkey with the emancipation and education of the female population in the large cities. Recreation, lighting, and consideration to leisure-time activities dominated in Schütte-Lihotzky's design. Although the Ministry of Education approved the design, and construction was scheduled to begin in June 1939, the extension of the girls' secondary school was never realized. The project was presumably dropped for financial reasons—the outbreak of World War II may have been the cause.[30] And Schütte-Lihotzky's mentor, Bruno Taut, had already passed away in December 1938, which likely triggered changes in employment relationships in the architectural department.[31]

28 On this matter, the architectural historian Sibel Bozdoğan wrote: "The project suggests that not only were the young women of the republic different from their mothers, but so were the buildings within which they were educated and socialized into Kemalist ideals." Bozdoğan, *Modernism and Nation Building*, 85.

29 See Margarete Schütte-Lihotzky, "Projekt zur Erweiterung des Mädchen Lyzeums win Ankara" (manuscript, 1939), UAUAK, NL MSL, PRNR 135.

30 In a letter to her sister, Schütte-Lihotzky writes that the extension in Ankara has been approved and building is due to commence in June 1939. Margarete Schütte-Lihotzky to Adele Hanakam, Moscow, n.d. [1939], UAUAK, NL MSL, Q/161. After her arrest, the architect put on record that she had not worked for the ministry since June 1939. Margarete Schütte-Lihotzky in the interrogation record of the Secret State Police, Vienna, January 24, 1941, Documentation Centre of Austrian Resistance (DÖW), Vienna.

31 Margarete Schütte-Lihotzky to Adele Hanakam, December 28, 1938, with the news of Taut's death, UAUAK, NL MSL, Korrespondenz von MSL (30er Jahre), Q/162.

32 See Burhan Toprak, "Schreiben zur Auflösung des Arbeitsverhältnisses mit der Akademie," March 13, 1939, reproduced in Demir, *Arşivdeki belgeler ışığında* (2008), 328.

33 See Leyla Baydar, "1923–1950 Cumhuriyet Dönemi Ankara Konutlarında İç Mekan Kurgusu," in *Ankara 1923–1950. Bir Başkentin Oluşumu*, ed. TMMOB Mimarlar Odası (Ankara: TMMOB Mimarlar Odası Ankara Şubesi, 1994), 47.

34 See Ernst Egli, "Mimari Muhit," *Türk Yurdu* 30 (224), vol. 4 (24) (1930): 32–36, here 35–36; Bruno Taut, "Türk Evi, Sinan, Ankara," *Her Ay Edebiyat ve Sanat* (February 1, 1938): 93–98, here 93; Wilhelm Schütte, "Bugünkü kültür ve ikametgâh," *Arkitekt* 1–2 (1944): 28–31, and 3–4 (1944): 66–70, here 67.

35 Figure showing *Lütfi Tozan* and *Nusret Evcen Evi* in Dogramaci, *Kulturtransfer und nationale Identität*, 127. On the latter, see Margarete Schütte-Lihotzky, "Beschreibung zur Skizze eines Landhauses in Cadde bostanı" (May 27, 1940), UAUAK, NL MSL, PRNR 138/16/TXT. In addition, the architect's floor plans for a house for Cambel Halet have been preserved; see UAUAK, NL MSL, 139/A/1–2.

Private Homes

Margarete Schütte-Lihotzky had not been working for the ministry since mid-1939. From then on, she had been active as a self-employed architect.[32] In January 1935, the Turkish newspaper *Ulus* asked what criteria had to be followed when building a modern house. In response, the editorial team published a series of articles over the course of several days on the Parisian Family Homes competition, which would serve as models for Turkey.[33] However, this shift to Western European house types and floor plans did not mean that historical Turkish house architecture would disappear. The majority of the Turkish population was far removed from the ideal of a European lifestyle. They could neither afford it nor did they want to completely abandon their traditions. Even in buildings for the upper classes, a synthesis of a modern floor plan and traditional architectural elements was advised. Many German-speaking architects were interested in Turkish architectural tradition anyway. Ernst Egli, Bruno Taut, and Wilhelm Schütte called for a serious discussion of the historical Turkish home in order to arrive at a reformulation of the concept.[34] Others tried to have their designs incorporate set pieces or aesthetic concepts from the historical Turkish home.

Similarly, Margarete Schütte-Lihotzky drew on architectural elements of local building tradition in her three house designs from 1940. Her *Lütfi Tozan* house in Ankara has a traditional bay window and a projecting roof. The house has a T-shaped floor plan typical of historical Turkish villa architecture. For her *Nusret Evcen Evi* house, to be situated picturesquely on the Bosporus, the architect proposed a "clay-tiled roof typical of the country."[35]

At the same time, however, her floor plan designs showed Schütte-Lihotzky to be the same kind of reform-minded architect she had already been in Frankfurt in the 1920s. For example, she integrated functional built-in elements and was particularly careful in her positioning of the children's rooms on the first upper floor. All three children's rooms in her *Evcen* house were to have access to a terrace, which could serve as an additional place to spend time during the summer and which provided access to the garden. At the same time, she integrated a separate washroom just for the children. This signaled a major improvement in their position within the family: "An extra washroom with a shower is planned for the children. It is situated so that the three children's rooms together with their terrace and their own washroom form a separate section of the house, which can even be separated from the staircase with a glass panel if desired."[36] The architect took account of the needs of the youngest family members as well as those of the adults; equality was therefore a central aspect of her design practices.[37]

Resistance and Return

While in Turkey, Margarete Schütte-Lihotzky continued to undergo the process of politicization that had already begun in the 1920s. In 1939, she finally became a member of the Communist Party and joined a Resistance group around the architect Herbert Eichholzer. In 1940, the two of them were on a secret trip as couriers in Austria and were arrested there. Margarete Schütte-Lihotzky was sentenced to prison whereas Herbert Eichholzer was executed.[38] With her Resistance work in Austria and arrest, Margarete Schütte-Lihotzky's Turkish intermezzo ended and she would not see her husband Wilhelm Schütte again until the end of 1946.[39]

Schütte-Lihotzky's time in Turkey was productive. She dealt with familiar architectural tasks as well as venturing into new terrain, including private homes. Margarete Schütte-Lihotzky carefully studied regional and climatic factors in Turkey and worked to improve conditions for national education. This deep interest in the structures of her host country arose from her understanding of her profession. Both in Frankfurt am Main and in the Soviet Union, her work was motivated by a sense of obligation to society; her plans came about as a result of her tackling specific challenges in the places she was living. Her architecture did not stand outside the fabric of society; it was an integral part of that fabric. In these efforts, she drew on earlier approaches and applied her reform goals to Turkey. Because her stay was limited and she held no senior position, Margarete Schütte-Lihotzky left fewer permanent traces behind than her male colleagues did. In addition, she did not carry out any flagship projects such

36 Schütte-Lihotzky, "Beschreibung zur Skizze eines Landhauses."

37 On Margarete Schütte-Lihotzky's and Wilhelm Schütte's own residence in Istanbul, see Burcu Dogramaci, "Margarete Schütte-Lihotzky and Wilhelm Schütte Apartment," METROMOD Archive, 2021, https://archive.metromod.net/viewer.p/69/2949/object/5140-10969688, last modified: September 18, 2021.

38 See Antje Senarclens de Grancy's essay in this volume and also Heimo Halbrainer, "Von der Kunst zur Politik," in *Herbert Eichholzer 1903–1943. Architektur und Widerstand*, exhibition catalog (Graz: Verein für Geschichts- und Bildungsarbeit, 1998), 60–81, here 80; Margarete Schütte-Lihotzky, *Erinnerungen aus dem Widerstand 1938–1945*, ed. Chup Friemert (Berlin: Volk und Welt, 1985), 144.

39 See Schütte-Lihotzky and Schütte, *Prinkipo*, 545.

as university or ministerial buildings; instead, she provided concepts for the construction of village schools, a modest field in terms of resources and prestige.

In the 1970s, the architect was asked to speak at a ceremony in Istanbul to honor her ex-husband Wilhelm Schütte, who had died in the meantime. In her address, she offered a brief summary of her time in exile: "They were eventful years. To both our minds, initially still part of those years of apprenticeship that took us to a variety of countries—later, though, years of a far-off global massacre—and the years of our separation from each other."[40] With these words, the architect pointed out the ambivalence of emigration, which had been a life-saving decision yet remained an existence with an unknown future.[41]

40 Schütte-Lihotzky, "Ansprache für Istanbul" (1978), 1.

41 This contribution was written as part of the author's ERC Consolidator Grant project "Relocating Modernism: Global Metropolises, Modern Art and Exile (METROMOD)," funded by the European Research Council (ERC) under the European Union's Horizon 2020 research and innovation program (grant agreement ID: 724649—METROMOD).

Forgotten Discourses on Architecture in Vienna after 1945

Monika Platzer

The reorientation in postwar Vienna brought about a communal welfare state that no longer polarized as Red Vienna had done in the 1920s but instead gave priority to meeting the needs of the population for stability and normality. The reminiscences of the project of a collective modernism that were evoked by the abstract skyscrapers on an election poster of the Communist Party of Austria (KPÖ) for the National Council elections of 1945[1] were therefore in direct contradiction to the postwar sociopolitical order being created.

In its efforts to reorient planning, social democracy in Vienna distanced itself from ideology and shifted away from the communal housing of Red Vienna, which was shaped by Austro-Marxism, toward a municipal welfare state with clear ties to the West. At the same time, anti-Communism was a point of consensus in the Second Republic that was shared across party and class lines.[2] In the forefront was Austria's reinvention of itself as a "special case," as a country that was deemed neither conquered nor liberated and that positioned itself as an intermediary between East and West.[3] After the disappointing showing of her party, the KPÖ, in the first provincial and national parliamentary elections, Margarete Schütte-Lihotzky's credo was this: "A common trait among us Communists is that we fight for our world view with a burning passion in our hearts while maintaining a sober approach to reality."[4]

This text is based on my book that accompanied the exhibition at the Architekturzentrum Wien in 2019: Monika Platzer, *Cold War and Architecture. The Competing Forces that Reshaped Austria after 1945* (Zurich: Park Books, 2020).

1 Carl Pick, KPÖ election poster for the National Council elections on November 25, 1945, Wienbibliothek im Rathaus (Vienna City Library), Plakatsammlung, P-460.

2 On this matter, see Manfried Mugrauer's essay in this volume.

3 Manfried Rauchensteiner, *Der Sonderfall. Die Besatzungszeit in Österreich, 1945 bis 1955* (Graz: Styria, 1985); Günter Bischof, *Austria in the First Cold War 1945–55. The Leverage of the Weak* (Basingstoke: Palgrave Macmillan,

1999); Gerald Stourzh, *Um Einheit und Freiheit: Staatsvertrag, Neutralität und das Ende der Ost-West-Besetzung Österreichs 1945–1955* (Vienna: StudienVerlag, 2005); Michael Gehler, "Vom Sonderfall zum Modellfall," in *Historische Debatten und Kontroversen im 19. und 20. Jahrhundert. Jubiläumstagung der Ranke-Gesellschaft in Essen, 2001*, ed. Jürgen Elvert and Susanne Krauß (Stuttgart: Franz Steiner Verlag, 2003), 175–205.

4 Margarete Schütte-Lihotzky, Referat zu den Wahlen, September 29, 1945, manuscript, University Archive of

The postwar life and work of the architect Margarete Schütte-Lihotzky oscillated between these two poles of enthusiasm and reality. My examination here begins with 1947 and correlates with the year of the city's first trade exhibition: *Wien baut auf* (Vienna builds).[5] The Stadtbauamt (central building authority in Vienna), which was assigned the largest area within this exhibition at city hall, presented its ideas on regional development and urban planning (fig. 1). Margarete Schütte-Lihotzky was on the team in charge of artistic design and was confronted with colleagues (Franz Schuster and Hugo Hassinger, among others) and planning content that showed the continuities and personnel linkages with National Socialism that existed in postwar Vienna. Both victims and perpetrators were working on the concepts for rebuilding a democratic society.

Vienna's geopolitical position within Europe was the subject of the first part of the exhibition, entitled *Weg zur Erneuerung* (Path to renewal). It called for a separation

Fig. 1. Setting up the *Wien baut auf* exhibition, 1947.

according to function and for an organic development of Vienna in the southern part of the city. A model study of the Per-Albin-Hansson-Siedlung, a public housing development in Wienerfeld, was exemplary for this new planning approach. The study featured "not a string of identical 'settlement elements,' but rather new organisms of living." The restorative new beginning for Vienna was characterized in many cases by the city simply continuing to build things already planned, as a comparison with the urban development plan from 1941 shows. This was a point not lost on Schütte-Lihotzky. She expressed her skepticism of and aloofness from the show's content in a note underlined in red: "870,000 schilling deficit for the exhibition *Wien baut auf* (mocked by the Viennese as *Wien bauscht auf* [Vienna is swelling]).[6]

the University of Applied Arts Vienna, Nachlass Margarete Schütte-Lihotzky (UAUAK, NL MSL), TXT/497–512.

5 *Wien baut auf. Zwei Jahre Wiederaufbau der Stadt Wien*, exhibition in the ballroom of the New City Hall, Vienna, September–October 1947.

6 Margarete Schütte-Lihotzky, Notiz, UAUAK, NL MSL, PRNR 152.

Communist Housing Program

Schütte-Lihotzky put her full energy into the new housing program, which the KPÖ submitted to the Vienna State Parliament in April of 1947.[7] In three construction phases, the plan was first to repair 30,000 damaged apartments and then to build 40,000 new apartments by 1951. The types of housing were to be 50 percent multistory apartment buildings and 50 percent "settlement houses" (*Siedlerhäuser*) with gardens. The plan was to build mostly two-room apartments but there were also provisions for three-room and one-room apartments, all with kitchen, shower, and toilet. The explanations about the housing program contain statements about construction organization and construction methods, calculations about the workers required, cost calculations, and a funding plan—all conceived by Schütte-Lihotzky.

7 Margarete Schütte-Lihotzky, "Das neue Wiener Wohnbauprogramm der kommunistischen Partei" (typescript, 1947), UAUAK, NL MSL, TXT/328–57.

There was no planning material in the archives, and it is questionable whether any drawings were even produced for the project. Schütte-Lihotzky had expertise from the Soviet Union on large-scale urban planning, which she wanted to apply extensively in the rebuilding of Vienna.

Unlike Red Vienna, the much-hated *Gangküchenhaus*—tenement block where the kitchen aired into the outside hallway—would now give way to mass housing that was not to be built by hand but rather assembled completely from prefabricated and standardized components. In her plans,

Schütte-Lihotzky envisioned making apartments available for the elderly, working singles, students, and large families, all with the same benefits of light, air, and sunlight.[8]

Neither the historical city nor its shortcomings were to be reconstructed. The calculations for the concept were based on the territory of Greater Vienna (*Groß-Wien*) as established by the Nazis, where there would have been sufficient space to bring in new housing, industries, and social infrastructure in line with Schütte-Lihotzky's urban planning program of deurbanization. However, the pre-1938 city limits were reinstated at the Allies' request.[9]

The KPÖ proposal on the housing program was rejected within the Vienna City Council by the Social Democratic Party of Austria (SPÖ). In that same year, on August 22, 1947, the City Council Committee approved the first phase of construction for the Per-Albin-Hansson-Siedlung, which kicked off the municipal housing program.[10]

The housing question remained a hotly contested issue between the SPÖ and the KPÖ. This is clear from the subject of a Vienna SPÖ election poster in 1949, where the KPÖ was demonized as a black dog and accused of lying. Continuity with Red Vienna was underscored with the slogan "SPÖ baut" (SPÖ builds) along with numerical and visual examples to back up that claim.[11]

The transnational urban-planning model of the garden city and the sociospatial organizing principle of the neighborhood, which also belonged to the planning repertoire of the Third Reich, became the "new," post ideological model of social urban development in Vienna after 1945 by way of the British "new towns" model.[12] The British played a significant role in "educational work" in the immediate postwar years. No other country enjoyed such extensive and continuous coverage in the City of Vienna's own magazine *Der Aufbau* as Great Britain did.[13] The ideological transformation of exiled Viennese Social Democrats that had begun in London contributed to the repositioning of the SPÖ after 1945 and the establishment of the national welfare state in the Second Republic.[14] Austria's alignment with the West and the anti-Communism associated with it changed the intellectual milieu of the postwar SPÖ in lasting ways.

8 Margarete Schütte-Lihotzky, "Licht, Luft, Sonne," *Stimme der Frau* 3, no. 21 (May 24, 1947), UAUAK, NL MSL, TXT/289.

9 Maren Seliger, "Groß- oder Klein-Wien?," *Studien zur Wiener Geschichte. Jahrbuch des Vereins für Geschichte der Stadt Wien* 51 (1995): 209–41, here 212.

10 See "Gemeinderatsausschüsse," *Amtsblatt der Stadt Wien* (September 6, 1947): 4.

11 See election poster of the Vienna SPÖ, 1949, "SPÖ baut, KPÖ lügt," Wienbibliothek im Rathaus (Vienna City Library), Plakatsammlung, P-1264.

12 Monika Platzer, "Great Britain's Contribution to Social Planning," in *Cold War and Architecture*, 41–69.

13 See, inter alia, Eduard F. Sekler, "Stevenage. Eine neue Stadt," *Der Aufbau* 2, no. 1/2 (Jan./Feb. 1947): 17–20.

14 Peter Pirker, *Subversion deutscher Herrschaft. Der britische Kriegsgeheimdienst SOE und Österreich (Zeitgeschichte im Kontext* 6) (Göttingen: V&R Unipress, 2012).

The Revival of CIAM Austria

It was thanks to Margarete Schütte-Lihotzky's international reputation that the Austrian section of CIAM (Congrès internationaux d'architecture moderne, or International Congresses of Modern Architecture) was able to be revived in 1947.[15] At the invitation of her Swiss colleagues, she participated in the first CIAM meeting of delegates in Zurich from May 25 to 29, 1947, as the sole representative of Austria.[16] Also taking part in the meeting were representatives from Belgium, England, France, Finland, the Netherlands, Italy, Poland, Sweden, Czechoslovakia, and Switzerland. After Schütte-Lihotzky's stay in Zurich, work began on establishing CIAM Austria. It was officially registered as an association on December 22, 1947.[17] The first postwar CIAM congress on the subject of reconstruction took place in Bridgwater, England in September 1947. Wilhelm Schütte and Margarete Schütte-Lihotzky attended the event as Austrian delegates.[18]

The clash between socialist realism and modernism at the second congress in Bergamo in 1949 severely disrupted East–West relations within the postwar CIAM.[19] From 1950 to 1955, members from Hungary, Czechoslovakia, and Poland no longer attended the congresses.[20] In 1952, a visit to Vienna by the CIAM secretary-general, Sigfried Giedion,[21] led to an ideological confrontation between the CIAM leadership and CIAM Austria. Giedion was staying in Vienna at the invitation of an organization known as Österreichisches College. At a social event to which Giedion was invited in February 1952, he made the following statement: CIAM Austria "is a 'Trojan horse' or Communist."[22]

Owing to her separation from Wilhelm Schütte, Margarete Schütte Lihotzky had already involuntarily withdrawn from the Austrian section effective from 1950 on. Giedion's statement shows the all-encompassing mentality that held sway during the Cold War, expressed not only in the political and ideological debate but also at a cultural and social level.

Discourses on Architecture during the Cold War

In contrast to Berlin, Vienna has not been perceived as the scene of a politicized architectural debate during the Cold

15 Monika Platzer, "Multiplier CIAM, Austria 1947–1959," in *Cold War and Architecture*, 237–42.

16 Margarete Schütte-Lihotzky, Bericht Österreich, June 26, 1947, ETH Zurich, gta Archives, CIAM Archives, 42-HMS-1-308.

17 CIAM Austria, Österreichische Gruppe der "Internationalen Kongresse für neues Bauen," Wiener Stadt- und Landesarchiv (WStLA), Sig. 1.3.2.119. A32.70/1948.

18 Margarete Schütte-Lihotzky, "Les Congrès Internationaux d'Architecture Moderne (CIAM)," *Der Aufbau* 3, no. 4 (April 1948): 92–95.

19 Sigfried Giedion, "Architects and Politics. An East–West Discussion, CIAM 8, Bergamo 1949," in *Architecture, You and Me. The Diary of a Development* (Cambridge, MA: Harvard University Press, 1958), 79–90.

20 Marcela Hanáčková, "Team 10 and Czechoslovakia. Secondary Networks," in *Team 10 East. Revisionist Architecture in Real Existing Modernism*, ed. Łukasz Stanek (Warsaw: Museum of Modern Art, 2014), 74.

21 Sigfried Giedion (1888–1968) was one of the founding members of CIAM in 1928 and influenced the programmatic and journalistic discourse

of CIAM until it was dissolved in 1959.

22 Nachlass Erich Boltenstern, Protokoll Mitgliederversammlung am 28.2.1952, 11.3.1952, Architekturzentrum Wien, Sammlung; Wilhelm Schütte to Sigfried Giedion, September 1952, typescript, ETH Zurich, gta Archives, CIAM Archives, 42-SG-40/219.

23 Platzer, *Cold War and Architecture.*

24 Ernst Plojhar (1920–2014) studied architecture at the Technische Hochschule (Technical University) in Vienna from 1938 to 1954 with a number of interruptions, joined the Communist Party in 1936, and worked as an editor at the Soviet information service and for "illustrative" propaganda from 1945 to 1953.

25 Wolfgang Mueller, "Österreichische Zeitung und Russische Stunde. Die Informationspolitik der sowjetischen Besatzungsmacht in Österreich 1945–1955" (master's thesis, University of Vienna, 1998), 14–16.

26 Margarete Schütte-Lihotzky, *Warschau heute* exhibition, Zedlitzhalle, Vienna, October 1952, UAUAK, NL MSL, Vorträge und Texte, TXT/381, 387–92; "Der polnische Arbeiter baut auf," PRNR 183.

War until recently. The latest research[23] shows that architecture exhibitions in Vienna were used by Great Britain, France, the United States, and the Soviet Union as a stage for cultural, ideological, economic, and technological transfers. The architecture on display and the accompanying discourses became instruments in an "educational program" for a new world and social order that reflected the global rivalry in the Cold War.

At the same time, the Allies were becoming important clients. Political issues were of central importance, and architecture served as a foil for propagandistic messages. Like her architectural comrade Ernst Plojhar,[24] Schütte-Lihotzky worked for the propaganda apparatus of the Soviet occupation forces, which, in turn, was closely interconnected with the KPÖ and its surrogate organizations in terms of personnel and organization.[25]

Schütte-Lihotzky stuck to the official line of Soviet propaganda in her commentary texts and accompanying lectures on two exhibitions she designed and developed for the Österreichisch-Polnische Gesellschaft (Austro-Polish Society): *Warschau heute* (Warsaw today) in 1952 and *Der polnische Arbeiter baut auf* (The Polish worker is building) in 1953.[26] The main focus was on popularizing the sociopolitical and economic achievements of the USSR and of the People's Republics allied with it.

The reconstruction plan for Warsaw followed the guidelines of socialist realism and ran counter to the ideas applied in the reconstruction of Western Europe. New Warsaw was deemed the epitome of successful social democratization and a Soviet architectural export. The magazine of the Österreichisch-Sowjetische Gesellschaft (Austro-Soviet Society), *Die Brücke*, among other publications, presented it as a heroic tale using the stylistic devices of photojournalism.[27] The article praised the workers' increased efficiency, noting that it had enabled the project to be realized and was not based on exploitive work conditions but rather achieved by the use of "collective work methods." Schütte-Lihotzky was personally in the city in 1952 to attend an international meeting of architects and reported repeatedly on the superlative aspects of "Warsaw as a reconstruction miracle" (fig. 2).[28]

Of interest in this context is the joint proposal submitted in 1955 by the already separated Schüttes and Fritz Weber for the reconstruction of the Heinrichshof, a building across from the Vienna State Opera.[29] Their design is spatially reminiscent of the kind of ensemble-based urban planning practiced in Moscow and Warsaw. The opera house and the new Heinrichshof, as well as the open space surrounding the two buildings, were to work together as a visually unified group (fig. 3). Shifting the building line back enabled an unimpeded view of one of Vienna's "most beautiful buildings" and "most beautiful urban vistas." In addition, the outdoor space received definition from colonnades, which extended the line of the wings to the Ring. A statue on axis with the opera house rounded out the aesthetic and the compositional parameters upon which the design was based. This counterproposal to the project by Carl Appel and Georg Lippert, which was already under construction, appeared in *Tagebuch*,

27 Hilde Mareiner, "Das Wunder von Warschau," *Die Brücke* 2 (1950): 11–14.

28 Margarete Schütte-Lihotzky, "Treffpunkt Polen. Neue Wege der Stadtplanung," UAUAK, NL MSL, TXT/382.

29 Grete Schütte-Lihotzky and Fritz Weber, "Noch einmal Heinrichshof," *Tagebuch* 10, no. 8 (April 9, 1955): n.p.

Was, wo und wie gebaut wird, wollen die ausländischen Architekten und Städtebauer genau studieren. Darum begaben sie sich zu allen wichtigen Baustätten. Auf unserem Bild: Architektin Grete Schütte-Lihotzky, die Autorin des nebenstehenden Artikels.

Fig. 2. International meeting of architects, Warsaw, 1952, from *Stimme der Frau*, 1952.

a cultural magazine funded by the KPÖ. In the article, the three architects publicly criticized Vienna's urban planning, calling instead for nonprofit urban planning of the kind found in the Soviet Union, where the representational buildings were arranged for easy use by the public around a central space with extensive squares and a major traffic axis.

The instrumentalization of architecture and urban planning in pursuit of sociopolitical goals was part of the repertoire of all occupying powers. The Marshall Haus in West Berlin served as the venue for the 1952 housing exhibition entitled *We're Building a Better Life*.[30] The title intentionally alludes to the GDR slogan "Mehr produzieren – besser leben" (produce more—live better), which was intended to motivate the "People of Workers" to increase their productivity through technology transfers with the USSR. The main attraction of the exhibition in West Berlin was a house within the exhibition space that allowed visitors to take part in the life of an American family by watching them through a window or from a balcony for a bird's eye view. During exhibition hours, the house was brought to life by a "model family" with two children, all played by professional actors. All objects shown in the home, including the refrigerator, the dishwasher, and the television, were in use.

The original plan for Vienna was to stage *We're Building a Better Life* in combination with the opening of the prefabricated housing project on Veitingergasse, but that project was not completed on time. It therefore opened as a special show on home furnishings in 1953 at an exhibition entitled *Gesünder leben, länger leben durch soziale Sicherheit* (A healthier, longer life through social security) put on by the Austrian Trade Union Federation at the Künstlerhaus in Vienna.[31] Parallel to that, 12 Marshall Plan allies presented their home furnishing products, including furniture, household appliances, and toys. The object of the show was to clearly express the array of products and services available from the cooperating countries of Western Europe as a united economic and consumption market.

Under the male pseudonym Karl Wahl, Schütte-Lihotzky wrote a critical commentary with the polemic title "Do Artists Have to Sell Themselves Out like This?"[32] She pointed

30 Greg Castillo, "Das 'ausgestellte' Haus und seine politische Rolle im Kalten Krieg in Deutschland," in *Wohnen zeigen. Modelle und Akteure des Wohnens in Architektur und visueller Kultur*, ed. Irene Nierhaus and Andreas Nierhaus (Bielefeld: Transcript, 2014), 57–76.

31 *Gesünder leben, länger leben durch soziale Sicherheit*, exhibition catalog, Künstlerhaus Wien, August 8–October 15, 1953 (Vienna: Vorwärts, 1953).

32 The typescript "Streiflichter zur Ausstellung 'Wir bauen ein besseres Leben' im Künstlerhaus" (UAUAK, NL MSL, TXT/281–327), which is dated September 1953 and has been preserved as part of the estate, was published under the pseudonym Karl Wahl in the journal *Tagebuch*: Karl Wahl [Margarete Schütte-Lihotzky] and Alfred Fischer, "Bilden Sie sich Ihre Meinung über 2 Ausstellungen. Müssen sich die Künstler so verkaufen? Versäumte Gelegenheiten," in *Tagebuch* 8, no. 19 (September 26, 1953): n.p [original title in German].

out the decline in living standards and the rise in unemployment while rejecting the "fashionable formalism" of the objects and criticizing the high prices of the products brought together there from the various countries. She presented detailed examples:

> A bookcase for 125,000 lira, that's 6,200 schillings. Or a goblet, holding a quarter liter of wine, from Murano, for 85 schillings, or white curtain fabric for 55 schillings per meter, although many people cannot afford the domestic fabric for 25 schillings. Many of the pieces of furniture are purely formalist—for example the table from Denmark, for 980 Danish krone = 3,700 schillings. [...] In between all these things are slogans about improving productivity. And: a serving cart from the USA, completely chrome plated; then three little tables that can be slid into each other with tabletops made out of mirrors—even from Austria, based on an attractive design by Oswald Haerdtl [...] for the "small" sum of 1,700 schillings. And all the while the loudspeaker makes its pitch: "Dear visitors, you can have all of these things, all of them, if we have a European customs union."[33]

33 Ibid.

Schütte-Lihotzky's sharp polemic about the unaffordable consumer products for the "general public" was in line with the reality of most visitors. At the same time her partisan mentality regarding East and West and the counterpropaganda is obvious.

Appealing to disadvantaged societal groups was a major component of Stalin's populism, and, consequently, his emancipatory efforts were also directed to women.[34] Without the female architects and engineers, the heroines of the rebuilding efforts, the modernization and urbanization project would have been doomed to failure. Traditionally male-dominated professions were opened up to women. It is therefore not remarkable that the magazine *Die Brücke* repeatedly highlighted the work of female architects.[35] An article about female architects involved in the construction of the high-rises on Smolensk Square in Moscow began with this brief statement:

> It has long been a matter of course in the Soviet Union that women work in nearly all professions. Positions of

34 Robert Maier, "'Die Frauen stellen die Hälfte der Bevölkerung unseres Landes.' Stalins Besinnung auf das weibliche Geschlecht," in *Stalinismus. Neue Forschungen und Konzepte*, ed. Stefan Plaggenborg (Berlin: Arno Spitz, 1998), 243–65.

35 On the cover, the architects Anna Kutyrna and Ludmilla Kirilzewa from Planning Studio No. 5 of the Moscow Institute for Housing, in *Die Brücke* 4 (1954).

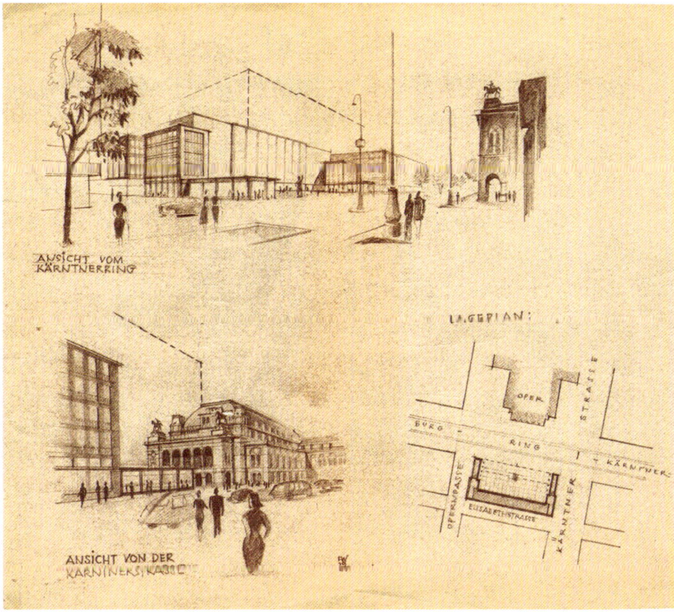

Fig. 3. Margarete Schütte-Lihotzky, Wilhelm Schütte, and Fritz Weber, "Heinrichshof" draft, 1955.

> responsibility and leadership are given to the candidate with the best qualifications regardless of whether that person is a man or a woman. Women and men work as equal colleagues in all work collectives and naturally receive equal pay for equal work. There are also women working in great numbers as scientists, engineers, technicians, skilled workers, etc. on the major structures for the transformation of nature and on the new high-rises.[36]

The alleged pay equality between men and women in the Soviet Union often did not match reality, as Thomas Flierl showed in his comparison of the employment contracts of Schütte-Lihotzky and her husband.[37] Moreover, Schütte-Lihotzky's didactic articles published in *Stimme der Frau*, the magazine of the Communist women's movement, fully meet the expectations of a traditional gender role for women as opposed to the emancipatory clichés being propagated.[38]

36 Jevgenija Taschlyk, "Auf dem Smolensker Platz, Moskau," in *Die Brücke* 8 (1952): n.p.

37 Thomas Flierl, "Wilhelm Schütte als Schulbauexperte in der Sowjetunion (1930–1937)," in *Wilhelm Schütte. Architekt. Frankfurt – Moskau – Istanbul – Wien*, ed. ÖGFA and Ute Waditschatka (Zurich: Park Books, 2019), 24–47, here 26.

38 Margarete Schütte-Lihotzky, "Hubers bekommen ein Kind," "Ohne Badezimmer," "Ein Fall aus meiner Praxis," "Die Poldi zieht nach Wien. Wo soll sie wohnen?," *Stimme der Frau* (1947–1950), UAUAK, NL MSL, TXT/195, 290, and 291.

The Bottom Line

After 1945, Schütte-Lihotzky was a tireless defender of conditions in the Soviet Union and stayed politically active in the KPÖ until the end of her days, unperturbed by the quashing of the Hungarian Revolution in 1956 and the Prague Spring in 1968. In her oeuvre up to the mid-1930s, Schütte-Lihotzky was committed to a rationalistic modernism; then, shortly before her return from the Soviet Union in 1937, she behaved more flexibly, employing her architectural language in a modified way to meet the new political situation.[39] In a lecture given to fellow party members in 1951, she addressed her stylistic about-face from functionalism to Soviet realism: "Functionalism was not suitable for expressing Soviet reality in all its fullness and depth."[40]

In postwar Vienna, she and like-minded colleagues had limited scope for action yet at the same time, the differences in world views in the Cold War led to an interaction between discourses being conducted locally and internationally. These discourses should be included in future examinations of architectural history.

39 Besides the formal shift toward socialist realism, a number of written sources also attest to her knowledge of the Stalinist purges. See Thomas Flierl's essay in this volume.

40 Margarete Schütte-Lihotzky, "Vortrag für Genossen und Genossinnen" (handwritten revised typescript, 1951), UAUAK, NL MSL, TXT/404.

Rereading Schütte-Lihotzky's 1956 China Diary: From the Walls of Beijing *siheyuan* to Vienna's Rinnböckstrasse

Helen Young Chang

On September 4, 1956, Margarete Schütte-Lihotzky went to China for the second time. The trip was arranged under the auspices of the Chinese Communist Party, which bade its Austrian counterpart to assemble an eight-member study group to tour and lecture in China for the wider purposes of cultural exchange.[1] In her diary, she notes that she had lain awake the previous two nights, anxious about making the long trip at 59, and alone.[2] But her worries seem to abate when arriving at Schwechat, the recently civilianized airport, where forced laborers had assembled planes for the German Luftwaffe not so long ago. She and her travel companions grouse over the renovated airport, how primitive and provincial it is, meanwhile munching on Frankfurter links, two apiece, served with bread and mustard. It was fantastic flying weather, she notes, quite hot for seven o'clock in the morning, and everyone, she tells us, was very excited, in top condition and the best of moods. But her use of "we" in German seems hopeful here, for she has only just met her

1 The People's Republic of China (PRC) invited foreign delegations to visit as part of a cultural diplomacy strategy to win United Nations recognition as the official China. Simone de Beauvoir was an official guest the previous year in 1955. The PRC would eventually replace the Republic of China (Taiwan) in the UN in 1971.

2 Reisetagebuch Reisebericht Chinareise 1956, University Archive of the University of Applied Arts Vienna, Nachlass Margarete Schütte-Lihotzky (UAUAK, NL MSL), TXT/420.

traveling partners and already professes to like them very much.

Over the next six weeks she will spy and inform on her travel companions for the Communist Party of Austria (KPÖ). In official reports, addressed to the Party (which I doubt she intended to leave in her archive, given the meticulous construction of her legacy), she will chronicle how she gains her colleagues' trust, weighs their comments and the depths of their feelings, political and otherwise. She will intuit their pasts, plumb their anecdotes for truth and, eventually, their potential use to the Party.[3]

3 Ibid.

Given the right circumstances, she writes, any of her travel colleagues could prove instrumental. One less convinced colleague could benefit from reading Engels, she says. Another, Professor Marinelli the zoologist, is marked as the most superficial and craven of her companions. But because he endures hours of rain on the founding day celebration of the young republic, fully riveted by the uniformed soldiers marching by, and only meters from Mao on the viewing platform where they are standing (figs. 1 and 2), she concludes that he must have some depth to him.

This is monstrous of course, but it is only one side of Schütte-Lihotzky's China trip. The other was chronicled and published in a 1958 article in *Der Aufbau*,[4] and though just as calculated in tone, it is bound by another set of ideological values. Its narrator is a foreigner without guile, a humanist and architect wholly immersed in the local ancient and new architectures, and who—as it happens—advocates on behalf of the Beijing residents. She is effusive in her praise of Chinese culture and architecture: the chopsticks that won't impart a metal taste in your mouth, round tables that place diners equidistant from the food served in the middle, the *Bienenfleiss* (industriousness) she encounters in every person, and Beijing as a singular urban jewel of Asia.

4 The article, "Altes Chinesisches Wohnhaus und neue Stadtplanung von Peking," was part of a longer book manuscript that was published posthumously: Margarete Schütte-Lihotzky, *Millionenstädte Chinas. Bilder- und Reisetagebuch einer Architektin (1958)*, ed. Karin Zogmayer (Vienna: Springer, 2007), 37–72.

In the original preface to her China writings, she says that her collection of essays is intended to further Europeans' understanding of the challenges facing Chinese cities. This account has its problems, however. When she wrote her text in 1956, she described a Beijing that no longer existed. What she called the most beautiful garden city in the world was

Fig. 1. Mao and Zhou Enlai in the VIP tribune at the parade celebrating the founding of the People's Republic of China in Beijing on October 1, 1956.

in the midst of being torn down. Its ancient walls, gates, and towers, which she revered, were being clawed apart. Her blatant elision obscures what she cannot say aloud: she felt deeply against the Chinese Communist Party's policies to destroy the old city. By the time Schütte-Lihotzky arrived, the few Beijing architects advocating for the old architecture had been publicly criticized and subjected to struggle sessions. For defending their city, they would pay with their reputations and eventually livelihoods. The lines they chose to cross are the same ones she treads lightly around, or in between, in her text, mindful of her position as an architect, a foreign observer, and a Communist. This is how we must reread her China diary.

Schütte-Lihotzky was less enthusiastic during her first visit to China in 1934, at the invitation of a delegation of

5 On the first China visit, see David Baum's essay and on the years in Moscow, see Thomas Flierl's essay in this volume.

6 En route to Beijing in 1956, as her plane enters Soviet airspace, Schütte-Lihotzky writes: "Suddenly flying over Soviet soil, it's somehow like coming home again after 19 years. I left the

Chinese pedagogues. At the time, the nation is overrun by civil war and foreign interests. She describes cows and coolies wandering the streets, the new architecture as international and characterless. She drafts her "Guidelines for Building Kindergartens and Nurseries," then proposes building a model kindergarten in Nanjing—and is bitter when she does not receive the commission.[5]

By the time of her second China visit, all of this is forgotten. The country has resurrected itself and so has she.[6] The ruling Communists have embarked on a modernization program Soviet-style, or full throttle. The summer before Schütte-Lihotzky visits, they have concluded the Hundred Flowers Movement, a brief period of liberalization where citizens are encouraged to speak their minds. (Later they will be punished for doing exactly that.)

When she returns to Vienna in mid-October 1956, thousands of Hungarians flee across the Austrian border to seek asylum; in dramatic language, the mayor exhorts the Viennese to welcome the refugees with open arms.[7] While Soviet forces suppress the Hungarian revolt, Schütte-Lihotzky finishes her informant reports and prepares to lecture on China in the new year.[8]

Fig. 2. Parade celebrating the founding of the People's Republic of China in Beijing on October 1, 1956.

Soviet Union from Odessa on August 12, 1937 and today, I am setting foot on Soviet soil again for the first time in over 19 years. […] A chapter in my life, seven years of living in the Soviet Union, had come to an end, a chapter that was to have a fundamental influence on the rest of my life. […] And now, after almost two decades, I see this world again […] I am reentering this country in such a different life situation, at such a different stage of my own development than the one in which I left it." Reisetagebuch Reisebericht Chinareise 1956, UAUAK, NL MSL, TXT/420.

7 5.11.1956: Hilfe für Flüchtlinge – Appell des Bürgermeisters, accessed November 22, 2022, https://www.wien.gv.at/presse/historisch-rk/1956/, "November 1956."

8 The Soviet actions intensify the Sino-Soviet split, which began with Khrushchev's "secret speech" denouncing Stalin in February 1956 and, more significantly, lead Mao to break with Soviet advisers and Beijing intelligentsia whose positions are echoed in Schütte-Lihotzky's China writings, and instead rely on technical plans as the Great Leap Forward to "remold thought." See Zhu Dandan, *1956: Mao's China and the Hungarian Crisis* (Ithaca: Cornell East Asia Series, 2013), 12.

Against this backdrop, her own doubts will intrude in spite of her efforts to forge an inner consistency. In her travel diary, she writes of how her colleagues lack the nerves and sensitivity to understand art (and perhaps Communists too?); how good it is to be a *Fachmann* (specialist) for once, not merely a *Funktionär* (functionary). She resigns herself to the failures of Soviet urban planning in Moscow and then in Beijing. Schütte-Lihotzky's tone, which Karin Zogmayer described as rational-naïve,[9] allows her to remain at the essential distance of an observer, albeit one with the absolute assurance that she is on the right path. But her personal diary, informant reports, and published China writings bear witness to something of a split mind. She is tapping around a rift between architecture and party, one that is temporal, physical, and material, and which will only be articulated years from now in her built work.

9 Schütte-Lihotzky, *Millionenstädte Chinas*, 25.

The Architect versus the Ideologue

On the way to Beijing in 1956, Schütte-Lihotzky's plane stops over in Moscow. Descending into the city, she notes a thousand twinkling lights, Moscow's new green spaces, and the city's eight new skyscrapers, which she deems "not wrong." But how dissonant the city has become, she writes.[10] She sees the city with one laughing eye and one crying eye. Laughing because the old architecture has been preserved. Streets have been widened and entire buildings uprooted and reassembled several paces back. Crying because of the new architecture built in the last 20 years. Technology has visibly outpaced the development of architecture, she writes, and the clash between old and new has obliterated the organic quality of Moscow.

10 Reisetagebuch Reisebericht Chinareise 1956, UAUAK, NL MSL, TXT/420.

It's not enough that the Soviets built; a city has to be built the right way. Here the architect prevails over the Communist. No ideology will cancel her understanding of the timeless qualities of good architecture and urbanism. But her criticism is only half-articulated. One suspects that after Moscow, she must realize what is in store for Beijing, another feudal city about to be remade into a Socialist city. That the Communists would be unable to learn from past mistakes; they would sooner stay on paths resembling known roads, or the technical and doctrinaire. Instead of redressing Soviet urban planning, she will choose an oblique approach: to highlight what she admires in Beijing, and what will disappear when the city undergoes its Socialist transformation.

Walls as "a Matter Political in Nature"[11]

Flying over Inner Mongolia on the way to Beijing, Schütte-Lihotzky describes the emergence of walls that seem to surround every farm, every single plot of land. She spots the Great Wall—she's first, of course—and cries out. The entire plane rushes to her side of the windows, but at this very moment, the machine lurches and her colleague, Dr. Tratz, is thrown against a seat. He breaks a rib and it's exactly the same one he's broken before. But that doesn't seem to stop him or anyone else from marveling and recounting the facts taking shape before their eyes: the wall's fortified towers every 100 to 200 meters, its total length four times that of Austria.

11 Quoted from Mao's 1958 Nanning Conference speech. See Li Rui, *My Personal Experience of the Great Leap Forward* (Shanghai: Yuandong, 1996), as cited in Jun Wang, *Beijing Record. A Physical and Political History of Planning Modern Beijing* (Singapore: World Scientific, 2010), 315.

This is just the start of Schütte-Lihotzky's unraveling of her admiration for Beijing's walls, and as they are dismantled in front of her eyes, they become more than just bricks and mortar. By 1956, one's willingness to destroy the walls is a litmus test for Party loyalty. For Schütte-Lihotzky, the struggle to preserve Beijing's cultural heritage mirrors an inner struggle: the walls are a material manifestation of a battle between two competing belief systems, architecture versus party. They are emblems of a humanist architecture, privacy, and inner freedom, and the homage she pays to them in her diary is an obituary at the same time.

Once inside China, she writes, one understands the tremendous role of walls in Chinese architecture and what important effects can be achieved with closed walls. "Starting with the Great Wall of China [...] to the enclosing walls of entire rural districts, to walls around every Chinese city, walls around every palace or temple, around every monastery—walls around almost every village, walls around every single farm (a farmstead without an enclosing wall is inconceivable there)—walls around every property in the city, walls that border roads on the left and right, only on the ground floor and without windowed walls to ward off the evil spirits in gardens and parks—walls in gray bricks, walls in red bricks, walls in splendid natural stone, and walls, plastered and painted with the beautiful Chinese red—walls with gray, yellow, or blue ceramic tile coverings—walls, walls, and yet more walls."[12]

12 Schütte-Lihotzky, *Millionenstädte Chinas*, 73. Here Schütte-Lihotzky closely paraphrases Osvald Siren, *The Walls and Gates of Peking* (London: The Bodley Head, 1924).

The many functions of city walls fascinate her, especially those of the traditional walled compounds where most Beijing residents lived. These delineated not only inside and outside, but also a gradation of public to semipublic to private spaces. In lines of keen observation, she notes how these walls fostered the inner lives of individuals: limiting one's own life to the outside, whereby the inner life might only be increased and increased.

Her admiration extends to inside the walled compounds: the *siheyuan* or single-story courtyard houses[13] which "for many of us architects," she writes, "had always been a model for living in very close connection with nature, far from the noise of the street."[14] These courtyard houses sheltered Beijing's poorest to richest residents, and even the emperor himself, and formed the basic building block of the city grid based on their standardized layout, dimensions, and orientation. Taken together, the logic of these cells forms the entire city map with its right angles and highly differentiated traffic and residential streets, yet overlaid with elements of nature, she writes, full of admiration, and continues: "This system, which was originally strictly prescribed, has been fully implemented in Beijing [...] and scattered extremely loosely in this strict system we see artificial bodies of water, ponds, hills, and parks—wonderful, deliberately created contrast between nature in motion and the clear forms of a highly cultivated urban architecture."[15]

13 Schütte-Lihotzky referred to these as *Pavillonhäuser* (pavilion houses).

14 Schütte-Lihotzky, *Millionenstädte Chinas*, 40.

15 Ibid., 50. In his 1930s memoir of pre-revolution China, historian George N. Kates also writes that the orientation of courtyards was planned so that you could walk through the city at any time of day and glance at the wall and the way the shadows lay, and know what time it was. George N. Kates, *The Years That Were Fat, Peking 1933–1940* (New York: Harper, 1952), 251.

In her diary, Schütte-Lihotzky included simple sketches of two single-unit courtyard houses, one oriented north-south, the other east-west. The main pavilion at the end of each compound, which also serves as the main living area, faces south. On both sides are *Ohrhäuser*, or the ears, where inhabitants sleep and the kitchen and bath are housed (fig. 3).

As with the walls, she lovingly makes a case for this traditional architecture, beginning with its dramatic entrance. In her China diary, Schütte-Lihotzky writes,

> A particularly charming feature of the Chinese home is the gradual transition from the stony streets teeming with people to the actual living quarters, the 'atrium' of the house, to the quiet courtyard surrounded by colonnades and columns entwined with plants. In the forecourt, behind the front gate, one first approaches what is known as the 'shadow wall,' which prevents passersby from looking into the housing complex, even when the front gate is open. Oleander, pomegranate trees, and other plants in pots stand in front of this small wall, which shields the household right at the entrance from the hustle and bustle of the world. From the forecourt with the shadow wall, one turns left into a garden-like corridor. Here, one feels completely removed from the big city. From there, one goes through an inner gate on the right into the courtyard, which gives a feeling of complete peace and harmony in wonderful proportions.[16]

16 Schütte-Lihotzky, *Millionenstädte Chinas*, 45.

Schütte-Lihotzky likens the interior spaces to a medieval cloister and asks, "Why does today's society dispense so completely with such places of tranquility in modern urban development, which we admire so much in ancient civilizations? The more collectivist our life becomes, the more we need such living systems, such concentration and resting places."[17]

17 Ibid., 52.

Following her meditation on walls and courtyard houses, Schütte-Lihotzky's writing abruptly changes. Her tone becomes more direct and laden with caution; perhaps one even slows when reading this part. She prefaces her suggestions with a sort of defense, one that grants her permission to criticize because it was requested of her. "Since we have always been asked for our opinion and criticism everywhere, I am permitted here, too—after everything I saw and heard there—to form my opinion about it and to back this up with photos."[18] Adequate housing, she argues, is the city's first and greatest need. This is the last of the Party's priorities, however, even as the capital's population tripled from one to three million after 1949.

18 Ibid., 62.

Population growth should be capped (growth is limited in any case by city walls, she says, as if there was no question they would remain), and immigration limited. Beijing

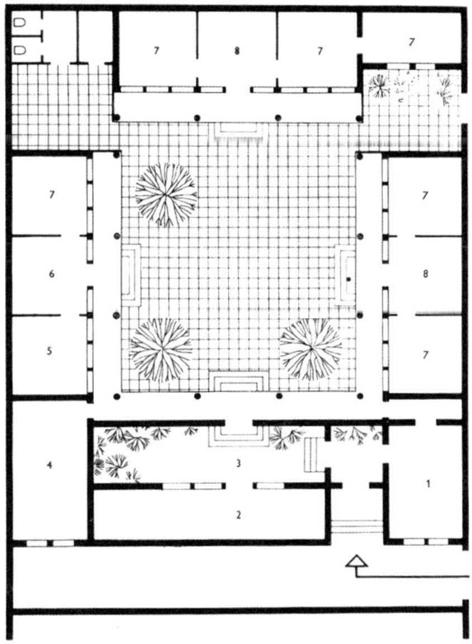

Wohnanlage an Nord-Süd-Straße
Maßstab 1 : 250

1 Pförtner
2 Empfangsraum
3 offener Gang
4 Küche
5 Bad
6 Arbeitsraum
7 Schlafraum
8 Wohnraum

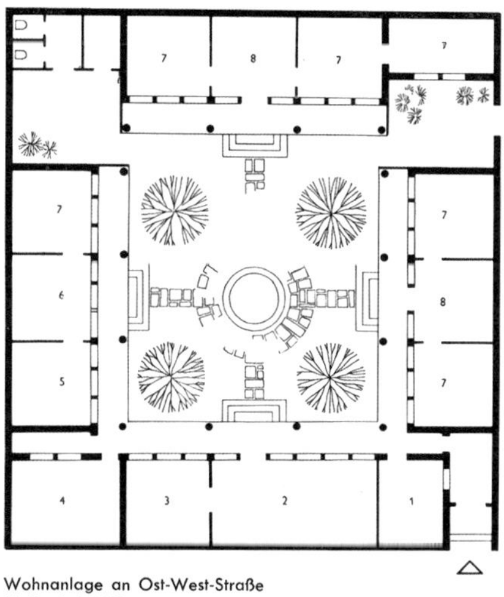

Wohnanlage an Ost-West-Straße
Maßstab 1 : 250

1 Pförtner
2 Empfangsraum
3 Fremdenzimmer
4 Küche
5 Bad
6 Arbeitsraum
7 Schlafraum
8 Wohnraum

Fig. 3. Layout plans for Chinese courtyard houses (siheyuan) by Margarete Schütte-Lihotzky, 1956.

should maintain its role and tasks as a cultural and administrative center, while a green belt is developed just outside the city walls, beyond which should come the factories, new industry, and the attached suburbs.[19]

Every new building, she says, must be approved by a central municipal organization. She writes: "Not a single valuable monument, whether temple or secular building, was demolished"[20] (and this is painful to read because of how untrue it is). If an old pailou (wooden gate structure) stands in the way of traffic, she adds, it will be carefully disassembled and then carefully reassembled in some nearby park. The restoration of old buildings is constant and done with the highest artistic skill, so that every eye is convinced.

High-rises are best added along the main axes of the city, such as Tiananmen, which she notes is already occurring, but only if their height does not surpass the 24-meter-high city gates, in order to preserve the silhouette of the city. For this same reason, all other buildings should remain low. Underused courtyard houses should be transformed into workshops, ateliers, printing houses, schools, kindergartens, or nurseries. Beijing must remain the jewel that it is, she writes.

Finally she ends with a warning: "Even in the new city and architecture that exploit all the technical achievements of our age, people must always be and remain the measure of all things. And it is this human scale that delights us about the Beijing home."[21] Don't succumb to gigantism, she admonishes, while her advice reveals that she is aware of the destruction and new construction already taking place.[22] To bolster her arguments, she quotes high officials in good standing such as Li Fuchun: "The spirit of the dangers of sudden material growth is countered by China's great ancient cultural traditions, which will avert this danger in time. The government warns of haste and exaggeration."[23] She also cites a February 1956 editorial in the Communist organ Shenbao, where city planners were reminded not to chase their fantasies.[24]

But succumbing to gigantism, haste, and exaggeration is exactly what happens. Though the Communists have only been in power since 1949, they manage to destroy more of the city in seven years than the previous half-century of con-

19 The plans of Soviet adviser to Beijing M. G. Barannikov for Beijing's industrial development were just the opposite. He writes: "As New China's national capital, [Beijing] should be a large industrial city as well, not only a city of culture, science, and art. The working class in Beijing now accounts for only 4 percent of the local population. In contrast, the figure is 25 percent for Moscow. That means Beijing is a consumption city, where most residents are merchants, not laboring people, hence the need for work to industrialize the city." See Jun Wang, *Beijing Record*, 104.

20 Schütte-Lihotzky, *Millionenstädte Chinas*, 58–59.

21 Ibid., 69.

22 In July 1955, Mao Zedong reportedly said that socialist construction should proceed at as high a speed as possible. See Jun Wang, *Beijing Record*, 332.

23 Schütte-Lihotzky cites the state's 1953–57 planning report. Vice Premier and head of the state planning commission Li Fuchun was a close and politically nimble associate of Mao, and eventually directed the disastrous Great Leap Forward. Schütte-Lihotzky, *Millionenstädte Chinas*, 69.

stant foreign occupations, the long and ruinous Civil War, and the atrocities of the Japanese invasion. By the time of Schütte-Lihotzky's visit in 1956, the city walls are almost completely torn down. In a *People's Daily* editorial,[25] residents were exhorted to use their hands to destroy the wall. Peering down from Tiananmen Square earlier that year, Mao proclaimed his desire to see a sea of smokestacks rising from the ancient garden city.

Schütte-Lihotzky does not name a single preservation-minded Beijing architect in her text. Most have already been attacked in public, including the still-revered architect and historian Liang Sicheng. He is dismissed from the Beijing Municipal Commission, ostracized, and subjected to public self-criticism.[26] Eventually, he will pay with his own life, as ominous lines in his diary hint: "Demolishing a city gate tower, you are cutting a piece of flesh off my body; taking off a brick from the city walls, you are peeling off an inch of my skin."[27] By the end of the decade, Beijing's walls will be completely dismantled. The homage Schütte-Lihotzky paid to Beijing's walls and courtyards in 1956, however, will emerge in a new form in her 1961 kindergarten on Vienna's Rinnböckstrasse.

The New, Freer Spirit of China's Future Generations

The kindergarten serves as a setting in the 1980 documentary film by Beatrix Novy and Günther Uhlig, *Das Bauen ist ja nicht das Primäre* (Building is not the primary thing). The three stand together in front of the kindergarten.[28] The wind that day is so strong the microphone can barely pick up their voices, and Schütte-Lihotzky is gesticulating vigorously with both arms, weather vane-like. The kindergarten's exterior wall is, in fact, as she says, not *feindlich* or hostile, but a wall of rather low height, extending to just above their heads, human-scale.

In July 2016, I come via subway to visit the kindergarten, passing by the back of a Penny Markt grocery store and its deafening compressors. Besides the kindergarten's front wall, which also serves as the windowless back of one of the kindergarten's pavilions, the only presence it has on the street is the profile of its pitched roof. This is the only giveaway that

24 Unattributed, but likely a February 1956 editorial written by Zhou Enlai, who made similar statements at the State Council meeting on February 8.

25 A *People's Daily* editorial read: "It is only the people who love the motherland, love the people, and love the party" who did not object [to pulling down the wall]. "The people all want to use their hands to destroy—you destroy a gray brick, I'll pull down a piece of stone, who can stand by idly? 'A single idiot can move a mountain,' so should citizens of every district help pull down the wall."

26 See Michael Meyer, *The Last Days of Old Beijing* (New York: Walker, 2008), 285.

27 Ibid., 286.

28 In a preceding scene, Schütte-Lihotzky explains her kindergarten design: "I find the Chinese way of building wonderful: to the front like this, to the back like that. [Here, she makes closed and open gestures with her hands.] Either I have family or I have community, but the street is not a community; it's only traffic now." *Das Bauen ist ja nicht das Primäre* (1980), directed by Bea Füsser-Novy, Gerd Haag, and Günther Uhlig, Tape 30, June 24, 1980, Insert 5, Architekturzentrum Wien Archive.

the building exists at all. When I step inside, the world goes quiet. For a fleeting moment, I am a 21-year-old student in Beijing again, stepping over a Chinese doorsill into the stillness of a courtyard house. The grass in the garden is overgrown and makes a bright, living carpet; the pergola captured in the documentary is still there, now thickly covered with vines.

Like the siheyuan, the kindergarten forms a square with its central courtyard, or in this case an atrium and four pavilions (fig. 4). It is oriented on an axis but one doesn't strictly experience it as such because the entrances are offset to the corners. There is a kind of movement in relationship to its symmetry, and herein lies another of the siheyuan qualities. Gone are the long, wide corridors of Schütte-Lihotzky's 1950 kindergarten at Kapaunplatz, and the absolute symmetry of her other pavilion-type kindergartens—Praunheim (1928) and her unrealized modular system for children's homes. At Rinnböckstrasse, one doesn't enter and immediately arrive; instead, it will take a while to get there.

Schütte-Lihotzky uses a version of the siheyuan shadow wall to shield the kindergarten from passersby. Like the north-south oriented siheyuan, it includes an open passage (figs. 5a and b). Beginning from the street, the progression into the building goes something like this: past the front gate, one sees the garden and descends a set of low steps and down an outside corridor the length of one entire pavilion, about 17 meters. At the end is the door. To enter, one must turn to step into the light-filled two-story atrium. Despite walking through the building at a uniform speed, the scenery—the garden, pergola, and atrium—is revealed in a series of jerks or revelations, which Gordon Cullen calls serial vision,[29] and it is how Schütte-Lihotzky choreographs an experience that builds from a public threshold to a calm, private, contemplative space.

29 Gordon Cullen, *The Concise Townscape* (London: Architectural Press, 1961), 9 and 182.

Approaching the kindergarten's north-east pavilion, one follows a similar sequence. Again, the door is placed on the corner. The visitor must turn and descend several steps into the cloakroom, turn again to pass through the cloakroom, and turn once again to enter the kindergarten space, also from the corner. Three turns in all are required to enter

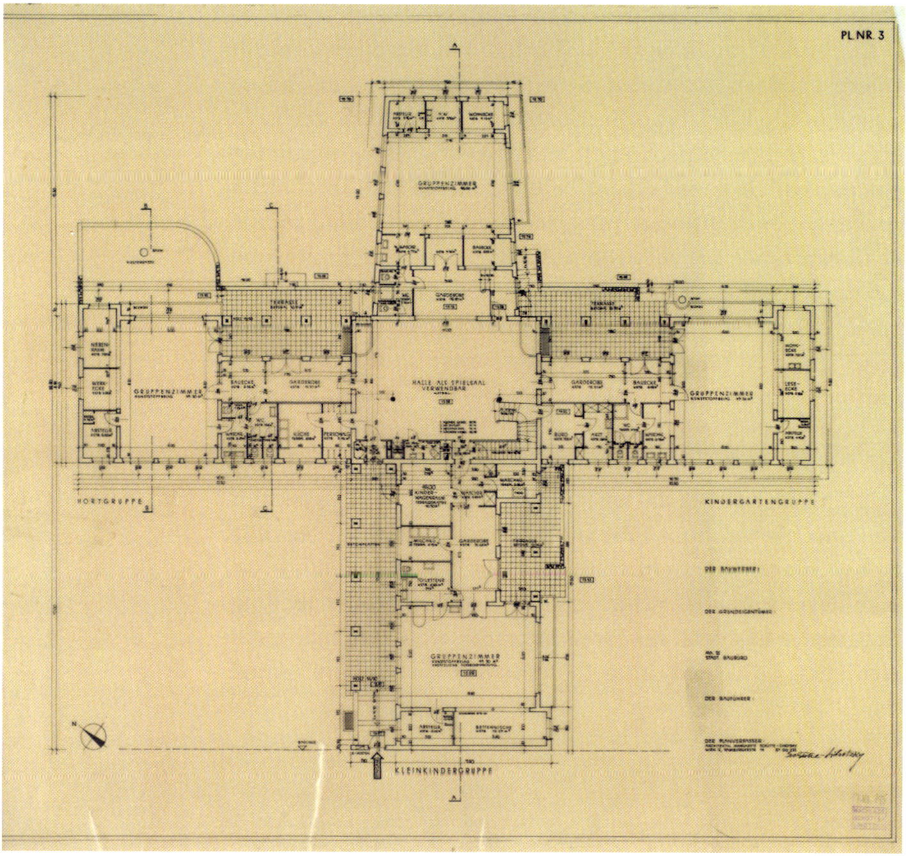

Fig. 4. Städtisches Kindertagesheim (municipal kindergarten), Wien 11, Rinnböckstrasse 47, plan of the ground floor.

the room, and the different views Schütte-Lihotzky curates along the way are dramatic in contrast: a narrow cloakroom versus the airy kindergarten with its windows facing the garden on three sides.

The atrium is similar to the siheyuan courtyard as well in that it is both an indoor and outside space, though covered with a roof. As pure interior walls typically don't have windows, the specific views created between atrium and pavilion, as well as between the main room and coat room, are a play on looking out versus in, what is here or there, what is contained or revealed.

Recently, the kindergarten adopted the practice of *Offene Arbeit* (open work), a German kindergarten concept where children are not tied to one room but can choose where in the kindergarten they want to be. Silvia, the caregiver, says the transparency and views within the kindergarten, which have "elastic" effects on its size in that its spaces are both intimate yet spacious, are well suited to this. At the entrance to every room is a board with magnets, one for each child. The board's two biggest categories are "*Ich bin da*" (I am here) and "*Ich bin zuhause*" (I am at home). The other pictured possibilities include symbols for the reading, music, or game rooms in the kindergarten's other pavilions. If children wish to leave their room, they takes their magnet, place it where they'd rather be, and go.

This is the material legacy of Schütte-Lihotzky's second and final trip to China, intimately linked to and made possible by her role and participation as a Party informant. While we may never know what impacts her reports had, her Beijing experience has been rendered into architecture. Traditional elements, borrowed from feudal siheyuan, are translated

Figs. 5a and b. Shadowing in Chinese houses: passage between shadow wall and inner courtyard, photo documentation by Margarete Schütte-Lihotzky on her visit to Beijing in 1956; next to it, Städtisches Kindertagesheim, Wien 11, Rinnböckstrasse 47, entrance area with pergola, around 1965.

into her kindergarten design, suggesting openness, transparency, individual privacy, and freedom for self-determination. In a twist of fate, what Schütte-Lihotzky wished for new Chinese architecture in 1934 has come true.[30] Her kindergarten on Rinnböckstrasse expresses "the new, freer spirit of future generations" rather than the reproduction of the old. This is Schütte-Lihotzky's last public commission from the City of Vienna at age 63. It marks the end of her career as a practicing architect. She will remain in the Party until the end of her life.

30 See Schütte-Lihotzky, *Richtlinien für den Bau von Kindergärten* (1934); "We must also avoid simply copying and importing European or American styles; instead, we must try to create new building forms using the existing means, materials, and constructions required by the climate and drawing on the experiences of Europe and America, which will document the new, freer spirit of future generations of China." UAUAK, NL MSL, TXT/235.

Consistently Modern? Margarete Schütte-Lihotzky as an Adviser to the Deutsche Bauakademie in the German Democratic Republic

Carla Aßmann

Among the many international destinations in Margarete Schütte-Lihotzky's postwar travels, the German Democratic Republic (GDR) holds a special place. She was drawn there not only for personal reasons but also to cultivate professional contacts, which several times even led to the prospect of promising contracts. These travels and contacts coincided with crucial times of upheaval in the development of architecture in the GDR, and Schütte-Lihotzky took a position on them with her work. The examination of Margarete Schütte-Lihotzky's interventions in the architectural debate within the GDR expands our knowledge of the role that the international exchange of ideas and views played in GDR architecture. Despite the now numerous scholarly studies proving that the exchange between architects also extended across the Iron Curtain,[1] one opinion has stubbornly persisted—namely, that the development of architecture in the GDR was strictly oriented toward the Soviet Union, cut off from the rest of the world, and hierarchically dictated by the political leadership.[2]

1 Also see Andreas Butter, "Showcase and Window to the World. East German Architecture Abroad 1949–1990," *Planning Perspectives* 33, no. 2 (2018).

Schütte-Lihotzky's client in Berlin was Kurt Liebknecht, president of the Deutsche Bauakademie (German Building Academy; renamed Bauakademie der DDR, Building Academy of the GDR, in 1973; referred to below as "Bauakademie") and a key figure on the GDR construction scene. The relationship also offers new insights into the actions of functionaries in these dynamic times of upheaval.

In the context of Schütte-Lihotzky's life and work, her contacts at the Bauakademie shed light on the significance of the professional and political network she had from her time in the Soviet Union but also on its limitations. Beyond that, further aspects of her dual role as party activist and female architect emerge. In particular, it becomes clear that her professional and political convictions did not always correspond with each other but also clashed.

In the spring of 1950, Margarete Schütte-Lihotzky traveled with Wilhelm Schütte to the capital city of the young GDR. After her imprisonment under the Nazi regime and a more than difficult start in the postwar period, it looked like the tide was finally turning for her again. In Vienna, a kindergarten was built according to her design, and together with her husband, she designed a multistory municipal apartment complex (*Gemeindebau*) for the Austrian capital.

In Berlin, the couple met with Kurt Liebknecht, a former colleague from the May Group in Moscow. Unlike most foreign architects, Liebknecht had taken on Russian citizenship and had remained in the Soviet Union until after World War II.[3] In 1948, he returned to East Berlin and after the founding of the GDR in the fall of 1949, became the director of the Institute for Urban Planning and Building Construction at the Ministry of Construction. Later, this institute would be merged with the Bauakademie, whose president was also Kurt Liebknecht, a post he held until 1961. The institute was responsible for drawing up the guidelines and frameworks for GDR architecture. At the same time, Liebknecht directed the central design institute, which stipulated and monitored the practical implementation of these guidelines.[4] This made Liebknecht the most influential figure in GDR architecture because the Minister of Construction, Lothar Bolz, was not a professional in the field.

2 This opinion continues to be present in public discourse—for example, Corina Kolbe, "Moskaus kleine Schwestern," *Der Spiegel* (August 31, 2018), accessed April 27, 2022, http://www.spiegel.de/einestages/berlin-dresden-leipzig-stalin-architektur-in-der-ddr-a-1221495.html. The disdain for GDR architecture is often associated with a general rejection of postwar modernism, culminating in demands for demolition, as in the case of architecture journalists Dankwart Guratzsch and Rainer Haubrich, who write mainly for the newspaper *Die Welt*; for example, Rainer Haubrich, "Kein Denkmalschutz für die elenden DDR-Bauten!," *Die Welt* (August 13, 2013), accessed April 27, 2022, https://www.welt.de/kultur/kunst-und-architektur/article118975328/Kein-Denkmalschutz-fuer-die-elenden-DDR-Bauten.html, and Rainer Haubrich, *Berlin. Glanz und Elend eines Stadtbilds* (Berlin: Nicolai, 2015), in particular 94–96 and 104–5.

3 Kurt Liebknecht, *Mein bewegtes Leben* (Berlin: VEB Verlag für Bauwesen, 1986); Werner Durth, Jörn Düwel, and Niels Gutschow, *Architektur und Städtebau in der DDR, Bd. 1: Ostkreuz. Personen, Pläne, Perspektiven* (Frankfurt am Main: Campus, 1998), 110–11.

For Schütte-Lihotzky, this reunion with an old colleague and comrade who had attained such influence presumably raised great expectations of receiving major contracts in the GDR as an architect. It even appeared as if this Socialist German state might offer opportunities for her to implement her plans for a comprehensive construction program for children's facilities, which had been ignored in Austria. During their stay in Berlin, Margarete and Wilhelm Schütte drafted a joint proposal for a design and construction program covering schools, children's facilities, housing construction, elements for urban and regional planning, and general design principles.[5] In addition, Schütte-Lihotzky presented her papers on children's facilities from 1945 and 1947, which had been disregarded in Vienna.[6]

The document reveals both architects' self-confidence about their ability to implement such an extensive architectural design and urban planning program in the GDR, a self-confidence they had gained from their experiences in New Frankfurt and in the Soviet Union. Moreover, it clearly indicates Schütte-Lihotzky's intention to manage the project from Vienna. At one point in the document she notes: "In general, elaborations can also be carried out without [us] being in the immediate vicinity of the institute."[7] The couple's hopes actually appeared to be coming true: Wilhelm Schütte was contracted by the Ministry of National Education to draw up a program and guidelines for school construction in the GDR and to build two schools as model structures.[8]

Margarete Schütte-Lihotzky landed a contract to create a program and guidelines for the construction of all kinds of children's facilities. Despite the importance assigned to state-run childcare, these services in the GDR had mostly been housed in unused buildings up to this point; the few new structures that existed were not specially designed for this purpose.[9] According to the planning in October 1950, the architect was to make her expertise available to a new working group for the construction of children's facilities.[10]

But the two architects' participation in the development of educational and children's facilities in the GDR would come to nothing. Schütte never received the written confirmation of his contract that he had been promised because it

4 Tobias Zervosen, *Architekten in der DDR. Realität und Selbstverständnis einer Profession* (Bielefeld: Transcript, 2016), 69–70.

5 Architect Professor Wilhelm Schütte and Architect Grete Schütte-Lihotzky, currently Berlin, June 1950, untitled document with the following sections: I. Schulbau, II. Bau von Kinderanstalten, III. Wohnungsbau, IV. Elemente für die Stadt- und Landesplanung (Zelle etc.), V. Form und Ausdruck in Architektur und Planung, Bundesarchiv (BArch) Berlin, DH 2/20040. The two pages of the document are in different places in the file.

6 "Programm zur Schaffung eines Zentral-Bau-Instituts für Kinderanstalten" (transcript/Stei), n.d.; Architect M. Schütte-Lihotzky, "Vorschläge zum Druck einer Entwurfslehre für Kinderanstalten," June 1947, both in BArch Berlin, DH 2/20040. The design program was able to be identified and dated using the quotations and information in *Margarete Schütte-Lihotzky, Soziale Architektur. Zeitzeugin eines Jahrhunderts*, exhibition catalog, MAK—Austrian Museum of Applied Arts, Vienna, ed. Peter Noever (Vienna: Böhlau, 1993), 193–94.

turned out that the Ministry of National Education was not competent in the matter and the planned alternative contract from the Ministry of Construction never materialized. A model school was built instead by the project planning office of the state of Saxony. The program that Schütte had drawn up for the construction of schools in the GDR ended up being filed away unused.[11]

The same fate was shared by Margarete Schütte-Lihotzky's paper in which she proposed developing standard types of buildings (*Typenbauten*) for children's facilities in the GDR.[12] This paper was an expanded version of her proposal for a central building institute. It featured exemplary designs and floor plans and was geared to the ideological and organizational requirements in the GDR.[13]

By contrast, a completed draft for a design theory for children's homes did not even make it to the GDR because Schütte-Lihotzky was not given a visa and the planned working group meeting did not take place.[14]

Why the sudden change of heart on the part of the contracting authorities? As the work of a committed Communist, Schütte-Lihotzky's program fully accorded with the ideological line in the GDR. Based on an oft-cited remark by Lenin that kindergartens were among the best ways "to liberate women [...], to reduce and put a stop to women being unequal to men in the role they play in society's production and in public life,"[15] she, too, cited the desirable and necessary entry of women into the workforce as justification for the construction of children's facilities.[16] Moreover, Schütte-Lihotzky emphasized the significance of the new buildings as facilities for rearing the future generation of Socialists: "From a young age, children in the new buildings will be brought up to live communally with other children, to help each other, to work collectively, and to be considerate of others."[17] This statement is also fully in line with the proclaimed child-rearing principles in German kindergartens in the GDR.[18]

Yet entrusting Schütte-Lihotzky with the planning and design of children's facilities would have contradicted the architectural policy of the GDR. Its declared goal was the *Vergesellschaftlichung* (socialization) of the architectural pro-

7 Schütte and Schütte-Lihotzky, untitled document, June 1950, 2.

8 See Architect Professor W. Schütte to Ministerium für Volksbildung, HA Unterricht und Erziehung, copy to Dr. Liebknecht, October 27, 1950, BArch Berlin, DH 2/20040.

9 Andreas Butter, *Neues Leben, neues Bauen. Die Moderne in der Architektur der SBZ/DDR 1945–1951* (Berlin: Hans Schiler, 2006), 234–35.

10 Ministerium für Volksbildung, Abteilung Planung und Statistik to the Institut für Städtebau und Hochbau, regarding building of children's homes, October 2, 1950, BArch Berlin, DH 2/20040.

11 Prof. Wilhelm Schütte, Architect, "Bau von Schulen in der Deutschen Demokratischen Republik," August 1950, BArch Berlin, DH 2/20040.

12 "Neue Kinder häuser in der DDR," by Architect Margarete Schütte-Lihotzky, Vienna, n.d. [presumably late summer/fall 1950], BArch Berlin, DH 2/20040.

13 Unfortunately the drawings have not been preserved, but Schütte-Lihotzky refers to them in the text.

14 Margarete Schütte-Lihotzky to Kurt Liebknecht, October 23, 1950, BArch Berlin, DH 2/20040.

fession. This meant that the design and planning offices that were *volkseigene Betriebe* (state-owned enterprises) were promoted to the detriment of self-employed architects, who were increasingly cut off from work opportunities. This approach by the Ministry of Construction elicited bitter protest.[19] Against this backdrop, the ministry was presumably concerned about its credibility and ability to hold sway if it had awarded this standout contract to the self-employed architect Schütte-Lihotzky. In addition, she lived in a non-Socialist country, and her program for children's facilities openly advocated contracting self-employed architects for independent work. In a prominent passage, the policy called for "planning, construction, and interior design to be entrusted to architects as trustees."[20]

In keeping with the goal of socializing all architectural tasks, the design of nursery schools was therefore entrusted on short notice to the planning offices of the *Länder* (the states within the GDR).[21]

At the same time, preparations were in full swing for the founding of the Bauakademie on January 1, 1951. Theoretical work and construction were to be pursued centrally there. Under the direction of the architect Karola Bloch, work began on the development of GDR type designs (*Typenentwürfe*).[22] However, it would take two years before a design program was actually in place. The style of these type designs (fig. 1) indicates another reason why Schütte-Lihotzky's program was not deemed tenable among top architecture policymakers.

In 1950, the development of architecture in the GDR made a dramatic about-face. Prior to this, reconstruction had oriented itself toward the modern architectural movement known as Neues Bauen, also in the Soviet occupation zone. Then, in an effort to find a design idiom specific to the GDR, the order came from on high to drop what was referred to as "formalism." Modernist buildings were defamed as Western decadence; Liebknecht reviled them as "primitive boxes."[23] Following the model of Socialist Realism in the Soviet Union, architecture was now to orient its style toward "national traditions" such as classicism in order to duly represent the "democratic substance" of the GDR. As in the

15 Quoted in Karola Bloch, "Grundrißschemas von Einrichtungen für das Kleinkind," *Deutsche Architektur* 1 (1953): 20–27, here 20.

16 Schütte-Lihotzky, "Neue Kinderhäuser," 1–2.

17 Ibid., 3.

18 There it said: "Willing and cheerful integration into the kindergarten community, in play and activity, careful performance of the small tasks and duties assigned." Quoted in Butter, *Neues Leben*, 233.

19 See Zervosen, *Architekten in der DDR*, 34–64.

20 Schütte-Lihotzky, "Neue Kinderhäuser," 2.

21 Prof. Hopp, Institut für Hochbau to the Ministerium für Planung, November 7, 1950, regarding project planning for nursery schools, BArch Berlin, DH 2/20040.

22 Initial guidelines were published by the Ministry of Construction on September 1, 1951, but these were far less detailed than Schütte-Lihotzky's program. See Karola Bloch, presentation on the development of types of day nurseries, held at the conference of the Ministry of Health on June 26, 1952 in Berlin, BArch Berlin, DH 2/3052.

Fig. 1. Karola Bloch, preliminary design for a daycare center for 45 children and day nursery for 34 children, Deutsche Bauakademie, Institut für Hoch- und Industriebau, Abteilung Kulturbauten und Erziehung, March 18, 1952.

23 Quoted in Andreas Schätzke, *Zwischen Bauhaus und Stalinallee. Architekturdiskussion im östlichen Deutschland 1945–1955* (Braunschweig: Vieweg, 1991), in particular 52.

Soviet Union, this architectural style tended toward the monumental in the GDR as well. The Stalinallee, a prestige project in East Berlin, is a case in point.

This orientation was officially ordered with the enactment of the "16 Grundsätze des Städtebaus" (16 principles of urban planning) by the Council of Ministers of the GDR in July 1950. Despite the political pressure, it was no mean feat to gain acceptance for this new approach among the GDR architects, most of whom had been steeped in Neues Bauen. Kurt Liebknecht was the man responsible for this task. Through his years of working in the Soviet Union and as one of the few who had previous experience in this realm, the style came to be known by the derogative nickname "Kulinatra": Kurt Liebknecht's national tradition.[24]

24 Liebknecht, *Mein bewegtes Leben*, 133.

Liebknecht must have discussed the new approach with Schütte-Lihotzky and her husband, especially since their stay in Berlin coincided with his return from the famous Moscow trip on which the doctrine had been drawn up.

Nonetheless, Schütte-Lihotzky's design program remained consistently modern. She called for and designed

Fig. 2. Margarete Schütte-Lihotzky, municipal kindergarten on Kapaunplatz, Vienna's 20th district, 1950–52, photo: Lucca Chmel.

low pavilions with large, low window fronts, which were to be built as standard types everywhere regardless of traditional regional styles. She called for walls and facades to be painted in bright colors. And she even explicitly urged architects "to forgo any suggestion of monumentality."[25]

Schütte-Lihotzky's kindergarten on Kapaunplatz in Vienna, which was completed in 1952, had all these characteristics and made for a program that was a modern, functional contrast to the Bauakademie designs (fig. 2).[26]

The contact between the former colleagues ended abruptly and was not revived again until 1954. At the time, the Bauakademie faced several problems. On June 17, 1953, protests in East Berlin against the raising of work quotas spread throughout the GDR and gave rise to a strong but short-lived movement for democratic rights. The protests were quickly ended with the help of the Soviet military, but the discontent over the GDR government remained. Architects in the GDR also began airing their dissatisfaction and pushed for reforms. However, the only concession made by the leadership was to decentralize the design work, a step that gave more responsibility to the Länder planning offices.[27] But their work angered the leading architects at the Bauaka-

25 Schütte-Lihotzky, "Neue Kinderhäuser," 4–6. Similarly, Wilhelm Schütte had stated in his school program: "The fresh, cheerful spirit that should prevail in the school does not need any stylistic ingredients in order to be architecturally reflected in the exterior and interior design of the school building. The visible use of efficient modern constructions, well-thought out technical composition [...] those will be the elements that will create the friendly, inviting, and at the same time dignified exterior of the new schools." Prof. Schütte, Architect, "Bau von Schulen in der Deutschen Demokratischen Republik," August 1950, p. 9, BArch Berlin, DH 2/20040.

demie because those offices did not stick to the guidelines the architects had issued. In addition, building in the "national tradition" style was expensive and underwent almost no further development. The imbalance between scarce resources and the gigantic need for construction led to ever greater difficulties. The focus shifted again to rationalizing construction by means of standard-type designs, but this approach was stuck in the planning phase.[28] In response to these problems, the Bauakademie undertook a "critical analysis of present-day architecture," which was then to be discussed at a public conference.[29]

In this situation, Liebknecht met up again with Margarete Schütte-Lihotzky and Wilhelm Schütte in East Berlin, who were both working together at the time for the Globus-Verlagshaus publishing house. Given the difficult state of affairs, Liebknecht apparently hoped to receive fresh impetus from abroad. His possibilities for action were limited, however, by the persisting propagandistic contradiction between architecture in line with national tradition and "decadent American formalism" as well as the condescending rejection of GDR architecture by the foreign trade press. So, he tried to revive his ties with old colleagues again, asking Schütte to do literature reviews[30] and beginning an exchange of letters with Werner Hebebrand.[31]

Schütte-Lihotzky was commissioned to assess the Bauakademie's design program for children's facilities as an external expert and to rate five existing facilities. She once again drew up a design theory for children's facilities and suggested that buildings be erected to serve as trial structures.[32]

She inspected two kindergartens on Stalinallee in Berlin and one children's home, which was also built in the national tradition style. In addition, she assessed the children's department store on Stalinallee and a kindergarten in Leipzig.[33]

Schütte-Lihotzky was especially harsh in her judgment of the kindergartens on Stalinallee, calling them "more reminiscent of old detention homes for children or hospitals than of homes for raising a happy community of our children."[34]

Schütte-Lihotzky's first point of criticism was the inefficiency of the designs. She calculated that much more space

26 On this matter, also see Christoph Freyer's essay in this volume.

27 See Zervosen, *Architekten in der DDR*, 96–102.

28 See Werner Durth, Jörn Düwel, and Niels Gutschow, *Architektur und Städtebau in der DDR, Bd. 2: Aufbau: Städte, Themen, Dokumente* (Frankfurt am Main: Campus, 1998), 172–80.

29 See Sachs, Forschungsinstitut für die Architektur der Bauten der Gesellschaft und Industrie, design, regarding letter from colleague Schütte-Lihotzky, November 11, 1954; Kurt Liebknecht to Margarete Schütte-Lihotzky, November 12, 1954; both BArch Berlin, DH 2/20064.

30 Wilhelm Schütte to Kurt Liebknecht, President of the Deutsche Bauakademie, April 19, 1954, BArch Berlin, DH2/20064.

31 This exchange of letters did not bring about the results hoped for, however, as is clear from what Liebknecht reported: Kurt Liebknecht to Margarete Schütte-Lihotzky, January 22, 1951, BArch Berlin, DH 2/20064.

32 Margarete Schütte-Lihotzky to Kurt Liebknecht, October 24, 1954, BArch Berlin, DH 2/20064.

33 Margarete Schütte-Lihotzky to the Deutsche Bauakademie, "Kritische

was allotted for hallways and utility rooms than in kindergartens in the Soviet Union or also in Vienna. In her view, this adversely affected the usable space for children,[35] and this expensive mode of construction had thus failed aesthetically, functionally, and pedagogically. The designs demonstrated a systematic neglect of all principles of progressive kindergarten construction such as a home-like atmosphere, connection to the outdoor space, promotion of community, and the prevention of disease by groups being spatially separated. The architect said of the kindergarten on Stalinallee: "There is nothing more repulsive than to run into a blank wall at the entrance, which is unfortunately the case at the D-Süd kindergarten" (fig. 3).[36] To name just a few more examples of her criticisms: the windows were so high that children could not look out of them; there was no connection to the yard outdoors; there was no provision made for cross-ventilation or for the isolation of sick children, no differentiation among the rooms, and no appealing color scheme; "all these possibilities for enhancing the architecture were completely disregarded there. Everything is sober, prosaic, and completely bland, devoid of architectural ideas or imagination."[37]

Schütte-Lihotzky rated the work of the Bauakademie as being of an "incomparably higher level" than the built facilities but criticized that a unique architectural character for children's facilities in the GDR still had to be developed.[38] In her conclusions, the architect offered to provide the urgently needed modular system for children's facilities herself—namely, by reworking her available standard-type designs.[39]

Surprisingly, her assessment met with strong support among the functionaries of the Bauakademie. They called for the assessment to be incorporated in the critical evaluation of overall architectural activities, and for Schütte-Lihotzky to take part in the associated conference.[40]

This all occurred against the backdrop of a simmering conflict with the municipal authority and the chief architect of Berlin, Hermann Henselmann. At stake was the issue of who had supreme power over the designs for public buildings. The thinking was that this assessment by a non-partisan expert from abroad with authority from her experiences and

Stellungnahme zu den besichtigten Bauten und Plänen von Kinderanstalten," September 24, 1954, BArch Berlin, DH 2/20064.

34 Ibid., 2–3.

35 Ibid., 4–7.

36 Ibid., 4.

37 Ibid., 12.

38 Ibid., 2 and 5.

39 Ibid., 13.

40 Liebknecht to Schütte-Lihotzky, November 12, 1954.

knowledge in the Soviet Union would strengthen the position of the Bauakademie because the Berlin municipal authority was responsible for the criticized buildings.[41] Moreover, the actual intention was to get Schütte-Lihotzky involved in developing standard-type designs.[42]

Once again, this prospect of Margarete Schütte-Lihotzky being able to gain greater influence as an architect would come to naught. This time it was the dynamics of outside events erupting and destroying her ambitions. On December 7, 1954, the head of the Communist Party of the Soviet Union (CPSU), Nikita Khrushchev, announced a new orientation in architectural policy at the All-Union Conference of Builders staged in Moscow. In keeping with the slogan "Mehr, besser und billiger bauen" (Build more, better, and cheaper),[43] the new orientation signaled a turn to industrial, unembellished, and stylistically modern architecture in the GDR as well. The planning that the Bauakademie had done up to that point for the evaluation conference and the type program also fell victim to the hectically introduced about-face.[44]

But this time, the contact with the Bauakademie was presumably not broken off. The preserved letters indicate that Schütte-Lihotzky exchanged professional views with her GDR colleagues that went beyond the issue of children's

41 Prof. Hopp to Kurt Liebknecht, November 1, 1954, BArch Berlin, DH 2/20064.

42 Sachs, design; Liebknecht to Schütte-Lihotzky, November 12, 1954.

43 This was the motto of the GDR's first building conference in April 1955; see Thomas Topfstedt, *Städtebau in der DDR 1955–1971* (Leipzig: Seemann, 1988), 11.

44 Kurt Liebknecht to Margarete Schütte-Lihotzky, January 22, 1955, and Kurt Liebknecht to Margarete Schütte-Lihotzky, March 15, 1955, both in BArch Berlin, DH 2/20064.

Fig. 3. Stalinallee D-Süd kindergarten, design: Projektierung Groß-Berlin VEB, 1953, developer: Magistrat von Groß-Berlin, condition in 2019.

facilities.[45] And in the meantime, yet another colleague from the May Group, the Swiss architect Hans Schmidt, was also working at the Bauakademie.

Continuously friendly, collegial, and rather informal relationships presumably also paved the way for Margarete Schütte-Lihotzky's half-year stay to conduct research at the Bauakademie in 1966. According to her recollections of that time, the new president of the Bauakademie, Gerhard Kosel, whom she also knew from the Soviet Union, asked her again to draw up an expert opinion as a specialist in children's facilities. In addition, she recalled that she offered him her modular system again.[46] In the documents of the Bauakademie, however, there is nothing preserved of Schütte-Lihotzky's extensive research work, in connection with which she inspected children's facilities throughout the GDR.

Although the architect likely continued to be unsparing in her criticism,[47] there were probably no ideological differences on architectural issues this time. The modernist design idiom now also served as an expression of GDR architecture, and the efforts to create standard-type designs made quick advances. The architectural critic Bruno Flierl was head of the theory group at the Institute for Urban Planning and Architecture at the Bauakademie at the time and recalls that Schütte-Lihotzky met at the Bauakademie with Hans Schmidt, who was also working on type design projects.[48]

It may be assumed that the disappearance of any and all traces of Schütte-Lihotzky's work is attributable to a gradual generational change on the GDR architectural scene. While Schütte-Lihotzky's old colleagues continued to appreciate their exchange with her, the younger architects probably felt less of a need for the now somewhat dated experiences and expertise of the architect, who was 69 years old at the time.

Not long after Schütte-Lihotzky's research stay, the article "Kleinkindereinrichtungen: Entwicklungstendenzen" (Young children's facilities: developmental trends) appeared in the most important architectural journal in the GDR, *Deutsche Architektur*.[49] The article also contained examples of kindergartens from the GDR and abroad but was written by Helmut Trauzettel, a GDR specialist in kindergarten con-

45 Schütte-Lihotzky also regularly sent her kind regards to the vice-president of the Bauakademie, Edmund Collein, via Liebknecht. Liebknecht, with whom the tone became significantly more familiar in the 1954/55 exchange of letters, also invited Schütte-Lihotzky to come at another time "in order to talk to us about the individual problems you face in your work" to make up for the canceled evaluation conference. Liebknecht to Schütte-Lihotzky, March 15, 1955.

46 "'Jetzt bin ich Persona grata.' Im Juni 1984 sprach Chup Friemert mit Margarete Schütte-Lihotzky in Wien," in Margarete Schütte-Lihotzky, *Erinnerungen aus dem Widerstand 1938–1945* (Hamburg: Konkret Literatur Verlag, 1985), 44–45.

47 Reporting on her visit to Rostock, the architect wrote to Hans Wetzler as follows: "Good new buildings for housing and poor facilities for children. My heart aches when I see how much national wealth was squandered [?] to make something so poor." Margarete Schütte-Lihotzky to Hans Wetzler, May 16, 1966, University Archive of the University of Applied Arts Vienna, Nachlass Margarete Schütte-Lihotzky (UAUAK, NL MSL, Q/164). I would like to thank Marcel Bois for pointing out this document. On Hans Wetzler,

struction who was 30 years younger than Schütte-Lihotzky. He even mentions her in the article but only as the architect of the kindergarten on Kapaunplatz in Vienna from 1951/52, without making any reference to her conceptual and theoretical work.[50]

Although her hopes of influencing the construction of children's facilities in the GDR had been dashed repeatedly, her contacts at the Bauakademie were important for Schütte-Lihotzky and her conception of herself. Whereas in Austria she was known and active in the postwar era primarily as a political person, as an anti-Fascist who stood up for women's rights and peace, in the GDR she was primarily an architect and was perceived as such. At the Bauakademie, she cultivated not only the contacts she had made earlier but also communicated with professional colleagues she was meeting there for the first time, and she stayed abreast of developments in the GDR.

Proof of the complementary role that Schütte-Lihotzky was viewed as playing in the GDR can also be found in a series of articles that she wrote in the 1980s for *form+zweck*, a GDR trade journal for industrial design.[51] While presenting herself in Austria as a contemporary witness to National Socialism and as a Resistance fighter, she published four articles in the GDR between 1981 and 1984 about her contributions to Neues Bauen;[52] a two-part interview about her work in the May Group appeared on the occasion of her 90th birthday.[53]

It was only in retrospect that her work became widely known to the public in the GDR as well, which can be attributed to the limited effectiveness of her network of former colleagues.

Unlike many other architects who no longer received contracts after the war, Schütte-Lihotzky never considered moving to the GDR. That said, she obviously had no fundamental reservations about the GDR state. For instance, she provided information to her comrade Liebknecht about an Austrian colleague who had been applying for work in the GDR.[54]

So, it must have been in her design work that the architect did not want to submit to the guidelines. Adjusting to architecture in the "national tradition"—the way that Hans

Margarete Schütte-Lihotzky's partner since the 1960s, see Marcel Bois, "Soziale Beziehungen und kommunistische Netzwerke. Annäherungen an Hans Wetzler (1905–1983)," in *Margarete Schütte-Lihotzky. Architektur. Politik. Geschlecht. Neue Perspektiven auf Leben und Werk*, ed. Marcel Bois and Bernadette Reinhold (Basel: Birkhäuser, 2019), 224–36.

48 Bruno Flierl in a telephone conversation with the author, September 5, 2018.

49 Helmut Trauzettel and Claudio Schrader, "Kleinkindereinrichtungen: Entwicklungstendenzen," *Deutsche Architektur* 7 (1967): 433–36.

50 Ibid., 434–35.

51 I am grateful to Tanja Scheffler, TU Dresden, for drawing my attention to this article.

52 Margarete Schütte-Lihotzky, "Arbeitsküche," *form+zweck* 4 (1981): 22–26; idem, "Volkswohnbau," *form+zweck* 2 (1982): 38–41; idem, "Erinnerungen an Gropius," *form+zweck* 2 (1983): 9; idem, "Die Wohnung der alleinstehenden berufstätigen Frau," *form+zweck* 2 (1984): 33–36.

53 "Damals in der Sowjetunion. Gespräch mit Margarete Schütte-Lihotzky, Teil 1: Aufbruch

Schmidt had done when relocating to the GDR[55] or Karola Bloch had done in kindergarten construction[56]—would have conflicted too greatly with her ideas about architecture. In this case, Schütte-Lihotzky's professional convictions proved irreconcilable with her political ones.

und Ankunft," *form+zweck* 4 (1987): 11–14; "Teil 2: Aufbaujahre," *form+zweck* 5 (1987): 8–15.

For Liebknecht and the Bauakademie, the contact with Schütte-Lihotzky was nonetheless of special significance precisely because she did live abroad in the West but was a Communist and could share experiences from the Soviet Union. Besides the general interest in international exchange, her judgment had the authority of "unbiased expertise," which could be drawn on in the arguments with the Berlin municipal authority. Liebknecht likely knew beforehand what her judgment of the Stalinallee kindergartens would be.

54 Letter from Architect Schütte-Lihotzky, no addressee, Klagenfurt, November 2, 1954. The context suggests that the addressee was Kurt Liebknecht, who had asked for information about the architect in question. BArch Berlin, DH 2/20064.

55 Schmidt designed the Max Kreuziger School in Berlin-Friedrichshain, which was completed in 1953 as a prime example of architecture in the national tradition.

I assume that Liebknecht not only instrumentalized Schütte-Lihotzky's work but also actually did respect it. The events of the years 1950 and 1954/55 show that even a prominent ideological hardliner like the president of the Bauakademie had more discriminating evaluation standards yet had to adapt to changing circumstances despite his position of power. An exchange of letters with Schütte-Lihotzky from 1988/89 allows us to surmise the political pressure Liebknecht was subjected to. Inspired by reading Schütte-Lihotzky's *Erinnerungen aus dem Widerstand* (Memories from the Resistance), he spoke for the first time about the dark side of his time in the Soviet Union, where he spent a year and a half in prison as a victim of Stalinist persecution.[57] Liebknecht also alluded to this aspect in heavily coded language in his 1986 biography.

56 As Bloch later explained: "You weren't allowed to design in a free and modern way, with large windows and irregular floor plans." Quoted in Butter, *Neues Leben*, 235.

57 Kurt Liebknecht to Margarete Schütte-Lihotzky, October 3, 1988, UAUAK, NL MSL, Korrespondenz privat.

Margarete Schütte-Lihotzky, for her part, never abandoned the hope that she would see her projects in the GDR carried out: even after her 90th birthday, she offered the journal *form+zweck* the right of first publication for a new design project for children's facilities.[58]

58 The editorial team, "Margarete Schütte-Lihotzky 90," *form+zweck* 1 (1987): 3.

Encounters

Friendship and Estrangement. Margarete Schütte-Lihotzky and Otto Neurath

Günther Sandner

Memory and Encounter

"Neurath was a giant, big and strong, with a long red beard and a bald head on which he wore a huge floppy black hat. A striking Andreas Hofer kind of figure, someone people on the street turned around to look at."[1] Margarete Schütte-Lihotzky described Otto Neurath repeatedly using these same words, first in a volume that Friedrich Stadler published in 1982 called *Arbeiterbildung in der Zwischenkriegszeit* (Workers' education in the interwar years) and lastly in her book *Warum ich Architektin wurde* (Why I became an architect), which was published after her death. What we know about their professional and personal relationship with each other has been gleaned mostly from memoirs such as these and a handful of letters. Schütte-Lihotzky's recollections of Neurath that are also connected to the rediscovery of his oeuvre in the German-speaking world, which did not set in until the 1970s and 1980s, will be revisited toward the end of this essay. Before that, the tale of a friendship and the tale of an estrangement will be told—two stories that occur in succession in certain respects yet cannot be precisely separated from each other chronologically.

Otto Neurath was born in 1882, making him about 15 years older than Schütte-Lihotzky. The two of them first met in the early 1920s (fig. 1). On July 25, 1919, Neurath had been

1 Margarete Schütte-Lihotzky, "Mein Freund Otto Neurath," in *Arbeiterbildung in der Zwischenkriegszeit. Otto Neurath – Gerd Arntz*, ed. Friedrich Stadler (Vienna: Löcker, 1982), 40–42, here 40. Margarete Schütte-Lihotzky, *Warum ich Architektin wurde* (Salzburg: Residenz, 2004), 79.

sentenced to one and a half years' imprisonment for "complicity in high treason" in his position as president of the Central Economic Office during the two Bavarian Soviet Republics. After massive political and diplomatic interventions and months of negotiations between the Austrian and Bavarian governments, he returned to Vienna in February 1920. There, he initially provided training for works council members and worked for a short-lived research institute for social economy before the settlement movement became the focus of his activity.[2]

His many years of work for the settlement movement marked his first attempt in the city of his birth, Vienna, to join social economic projects that he himself had developed as an economist and socialization theoretician. In January 1921, he took over at the helm of the newly founded Main Association for Settlements and Allotment Gardens and in October of that same year became secretary-general of the Austrian Settlement and Allotment Garden Association (Österreichischer Verband für Siedlungs- und Kleingartenwesen, ÖVSK), for whose founding he had personally laid the groundwork.[3]

Grete Lihotzky returned to Vienna in the summer of 1920 from the Netherlands, where she had lived and worked for several months as an escort to poor, starving Viennese children who had been sent there to convalesce. In an interview in 1984, she estimated the time of her return as "around about June."[4] Wanting to make a name for herself as an architect, she took part in a competition for an allotment garden colony on Schafberg, a large hill in the far west of Vienna. She became acquainted with the director of the settlement office, Max Ermers, and through him, met Adolf Loos in the fall of 1920. Loos ultimately motivated her to become involved in the settlement movement.[5] From 1922 to 1925, she worked as an architect in the building office of the ÖVSK.[6]

2 Also see S. E. Eisterer's essay in this volume.

3 Günther Sandner, *Otto Neurath. Eine politische Biographie* (Vienna: Zsolnay, 2014), 168–89.

4 Margarete Schütte-Lihotzky, *Erinnerungen aus dem Widerstand 1938–1945*, ed. Chup Friemert (Hamburg: Konkret Literatur Verlag, 1985), 17.

5 Ibid., 18.

6 Elisabeth Holzinger, "Widerstand in Zeiten des Terrors," in Margarete Schütte-Lihotzky, *Erinnerungen aus dem Widerstand. Das kämpferische Leben einer Architektin 1938–1945* (Vienna: Promedia, 2014), 7–20, here 14.

A Friendship

It was in the ÖVSK that Otto Neurath and Margarete Lihotzky became acquainted with each other. "My work brought me into daily contact with Neurath for years on end. In addition, I was also a personal friend of his," she wrote much later, summing up this time in her life.[7] Lihotzky was also responsible for founding an office known as Warentreuhand (merchandise trust) within the ÖVSK. Its purpose was to enable settlers to acquire suitable furniture at low prices.[8] With the help of Otto Neurath, she received her first contract from the City of Vienna, under which she worked with others on the Winarsky-Hof, a multistory municipal housing complex erected in the 20th district of Vienna in 1924.[9]

The friendly collaboration between the two was of short duration, however. Lihotzky fell ill with tuberculosis in 1924, and when she returned from her sick leave, Neurath was no longer active in the ÖVSK. In addition, the Social Democratic government had changed its housing construction policy. While settlements increasingly faded into the background, city policymakers began pushing multistory municipal housing complexes (*Gemeindebauten*) within preexisting urban areas. The Austrian Broadcasting Corporation (Österreichischer Rundfunk, ORF) completed a documentation on Neurath in 1990 called *Der unbekümmerte Denker* (The freewheeling thinker). In an interview from that piece, Schütte-

7 Margarete Schütte-Lihotzky, "Zeitzeugin," in *Vertriebene Vernunft II. Emigration und Exil österreichischer Wissenschaft 1930–1940, Teilband 2*, ed. Friedrich Stadler (Münster: LIT, 2004), 629–33, here 630.

8 Schütte-Lihotzky, *Erinnerungen* (1985), 18–19.

9 Schütte-Lihotzky, *Warum ich Architektin wurde*, 63–65, 101–4.

Fig. 1. Otto Neurath, 1920s, photograph.

Lihotzky talked about the three to four years Neurath and she were active together in the settlement movement.[10]

10 Margarete Schütte-Lihotzky (interview), in Karo Wolm, *Otto Neurath 1882–1945. Der unbekümmerte Denker*, ORF production, Vienna, 1990.

Grete Lihotzky was also involved, at least on the periphery, in the founding of the Gesellschafts- und Wirtschaftsmuseum (Social and Economic Museum). In this social museum, Otto Neurath and his team developed the Vienna Method of Pictorial Statistics, whose pictorial symbols are still known today, mainly under the later name Isotype.[11] In her essay for the book project on contemporary history entitled *Vertriebene Vernunft* (Banished reason), she recounts that Otto Neurath wrote a short exposé for a museum project, packed it up, and took a taxi to the leading figures in the municipal administration and to parliamentarians and city council members. She went on to write: "He returned to the taxi with a triumphant smile and nothing else in his pocket but two pieces of paper signed by Seitz, Renner, Deutsch, and others. That was the very beginning of the Museum für Siedlungs- und Städtebau (Museum for Settlement Construction and Urban Planning) in Vienna, from 1925 on known as the Gesellschafts- und Wirtschaftsmuseum (Social and Economic Museum), which would later become world famous." How could she have such precise knowledge of this episode? "I rode along with him," she revealed in her text.[12] That must have been in 1923.

11 Isotype stands for International System of Typographic Picture Education.

12 Schütte-Lihotzky, "Zeitzeugin," 630.

How could their friendship be described? Let us start by reading how Margarete Schütte-Lihotzky characterized Otto Neurath in retrospect: "Besides being highly engaged in a variety of activities centered on intellect and reason, he also wrote fairy tales at the time and painted small, fanciful, intertwined animals on wood in meticulous detail. This giant—Neurath always signed letters and cards not with his name but with elephants, happy and sad, laughing and crying, running, jumping, sitting—was imbued with a subtly reacting and imaginative sensibility. Several of these fairy tales and paintings are still in my possession today."[13]

13 Schütte-Lihotzky, *Warum ich Architektin wurde*, 80.

Margarete Schütte-Lihotzky's estate does in fact contain several of these fairy tales and paintings by Otto Neurath. At least some of these consistently literary texts have also been published.[14] However, Otto Neurath did not appear in name as the author of these stories. He invented not only Chinese

14 This relates to Sa-Le-Fe, "Das Fremde," *Die Wage* 4 no. 5 (1923): 156–59, and La-Se-Fe, "Das Gespräch von der Weihe des Berufes," *Die Wage* 4 no. 15 (1923): 463–67. While these and another of Neurath's texts appeared under a pseudonym, he published literary texts under his real name in the *Österreichischer Arbeiter-Kalender* from 1927 to 1930.

literary figures but also the appropriate Chinese authors to go with them, such as a La-Se-Fe and a Sa-Le-Fe. In other words, the original Chinese stories, of which these texts purported to be the translations, did not even exist. Nonetheless, the name La-Se-Fe appears in a German-language literary history of China. As Sebastian Meissl aptly wrote: the egg landed "in the literary historian's nest."[15] The translator of the Chinese tales, a Peter Zirngibel from Dresden, was clearly not a real person either, just another one of Otto Neurath's pen names.

One of these literary texts, the typescript "Der gestaltende Gott" (The creative god), bears the note "Autumnal thoughts 1923" and the dedication "To my dear creative friend." It is an allegorical story about creative genius, about the utopia of a new age, about obstacles and hindrances on the path there, but also about assurance and encouragement. Another story in the estate is dedicated to a Li-Ha, namely by "der Masslose" (the unbridled one), yet another also to Li-Ha, "das tanzende Sonnenstrählchen" (the little dancing sunbeam). Li-Ha undoubtedly stood for Grete Lihotzky,[16] and it is not difficult to guess who was being referred to as the unbridled one. In any event, all this points to a very close, perhaps even intimate relationship between the two.

Neurath regularly wrote literary texts of this sort from the early 1920s till about 1930. They are parables and discourses that in certain ways create a bright counterworld, a world of love and happiness, which is a key concept in his ethics and in his utopian writings. They also represent a counterproject to Oswald Spengler's *The Decline of the West*, which he covered thoroughly in his book *Anti-Spengler*.[17]

A certain tension between the ability to create an individual way of life and the collective achievement of aspirations for happiness is an omnipresent theme in these texts,[18] which can be considered part of Neurath's scholarly and political work, perhaps not in style but certainly in substance.

Along with these texts, Schütte-Lihotzky's estate contains at least one "painting" by Neurath, a fanciful Christmas card from 1922 (fig. 2). The small collection of documents also clarifies what had been an unanswered question up to that point—namely, why Otto Neurath was called Peter instead of Otto in so many letters from old friends from his

15 Sebastian Meissl, "Vom Literaturhistoriker zum Literaten. Wege und Umwege Otto Neuraths," in Stadler, *Arbeiterbildung*, 112–18, here 118, note 29.

16 Schütte-Lihotzky also signed a letter to Otto Neurath on November 14, 1938 with the name Li-Ha (Nachlass Otto und Marie Neurath, Österreichische Nationalbibliothek (ÖNB), Handschriftensammlung, Sig. 1224/17).

17 Otto Neurath, *Anti-Spengler* (Munich: Georg D. W. Callwey, 1921).

18 Meissl, *Vom Literaturhistoriker zum Literaten*, 117.

time in Vienna. His boyhood friend Dora Lucka, for instance, continued even in exile in England to use forms of address such as "Lieber Peter" (Dear Peter), "Lieber Peterfreund" (Dear Peter Friend), "Lieber Oberpeter" (Dear Peter-in-Chief) or—for Otto and Marie Neurath together—"Liebe Peterleute" (Dear Peter People).[19] The signature on the greeting card to Grete Lihotzky reads: "Herzliche Grüße, Peter Pan" (Warm regards, Peter Pan). Otto Neurath as Peter Pan, the adventurous child who never grows up.

19 The extremely extensive correspondence between Otto Neurath and Dora Lucka can be found in Otto and Marie Neurath's estate in the Austrian National Library's collection of handwritten documents (Nachlass Otto und Marie Neurath, Handschriftensammlung der ÖNB). Also see Sandner, *Otto Neurath*, 287–88.

Fig. 2. Christmas card from Otto Neurath to Margarete Lihotzky, 1922, lacquer paint on cardboard.

In 1926 Grete Lihotzky moved to Frankfurt am Main. Little is known about the contact the two had with each other in the years that followed, but they did at least work on the same project again a few years later, in 1932: the Wiener Werkbundsiedlung (social housing settlement in Vienna) and the associated exhibition staged by the Werkbund (association of craftsmen). Along with a host of other prominent architects, Schütte-Lihotzky designed two cubical housing units for this settlement project. But at the time the Werkbundsiedlung was being built, she was living in Moscow and was not able to supervise construction on site.[20] Otto Neurath, for his part, had a multifaceted role in the project. He was involved in planning and concept design, personally conducted tours through the exhibition, and wrote two articles for the *Arbeiter-Zeitung* on it.[21] However, the two of them probably did not encounter each other at the Werkbund exhibition in Vienna.

Estrangement

After her stay in Frankfurt, Margarete Schütte-Lihotzky, as she was called after her marriage in 1927, spent the years 1930 to 1937 in Moscow. That was followed by stays in London and Paris until she was appointed to a position at the Academy of Fine Arts in Istanbul.[22] While still in Paris prior to her departure to Istanbul, she paid a visit to Otto Neurath and his then colleague and later wife, Marie Reidemeister, in Den Haag, where the two of them lived after fleeing Austria in 1934. Otto Neurath's wife at the time, Olga Neurath (née Hahn), had also been living in Den Haag until her death on July 20, 1937. This meeting led to a rift. In her memoirs, Schütte-Lihotzky describes the visit:

> In 1937 I visited him [Otto Neurath] in Den Haag. I stayed at his house for five days but they were excruciating days. We no longer understood each other politically. There were countless, futile debates. Marie Reidemeister wanted to act as mediator; I personally did not even want to touch on political topics anymore. After all, there were still so many other things that connected us. But he kept returning to political issues time and again and tormented himself and me without achieving the recon-

20 Iris Meder, Margarete Schütte-Lihotzky, Wien–Moskau" in *Werkbundsiedlung Wien 1932. Ein Manifest des Neuen Wohnens*, ed. Andreas Nierhaus and Eva-Maria Orosz (Vienna: Müry Salzmann, 2012), 220.

21 Otto Neurath, "Glückliches Wohnen. Die Bedeutung der Werkbundsiedlung für die Zukunft," *Arbeiter-Zeitung* (June 19, 1932): 10; Otto Neurath, "Ein Schlußwort zur Werkbundsiedlung," *Arbeiter-Zeitung* (August 6, 1932): 6.

22 Also see Burcu Dogramaci's essay in this volume.

ciliation that was so desired. It was there that he showed how obstinate he could be—both an advantage and a disadvantage in his life! He stood on the station platform in Den Haag as my train departed with a despondent look on his face that I will never forget. Back then was the last time I saw him.[23]

What were their political differences? Astonishingly, Schütte-Lihotzky does not address them at all. In Red Vienna, both of them, Otto Neurath and Grete Lihotzky, had been members of the Social Democratic Workers' Party (SDAP). Otto Neurath had already joined the SDAP in 1918; Grete Lihotzky did so several years later. But unlike Neurath, she already left the party again in 1927. Her comment on this step: "After the events in Austria on July 15, 1927, I resigned from the Austrian Social Democratic Party with a somewhat pathetic letter after being a member for two and a half years."[24] Otto Neurath played an indirect role in this resignation, at least by Schütte Lihotzky's account. After she arrived in Frankfurt, it was Neurath who brought her together with Carl Grünberg, the well-known socialist economist and director of the Frankfurt Institute for Social Research. He had an influence on the Austrian architect that Schütte-Lihotzky described as follows: "It was Carl Grünberg who opened my eyes about Austrian social democracy and proved to me that it would not lead the country to Socialism."[25] Despite her positive attitude toward the Soviet Union, she did not join the Communist Party either in Frankfurt or in Moscow. It was not until 1939 during her stay in Turkey that she became a member.

Otto Neurath had already had his own experiences in the Soviet Union. He cooperated with a pictorial statistical institute in Moscow, the Izostat, from 1931 to 1934. The project involved having a small team train Soviet colleagues in the Vienna Method of Pictorial Statistics. This collaboration led to him being accused of Soviet propaganda, especially later on.[26] It is not possible to elaborate on the project in this essay.[27] In any event, it ended negatively in a material sense because a final installment of USD 6,000 was no longer paid out by the Soviet authorities, and Neurath faced massive monetary problems in Den Haag for several years after going into exile in the Netherlands following the events of February 1934.[28]

23 Schütte-Lihotzky, *Warum ich Architektin wurde*, 82–83.

24 Ibid., 120.

25 Ibid.; Marcel Bois, "Margarete Schütte-Lihotzky und das Frankfurter Institut für Sozialforschung," *maybrief* 049 (June 2018): 16–17.

26 Clive Chizlett, "Damned Lies. And Statistics. Otto Neurath and Soviet Propaganda in the 1930s," *Visible Language* 26 (1992): 298–321; Robin Kinross, "Blind Eyes, Innuendo and the Politics of Design. A Reply to Clive Chizlett," *Visible Language* 28 (1994): 67–79.

27 Julia Köstenberger, "Otto Neuraths 'Wiener Methode' im Dienste der sowjetischen Propaganda," in *Gegenwelten. Aspekte der österreichisch-sowjetischen Beziehungen 1918–1938*, ed. Verena Moritz et al. (Vienna: Residenz, 2013), 275–82; Emma Minns, "Picturing Soviet Progress: Izostat, 1931–4," in *Isotype. Design and Contexts 1925–1971*, ed. Christopher Burke, Eric Kindel, and Sue Walker (London: Hyphen, 2013), 257–80.

28 Sandner, *Otto Neurath*, 231 and 236.

Otto Neurath had pinned certain hopes on the Soviet Union and did not want to pass up the opportunity to further spread his pictorial statistical method. But he remained a Social Democrat his whole life and had also obtained the consent of the SDAP in advance for his collaboration in Moscow.[29] In letters from that period, he refers to himself—be it ironically or cynically—as a "Social Fascist," which was the derogatory term the Communists applied to the Social Democrats.[30] Although he left behind no text that could be called a systematic analysis of the Soviet Union, many of his handwritten notes in pertinent books on the subject indicate that he had adopted a decidedly detached attitude toward that country. Later, Marie Neurath wrote Schütte-Lihotzky that he had been shocked by the "inhumanity that was becoming ever more apparent."[31]

As a later letter from Schütte-Lihotzky indicates, she and Neurath had met in Moscow in the early 1930s. Marie Neurath, whose name was still Reidemeister at the time of the meeting,[32] later wrote to Schütte-Lihotzky that a "friendly skepticism" toward the Soviet Union prevailed in those conversations.[33] The political disputes of the time still resonated when the two of them corresponded in 1981 about the publication of *Arbeiterbildung in der Zwischenkriegszeit*. Marie Neurath was not the publisher but she proofread Schütte-Lihotzky's text, "Mein Freund Otto Neurath" (My friend Otto Neurath), from which the opening quotation of this essay is taken. In an initial version, Schütte-Lihotzky asserted that Otto Neurath had already "arrived at the far-right fringe of social democracy" at the time of their quarrel in Den Haag.[34] Marie Neurath emphatically disagreed: "Neurath did not move to the right."[35] She called Schütte-Lihotzky a "devout Communist" or in fuller context: "The misfortune for us was that you had become a devout Communist."[36] Schütte-Lihotzky was indignant: "I was not a Communist at the time and did not feel like one and can therefore also not say that I was one. Let alone devout."[37] According to Schütte-Lihotzky, Neurath had kept bringing the conversation in Den Haag back to the Soviet Union and pushed her into a corner argumentatively. At that point she had long since lost all desire to talk about politics anymore, but he would not stop.

29 Ibid., 233.

30 Otto Neurath to Martha Tausk, Easter Monday 1932 or 1933 (International Institute of Social History, Amsterdam, Martha Tausk Papers); see Sandner, *Otto Neurath*, 232.

31 Marie Neurath to Margarete Schütte-Lihotzky, November 22, 1981, University Archive of the University of Applied Arts Vienna, Nachlass Margarete Schütte-Lihotzky (UAUAK, NL MSL).

32 Otto Neurath und Marie Reidemeister married in England in 1941.

33 Marie Neurath to Margarete Schütte-Lihotzky, December 22, 1981, UAUAK, NL MSL.

34 Margarete Schütte-Lihotzky, "Mein Freund Otto Neurath," UAUAK, NL MSL (typescript), 5. Interestingly, Marie Neurath's corrections also contain errors which are then found in the final version of Schütte-Lihotzky's essay; these include the claim that Otto Neurath was president of the Central Economic Office under Kurt Eisner's government. In fact, he only became so after Eisner's murder (see Sandner, *Otto Neurath*, 122–32).

35 Marie Neurath to Margarete Schütte-Lihotzky, November 15, 1981, UAUAK, NL MSL.

36 Ibid.

37 Margarete Schütte-Lihotzky to Marie Neurath, [November] 1981, UAUAK, NL MSL.

38 Margarete Schütte-Lihotzky to Otto Neurath, November 14, 1938, Nachlass Otto und Marie Neurath, ÖNB, Handschriftensammlung, Sig. 1224/17.

39 See Hans Schafranek, *Widerstand und Verrat. Gestapospitzel im antifaschistischen Untergrund* (Vienna: Czernin, 2017), 81–82.

40 Schütte-Lihotzky, *Warum ich Architektin wurde*, 82; Schütte-Lihotzky, "Mein Freund Otto Neurath," 42.

41 Schütte-Lihotzky, "Zeitzeugin," 631; in almost identical wording: Schütte-Lihotzky, *Warum ich Architektin wurde*, 83.

42 Austrian Science Fund (FWF), P 31500-G32.

What were the consequences of this rift? A political estrangement had obviously occurred, probably also a personal one, but by no means a complete break. A letter from Istanbul dated November 14, 1938, the only letter from Schütte-Lihotzky in the Neurath estate at the Austrian National Library, shows that the two resumed contact again after one year at the latest. In the letter, Schütte-Lihotzky invited Otto Neurath and Marie Reidemeister to visit her in Istanbul and offered to let them stay in a guest room in her lovely apartment.[38] The visit did not materialize, however.

In December 1940, Margarete Schütte-Lihotzky returned to Vienna on behalf of the party to become an activist in the Communist Resistance. Just weeks later, she was betrayed by a Gestapo informer[39] and sentenced to 15 years' imprisonment. In her memoirs, she writes that she found out after the war that Otto Neurath had immediately organized a fund-raising campaign for her upon hearing about her conviction in National Socialist Vienna. He wanted to use the collected money to make her life easier after she was released. She writes: "This touching action proves that in him, I have lost a good, loyal, and caring friend, who brightened my youth and who had a not insignificant influence on my development."[40] After the end of the war and National Socialism, Margarete Schütte-Lihotzky tried to reorganize her professional life in Vienna. But as a Communist, she received virtually no public contracts in postwar Social Democratic Vienna. The literature contains reference after reference indicating that she was given almost no opportunities to bring her competence and experiences to bear. She wrote this about Otto Neurath: "In the fall of 1945, he wanted to return to Austria, but just a few days prior to his planned departure, he met his sudden death."[41] Yet in truth, Otto Neurath had already concentrated his future plans on his new home of England, the country to which he had fled from Den Haag in May 1940 before the advancing troops of National Socialist Germany. His sudden and also somewhat surprising death in Oxford on December 22, 1945 foiled those plans.[42]

Margarete Schütte-Lihotzky and Herbert Eichholzer. A Relational Fabric and Its Implications

Antje Senarclens de Grancy

At the end of September 1945, a few months after the end of the war, a two-page text by Margarete Schütte-Lihotzky appeared in a commemorative volume for a memorial service bearing the same name: *Unsterbliche Opfer, gefallen im Kampf der Kommunistischen Partei für Österreichs Freiheit* (Immortal victims, fallen in the fight of the Communist Party for Austria's freedom).[1] In a text entitled "Ein Architekt des Volkes" (An architect of the people), she depicted the life and work of the Graz architect Herbert Eichholzer (fig. 1), who had been executed in Vienna in 1943 for "making preparations for high treason."[2] She wrote about him specializing in housing construction and cited several of his buildings, but equally important to her was to recount his "pure, unambiguous convictions" and his "confident and courageous attitude in prison and before the court."

The facts about Herbert Eichholzer's role and activity in the Communist Resistance and about his arrest and conviction are largely known today thanks to contemporary historical research conducted in recent decades.[3] In March 1938, Eichholzer was forced to leave Austria immediately after the *Anschluss* (the annexation of Austria by Nazi Germany) because of his personal political history.[4] He traveled via Trieste and Zurich to Paris, where he was active as a political refugee in the Central Association of Austrian Émigrés and

1 [Margarete Schütte-Lihotzky], "Ein Architekt des Volkes," in *Unsterbliche Opfer. Gefallen im Kampf der Kommunistischen Partei für Österreichs Freiheit*, ed. Kommunistische Partei Österreichs (Vienna: Kommunistische Partei Österreichs, [1945]), 69–70. The memorial service took place in the Great Hall of the Konzerthaus in Vienna on September 29, 1945. See "Unsterbliche Opfer. Ein Gedenkbuch für die Helden der Kommunistischen Partei," *Österreichische Volksstimme* (September 30, 1945).

2 Dietrich Ecker, "Architekt Herbert Eichholzer 1903–1943" (doctoral dissertation, TU Graz, 1984); Antje Senarclens de Grancy and Heimo Halbrainer, *Totes Leben gibt es nicht. Herbert Eichholzer*

1903–1943. Architektur – Kunst – Politik (Vienna: Springer, 2004).

3 See in particular the research conducted by Heimo Halbrainer, "Ein Leben für soziale Architektur und Freiheit," in *Totes Leben*, Senarclens de Grancy and Halbrainer, 22–74, here 60–74; Heimo Halbrainer, "'Postanschrift Villa Leskoschek in Graz' – Das Haus als Treffpunkt des politischen und kulturellen Widerstands," in *Hilmteichstraße 24. Haus Albrecher-Leskoschek von Herbert Eichholzer*, Heimo Halbrainer, Eva Klein, and Antje Senarclens de Grancy (Graz: CLIO, 2016), 97–135; and *Herbert Eichholzer. Architektur und Widerstand*, exhibition catalog, ed. Heimo Halbrainer (Graz: CLIO, 1998).

4 Eichholzer had already been a member of the Association of Socialist Students as a student and joined the Republikanischer Schutzbund (Republican Defense League) in 1932. He took part in the February Uprising in 1934 and was imprisoned along with his then co-worker and partner Anna Lülja Simidoff (later married name Praun). After being released from prison, he may have joined the illegal Communist Party, or was at least a sympathizer. See Halbrainer, "Ein Leben," 23–74.

Fig. 1. Herbert Eichholzer, mid-1930s, photograph.

tried unsuccessfully for several months to find work as an architect. From the summer of 1938 onward, the Executive Committee of the Communist Party of Austria (KPÖ) was located in Paris and coordinated Resistance activities against the National Socialist regime from there. After a lengthy correspondence with Clemens Holzmeister, who was busy planning the Turkish government precinct in Ankara, Eichholzer finally received an invitation to work in Holzmeister's studio in Istanbul.

Right after arriving in Turkey, he contacted Margarete Schütte-Lihotzky. She had already been working for several months in Istanbul together with her husband Wilhelm Schütte at the intercession and invitation of Bruno Taut.[5] Nearly a half century later she wrote:

In November 1938 a charming young man, an Austrian architect, [came] to us at the Academy [of Fine Arts in Istanbul]. He said he knew me by name, came from Paris, and was working for Professor Clemens Holzmeister in Tarabya, an exclusive residential area on the Bosporus. That was my first encounter with Herbert Eichholzer. He built up the foreign chapter of the KPÖ in Turkey, which would become significant for the Resistance in Austria and for its ties to the KPÖ Executive Committee abroad.[6]

In March 1940, Eichholzer set off for Austria—redubbed the "*Ostmark*" (Eastern March) by the National Socialists—to create and coordinate Communist Resistance cells. Margarete Schütte-Lihotzky followed in December of that same year as a courier.[7]

Remembering this architect, murdered at age 39 and virtually unknown for decades, appears to have been of special significance to Schütte-Lihotzky till the end of her life. In this essay, I will attempt to shed light on the relational fabric between these two individuals along three different axes: their shared interests, their role as contemporary witnesses, and their conception of themselves. In the process, I will try to find clues about the role Herbert Eichholzer could have played in Margarete Schütte-Lihotzky's life.[8]

Points of Contact and Commonalities

In a 1982 interview, Schütte-Lihotzky noted that her stay in Istanbul was the first time in her life that she had had time to "educate myself a little on [basic] political theory."[9] She said she read various things: "Marx and Engels, for example, I hardly had any time earlier, so it was actually from that point forward that I considered myself to be a Communist." The discussions and conversations in the group around Eichholzer[10] also helped her to fortify her own convictions during the barely 16 months that she and Eichholzer were both living in the city:

> For each of us, it was a time of satisfying, meaningful work: theoretical analysis of Marxism in direct connection with the Resistance in Austria, with the possibility of us lending practical support.[11]

5 See Burcu Dogramaci, "Architekt, Lehrer, Autor. Wilhelm Schütte in der Türkei (1938–1946)," in *Wilhelm Schütte. Architekt. Frankfurt – Moskau – Istanbul – Wien*, ed. ÖGFA and Ute Waditschatka (Zurich: Park Books, 2019), 48–62.

6 Margarete Schütte-Lihotzky, *Erinnerungen aus dem Widerstand. Das kämpferische Leben einer Architektin von 1938–1945* (Hamburg: Konkret-Literatur-Verlag, 1985), 50–51.

7 The subsequent events in both their lives are well-known: betrayal, arrest, conviction, and imprisonment or—in the case of Eichholzer—execution. See Schütte-Lihotzky, *Erinnerungen* (1985), and Elisabeth Boeckl-Klamper's essay in this volume.

8 In terms of sources, the relationship between Schütte-Lihotzky and Eichholzer is a very asymmetrical one. Only Schütte-Lihotzky's memories of Eichholzer have been preserved, recorded in texts and in television and radio interviews over decades. Eichholzer, on the other hand, left no diaries and only a few letters, in which there is no reference made to Schütte-Lihotzky.

9 Transcript of the tape recording of an interview with Margarete Schütte-

Lihotzky, 1982, Documentation Centre of Austrian Resistance (DÖW), Vienna, no. 19584, sheet 6.

10 Apart from Schütte-Lihotzky, members of the Resistance group around Eichholzer in Istanbul also included Wilhelm Schütte, Herbert Feuerlöscher, and Ines Victoria Maier.

11 Schütte-Lihotzky, *Erinnerungen* (1985), 51.

12 Before 1938, Eichholzer was able to work for barely 10 years as a self-employed architect in Graz after and alongside internships in Paris and work abroad in Greece, Turkey, and the Soviet Union. With the exception of a building to house workers in the Styrian town of Judenburg, he did not receive any public building contracts.

13 See Schütte-Lihotzky, *Erinnerungen* (1985), 50; Halbrainer, "Ein Leben," 57.

14 After completing her studies, Lihotzky worked in the Netherlands and later in Frankfurt and Moscow; she traveled to China and Japan in 1934, and also spent around a year in France. Eichholzer traveled to Abyssinia (now Ethiopia) in 1927, worked as a building manager for steel houses in Greece and Turkey, and worked in Paris in 1929 and in Moscow in 1932.

Although Eichholzer was six years younger than Schütte-Lihotzky and had less professional experience than she did,[12] the two of them quickly formed a trusting relationship with each other. It was probably grounded in their decision to participate in the Communist Resistance[13] and in their unconditional willingness to take on personal risk, yet it extended beyond a shared partisan commitment. Both Schütte-Lihotzky and Eichholzer were highly mobile in their younger years as far as work activities or internships abroad were concerned and had experienced Asia and Africa, respectively, on extensive travels in those regions.[14] Although they had never met each other personally before, either in Vienna or while working in Moscow or Paris, they had a number of common acquaintances and colleagues in the field of architecture. One example is Le Corbusier,[15] who was especially important for Eichholzer; another is Ernst May. They also had a unifying frame of reference on current issues and suggested solutions from the modern architectural movement Neues Bauen and from contemporary housing construction.

Early on, both had recognized for themselves that it would not suffice to be an "architect, body and soul"[16] and to spread their own views as widely as possible through projects, lectures, or exhibitions. Instead, "the primary focus for the architect must be to fight for the kind of social structure without which his architectural ideas cannot be realized."[17] Eichholzer's political engagement in social democracy had already resulted in him serving several weeks of imprisonment in 1934 after the February Uprising, the Austrian civil war.

Among their most important commonalities were the experiences both of them had had in the Soviet Union. Eichholzer's multimonth stay in Moscow from September to December 1932 fell within the years that Margarete Schütte-Lihotzky was active there. Eichholzer worked in the proximity of the May Group, and both of them were involved in the Standartgorproekt.[18] Besides the architects from Frankfurt, the May Group also consisted of about 150 foreigners, who, like Eichholzer, were looking for work in the Soviet Union because they were unemployed or in want of contracts.[19] In October 1932, Eichholzer wrote the following in a letter to his office colleague in Graz, Rudolf Nowotny:

> After four weeks of well-paid idleness, I have finally ended up in a large planning trust (it is the largest one here). The Mai [May] Brigade also works here, then Stam, Hans Schmied [Schmidt] (Basel), and other such greats; Bruno Taut is in the neighboring trust.[20]

Eichholzer was given the task of developing a standard type of housing with facades facing north and south but was personally more interested in designing a boarding house with 24 residential units per floor (fig. 2). Disappointed by the working conditions in the Soviet Union and the misery he witnessed there, he already returned to Graz in December 1932.[21]

One person who paid a special role in the relational fabric between Margarete Schütte-Lihotzky and Herbert

Fig. 2. Herbert Eichholzer, model of a boarding house for Moscow, 1932/33, photograph.

15 Margarete Schütte-Lihotzky, *Warum ich Architektin wurde*, ed. Karin Zogmayer (Salzburg: Residenz, 2004), 65 and 188.

16 [Schütte-Lihotzky], "Ein Architekt des Volkes," 69.

17 Ibid.

18 Remembered record of a conversation between Dietrich Ecker and Margarete Schütte-Lihotzky, May/June 1985, Archive of TU Graz, Nachlass Dietrich Ecker, Bestand Herbert Eichholzer (NL Ecker, Bestand Eichholzer), Karton 3, Ordner 5. See Thomas Flierl (ed.), *Standardstädte. Ernst May in der Sowjetunion 1930–1933. Texte und Dokumente* (Berlin: Suhrkamp, 2012).

19 See Thomas Flierl's essay in this volume and also Thomas Flierl, "'Vielleicht die größte Aufgabe, die je einem Architekten gestellt wurde.' Ernst May in der Sowjetunion (1930–1933)," in *Ernst May (1886–1970). Neue Städte auf drei Kontinenten*, ed. Claudia Quiring et al. (Munich: Prestel, 2011), 156–95, here 157.

20 Herbert Eichholzer to Rudolf Nowotny, October 14, 1932, Archive of TU Graz, NL Ecker, Bestand Eichholzer, Karton 3, Ordner 5.

21 Herbert Eichholzer, "Architektur in Sowjet-

russland – ein Weg zurück!," *Tagespost* (December 25, 1932).

22 Interview by Edith Friedl with Margarete Schütte-Lihotzky in Vienna on November 1, 1999, quoted in Edith Friedl, *Nie erlag ich seiner Persönlichkeit. Margarete Schütte-Lihotzky und Adolf Loos. Ein sozial- und kulturgeschichtlicher Vergleich* (Vienna: Milena, 2005), 207.

23 See Antje Senarclens de Grancy, "Herbert Eichholzer und Clemens Holzmeister. Eine (un-)mögliche Beziehung zwischen Architektur und Politik," in *Gibt es eine Holzmeister-Schule? Clemens Holzmeister (1886–1983)*, ed. Christoph Hölz (Innsbruck: Innsbruck University Press, 2015), 217–44.

24 Remembered record of a conversation between Ecker and Schütte-Lihotzky.

25 Herbert Eichholzer's death sentence included the following statement on his work for Holzmeister: "Holzmeister's group of employees was entirely opposed to National Socialist governance, which was mainly due to the fact that the senior managers Waldapfel and Reichel were fully Jewish. He came into closer contact with the architect Ines Victoria Maier, who was later sent to the Ostmark as a courier by

Eichholzer was the Austrian architect Clemens Holzmeister, particularly because the media and trade publications had incorrectly and repeatedly reported—and still do today—that Schütte-Lihotzky had been a co-worker of Holzmeister. She herself corrected that misunderstanding in an interview: "I never worked with Holzmeister; I was simply in Istanbul at the same time he was."[22]

Both Eichholzer and Schütte-Lihotzky appear to have been impressed even in their younger years by Feuerhalle Simmering, a crematorium that Holzmeister completed in 1922 on a site opposite the main gate of Vienna's Central Cemetery. Since the early 1930s, Eichholzer had been friends with Holzmeister, who was 17 years his senior,[23] and had often visited him in Vienna and at his house on Hahnenkamm, a mountain in Tyrol. His closeness to Holzmeister may come as a surprise, given that the older architect was on the other end of the political spectrum as a prominent and powerful representative of the *Ständestaat* government (the corporative authoritarian system in Austria from 1934 to 1938). Later the rift between them on architectural matters widened, probably also because of the dramatic political events. Schütte-Lihotzky recalled that Eichholzer had been "unhappy working for Holzmeister" in Istanbul because of the architecture involved: "They never discussed architecture."[24] Today, it is no longer possible to reconstruct to what extent and in what detail Holzmeister himself knew about the Resistance activities[25]—still, two of his employees in Istanbul did participate: besides Eichholzer, his former Chilean student at the Academy of Fine Arts in Vienna, Ines Victoria Maier.[26]

Despite their diverging political and ideological views and commitments, Schütte-Lihotzky had no reservations about Holzmeister in the decades following the war, although she did refer to herself at the time as a "persona non grata" because she had remained a Communist. In 1961, she congratulated Holzmeister on his 75th birthday in almost effusive terms in *Stimme der Frau*, the journal of the Communist women's movement in Austria (fig. 3).[27] She noted that he had spent the "unfortunate Nazi era" in Turkey, had trained hundreds of architects as a teacher, and was "deeply connected

Brigitte

Clemens Holzmeister:

Baumeister und Künstler

Der in Österreich und weit über die Grenzen unseres Landes bekannte Architekt Professor Clemens Holzmeister feiert am 27. März sein 75. Geburtstagsjubiläum.

Wir freuen uns, daß er trotz seines vorgerückten Alters heute wie eh und je auf der Höhe seiner Schaffenskraft steht. Hat er doch erst vor kurzem eine der größten Kulturstätten unseres Landes, das neue Salzburger Festspielhaus als sein Werk der Öffentlichkeit übergeben.

Holzmeister begann seine Laufbahn in Innsbruck, er wurde zum ersten Male durch den Bau des Wiener Krematoriums den breiten Massen der Wiener bekannt. Zwischen diesem, damals so fortschrittlichen Bau, der schwer erkämpft werden mußte, und dem Salzburger Musentempel liegen unzählige Bauwerke, die nach seinen Ideen und Plänen errichtet wurden. Die unglückliche Nazizeit verbrachte Clemens Holzmeister in der Türkei, wo er außer dem Palais für den damaligen Staatspräsidenten Kemal Ata Türk durch viele andere Gebäude das Gesicht des heutigen Ankara weitgehend mitbestimmte.

Clemens Holzmeister hat als Lehrer Hunderte von Architekten herangebildet, er ist zutiefst mit der österreichischen Kunst, vor allem dem Barock, verbunden. Anläßlich seines Jubiläums wollen wir ihm, dem verdienten Baumeister und Künstler unseres Landes, herzlich gratulieren und wünschen, daß ihm auch weiterhin so viel Schaffenskraft erhalten bleibe.

Architektin Grete Schütte-Lihotzky

Fig. 3. Margarete Schütte-Lihotzky, "Clemens Holzmeister: Baumeister und Künstler," on Holzmeister's 75th birthday, *Stimme der Frau*, 1961.

to Austrian art, especially Baroque." Finally, she said this in a 1994 interview: "I do not fully subscribe to Holzmeister's architecture. But I was on very good terms with him."[28]

Contemporary Witnesses

In the 1960s, a younger generation of architects and architectural historians sought to overcome the traumatic period of National Socialism and the dull postwar functionalism thereafter by taking a look at the preceding era. This rediscovery of the past also helped them to arrive at their own

the foreign apparatus of the Communist Party of Austria." Verdict of the People's Court against Herbert Eichholzer, September 9, 1942, 7 J 257/41, Bundesarchiv Berlin, R 3017/26246, sheet 4.

26 See Sophie Hochhäusl, "Spatial Histories of Dissidence: Imagination, Memory, and Resistance in Istanbul, Vienna, and Santiago de Chile, 1938–1945," *ARQ*, no. 105 (2020): 40–61; Christine Kanzler, "Maier Ines Victoria, Deckname: Wera," in *biografiA. Lexikon österreichischer Frauen, Band 2*, ed. Ilse Korotin (Vienna: Böhlau, 2016), 2076–77; Schütte-Lihotzky, *Erinnerungen* (1985), 119–20.

27 Grete Schütte-Lihotzky, "Clemens Holzmeister. Baumeister und Künstler," *Stimme der Frau* (1961): 21.

28 Quoted in Friedl, *Nie erlag ich*, 207.

positions regarding a hegemonic understanding of history and culture. Parallel to that, there was an international awakening of interest in interwar architecture and a historization of modernism, now being described as "classic." In 1968, Dietrich Ecker, a member of the Graz architecture firm Team A, began doing research on "modernist architecture" in Styria. In the process he happened upon Herbert Eichholzer, who had virtually been forgotten by that time. Ecker sought out still living witnesses of the period, conducted interviews, and performed the painstaking pioneering task of collecting archive materials. In the summer of 1970, he wrote to Clemens Holzmeister, who had been teaching at the Academy of Fine Arts in Vienna again since 1949. Holzmeister forwarded Ecker's letter without comment to Anna-Lülja Praun (née Simidoff), Eichholzer's former co-worker and life partner,[29] and evidently sent no reply himself.

It was not until 1985, a few months after completing his dissertation on Eichholzer,[30] that Ecker contacted Margarete Schütte-Lihotzky. His attention was presumably first drawn to this significant contemporary witness by the publication of her book *Erinnerungen aus dem Widerstand* (Memories from the Resistance) that same year and the media interest it sparked.[31] In his interview with Schütte-Lihotzky, she said this about Clemens Holzmeister, two years dead at that point, and about him giving Eichholzer—consciously or unconsciously—the financial wherewithal to pursue Communist Resistance activity: "It is impossible that Holzmeister does not remember." She added that she had even talked with him herself about Eichholzer.[32]

From the contemporary witness Schütte-Lihotzky, we learn about a series of moments that, like puzzle pieces, enable us for the first time to understand Eichholzer's way of thinking. She shared information mostly about his theoretical views, correcting the opinion of many contemporary witnesses from his time in Graz up to 1938, who repeatedly referred to him as a *Salonsozialist* (champagne Socialist) or *Edelkommunist* (armchair Communist). Possibly in the hopes of rehabilitating the architect in anti-Communist postwar Austria, Gustav Scheiger, for instance, the former secretary of the Sezession Graz, which decisively shaped

29 Anna-Lülja Praun to Dietrich Ecker, July 17, 1970, Archive of TU Graz, Bestand Herbert Eichholzer, Karton 3, Ordner 5.

30 Ecker, "Architekt Herbert Eichholzer."

31 In his dissertation, Ecker mentions Schütte-Lihotzky only in a list of some of Ernst May's co-workers in Moscow. He was apparently not yet aware of her involvement in the Resistance group in Istanbul. Ecker, "Architekt Herbert Eichholzer," 76.

32 Remembered record of a conversation between Ecker and Schütte-Lihotzky.

Eichholzer, described him in 1956 as a Communist "at least in line with Picasso, Joliot-Curie, Bertolt Brecht, and many other significant minds, whom a not altogether objective public thought they could dismiss with the label 'champagne Bolshevik.'"[33]

By contrast, Margarete Schütte-Lihotzky talked about Eichholzer as a "committed Marxist."[34] The social and political radicalization in Austria prior to the *Anschluss* and the special circumstances he faced in exile appear to have brought Eichholzer to a more finely honed position and a more precise theoretical analysis. We also find out from the contemporary witness Schütte-Lihotzky that during his months of exile in Paris, Eichholzer sought to apply Marxist theory to fathom the development of architecture, which under the banner of National Socialism had become an ideological instrument of a terror regime. She wrote that "in a larger theoretical paper entitled 'Faschistische Architektur' (Fascist architecture) [he] examined the trends in architecture in the Third Reich using the scientific method of dialectical materialism."[35] This unpreserved manuscript may have been him staking out a counter-position to a draft text by the architect Franz Schacherl about the "Architectural Style of Dictatorships" for the second issue of the anti-Fascist journal *Plan* slated for release in the spring of 1938. Eichholzer also played a major role in this journal.[36]

Memory and Conception of Self

Schütte-Lihotzky's 1945 text "Ein Architekt des Volkes" mentioned at the outset of this essay is not formulated as a personal memoir of a like-minded political companion[37] but rather as an attempt to capture Eichholzer's personality from a greater distance and above all, to reveal him as a socially responsible architect even when faced with the ultimate consequence. The essay is a clear exception to Schütte-Lihotzky's writings from the 1920s when she published mostly texts about her own projects and general issues of rational construction. It is the first of her essays about her contemporaries and architectural colleagues.[38] It was followed—but not until several decades later—by a series of memoirs about former like-minded companions at various stages in her life

33 Gustav Scheiger, "Ist der Architekt Herbert Eichholzer vergessen?," *Österreichisches Tagebuch* (November 3, 1956).

34 Remembered record of a conversation between Ecker and Schütte-Lihotzky.

35 [Schütte-Lihotzky], "Ein Architekt des Volkes," 70.

36 See Otto Basil to Herbert Eichholzer, January 20, 1938, 3, in Archive of TU Graz, NL Ecker, Bestand Eichholzer, Karton 3, Ordner 5. On *Plan*, see Günter Eisenhut, "Das erste Heft der legendären Kulturzeitschrift 'Plan'," in *Totes Leben*, Senarclens de Grancy and Halbrainer, 82–91.

37 The last contact between the two came in the form of messages and greetings they sent to each other from prison to prison in the last few months of 1942. See Schütte-Lihotzky, *Erinnerungen* (1985), 120–22.

38 See "Schriftenverzeichnis," in *Margarete Schütte-Lihotzky, Soziale Architektur. Zeitzeugin eines Jahrhunderts*, exhibition catalog, MAK—Austrian Museum of Applied Arts, Vienna, ed. Peter Noever (Vienna: Böhlau, 1996), 293–97.

such as Adolf Loos, Otto Neurath, Oskar Strnad, Walter Gropius, Josef Frank, and Ernst May, which appeared in the 1970s and 1980s in journals and exhibition catalogs. However, these figures differ from Eichholzer in that they were already in well-established positions prior to the war, and their significance was already more or less acknowledged internationally or they had already been rediscovered by architectural researchers.

Herbert Eichholzer was a man whom the public forgot and whose memory it repressed. For decades, Schutte-Lihotzky repeatedly demanded that he be remembered and sought to correct the imbalance in the attention he was given. For instance, Jan Tabor recounts an initial meeting with her in 1978, initiated by Harald Sterk, the then art critic at the *Arbeiter-Zeitung*. She did not want to answer questions about Loos, Frank, May, Le Corbusier, or Taut: "She wanted to talk about Herbert Eichholzer, the talented architect from Graz, who had also returned to Austria from Turkey and had been executed in 1943. She wanted recognition for him."[39]

39 Jan Tabor, "'Sie waren so elegant.' Margarete Schütte-Lihotzky (1897–2000)," *Falter* (January 26, 2000).

Schütte-Lihotzky often said that she was the only one to survive from her narrower circle of Resistance comrades for a free Austria. That is why she published her 1985 book *Erinnerungen aus dem Widerstand* (Memories from the Resistance). It attracted international attention, also in the context of a new remembrance culture in Austria following the Waldheim Affair in 1986.

Remembering Eichholzer in particular probably also served a function for her in processing her own life story, he having had the same profession as she did, architect, and as such, the same role in society. It sounds like she was talking about herself when she wrote this in 1945:

> He belonged to that unfortunately still small group of architects who fully and completely felt the misery of the masses and through their professional work wanted to help if not to eliminate this misery at least to alleviate it. These were the architects who put their own artistic ambitions far behind their desire to serve the general public, who considered it much more important to do their own small individual part in raising the living standards of the masses than to build villas for rich

> people. He recognized very early on that the realization of his professional ideals depended on the structure of society. He inevitably moved from the issues of housing construction to those of urban planning as a whole, to those issues in which a serious, responsible architect must grapple with the problems of the distribution of property, the overall economy, and society.[40]

In other words, Eichholzer possibly took on the role of an alter ego in Schütte-Lihotzky's memoirs—or at least that of a younger male identification figure. For her, too, the question arose of how far the commitment to architecture had to extend and what consequences one had to be willing to bear. In view of her own horror about the senselessness of her comrades' deaths, her remembrance of Eichholzer also gave her the opportunity to interpret her own work in the Resistance. In the mid-1990s, she made the following statement in a conversation with Gabu Heindl and Martin Engelmeier: "Herbert Eichholzer was executed. Many died for their convictions. It is still better than being indiscriminately shot dead as a soldier on the battlefield."[41] And on her decision to participate in the Resistance, she said this in 1982:

> You should finish what you start; I cannot suddenly say, oh, I am not going after all; that did not even enter my mind. And you walk into this danger probably similar to the way a soldier does; you might think: one guy will be hit by a bullet, the other guy might not. I think that there is nothing more to it. If you really want to do something and believe it is necessary, you go ahead and do it [...].[42]

40 [Schütte-Lihotzky], "Ein Architekt des Volkes," 69.

41 Gabu Heindl and Martin Engelmeier, "Architektur und Widerstand. Auszüge aus Gesprächen mit der Architektin Margarete Schütte-Lihotzky über ihre Widerstandsarbeit im 2. Weltkrieg," *pblattform BOKU-live*, no. 4/95 (May 1995), online at https://www.yumpu.com/de/document/view/6413109.

42 Lihotzky, DÖW Vienna, 7.

Wilhelm Schütte—In the Shadow of Lihotzky?

David Baum

Wilhelm Schütte was already 12 years deceased and Margarete Schütte-Lihotzky 83 years old when she received the Award of the City of Vienna for Architecture in 1980.[1] It was the first time she had attracted notice outside narrower professional circles. In the 1970s, interest in the history of New Frankfurt increased, and Schütte-Lihotzky was one of the few direct participants left from Ernst May's entourage with whom people could still talk about that era. Faced with a barrage of inquiries and interviews, she saw herself virtually forced to turn her attention to "her" archive. In 1978, on the 10th anniversary of Wilhelm Schütte's death, she held an address in Istanbul before his former students.[2] In 1985, she released her *Erinnerungen aus dem Widerstand* (Memories from within the Resistance) and at age 90 or so, began to write her professional memoirs, which were published posthumously in 2004 under the title *Warum ich Architektin wurde* (Why I became an architect).[3]

Margarete Schütte-Lihotzky died in 2000 at the age of nearly 103, thereby outliving her former husband—they had been divorced since the 1950s—by more than 30 years. It is understandable that she recounted events from her own subjective perspective, that she was no longer able to convey all the facts accurately at her advanced age, and that she made omissions, consciously or unconsciously. In any event, from today's standpoint, this married couple's collaboration, even after their separation, gave rise to a bigger output than was previously known. Schütte-Lihotzky's estate contains material bearing Wilhelm Schütte's handwriting. The author-

1 This chapter is a modified version of the following essays: David Baum, "Wilhelm Schütte und die Ära des Reformschulbaus im Neuen Frankfurt (1925–1930)," and "Wilhelm Schütte als Vermittler und Architekt im Nachkriegs-Wien (1947–1968)," in *Wilhelm Schütte. Architekt. Frankfurt – Moskau – Istanbul – Wien*, ed. ÖGFA and Ute Waditschatka (Zurich: Park Books, 2019), 8–23, 64–91.

2 Margarete Schütte-Lihotzky, "Ansprache für Istanbul" (typescript/manuscript, June 1978), University Archive of the University of Applied Arts Vienna, Nachlass Margarete Schütte-Lihotzky (UAUAK, NL MSL), TXT/274.

3 Margarete Schütte-Lihotzky, *Erinnerungen aus dem Widerstand*, ed. Chup Friemert (Hamburg: Konkret Literatur Verlag, 1985); Margarete Schütte-Lihotzky, *Warum ich Architektin wurde*,

ship of many of the works would have to be ascribed to both of them, even those labeled as being by just one of them. They conducted business as "the Schüttes." Nonetheless, this essay is devoted to her creative partner, who has been in her shadow due to the reception she received as one of the first female architects.

Origins and Studies

Wilhelm Schütte was born in the German town of Heissen near Mülheim an der Ruhr on August 14, 1900,[4] and grew up in Cologne, where his father, a pastor, took over a parish in 1902.[5] After completing the special wartime school-leaving examination (*Notreifeprüfung*) during World War I in 1917, he began gaining initial practical experience on construction sites and at construction site offices. Parallel to that, he enrolled in building engineering at the technical university in Aachen (now RWTH Aachen) in 1918 but still had to perform military service from June to November.[6] In 1918/19, Schütte transferred to the technical university in Darmstadt, where he often passed the foot of the Mathildenhöhe hill with its buildings by Joseph Maria Olbrich, Peter Behrens, and others.[7] After receiving his intermediate diploma in October 1920, Wilhelm Schütte practiced as an architect and site manager for Karl Doll in Essen. From 1921 on, he studied architecture at the technical university in Munich and in 1922 worked for Martin Elsaesser in Cologne. During the winter semester of 1922/23, Schütte completed his studies in Munich with Theodor Fischer, who employed him in his office until September 1923. Schütte continued his work at the Postbauschule (postal building school of the Bavarian Post Office) as a *Baureferendar*—that is, as a graduate building engineer in preparatory service for a higher civil service position. There, he planned and built a postal building in Berchtesgaden to serve as housing and for overnight stays.[8]

Head of the School Construction Department for New Frankfurt

On passing his *Regierungsbaumeister* (civil service architect) examination, Wilhelm Schütte became one of the first employees to work on New Frankfurt from November 1, 1925

ed. Karin Zogmayer (Salzburg: Residenz, 2004).

4 Paul Wilhelm Ferdinand Schütte, Auszug aus dem Taufregister der evangelischen Gemeinde Heißen, April 4, 1902. Sonderbestand "Wilhelm Schütte" im Nachlass Margarete Schütte-Lihotzky (UAUAK, NL MSL, WS 0207/Q).

5 See D. Rosenkranz, edited by W. Heynen, "Die Mülheimer Pfarrer von 1610 bis 1960," in *350 Jahre (1610–1960) Evangelische Kirchengemeinde Mülheim am Rhein* (Essen: Evangelische Kirchengemeinde Mülheim am Rhein, 1960), 45–51, here 47.

6 Diplomvorprüfungsakte, Historical Archive of TU Darmstadt, 102 no. 9035.

7 Residential address: Im Geissensee 11, ibid.

8 See Zeugnisse, UAUAK, NL MSL, WS 0212/1,2/Q.

9 Zeugnis Städtisches Hochbauamt Frankfurt am Main, October 10, 1930, UAUAK, NL MSL, WS 0245/1/Q.

10 Wilhelm Schütte, "Vom Neuen Bauen in Frankfurt am Main. I. Haus May in Ginnheim bei Frankfurt am Main," *Der Baumeister* 3 (1927): 61–65.

11 Zeugnis Städtisches Hochbauamt.

on.[9] He soon began reporting on this activity in a series of articles for the journal *Der Baumeister*.[10] The first task Wilhelm Schütte was assigned by the Hochbauamt (central building authority in Frankfurt) was "Design Development and Supervision of Construction for the Konrad Haenisch School with Children's Facilities."[11] This project was the first new school building in New Frankfurt, and its design already incorporated the findings of the New Education movement.[12] Schütte subsequently participated in all projects for new school buildings in Frankfurt during the interwar years.[13]

From 1927 on, he was already preparing concepts for pavilion-style schools.[14] The Frankfurt guidelines for the planning of new school buildings were presented in July 1928. The preceding discussions between educators and architects had taken place in the new department for school construction, which was run by Schütte.[15] Perhaps the most influential of the advising educators was Fritz Karsen. He and Bruno Taut planned a school in Berlin-Neukölln (Dammwegschule).[16] Schütte and Karsen wrote articles together for *Der Baumeister* and for the *International Review of Education/ Internationale Zeitschrift für Erziehungswissenschaft*.[17] In 1928 the Taut–Karsen plan for this comprehensive school on Dammweg was published and a trial classroom building was erected.[18] This was presumably the model for developing a prototype for Ernst May's design for a New Education type school (Reformschule am Bornheimer Hang) in Frankfurt, which was presented that same year. Schütte's experimental building gave rise in the spring of 1930 to the "*Pavillon der Freiklassen*" (pavilion of open-air classrooms) at the Frankensteinerschule. It was not far from the apartment into which the Schüttes had moved as newlyweds in the spring of 1927.[19] Shortly before, they had been represented at the exhibition *Die neue Wohnung und ihr Innenausbau* (The new apartment and its interior finishings) with two exhibits: a standard-type allotment garden hut and an expandable "Li-Schü" weekend house. "If everything we create together turns out to be as good as the weekend house, we can be satisfied," Schütte-Lihotzky wrote[20] (fig. 1). For the city schools in Frankfurt, Wilhelm Schütte developed standard types of school furniture, in some cases the same model in four differ-

12 Also known as the New School Movement; the German term is *Reformpädagogik*. See Kurt Schäfer, *Schulen und Schulpolitik in Frankfurt am Main, 1900–1945* (Frankfurt am Main: Waldemar Kramer, 1994), 237.

13 On the individual schools, see Baum, "Wilhelm Schütte und die Ära des Reformschulbaus," 12.

14 Zeugnis Städtisches Hochbauamt.

15 See Jutta Friess, *Der Frankfurter Reformschulversuch 1921–1937. Verdrängt und vergessen* (Frankfurt am Main: Brandes & Apsel, 2007), 214–38.

16 See Ute Maasberg and Regina Prinz, "Verzeichnis der Werke," in *Bruno Taut 1880–1938. Architekt zwischen Tradition und Avantgarde*, ed. Winfried Nerdinger et al. (Stuttgart: Deutsche Verlags-Anstalt, 2001), 310–95, here 374–75. Karsen was also a lecturer in practical pedagogy at Goethe University and was frequently in Frankfurt, a center of the New Education movement in the Weimar Republic. Whenever his brisk construction activity permitted during this time in Berlin, Taut also came to this city on the Main River. See Schütte-Lihotzky, *Warum ich Architektin wurde*, 192.

17 Wilhelm Schütte, "Grundsätzliches über

Fig. 1. Margarete Schütte-Lihotzky and Wilhelm Schütte near Frankfurt am Main, 1928; written on the reverse: "Oh what a shame! Where there is much light, there is also much shadow!"

ent sizes, and furniture for special classes, classrooms for industrial arts, handicrafts, labs, etc.[21]

At the CIAM (Congrès internationaux d'architecture moderne, or International Congresses of Modern Architecture) Congress in Frankfurt in 1929, Wilhelm Schütte gave a guided tour through the Römerstadtschule, a school he had planned under Elsaesser's direction.[22] In the exhibition bearing the same name as the congress, *Die Wohnung für das Existenzminimum* (Dwelling for minimal existence), the Schüttes displayed their floor plan for a "factory worker's apartment." The opening day coincided with the Black Thursday stock market crash in New York, lending the show a striking topicality given its theme of economical construction.

Other designs were scrapped, such as those by Elsaesser and Schütte for the pavilion-style school planned for the Bonames district in Frankfurt.[23] The first complex of open-air classrooms was the primary school Volksschule Praunheim (Eugen Kaufmann, Wilhelm Pullmann) featuring three pavilions with four classrooms each. It was opened in August 1930.[24] The second open-air school followed a month later on Bornheimer Hang (Ernst May, Albert Löcher).[25] May and

neue Volksschulen;" Fritz Karsen, "Schulbau und Pädagogik," *Der Baumeister* 12 (1930): 461–99, plates 64–71; Wilhelm Schütte, "Der moderne Volksschulbau;" Fritz Karsen, "Die Dammwegschule Neukölln," *Internationale Zeitschrift für Erziehungswissenschaft* 1 (1931–32): 87–91 (and eight pages of figures).

18 See Gerd Radde, "Fritz Karsen. Ein Berliner Schulreformer der Weimarer Zeit" (Frankfurt am Main: Peter Lang, 1999), 330. The trial classroom building, which was recognized as a historic place worthy of preservation, was reopened in 2001 after being renovated. See Dorothée Sack (ed.), "Der Versuchspavillon der Schule am Dammweg von Bruno Taut in Berlin-Neukölln," *Aufbaustudium Denkmalpflege der TU Berlin* 1 (2000), accessed February 6, 2023, https://tu-berlin.hosted.exlibrisgroup.com/permalink/f/1ljtibe/TUB_ALMA_DS21512103970002884; Ulrich Brinkmann, "Versuchspavillon der Dammwegschule rekonstruiert," *Bauwelt* 13 (2001): 4–5.

19 Margarete Schütte-Lihotzky to Adele Hanakam, Frankfurt am Main, [March 31, 1927], UAUAK, NL MSL n.d./26. The civil wedding ceremony took place in Frankfurt am Main on April 12, 1927.

Löcher's arrangement of the pavilions resembles the one used by Elsaesser and Schütte in their project for Bonames. The school on Bornheimer Hang (Schule am Bornheimer Hang) is deemed the perfect finale to the New Frankfurt era and obviously incorporates a substantial part of the theoretical and practical preparatory work Schütte carried out for the project. He was invited to the opening ceremony as a member of the small group of "city architects participating in the construction" of the school.[26] A short time later, on October 8, 1930, Ernst May and about 20 colleagues, mostly from the Hochbauamt, gathered at Schlesischer Bahnhof (Silesian Station) in Berlin to board a train for Moscow.[27]

As a Specialist with the May Group in the Soviet Union

The group selected by May included both Margarete Schütte-Lihotzky and Wilhelm Schütte, who "prior to his arrival in the USSR [was] already known" as a school specialist.[28] Together with Werner Hebebrand, Schütte won the competition for a "polytechnic station" to develop and test "polytechnic education": a "gigantic school [...] similar to Karsen's but much larger."[29] After an intensive planning phase for standard-type projects, Schütte wrote an article presenting the school center for 4,000 secondary and university students together with a "*Dreikomplexschule*" (a triple-complex school) for 960 secondary students and an "*Einkomplekt-Schule*" (a single-complex school) for 320 secondary students.[30]

The first project Schütte carried out in the Soviet Union was probably the school in Magnitogorsk (1931/32). It forms the backbone of the first *kvartal*, the first grouping of buildings in the new industrial city for which the May Group had drawn up the general development plan. A three-story section of the school stands on the central axis of the *kvartal* and has a two-story classroom wing projecting perpendicularly from it on both sides for a good 150 meters. Schütte designed his standardized school types initially at the Moscow planning trust Standartgorproekt.[31] The type for 960 secondary students was successfully built in Stalinsk in Kuznetsk, as Hebebrand reported after a visit to Siberia at the end of 1933.[32] The school type for 320 secondary students—

20 Ibid. In addition to their work for the Hochbauamt, Wilhelm and Margarete jointly entered competitions such as the "Tuberculosis Hospital in Marburg an der Lahn," the "Elbstrand Hotel in Salesel, Northern Bohemia," and the "Teacher Training College in Kassel," and also undertook private commissions such as "Haus Strasburger" in Frankfurt am Main and "Haus Chabot" in Amsterdam. See *Margarete Schütte-Lihotzky. Soziale Architektur. Zeitzeugin eines Jahrhunderts*, exhibition catalog, MAK—Austrian Museum of Applied Arts, Vienna, ed. Peter Noever (Vienna: Böhlau, 1993), 286.

21 See David Baum, "Wilhelm Schütte – Soziale Architektur" (master's thesis, University of Art and Design Linz, 2016), 54–59.

22 See Claudia Quiring, Thomas Flierl, and David Baum, "Schütte, Wilhelm," in *Akteure des Neuen Frankfurt*, ed. Evelyn Brockhoff (Frankfurt am Main: Societäts-Verlag, 2016), 175–76.

23 See Martin Elsaesser, *Bauten und Entwürfe aus den Jahren 1924–1932, Teil II. Schulen, Kirchen und Schwimmbäder* (Berlin: Bauwelt-Verlag, 1932), 188. Three projects he was no longer able to bring into concrete existence were the vocational and home economics

kept ultra-simple due to the shortage of building materials—had been selected in 1932 for the entire Soviet Union. It is still unknown whether this school type was ever actually built.[33]

In the autumn of 1932, Schütte worked on an exhibition about school construction.[34] There was a plan to present his Magnitogorsk school at an exhibition on Soviet architecture at the Fourth CIAM Congress in Moscow in 1933.[35] In the meantime, Schütte und Schütte-Lihotzky had transferred to OZDiP, the Central Institute for the Protection of the Health of Children and Adolescents, where they created a number of further designs for education buildings.[36]

To Japan to Bruno Taut—To China as a Consultant for School Construction

In the fall of 1933, the Schüttes planned to take a trip to Japan[37] and a side trip from there to China. Chinese specialists consulted with Wilhelm Schütte as a school construction expert,[38] and Bruno and Erika Taut had been in Japan since May of that same year.

Taut had lived and worked for one year in Moscow before that, but probably knew Schütte since the two of them worked with Fritz Karsen in the late 1920s. In early May 1934 he noted: "Everything is very pleasant with the Schüttes. He is making big gains, and we are on pleasant terms, [...] he takes in everything quietly, and there seems to be a good core behind his dry outward manner (34 years old, 'young generation'—F. K. is right)."[39]

During their visit, Taut created his trailblazing portfolio of drawings and gouaches on the Katsura Villa, which he visited with the Schüttes a second time, staying for nearly five hours.[40] In China, "[we] actually [wanted] to stay just one week and return to here [Japan], where the Tauts had already arranged another lovely travel itinerary for us, but a telegram came again today from Nanjing, expressing a fervent desire that we stay longer [...]. We certainly would have preferred to have used the time off to rest in the cultivated atmosphere of Japan with its wonderful landscape, but professionally, the matter with China is naturally a big honor for Wilhelm, and we can't wait to see whether further work will come of it."[41] As Margarete went on to tell her sister, Wilhelm

school for which he had submitted several versions; the planned addition of a kindergarten to complete the Römerstadtschule; and a standard type of school gym he had developed for Frankfurt suburbs.

24 See "Die neue Hindenburgschule," *Frankfurter Zeitung* (August 21, 1930).

25 Albert Löcher was the head of the model-making department, which—like Schütte's school construction department—came under Elsaesser's Department E (individual and large buildings). Visualization using clear models was especially important for the implementation of projects in view of the difficult economic situation.

26 Mag. Akte SchulA 4571, Institute for the History of Frankfurt (ISG).

27 Margarete Schütte-Lihotzky to Adele Hanakam, Gießen, October 6, 1930, UAUAK, NL MSL 1930/10/6.

28 Zeugnis, signed Schurpe, Molkov, Ivanovski (trans. from Russian), Austrian Society of Architecture (ÖGFA), Vienna, Archiv Schütte; original (Moscow, June 4, 1933) and trans. into French: UAUAK, NL MSL, WS 0236/1-2/Q.

29 Margarete Schütte-Lihotzky to Adele Hanakam, Moscow, [end of Jan. 1931], UAUAK, NL MSL n.d./6.

was celebrated at a banquet in Shanghai as "more or less 'the greatest school builder in the world.'"[42] But at the end of June during a short stay with the Tauts in Kyoto on her way home, she reported with disappointment that old China "[is] nothing but a museum (even Beijing despite its huge size), Shanghai and Nanjing [are] ugly, and the modern Chinese [are] soft, lacking in self-initiative." She went on to say that the Chinese would have to build but the state had no money and private individuals did not want to take any risks.[43]

Final Years in Moscow and a Search from Paris for a Place of Exile

Back in Moscow, Schütte was busy planning a club for metallurgists in Novokuznetsk and producing further school designs. This latter work included a joint project with his wife involving two schools for the Ukrainian city of Makiivka (it has not been verified to date whether they were ever built), a project for Kybishev, and a school built in Moscow with a relief by the German sculptor Will Lammert, who had fled to the Soviet Union from France in 1934.[44] As built, it resembles a primary school André Lurçat did in Moscow, which was erected at almost the same time in 1935.[45] In Moscow since 1934, Lurçat published in the Soviet trade press nearly exclusively about school construction, just as Schütte did. He likely discussed pertinent issues on this subject with the Schüttes.[46]

Following the bad experiences their friend Hebebrand had had with the issuing of his new passport by the German embassy in Moscow, the Schüttes decided to leave the country before their passports expired in August 1937. While they were traveling by ship from Odessa to Trieste, Bruno Taut invited them to follow him to the Academy of Fine Arts in Istanbul. "But we wanted to be in more Western climes again and traveled on to Paris to obtain new passports and then, from there to England."[47] They arrived in the French capital while the World's Fair was underway. Wilhelm Schütte worked on a competition for a girls' school in Bagneux near Paris for Pierre Forestier, a pupil of Perret.[48] Margarete Schütte-Lihotzky designed the kindergarten for this school. Tibor Weiner, who was with the group headed by Hannes

30 Wilhelm Schütte, "Schulen des vollen Tages und des runden Jahres – Zum Schulbau in Russland," *Wasmuths Monatshefte für Baukunst und Städtebau* 6 (1932). 282–84.

31 See Thomas Flierl, "Wilhelm Schütte als Schulbauexperte in der Sowjetunion," in ÖGFA and Waditschatka, *Schütte*, 24–47.

32 Margarete Schütte-Lihotzky to Adele and Josef Hanakam, Moscow, December 19, 1933, UAUAK, NL MSL 1933/3/19.

33 See Schütte, "Schulen des vollen Tages," 284.

34 Margarete Schütte-Lihotzky to Adele Hanakam, Moscow, October 31, 1932, UAUAK, NL MSL 1932/10/12.

35 See Flierl, "Schütte als Schulbauexperte," 33.

36 Ibid., 33–41.

37 Margarete Schütte-Lihotzky to Adele Hanakam, Moscow, October 30, 1933, UAUAK, NL MSL 1933/10/30

38 See Chup Friemert's interview with Margarete Schütte-Lihotzky, in Schütte-Lihotzky, *Erinnerungen* (1985), 34.

39 See Manfred Speidel (ed.), *Bruno Taut in Japan. Das Tagebuch. Zweiter Band 1934* (Berlin:

Meyer in Moscow, also participated. Beyond that, Schütte planned—presumably with Forestier—the conversion of a "manor and forts into a preventorium,"[49] but overall, contracts remained few and far between. After repeated invitations from Taut, the Schüttes finally submitted their applications to the Turkish Ministry of Culture in mid-March 1938:[50] "Despite this offer [and the application submitted on receiving it] we continued on our way to London to look for work there."[51] But it became increasingly hopeless to find work in London, even more so than in Paris.

In Tatbikat Bürosu Working for Taut

Wilhelm and Margarete Schütte arrived in Istanbul on August 24, 1938, with favorably negotiated employment contracts in hand. Right after arriving, the two began working in the Ministry of Education's building office that Taut ran at the Academy of Fine Arts in Istanbul.[52] Initially, this work consisted of the "preparation of systematic solutions for school construction for the Turkish Ministry of Culture," and of excursions "in Istanbul and in Ankara and environs."[53]

In what was possibly a revision of a preliminary project by Taut,[54] the Schüttes designed a temporary building as decoration for the Karaköy bridgehead of the Galata Bridge in Istanbul to mark the 15th anniversary of the founding of the Turkish Republic.[55] After Atatürk's death in November, Schütte designed a "Decoration for TAXIM Square to mark November 20, 1938" as part of the leader's funeral service. It is unknown whether the design was ever implemented.[56] On November 15, Taut was in bed severely ill when he completed his last sketch for the burial in Ankara: his design of the catafalque.[57]

Hamam Önü Middle School in Ankara-Cebeci had been in the works by Taut and his colleague Hillinger since May 1938. Starting in October 1938, both Schüttes joined this project.[58] At the same time, Schütte began planning a higher-level teacher training school in Istanbul. He then drew up school construction programs and in 1939 finalized the project for a middle school for Ankara-Yenişehir[59] as a further development of his standard type of open-air classrooms in Frankfurt and as a follow-up to his projects for Makiivka and Bagneux. His

Gebr. Mann, 2015), 134. By F. K., Taut obviously means Fritz Karsen.

40 Ibid., 135–36.

41 Margarete Schütte-Lihotzky to Adele Hanakam, Nara, May 15, 1934, UAUAK, NL MSL 1934/5/15.

42 Margarete Schütte-Lihotzky to Adele Hanakam, Nanjing, May 29, 1934, UAUAK, NL MSL 1934/5/29.

43 See Speidel, *Taut in Japan. Zweiter Band*, 166.

44 See Baum, "Schütte – Soziale Architektur," 160–71 and 178–81.

45 See Jean-Louis Cohen, *André Lurçat, 1894–1970. Autocritique d'un moderne* (Liège: Mardaga, 1995), 196–98.

46 Ibid., 205.

47 See typescript, UAUAK, NL MSL, TXT/418, 20. Also see Schütte-Lihotzky, *Erinnerungen* (1985), 48.

48 The submission deadline was April 16, 1938. See *L'Architecture d'aujourd'hui* 2 (February 1938): 80.

49 Letter of application "An das Kulturministerium Ankara," March 18, 1938, ÖGFA, Archiv Schütte.

50 See Schütte-Lihotzky, "Ansprache für Istanbul."

51 See Schütte-Lihotzky, *Erinnerungen* (1985), 48.

"Changes to the Theater Project for Ankara,"[60] dated end of April 1940, might be the successor project to an opera house project on which Taut had been working.[61] As a private commission, Margarete and Wilhelm Schütte designed a villa in Ankara for Lütfi Tozan in August 1940.[62] At the beginning of July 1939, the couple attended the International Congress for Housing and Town Planning in Stockholm, where they also paid a visit to Josef Frank.[63] Astoundingly, they opted for the route via Berlin, as a Vienna residence registration form shows.[64] A year and a half later during another stay in Vienna, Margarete Schütte-Lihotzky was arrested by the Gestapo in Café Victoria am Schottentor.[65]

Teaching at the Academy of Fine Arts in Istanbul

The focus of Wilhelm Schütte's work at the Academy of Fine Arts in Istanbul gradually shifted from the building office to teaching. In December 1939, he was hired as a teacher.[66] Along with his lectures, he taught perspective and made preparations for creating a collection of building materials. This work was likely in connection with studies on rebuilding a region in Anatolia that had been devastated by a serious earthquake at the end of 1939.[67] Besides prefabricated elements to ensure stability, preference was given to the use of building materials available in the area. He held his lectures as a member of the decoration department, which had been headed by the French designer and decorator Louis Süe since 1939.[68] Besides Süe, Rector Burhan Toprak appointed another Frenchman, Henri Prost, as a professor for urban planning in 1941;[69] André Lurçat had been considered as a possible successor to Taut in 1939.[70] From March 1941 on, Schütte taught as a design lecturer and in 1942 was appointed professor for architectural design.[71] He wrote numerous articles for the trade journal *Arkitekt*.[72] In late 1943, he published a proposal in *Der Baumeister* based on a resource-saving study for earthquake-prone regions. It was likely not intended as support for the Third Reich, but rather addressed to decision-makers to remind them that his wife, then imprisoned in Germany, had expertise in the rationalization of housing construction.[73]

52 See Burcu Dogramaci, "Architekt, Lehrer, Autor. Wilhelm Schütte in der Türkei (1938–1946)," in ÖGFA and Waditschatka, *Schütte*, 40–66, here 49–50.

53 Schütte-Lihotzky, "Ansprache für Istanbul."

54 See Maasberg and Prinz, "Verzeichnis," 392, and Dogramaci, *Schütte in der Türkei*, 51.

55 See Margarete Schütte-Lihotzky, *Soziale Architektur*, 173. Also see Burcu Dogramaci's essay in this volume.

56 Wilhelm Schütte, "Bericht über die Tätigkeit von Architekt W. Schütte im 'Tatbikatbürosu' von Güzel Sanatlar Akademisi Istanbul von September 1938 bis September 1939," ÖGFA, Archiv Schütte. Also see Dogramaci, *Schütte in der Türkei*, 52.

57 See Maasberg and Prinz, "Verzeichnis," 395.

58 Ibid., 393.

59 See Schütte, "Bericht über die Tätigkeit."

60 "Juni 1940. Bericht über die Arbeiten von Architekt Schütte," ÖGFA, Archiv Schütte.

61 See Bernd Nicolai, *Moderne und Exil. Deutschsprachige Architekten in der Türkei 1925–1955* (Berlin: Verlag für Bauwesen, 1998), 146–47,

Internment 1944 to 1946

When the Turkish Republic ended its neutrality in World War II in August 1944, German citizens were expelled from the country. Emigrés threatened with persecution were granted protection but were obligated to live in an Anatolian city assigned to them. In the case of Wilhelm Schütte, the city was Yozgat,[74] where he would spend nearly two years. He started a public library, which was made available to the internees in particular, and planned an addition to the local secondary school.[75] While most internees were able to return to their Turkish places of residence at the end of 1945,[76]

Fig. 2. Margarete Schütte-Lihotzky and Wilhelm Schütte in Sofia, November 1946.

and Maasberg and Prinz, "Verzeichnis," 391.

62 See Baum, "Schütte – Soziale Architektur," 204–5.

63 See Schütte-Lihotzky, *Warum ich Architektin wurde*, 77. This was the 17th International Congress for Housing and Town Planning, July 8–15, 1939.

64 "Moved out on: July 5, 1939 to (place, district, street no.): Berlin—Stockholm," Meldezettel für Unterparteien, July 3–6, 1939, Wiener Stadt- und Landesarchiv (WstLA), Akt 2.5.1.4.K11.Schuette-Lihotzky Margarethe. 23.1.1897.

65 See Schütte-Lihotzky, *Erinnerungen* (1985), 73, and Elisabeth Boeckl-Klamper's essay in this volume.

66 See Dogramaci, *Schütte in der Türkei*, 56.

67 See "Juni 1940. Bericht über die Arbeiten von Architekt Schütte," ÖGFA, Archiv Schütte.

68 See Joanna Banham (ed.), *Encyclopedia of Interior Design* (London: Routledge, 2015), 1253–55.

69 Ataman Demir, *Arşivdeki belgeler ışığında Güzel Sanatlar Akademisi'nde yabancı hocalar: Philipp Ginther'den (1929)–(1958) Kurt Erdmann'a kadar* (Istanbul: Mimar Sinan Güzel Sanatlar Üniversitesi, 2008), 14.

70 See Cohen, *André Lurçat*, 214.

71 Vertrag vom 13.3.1941, UAUAK, NL MSL, WS 0247/1-3/Q, Vertrag vom 20.2.1942, reproduced in Demir, *Arşivdeki belgeler*, 311–12.

72 See Baum, "Schütte – Soziale Architektur," 349–50.

73 Wilhelm Schütte, "Von der Notunterkunft zur vollwertigen Wohnung," *Der Baumeister* (Oct.–Dec. 1943): B124–B126.

74 Wilhelm Schütte, in Yozgat at the time, July 26, 1945 (date added by hand), typescript, ÖGFA, Archiv Schütte.

75 Mayor Sadri Aka to Wilhelm Schütte, Yozgat, 1944, UAUAK, NL MSL, WS 0257/Q. Also see Dogramaci, *Schütte in der Türkei*, 61.

76 See Burcu Dogramaci, *Kulturtransfer und nationale Identıtat. Deutschsprachige Architekten, Stadtplaner und Bildhauer in der Türkei nach 1927* (Berlin: Gebr. Mann, 2008), 36.

77 See Dogramaci, *Schütte in der Türkei*, 61.

78 See Schütte-Lihotzky, *Erinnerungen* (1985), 37–38.

79 Stamp on entry to Bruckneudorf on December 31, 1946, Bulgarian

Schütte had to wait until June 1946 for his release.[77] His wife, now free from prison, had traveled from Vienna to meet him partway and had been staying in Sofia since February. It was there that the two of them met again in October of that same year, after nearly six years of separation[78] (fig. 2). From Sofia, they traveled to Vienna via Belgrade and Budapest, arriving at the turn of the year 1946/47.[79]

Initial Work in Vienna and the CIAM Working Group

Probably one of the first work tasks of Schütte and his wife involved their participation in *Wien baut auf* (Vienna builds), an exhibition staged at the City Hall from September to December 1947.[80] On July 7, 1947, he obtained Austrian citizenship.[81] A short time later, the Schüttes took part in the first postwar congress of the CIAM in the English town of Bridgwater. In preparation for the event, Sigfried Giedion had invited Schütte-Lihotzky to Zurich "because every connection to Austria has been broken off for a long time."[82] In collaboration with Fritz Cremer, professor of the sculpting class at the Academy of Applied Arts in Vienna (now University of Applied Arts Vienna) from 1946 to 1950, Schütte designed a memorial for the victims of Fascism (1947–48) for the City of Vienna. It was unveiled in November 1948.

The City of Vienna and the building owners announced a competition in 1948 for redesigning Stephansplatz (St. Stephen's Square) in Vienna. No major urban planning project was likely to be implemented, so Oswald Haerdtl, Wilhelm Schütte, and Karl Schwanzer joined together to form a team, which was thus made up of the leading minds of the new CIAM Austria. The latter was founded on May 11, 1948—Le Corbusier, André Lurçat, and Marcel Lods were all staying in Vienna at the time.[83]

In an initial version of the Stephansplatz project, the "Arbeitsgruppe CIAM" (CIAM working group) went beyond the announced scope of the competition. They envisaged the west side of the square being formed by a continuous facade built over the side streets joining the square. Across from the cathedral portal was to be a lancet arch entrance to a large courtyard modeled on the Galleria Vittorio Emanuele II in Milan. The project was further developed under the aegis of

Schütte for CIAM 7 in Bergamo at the end of July 1949 and was presented there.[84] It would be the final CIAM congress in which Margarete Schütte-Lihotzky also took part.[85]

Exhibitions and Activities Arranged by Schütte as the First Delegate of CIAM Austria

In the early years of CIAM Austria, Wilhelm Schütte sought to bring exhibitions to Austria, including the *Schweizerische Architekturausstellung* (Swiss architecture exhibition)[86] and *Neues Wohnen. Deutsche Architektur seit 1945* (New dwelling. German architecture since 1945).[87] Encouraged by Josef Frank, he contacted Svenska Slöjdföreningen (now Svensk Form) in Stockholm in 1948, asking whether they could put together materials for an exhibition in Vienna.[88] In February 1949, *Französische Baukunst* (French architecture), an exhibition he had arranged, was opened at the technical university in Graz "with an associated show featuring French posters," which can also be traced to a proposal of his.[89]

At the same time, Schütte advocated sending young colleagues abroad—for instance, Othmar Egger, who took part in the CIAM Summer School in London in 1949.[90] In June 1952, Schütte was accompanied to the CIAM meeting in Sigtuna by the Graz professor Karl Raimund Lorenz.[91] The event was co-organized by Fred Forbat, a colleague with whom the Schüttes had shared an apartment in Moscow and who had emigrated to Sweden, where Schütte saw again him "after such a long time."[92] At CIAM 9 in Aix-en-Provence in 1953, by contrast, "the next generation of architects [were to be] more strongly represented."[93] The individuals from Vienna who were registered were Karl Bayer, Monika Euler, Fred Freyler, Gustav Peichl, Hugo Potyka, Herbert Prehsler, Sepp Stein, and Erich Sulka, all accompanied by Eduard Sekler.[94] The "Jugendgruppe Graz" (Graz youth group) consisted of the later renowned team of Fritz Eller, Erich Moser, and Robert Walter, accompanied by Wilhelm Aduatz, Rambald von Steinbüchel-Rheinwall,[95] and Karl R. Lorenz.[96] The CIAM work meeting in La Sarraz in September 1955 had three registered teams who were preparing their projects: the "blaue Gruppe"[97] (blue group; group from TH Wien, today's TU Wien) and the "ABC" group, represented by Herbert

identity card, issued November 19, 1946, UAUAK, NL MSL, WS 0232/Q.

80 "An den Magistrat der Stadt Wien" (application for naturalization, concept), typescript, UAUAK, NL MSL, WS 0203/1/Q. His involvement in the exhibition *Wien 1848*, also in Vienna City Hall, is provided as evidence. Margarete Schütte-Lihotzky and Wilhelm Schütte to Viktor Matejka, Vienna, December 24, 1947, UAUAK, NL MSL, PRNR 154.

81 "Urkunde über die Verleihung der Staatsbürgerschaft," typescript, UAUAK, NL MSL, WS 0220/Q.

82 Sigfried Giedion to Margarete Schütte-Lihotzky, Zurich, April 29, 1947, ÖGFA, Archive, Mappe 28.

83 It is not correct that Roland Rainer was a founding member (Schütte-Lihotzky, *Warum ich Architektin wurde*, 189). See "Mitgliedsliste," April 1952, typescript, ÖGFA, Archive, Mappe 28.

84 See Oswald Haerdtl, "Die Architektur von Heute und die Tendenzen der angewandten Kunst," presentation, Vienna, May 16, 1950, in Adolph Stiller, *Oswald Haerdtl. Architekt und Designer. 1899–1959* (Salzburg: Anton Pustet, 2000), 174–83, here 179.

85 Schütte-Lihotzky, *Warum ich Architektin wurde*, 189.

86 See Wilhelm Schütte to Sigfried Giedion, Vienna, June 6, 1948, ÖGFA, Archive, Mappe 28.

87 See Alfons Leitl to Wilhelm Schütte, Rheydt, June 18, 1949, ibid.

88 Wilhelm Schütte to Svenska Slöjdförenigingen, Vienna, June 11, 1948, ibid.

89 Wilhelm Schütte to Friedrich Zotter, Vienna, December 16, 1948, ibid.

90 Othmar Egger to Wilhelm Schütte, Graz, September 27, 1949; also see Wilhelm Schütte to Sigfried Giedion, Vienna, January 8, 1950, ibid.

91 Georg Plankensteiner, "Univ.-Prof. Arch. Dipl.-Ing. Karl Raimund Lorenz (1909–1996). Leben und Wirken einer Architekten- und Lehrerpersönlichkeit" (doctoral dissertation, TU Graz, 2001), 238.

92 Wilhelm Schütte to Fred Forbat, Vienna, March 20, 1952, typescript/copy, ÖGFA, Archive, Mappe 28.

93 Circular from Wilhelm Schütte to Fellerer, Wörle, Wachberger, Thurner, Legler, Auböck, and Schlesinger, around May/June 1953, ibid.

94 Eduard Sekler to Wilhelm Schütte, Vienna, May 22, 1953, ibid.

95 Friedrich Zotter to Wilhelm Schütte, Graz, February 24, 1953, ibid.

Prader and Fred Freyler respectively, and the "arbeitsgruppe 4."[98] Schütte addressed the chair of CIAM Switzerland, Alfred Roth, asking "whether it would be possible to maybe bring along one or two of the highly ambitious younger architects to La Sarraz." What he meant was whether all members of arbeitsgruppe 4 could participate—in other words, Holzbauer, Kurrent, and Spalt.[99]

Gemeindebauten

Together, Margarete Schütte-Lihotzky and Wilhelm Schütte built a multistory municipal apartment complex (*Gemeindebau*) on Barthgasse in Landstrasse, Vienna's third district, in 1949/50. The planned color scheme—rust red facade, gray base, and dark blue window frames—is preserved in a color study but was never carried out.[100] This color scheme is unusual for buildings in Vienna and points to the Pompeii red favored by Ernst May—for instance, in the Römerstadt Settlement in Frankfurt—and to the blue used there for the window frames.[101] Another apartment complex was erected in 1953/54 on Ebner-Rofenstein-Gasse in Vienna in a non-densely built area on former meadowland in Lainz close to the Werkbundsiedlung. It consists of seven plain two-story buildings arranged on a property that extends lengthwise. The third housing contract for the City of Vienna and also the last that Wilhelm Schütte was able to carry out is a housing complex on the outskirts of the city on Neuwaldegger Strasse in Hernals, Vienna's 17th district, consisting of two rows of three-story structures (1965–67). The glazed staircases lend structure to the street facade and to the entrance side of the courtyard wing; the entrance areas are additionally set off by abstract mosaics.[102]

Temporary Buildings and Memorials

From 1948 to 1953, Margarete Schütte-Lihotzky and Wilhelm Schütte helped to plan the festivals organized by the *Volksstimme*, the daily newspaper of the Communist Party of Austria (KPÖ).[103] They have taken place every year since 1946 in the Prater Park in Vienna: first in the Prater stadium and then from 1947 on, in the open air on the Jesuitenwiese meadow due to the large crowds and from 1949 on, also on the Arenawiese meadow.[104] For instance, the Schüttes designed a pavilion on the Jesuitenwiese in 1948 for an exhibition celebrating 30 years of Communist literature and the Communist press. It featured materials from the Resistance fight, among other items. A comparable task was the design of the festival rostrum for the Pentecost youth meeting of the Communist Free Youth (KJÖ) in front of Parliament in 1951.[105] The organizer expected 50,000 visitors from all federal provinces. To kick off the event, groups of artists performed along the Ringstrasse, from Stalinplatz (now Schwarzenbergplatz), where the memorial to the Red Army still stands today, all the way to Parliament.[106] In front of Parliament was a rostrum, which Wilhelm Schütte had designed to resemble a huge triumphal arch and which bore a banner with the words "Peace and Freedom."

Schütte collaborated in 1947/48 with the sculptor Fritz Cremer on the Memorial for the Victims of Fascism at the Central Cemetery in Vienna. In 1949/50, the two of them planned the French memorial at Mauthausen together with André Bruyère. Schütte designed the memorial stones for the former branch camps of Melk, Hartheim, Ebensee, and Gusen, the Gusen Memorial Site, and the overall concept for the Memorial Park at Mauthausen. He supervised construction of the Polish and presumably the Soviet, Italian, and Spanish memorials and designed the *Weiheraum* memorial in the former execution room at the Regional Court for Criminal Matters in Vienna.[107]

Publisher's Buildings and Bookstores

From 1949 on, the Schüttes jointly planned the adaptation of a former factory premises for the publisher Grazer Volksverlag.[108] The alterations and extensions were completed in 1955, creating Volkshaus Graz, which would serve as the headquarters of the KPÖ of Styria and Graz and other organizations, as well as the regional center for the party's political and cultural life.[109] Wilhelm Schütte teamed up with Margarete Schütte-Lihotzky, Fritz Weber, and Karl Eder to build the "Globus" printing and publishing building for the KPÖ at Höchstädtplatz in Brigittenau, Vienna's 20th district, from 1954 to 1956. It consists of the eight-story office wing

96 Karl Raimund Lorenz to Wilhelm Schütte, Graz, July 11, 1953, ibid.

97 See Maja Lorbek, "CIAM Austria. Eine chronologische Spurensuche," in *Moderat Modern. Erich Boltenstern und die Baukultur nach 1945*, ed. Judith Eiblmayr and Iris Meder, exhibition catalog, Wien Museum (Salzburg: Anton Pustet, 2005), 137–43, here 143; see also Monika Platzer, *Cold War and Architecture. The Competing Forces That Reshaped Austria after 1945* (Zurich: Park Books, 2020), 260–67.

98 See Baum, "Schütte als Vermittler," 76–77; see also Ute Waditschatka, "Im Vordergrund das Bauen, Teil 1: Zur Werkgeschichte der arbeitsgruppe 4," in *arbeitsgruppe 4. Wilhelm Holzbauer, Friedrich Kurrent, Johannes Spalt. 1950–1970*, ed. Architekturzentrum Wien (Salzburg: Müry Salzmann, 2010), 20–77, here 51.

99 Wilhelm Schütte to Alfred Roth, Vienna, August 3, 1955, ÖGFA, Archive, Mappe 28.

100 See Margarete Schütte-Lihotzky, *Soziale Architektur*, 209.

101 See Christoph Mohr, "Das Neue Frankfurt und die Farbe," *Bauwelt* 28 (1986): 1059–61.

102 Three mosaics each by Fritz Riedl and Robert Pick (1966–67); see

Fig. 3. Margarete Schütte-Lihotzky at the Wilhelm Schütte memorial exhibition staged by the Austrian Society of Architecture in Vienna, November 1968.

and the printing building with its striking shed roof as well as the four-story personnel wing featuring the large hall later named for Margarete Schütte-Lihotzky, and the wing containing the rotary presses for printing newspapers.[110]

In Vienna, the Globus-Verlag publishing house operated five bookstores, where customers could acquire leftist and Socialist literature that "could not be sold [through normal distribution channels] because of the boycott."[111] Wilhelm Schütte remodeled the Zentralbuchhandlung (central book store) in 1957 and 1961.[112] He also planned and carried out the modification of the business facade for the Arbeiterbuchhandlung (workers' bookstore) on Laxenburger Strasse in Favoriten, Vienna's 10th district. It has strong similarities to the plans that Margarete Schütte-Lihotzky envisaged in 1952 but only partially implemented.[113] Another bookstore planned by Wilhelm Schütte for the KPÖ publishing house was the Volksbuchhandlung (people's bookstore) in the center of Graz (1964).[114]

Wiener Wohnen, description of housing complex at Neuwaldegger Strasse 3, accessed August 8, 2022, https://www.wienerwohnen.at/hof/1077/1077.html.

103 See Baum, "Schütte – Soziale Architektur," 250–53.

104 See Ilse Grusch, *Das Volksstimmefest. Geschichte eines Wiener Volksfestes* (master's thesis, University of Vienna, 2000), 27–36.

105 Pentecost youth meeting, May 12–14, 1951. The festivities at the Eislaufverein ice rink were designed by Schütte-Lihotzky (a "festival of 150,000" remains unspecified); see Margarete Schütte-Lihotzky, *Soziale Architektur*, 290, no. 176.

106 "Das Programm des Jugendtreffens der 50.000 für Frieden und Freiheit," 1951, Zentrales Parteiarchiv der KPÖ, Vienna.

107 See Baum, "Schütte – Soziale Architektur," 244–49, 258–61, 310–13, 328–31, and Andreas Vass, "Zwischen Dekor und Gedenken. Versuch zur politischen Rhetorik der Architektur von Wilhelm Schütte," in ÖGFA and Waditschatka, *Schütte*, 110–29.

108 See Baum, "Schütte – Soziale Architektur," 266–69.

109 See Friedrich

Floridsdorf Open-Air School and "Building Schools"

Lighting classrooms from two different sides is a principle that Schütte had developed early on. He actually implemented this principle and the connection of classrooms to the outdoors from 1959 to 1961 with his open-air school in Floridsdorf, Vienna's 21st district.[115] Although he was well known as an expert, Schütte was kept from carrying out projects for years because of his political convictions, but here he was finally able to turn his ideas into reality. The school conforms to concepts that he had been developing together with educators since the 1920s and that were now applied to trailblazing school buildings. The design is a consistent continuation of the principle of the open-air classrooms for pavilion-style schools in Frankfurt am Main and resembles his plans for schools in Makiivka in 1934, Bagneux in 1938, and Ankara-Yenişehir in 1939.

In October 1966, the Zentralvereinigung der Architekten Österreichs (Central association of Austrian architects, ZV) staged an exhibition at the Bauzentrum in Palais Lichtenstein entitled *Schulen bauen* (Building schools). Although it was put together by a team,[116] Wilhelm Schütte was considered the guiding spirit of the enterprise. Part of the exhibition was devoted to plans for standard types of primary and lower secondary schools in accordance with UNESCO guidelines.[117] In another project for the Austrian UNESCO Commission, Schütte teamed up with Lukas Lang, Peter Czernin, Georg Bachmayr-Heyda, and Karl Fostel (Sonett company) to develop a series of school furniture: tables and chairs made of flat tubular steel and parts shaped from compreg. Friedrich Kurrent remembers that Schütte overexerted himself working on this school building exhibition.[118] Two days prior to the opening, he suffered a heart attack—"working was no longer conceivable."[119] In the short time he had left, Wilhelm Schütte joined Lukas Lang in attending the Ninth Congress of the International Union of Architects (UIA) in Prague in 1967 as representatives of the School Construction Commission of the Austrian Section.[120] Schütte, his friend Fritz Weber, and Lang traveled to Dresden in October 1967 at the invitation of Helmut Trauzettel[121] in order to present and discuss the exhibition materials.[122] After a

Achleitner, *Österreichische Architektur im 20. Jahrhundert, Bd. II: Kärnten/Steiermark/Burgenland, Salzburg/Wien* (Salzburg: Residenz, 1983), 347.

110 On the history and establishment of Globus, see Christina Köstner, "Wie das Salz in der Suppe. Zur Geschichte eines kommunistischen Verlages. Der Globus Verlag" (master's thesis, University of Vienna, 2001), and Fritz Weber, *Mosaiksteine meines Weltbildes* (Vienna: Globus, 1991). Also see Gabriele Kaiser, "'Wir legen den Grundstein für das Haus der Wahrheit.' Der Neubau der Globus Zeitungs-, Druck- und Verlagsanstalt (1954–1956)," in ÖGFA and Waditschatka, *Schütte*, 138–51.

111 "Die Buchhandlungen," in Köstner, "Salz in der Suppe," 74–81.

112 See Friedrich Achleitner, *Österreichische Architektur im 20. Jahrhundert, Bd. III/1: Wien 1.–12. Bezirk* (Salzburg: Residenz, 1983), 70.

113 See Baum, "Schütte – Soziale Architektur," 324–27.

114 With the exception of the former central bookstore, which has now changed, the bookstores mentioned no longer exist.

decline in his state of health and an associated hospital stay, Wilhelm Schütte died on April 17, 1968 as a result of a second heart attack. In November of that same year, the Austrian Society of Architecture (Österreichische Gesellschaft für Architektur, ÖGFA) staged a memorial exhibition on the life and work of Wilhelm Schütte (fig. 3). Along with parts of his estate, he had bequeathed shares of stock to the society to enable one to three young architects each year to broaden their horizons: "Study tours must go to the countries in the East! Peace!"[123]

115 See Wilhelm Schütte, "Das Schulzimmer und seine natürliche Belichtung," *Bauen+ Wohnen* 6, no. 4 (1952): 184–87; see also Wilhelm Schütte, "Sonderschule Wien 1961," *Schul- und Sportstättenbau* 1 (1966): 29–31.

116 Peter Czernin, Lukas Lang, Wilhelm Schütte, Franz Schuster, Anton Schweighofer, Herbert Thurner, Robert Weinlich.

117 See Lukas Lang, "Schulen bauen," *Der Aufbau* 11/12 (1966): 387; also see Maja Lorbek, "Schulen bauen als rationelle Programmatik und internationale Expertise," in *Schütte*, ÖGFA and Waditschatka, 152–63.

118 See Ute Waditschatka and David Baum's interview with Friedrich Kurrent, Vienna, May 12, 2018, author's private archive.

119 Schütte-Lihotzky, "Ansprache für Istanbul."

120 See Ute Waditschatka and David Baum's interview with Lukas Lang, Altmünster am Traunsee, May 17, 2018, author's private archive; see "Bericht der Österreichischen Sektion der UIA über den IX. Kongress der UIA Prag 1967," UAUAK, NL MSL, WS 0197/Q.

121 Helmut Trauzettel (1927–2003), GDR school construction expert, 1964–89 member of the UIA group for school and cultural buildings, from 1966 professor of residential and social buildings at TU Dresden; see Luise Helas, "Die Nachkriegsmoderne in Dresden," in *Dresden und seine Architekten. Strömungen und Tendenzen 1900–1970,* Bernhard Sterra et al. (Husum: Verlag der Kunst Dresden, 2011), 137–58, here 147.

122 See Fritz Weber, "Wilhelm Schütte," in *Wilhelm Schütte. 1900–1968, Gedächtnisausstellung der Österreichischen Gesellschaft für Architektur in der Zeit vom 9.–27.11.1968* (Vienna: ÖGFA, 1968). Also see Fritz Weber, "Wilhelm Schütte – ein Nachruf," in *Schütte*, ÖGFA and Waditschatka, 92–95, here 94.

123 Legate im Todesfalle, ÖGFA, Archiv Schütte.

The Political
Margarete Schütte-Lihotzky

"Followed a False Ideology till Her Dying Day." Margarete Schütte-Lihotzky as a Communist Intellectual

Marcel Bois

In early summer 2000, a heated debate arose in the Römer, the city hall of Frankfurt am Main and the seat of its city council. The chair of the Green group in the council called a politician from the Christian Democratic Union of Germany (CDU) a "Cold Warrior." The group chair of the Social Democratic Party of Germany (SPD) responded by equating the position of the CDU with US Senator Joseph McCarthy's witch hunt on Communists in 1950s America.[1] Various other public representatives who appeared in the press on the days following the incident also expressed indignation about the Christian Democrats: the director of the Städelschule responded to the discussion "with dismay" while a member of the urban development advisory committee distanced himself from the "slander" of the CDU.[2]

The controversy arose because of a motion filed by the Social Democrats to name a street after the architect Margarete Schütte-Lihotzky. Schütte-Lihotzky, who had died in January 2000 shortly before her 103rd birthday, had

1 "Wie kommunistisch darf eine Einbauküche sein?," *Frankfurter Neue Presse (FNP)* (June 7, 2000).

2 Kasper König, "Die Küche, die alte Dame und die Politik," *FNP* (June 9, 2000).

lived and worked in Frankfurt in the second half of the 1920s. The director of the Stadtbauamt (municipal building authority) at the time, Ernst May, had brought her to the city, where she would soon create her best-known work: the Frankfurt Kitchen, a precursor to the modern built-in kitchen. It would be installed in 10,000 apartments in New Frankfurt.

The Social Democrats wanted to honor her service to social housing construction in the city. The CDU rejected the initiative, however, as did the far-right-wing Republicans. As justification, the CDU said that Schütte-Lihotzky had been a member of the Communist Party of Austria (KPÖ) and a "professed Stalinist" since 1939. The chair of the CDU group in the council, Karlheinz Bührmann, declared that the architect had "followed a false ideology till her dying day." The CDU city councillor Thomas Rätzke chimed in, noting that Schütte-Lihotzky had been "enthusiastic about Stalin."[3]

Despite all the polemics, things soon calmed down. The initiative passed by a majority vote, whereupon a public park was finally named after her in the Praunheim district of the city in January 2001.[4] All the same, the course of events was remarkable because it points out that Schütte-Lihotzky was

3 CDU, "Schütte-Lihotzky als 'Stalinistin' untragbar," *Frankfurter Rundschau* (June 7, 2000); "Wie kommunistisch darf eine Einbauküche sein?," *FNP* (June 7, 2000).

4 "Grünanlage nach Schütte-Lihotzky benannt," *Frankfurter Allgemeine Zeitung* (January 4, 2001).

Fig. 1. Margarete Schütte-Lihotzky speaking at a peace demonstration in Vienna on June 9, 1961.

not only a well-known architect but also a person active and interested in politics. She did in fact belong to the Communist Party for more than 60 years and served for more than two decades as chair of the KPÖ-affiliated League of Democratic Women of Austria (Bund demokratischer Frauen Österreichs, BDFÖ). Furthermore, she staged exhibitions for the Austrian Peace Council (Österreichischer Friedensrat), worked on the board of the KZ-Verband (National Association of Austrian Resistance Fighters and Victims of Fascism), and was on the board of the Austrian Committee for European Security and Cooperation. Schütte-Lihotzky regularly used her prominence to solicit support for the Communist movement. She not only signed election appeals but also took part in numerous conferences in Austria and abroad, gave speeches, and wrote articles on political topics. Thanks in no small part to a short book she published in 1985, the public paid special attention to her Resistance work against the National Socialists, which had landed her in prison for more than four years. The book has gone through several editions in the meantime and served as the basis for a feature film.[5] In her final decades, she presented herself increasingly as a contemporary witness

Fig. 2. Margarete Schütte-Lihotzky giving a speech at a demonstration against nuclear armament and war, Vienna, 1961.

5 The 2014 edition is always cited below: Margarete Schütte-Lihotzky, *Erinnerungen aus dem Widerstand. Das kämpferische Leben einer Architektin von 1938–1945*, with a foreword by Elisabeth Holzinger (Vienna: Promedia, 2014). The feature film was entitled *Eine Minute Dunkelheit macht uns nicht blind* (1986) and was directed by Susanne Zanke.

6 Elisabeth Holzinger, "Widerstand in Zeiten des Terrors," in Schütte-Lihotzky, *Erinnerungen*, 7–20, here 19.

7 In addition to the author's works, mention should be made here of, for example, *Margarete Schütte-Lihotzky. Spuren in Wien*, ed. Christine Zwingl (Vienna: Promedia, 2021); Thomas Flierl, "Mit einem Karton voller Briefe auf Zeitreise," in *Mach den Weg um Prinkipo, meine Gedanken werden Dich begleiten! Der Gefängnis-Briefwechsel 1941–1945*, Margarete Schütte-Lihotzky and Wilhelm Schütte, ed. Thomas Flierl (Berlin: Lukas Verlag, 2021), 409–576.

to the Nazi terror. Although she wrote no texts on political theory, she regularly stated her position on current social issues. In view of these activities, this creative artist can undoubtedly be called a Communist intellectual.

This role of Schütte-Lihotzky has been little researched to date. Elisabeth Holzinger noted several years ago that "Margarete Schütte-Lihotzky may be well known as an architect in the meantime but too little is known about her as a political person."[6] Her political engagement has been mentioned regularly in scholarly studies and biographical summaries, but individual aspects of it have not been subject to closer examination until recent years.[7] Unlike her architectural work, this side of her life has not yet been systematically analyzed and interpreted. Conversely, Schütte-Lihotzky also remains unmentioned in works about Communist intellectuals, for instance in Thomas Kroll's comparative study of actors from France, Italy, Great Britain, and Austria in the initial decades after the war. Schütte-Lihotzky does not come up there even though Kroll examined the lives of 91 prominent KPÖ members from Austria for this book.[8] Nor was she mentioned in Doris Danzer's study on German-speaking Communist intellectuals.[9] For this reason, an attempt will be made here to analyze Schütte-Lihotzky's lifelong political engagement and to put it in a historical context.

This essay sets out to answer a number of questions in this regard: How did Schütte-Lihotzky become politicized; how did she make her way to Communism? How did her views change? What contemporary social developments and what biographical experiences played a role in this process? Who influenced her? What issues were important to her? At what points was her political development typical, at what points less so?

This analysis will build on Kroll and Danzer. Both of them distanced themselves in their studies from earlier research that had interpreted the political engagement of Communist intellectuals as an irrational position and as a blindness of their own making.[10] In contrast to the polemics of the Cold War, which considered the intellectuals to be mere puppets of Moscow, the two authors tried to take these individuals' views seriously and to explain their conversion

8 Thomas Kroll, *Kommunistische Intellektuelle in Westeuropa. Frankreich, Österreich, Italien und Großbritannien im Vergleich (1945–1956)* (Cologne: Böhlau, 2007).

9 Doris Danzer, *Zwischen Vertrauen und Verrat. Deutschsprachige kommunistische Intellektuelle und ihre sozialen Beziehungen (1918–1960)* (Göttingen: V&R Unipress, 2012).

10 A prime example of this is François Furet, *The Passing of an Illusion: The Idea of Communism in the Twentieth Century* (Chicago: University of Chicago Press, 1999).

to Communism as part of their life stories and embedded in social developments.[11] Schütte-Lihotzky's political career will now also be examined here in this sense and on the basis of numerous primary sources.[12]

11 Kroll, *Intellektuelle*, 3–7; *Danzer, Vertrauen*, 25.

12 This essay touches in numerous places on topics and aspects that are expanded upon in other texts in this volume. No separate references will be made to these texts, however, apart from this general note.

The Path to Communism

At first glance, the path that led Margarete Schütte-Lihotzky to Communism appears to be rather unusual. Unlike many other men and women of her age group, she did not join the movement in the years after World War I, when she was young herself and the movement was on the upswing. Instead, she first became a KPÖ member at age 42—at a time when the luster of the Russian Revolution had long since faded away.

It was the time of the Stalinist terror in the Soviet Union. Having lived in the country from 1930 to 1937 with her husband Wilhelm Schütte, Schütte-Lihotzky had witnessed the arrests of individuals undesirable to the regime as well as the disappointment about the state reneging on a number of political and social achievements from the revolutionary period. Yet neither those experiences nor the fact that the USSR ultimately allied itself with Nazi Germany in 1939 deterred her from joining the Communist movement. A great many Communists became proverbial apostates from the faith at the time.[13] But the committed anti-Fascist chose precisely this point in time, the year of the Hitler–Stalin Pact, to become a member of the KPÖ. How did all that fit together?

To answer this question, specific characteristics of Austrian Communism must be taken into consideration. The KPÖ was one of the first Communist parties to be established worldwide. Nonetheless, after a "tumultuous start" that saw membership swell to more than 40,000 in June 1919, the party soon faded into political insignificance.[14] During the First Republic, it was always overshadowed by the Social Democratic Workers' Party of German Austria (SDAP), which ruled the capital city of the country continuously till 1934 and implemented a widely acclaimed municipal reform program there. Red Vienna was shaped not only by far-reaching improvements in social, health, and educational policies, but above all by extensive housing construc-

13 See Bernhard H. Bayerlein, *"Der Verräter, Stalin, bist Du!" Vom Ende der linken Solidarität, Komintern und kommunistische Parteien im Zweiten Weltkrieg 1939–1942* (Berlin: Aufbau, 2008).

14 Walter Baier, *Das kurze Jahrhundert. Kommunismus in Österreich. KPÖ 1918 bis 2008* (Vienna: Edition Steinbauer, 2009), 17–26.

tion projects. Hundreds of apartment blocks with a total of 64,000 residential units were built there.[15]

15 Eve Blau, *The Architecture of Red Vienna, 1919–1934* (Cambridge, MA: MIT Press, 1999), 2.

The young architect was fascinated by this development. Even during her studies, she had geared her designs to the needs of the poorer social classes. After the war, she supported the Vienna settlement movement—a "poor people movement,"[16] whose members squatted on land and built simple dwellings there in response to the severe housing shortage. In 1924 she joined the SDAP because, as she later wrote, she was "impressed by the accomplishments of social democracy in Vienna in the fields of housing, health, and schooling as well as in cultural policy."[17] Unfortunately, no further sources on Lihotzky's party membership have yet been found. However, one can assume that Otto Neurath played a key role in her becoming politicized and joining the party. The prominent Social Democrat had run the office for central economic planning in the short-lived Bavarian Soviet Republic. Lihotzky became acquainted with him while working for the Viennese Settlement Association in the early 1920s. Both shared a years-long friendship, which ended in the 1930s as the architect moved ever closer to Communism.[18]

16 Klaus Novy, "Selbsthilfe als Reformbewegung. Der Kampf der Siedler nach dem 1. Weltkrieg," in *Arch+* 55 (February 1, 1981): 26–40, here 36.

17 Margarete Schütte-Lihotzky, *Warum ich Architektin wurde*, ed. Karin Zogmayer (Salzburg: Residenz, 2004), 117.

18 Ibid., 79–83.

The radicalization process that would ultimately lead Lihotzky to the KPÖ began during her migration period. By her own account, when she went to Frankfurt in 1925 she was appalled by the political disinterest of her colleagues there. Nor could she identify with the politics of the local SPD. She warded off any attempt to win her over to the party and finally also left Austrian social democracy behind in the summer of 1927. The contacts she had at the University of Frankfurt Institute for Social Research had a large part to do with that step. She had come to know its founding director, the "old, significant Marxist" Carl Grünberg, through Neurath[19] and was also in contact with Grünberg's assistant, Hendryk Grossmann, during this same period.[20] It would ultimately be Grünberg "who opened my eyes about Austrian social democracy and proved to me that it would not lead the country to Socialism."[21]

19 Ibid., 118–20.

20 Margarete Schütte-Lihotzky to Genossin [Asja] Lacis, January 8, 1977, University Archive of the University of Applied Arts Vienna, Nachlass Margarete Schütte-Lihotzky (UAUAK, NL MSL), Korrespondenz privat.

21 Schütte-Lihotzky, *Architektin*, 120.

At this point, she began to explore the culture of the young Soviet Union, reading books by the Communist authors John Reed and Nikolai Ognev, watching the movies of Sergei Eisenstein, and attending lectures by the filmmaker Dziga Vertov: "So, even as a person free of party affiliation, I already felt a cultural connection to the Soviet Union."[22] In fact, this type of cultural connection was by no means uncommon. The historian Ulrich Eumann thinks that Soviet literature and films were of "special significance" precisely to those individuals who encountered Communism in Germany in the second half of the 1920s: "All told, *Battleship Potemkin* may well have won over more people to the Communist Party of Germany in the long term than many a successful membership drive by thousands of comrades."[23]

Then, in 1930, Schütte-Lihotzky moved to Moscow. She went to the Soviet Union with a group of architects headed by Ernst May. It was at the time of Stalin's first five-year plan, which called for the construction of entire workers' cities such as Magnitogorsk. At this juncture, she "already [felt] attracted to the Communists," she reported later.[24] This attitude was reinforced by the fact that the Soviet state was her employer and paid her an above-average salary.[25] That, too, was no exception. In the early 1930s, many Western immigrants enjoyed privileges over the Soviet population. They received higher pay, special allotments of food, and support from the International Red Aid. They were offered trips in exchange for translating authors' works free of charge. "These privileges made visitors close their eyes to many of the deficiencies of the system," Ludmila Stern assessed in her study on Western intellectuals in the Soviet Union.[26] So, one rarely finds complaints about living standards or political conditions in their letters home to friends and relatives. The same is true of Schütte-Lihotzky. "You would be amazed how happy life here has become, so much more focused on happiness and enjoyment, for everyone, compared to 1932," she wrote her sister in January 1935.[27]

During the years of industrialization, Schütte-Lihotzky observed with fascination how the Soviet Union transformed itself from an agrarian state into an industrial one in a very short span of time. Later, she described this period as a "time of great, very remarkable development throughout the country, not just industrially and materially but culturally as

22 Ibid., 204–6, quote on 206.

23 Ulrich Eumann, "'Kameraden vom roten Tuch.' Die Weimarer KPD aus der Perspektive ehemaliger Mitglieder," *Archiv für die Geschichte des Widerstands und der Arbeit* 16 (2001): 97–164, here 105.

24 Schütte-Lihotzky, *Erinnerungen*, 23.

25 The architect earned 350 rubles per month. In addition, 50 US dollars were transferred to a foreign account of her choice. She had to pay only 10 percent tax on her income. Margarete Schütte-Lihotzky's employment contract with the Central Bank for Municipal Economy and Housing, Moscow, October 1, 1930, UAUAK, NL MSL, Q 1-34 Preis + Zeugnisse + Bestätigungen, Q 22/2, sheets 2 and 4. By way of comparison, the average income of a Soviet worker in 1930 was between 80 and 110 rubles per month. Aleksandr A. Il'iukhov, *Kak platili bol'sheviki. Politika sovetskoĭ vlasti v sfere oplaty truda v 1917–1941* (Moscow: Rosspen, 2010), 389 and 404–5. I would like to thank Gleb J. Albert for pointing out these comparative figures.

26 Ludmila Stern, *Western Intellectuals and the Soviet Union, 1920–40. From Red Square to the Left Bank* (London: Routledge, 2007), 35.

well."[28] This same attitude can be observed even in otherwise critical Communists such as Clara Zetkin. The rapid pace of development led her, too, to turn a blind eye to coercion and terror.[29]

As an architect, Schütte-Lihotzky was certainly also fascinated by the fact that gigantic sums were spent on urban planning and housing development while in Central Europe, resources for these kinds of projects had all but dried up because of the global economic crisis of 1929. Two billion rubles were allocated to the "May Group," the group of architects to which Schütte-Lihotzky belonged. According to Thomas Flierl, this volume of funding "was a gigantic sum at the time, and would amount to about nine billion euros converted to today's currency."[30] Nonetheless, conflicts arose time and again with the contracting authorities. This situation, in particular, prompted many German-speaking architects such as Ernst May and Bruno Taut to leave the Soviet Union from 1933 on.[31] It is striking that Schütte-Lihotzky and her husband stayed in the country substantially longer than most of their colleagues. She did not emigrate until 1937, the year of the "Great Purges"—but by her own account not due to the repressions but rather because their passports had expired and Nazi Germany was the only place they could have returned to.[32]

But her fascination for the set-in-stone "Building of Socialism" in the Soviet Union was not the only thing that led Schütte-Lihotzky ever closer to the Communist movement. It was also the establishment of National Socialist despotism in Germany and later also in Austria. Even while still in the Soviet Union, she was already planning to join the Resistance against the Nazi regime. After her departure, she met Austrian exiles in London who had close ties to the Communist Party. In Paris she talked with Communists about her possible participation in the Resistance. She finally took that step in 1939 in Turkey, where she met her colleague Herbert Eichholzer, who was forming a foreign chapter of the KPÖ there.

Anti-Fascism therefore had a great deal to do with Schütte-Lihotzky joining the party. At that point, her path to Communism matched the typical ideal. After the loss of the

27 Margarete Schütte-Lihotzky to Adele Hanakam, January 31, 1935, UAUAK, NL MSL, Korrespondenz von MSL (1930er-Jahre).

28 "Stalinismus" manuscript, UAUAK, NL MSL, Erinnerungen SU.

29 Marcel Bois, "Clara Zetkin und die Stalinisierung von KPD und Komintern," in *Clara Zetkin in ihrer Zeit. Neue Fakten, Erkenntnisse, Wertungen*, ed. Ulla Plener (Berlin: Dietz, 2008), 149–56.

30 Thomas Flierl, "Planstädte für ein planloses Land. Ernst May in der Sowjetunion 1930–1933," in *Standardstädte. Ernst May in der Sowjetunion 1930–1933. Texte und Dokumente*, ed. Thomas Flierl (Berlin: Suhrkamp, 2012), 33–164, here 52.

31 Ursula Muscheler, *Das rote Bauhaus. Eine Geschichte von Hoffnung und Scheitern* (Berlin: Berenberg, 2016), 81–89.

32 Schütte-Lihotzky, *Erinnerungen*, 23.

February Uprising of 1934, the KPÖ changed "from a small party with little influence to the major force in the Austrian workers' movement," as Manfred Mugrauer emphasizes.[33] Many disappointed Social Democrats joined the Communist Party, which would soon become the most important actor in the anti-Fascist Resistance. Kroll, too, emphasized that anti-Fascism was a major motivation for many intellectuals to join the party. For instance, he wrote that "the orientation toward Communism [occurs] in situations of social and political crisis that shake what till then had been the firmly established world view."[34]

Schütte-Lihotzky's anti-Fascist activities would ultimately land her in prison. In December 1940, she traveled to Vienna to contact the local Resistance movement. But a Gestapo informer blew the group's cover.[35] On January 22, 1941, a few days before her planned departure, the architect was arrested and sentenced to 15 years' imprisonment.[36] Schütte-Lihotzky did most of her time at the Aichach women's prison in Bavaria, where she was liberated by US soldiers on April 29, 1945.

The "Second Exile"

When Schütte-Lihotzky returned to the Austrian capital in September 1945, there was no doubt in her mind that she would "work in Vienna again and make available to my native city the specialized skills I have acquired in a wide variety of countries over such a long period," as she later emphasized. "After years of forced inactivity in Nazi prisons, I returned home with great hopes and the passionate desire to devote my professional energy to rebuilding Vienna."[37]

The metropolis had sustained heavy damage in the war. After the municipality had cleared away the rubble, it began erecting new buildings from 1947 on. In the 1950s, about 5,000 new apartments were built each year.[38] From the perspective of the City of Vienna, it would have been completely logical to also entrust Schütte-Lihotzky with building projects. She was viewed as an expert in social housing construction because of her experiences in Red Vienna, in New Frankfurt, and in the Soviet Union. Yet she waited a long time in vain for municipal construction contracts, and many

33 Manfred Mugrauer, "Die Kommunistische Partei Österreichs. Zum Stand der Forschung über die Geschichte der KPÖ," *Jahrbuch für Historische Kommunismusforschung* 2013: 211–34, here 217.

34 Kroll, *Intellektuelle*, 628.

35 Hans Schafranek, *Widerstand und Verrat. Gestapospitzel im antifaschistischen Untergrund 1938–1945* (Vienna: Czernin, 2017), 81–84.

36 Verdict of the People's Court against Erwin Puschmann, Franz Sebek, Anna Haider, Franz Haider, Margarete Schütte, Karl Lisetz, September 22, 1942, Documentation Centre of Austrian Resistance (DÖW), Vienna, no. 19793/144.

37 Margarete Schütte-Lihotzky, "Berufsverbote auch in Österreich praktiziert" (manuscript, September 1976), UAUAK, NL MSL, TXT/508, sheet 3.

38 Gustav Bihl, "Wien 1945–2005. Eine politische Geschichte" in *Wien. Geschichte einer Stadt, Bd. 3: Von 1790 bis zur Gegenwart*, ed. Peter Csendes and Ferdinand Opll (Vienna: Böhlau, 2006), 545–650, here 585–89.

of her bids were rejected. It was not until several years after her return that she and her husband received a joint contract to build a smaller-scale *Gemeindebau* (municipal housing complex) "of the kind awarded to novice architects."[39] The only contracts that followed over the next 15 years were one residential building, a child day-care center, and a kindergarten, whereby Schütte-Lihotzky had submitted the design for the kindergarten anonymously.

Given this poor yield, Schütte-Lihotzky conjectured with the then vice-mayor Felix Slavik in February 1960 that "objective professional considerations are not the decisive factors" for the numerous rejections from the city.[40] Later, in September 1976, when she was retired from her profession, she wrote a text about the matter. Excerpts of it appeared as an interview in the Communist newspaper *Volksstimme*.[41] In it, she complained that "many of the architects who faithfully served the Nazi regime received large contracts from the City of Vienna and were thus allowed to leave visible accomplishments for posterity." However, this was something she was "denied as a person persecuted by the Nazi regime and as a Communist."[42] The title of her manuscript, "Berufsverbote auch in Österreich praktiziert" (Professional bans also imposed in Austria), alluded to the corresponding practice in the Federal Republic of Germany. There, individuals deemed hostile to the constitution were removed from the civil service or not even accepted into it in the first place. This practice was based on the *Radikalenerlass* (Anti-radical decree) of 1972[43] and affected primarily members of the German Communist Party (DKP), a sister party of the KPÖ. Initially, Schütte-Lihotzky relativized the matter: "Of course, professional bans are not anchored in Austrian law, as is the case in the Federal Republic. But," she continued, "for something to become a reality in a city like Vienna, it suffices for the executive committee of the Socialist Party to issue an instruction, a mere expression of its will." To substantiate her charges against the Socialist Party of Austria (SPÖ), she presented a chief witness: "Senate Councillor Böck—he passed away long ago—was kind enough to confide the following to me: based on a decision of the SPÖ executive committee, the Stadtbauamt was explicitly prohibited from

39 Schütte-Lihotzky, "Berufsverbote" (as note 37), sheets 3–4.

40 Margarete Schütte-Lihotzky to Felix Slavik, [February 1960], UAUAK, NL MSL, Korrespondenz Inland.

41 Schütte-Lihotzky, "Berufsverbote" (as note 37); "Beispiel: Berufsverbot in Österreich. Wie eine Expertin für Sozialen Wohnungsbau von der Gemeinde Wien kaltgestellt wurde," *Volksstimme*, [1976], UAUAK, NL MSL, TXT/499.

42 Schütte-Lihotzky, "Berufsverbote" (as note 37), sheets 6–7.

43 See Dominik Rigoll, *Staatsschutz in Westdeutschland. Von der Entnazifizierung zur Extremistenabwehr* (Göttingen: Wallstein, 2013); Alexandra Jaeger, *Auf der Suche nach "Verfassungsfeinden." Der Radikalenbeschluss in Hamburg 1971–1987* (Göttingen: Wallstein, 2019).

awarding contracts to the architect Schütte-Lihotzky, as a KPÖ member and, in particular, as president of the BDFÖ." She said she had "long been silent on the matter in order not to repay the Senate Councillor's trust with a posthumous citing of his name."[44]

Latent anti-Communism did in fact prevail in postwar Austria, and its champion, according to Oliver Rathkolb, was "a compact, extremely pro-Western [form of] social democracy that was strictly anti-Communist in its ideology."[45] Thus, it is certainly conceivable that the SPÖ, whose candidates had won every mayoral election since 1945, did indeed exclude Schütte-Lihotzky from public construction contracts. This interpretation is also backed up by the fact that other Communist architects suffered a similar fate. Schütte-Lihotzky's husband, who had lived apart from her since 1951, was also "excluded for years from putting his ideas into practice because of his convictions" and received very few contracts from the City of Vienna.[46] And anti-Communism was also felt in other cultural areas. The best-known examples are certainly the charges against the Austrian PEN Club accusing it of acting as a Communist "bridgehead" and the Brecht boycott from 1953 to 1962, when none of the established theaters in the city put on works by the German playwright. Artists working for the Russian film industry or at Das Neue Theater in der Scala, a theater supported by the Soviet occupying power, were also marginalized. They often had no alternative than to emigrate to the GDR. Communist scholars and scientists such as the historian Leo Stern and the biochemist Samuel Mitja Rapoport, a good friend of Schütte-Lihotzky, went this route because they saw no chance of continuing their academic careers in Vienna.[47]

Apart from anti-Communism, there were other reasons contributing to the professional exclusion of Schütte-Lihotzky. For instance, exceedingly few women who had belonged to the female avant-garde in architecture in the 1920s managed to regain a foothold in the profession after the war. During the Nazi regime, many of them had to abandon their work, were persecuted, and even murdered, as was the case with Friedl Dicker-Brandeis and Zsuzska Banki.[48] For Schütte-Lihotzky, her years in exile were an

44 Schütte-Lihotzky, "Berufsverbote" (as note 37), sheets 1 and 4–5.

45 Oliver Rathkolb, "Kalter Krieg und politische Propaganda in Österreich," in *Kalter Krieg in Österreich. Literatur – Kunst – Kultur*, ed. Michael Hansel and Michael Rohrwasser (Vienna: Zsolnay, 2010), 11–34, here 30.

46 David Baum, "Wilhelm Schütte—Soziale Architektur" (master's thesis, University of Art and Design Linz, 2016), 315.

47 On anti-Communism in culture and science, see Manfred Mugrauer, *Die Politik der KPÖ 1945–1955. Von der Regierungsbank in die innenpolitische Isolation* (Göttingen: V&R Unipress, 2020), 545–48.

48 One exception among them was Lucy Hillebrand, who, having had to give up her job in 1934 as a "half-Jew," returned to work as an architect in the Federal Republic of Germany. See the biographical sketches in Uta Maasberg and Regina Prinz, *Die Neuen kommen! Weibliche Avantgarde in der Architektur der zwanziger Jahre*, 2nd ed. (Hamburg: Junius, 2005), 54–115.

49 On her relationship with the individual people, see Schütte-Lihotzky, *Architektin*, 15–28 and 49–83.

additional factor. After nearly 20 years abroad, professional networks in Austria had simply vanished for her. After 1945, none of her prominent mentors from the interbellum years were in Vienna anymore. Oskar Strnad, her professor at the Kunstgewerbeschule (School of Arts and Crafts; today's University of Applied Arts Vienna), had since died, as had Adolf Loos and Otto Neurath, with whom she had worked in the settlement movement. Ernst Egli had relocated to Switzerland and Josef Frank to Sweden.[49]

Schütte-Lihotzky's anti-Fascist Resistance activity was also certainly less than beneficial to her professional relaunch. For large parts of the population, Resistance fighters were considered "traitors to the Fatherland" in the immediate postwar period.[50] Wolfgang Neugebauer, the long-time head of the Documentation Centre of Austrian Resistance (DÖW), noted that the topic of the Resistance almost became "a political taboo" at the end of the 1940s.[51] A cloak of silence was laid over the actors involved. That is precisely what happened to Margarete Schütte-Lihotzky as well. Not only was she excluded professionally, she also disappeared for decades from the public eye. Between 1953 and 1985 she did not take part in a single exhibition. She did not appear on Austrian radio or television for a period of more than 20 years.[52]

Kroll points out that this situation was not unique. In fact, a number of returning Communist intellectuals faced political and social isolation in the postwar period. He uses the term "second exile" for this experience of exclusion, which was a major biographical turning point for many of them.[53] Helga Embacher even posits that for several Communists it was not their actual exile that broke them but rather the "shock of re-emigration."[54]

Non-Partisan Alliances and Internal Loyalty to the Party Line

Schütte-Lihotzky was not broken by her experience of exclusion. And unlike many of her comrades, she opted not to emigrate to the GDR. She remained in Vienna even after entering into a relationship with the Austrian Communist Hans Wetzler, who lived in East Berlin.[55] Ultimately, that decision paid off. The architect lived long enough to witness

50 Helga Embacher, "Eine Heimkehr gibt es nicht? Remigration nach Österreich," in *Exilforschung. Ein Internationales Jahrbuch* 19 (2001): 187–203, here 194–95.

51 Wolfgang Neugebauer, "Widerstandsforschung in Österreich," in *Das große Tabu. Österreichs Umgang mit seiner Vergangenheit*, ed. Anton Pelinka and Erika Weinzierl, 2nd ed. (Vienna: Verlag Österreich, 1997), 163–73, here 163.

52 See the overview of her participation in exhibitions and also TV and radio contributions in *Margarete Schütte-Lihotzky. Soziale Architektur. Zeitzeugin eines Jahrhunderts*, exhibition catalog, MAK—Austrian Museum of Applied Arts, Vienna, ed. Peter Noever (Vienna: Böhlau, 1996), 279 and 297.

53 Kroll, *Intellektuelle*, 312.

54 Embacher, "Heimkehr," 199.

55 Marcel Bois, "Soziale Beziehungen und kommunistische Netzwerke. Annäherungen an Hans Wetzler," in *Margarete Schütte-Lihotzky. Architektur. Politik. Geschlecht. Neue Perspektiven auf Leben und Werk*, ed. Marcel Bois and Bernadette Reinhold (Basel: Birkhäuser, 2019), 224–36. This essay is not

Fig. 3. Photograph of Schütte-Lihotzky's life partner Hans Wetzler, Radstadt, 1976.

her rediscovery by the public. From the late 1970s on, she was present in the Austrian media again and received numerous tributes and honorary doctorates.

Before reaching that point, however, Schütte-Lihotzky moved closer to the Communist Party, intensifying her political engagement to a striking degree in the postwar era. Her activities revolved mainly around three sets of topics: women, peace, and anti-Fascism.

Already active in the Communist women's movement since the late 1940s, the Viennese native became president of the BDFÖ, an association founded in 1948 that was closely allied with the KPÖ. She retained this position until 1969 and later became honorary president of the BDFÖ. She held speeches at demonstrations and rallies and participated in

included in the present English translation.

56 Margarete Schütte-Lihotzky, speech manuscript, July 20, 1961 (TXT/478); article: "Der Moskauer Weltkongress der Frauen. Eine macht-

volle Manifestation für Frieden und Fortschritt" (TXT/494); Margarete Schütte-Lihotzky, "Bericht über meine Reise nach Mailand und der Teilnahme an einer Jubiläumsfeier der italienischen Frauen am 31.1.1965," February 1965, UAUAK, NL MSL, TXT/486.

57 Holzinger, *Widerstand*, 18.

58 "Oesterreichische Intellektuelle für Pariser Weltfriedenskongreß," *Österreichische Volksstimme* (March 31, 1949): 2; "Aus der Arbeit des Österreichischen Friedensrates," *Mitteilungen des Österreichischen Friedensrates* 1, no. 3 (December 1949): 4.

59 See the relevant speech manuscripts in UAUAK, NL MSL, TXT/514–26.

60 Weltfrauentreffen in Wien, May 23–25, 1962, Ablauf der Arbeiten, March 23, 1962, UAUAK, NL MSL, TXT/455–96.

61 Benjamin Gilde, *Österreich in KSZE-Prozess 1969–1983. Neutraler Vermittler in humanitärer Mission* (Munich: Oldenbourg, 2013), 45, note 135.

62 Österreichisches Komitee für Europäische Sicherheit und Zusammenarbeit [circular letter to members], October 15, 1987, UAUAK, NL MSL, TXT/527.

numerous international conferences and delegation trips. For instance, she held lectures in front of Cuban women in the summer of 1961, appeared as an Austrian delegate at the World Congress of Women in Moscow in 1963, and met with representatives of Italian women's groups in Milan in February 1965.[56] In the 1960s, she was one of the founders of a non-partisan women's committee that showed political films for three decades at the Urania, a public educational institute in central Vienna. The first showing was prompted by anti Semitic protests that had led to *The Diary of Anne Frank* being canceled at several Austrian movie theaters in 1959.[57]

There is evidence that she engaged in her first activities in the peace movement in the late 1940s, when she participated in the preparations for the World Congress of Partisans of Peace in Paris. At that time, Schütte-Lihotzky became a member of the leadership of the Austrian Peace Council.[58] Later she appeared as a speaker at various events in West Germany, where a broad social movement against nuclear weapons had formed with the name "Kampf dem Atomtod" (fight against nuclear death). She spoke, for instance, at a "Day of Reflection" in Nuremberg in November 1959, at an international peace meeting at Lake Constance in June 1960, and also at the Evangelical Academy in Berlin in July 1962. As a citizen of neutral Austria, she always emphasized the necessity of complete demobilization.[59] In March 1962, she opened a World Gathering of Women for Disarmament in Vienna in her capacity as BDFÖ president.[60] Schütte-Lihotzky found another field of activity in the early 1970s when she joined an Austrian Committee for European Security and Cooperation that had been formed by KPÖ members. The committee was an observer of negotiations at the Conference on Security and Co-operation in Europe (CSCE) in Helsinki. Although this committee had no impact on CSCE politics in Austria,[61] it did give the architect a chance to cultivate and expand her numerous contacts abroad. In 1970 and 1973 she took part in various international meetings—for example, in Brussels and in the Swedish city of Ystad. In 1987, at the age of 90, Schütte-Lihotzky was still a member of the executive board of the Austrian Committee.[62]

Her anti-Fascist commitment was strongly shaped by biographical experiences, a fact that came through in her work in the executive committee of the KZ-Verband.[63] "[During my] four years behind bars, I came to know German Fascism firsthand in its most brutal form, not just by what I personally suffered but also through the bond of fate I shared with numerous comrades, many of whom lost their lives to the executioner's ax," she wrote. "We all swore back then that everything that could ever again lead to Fascism must be nipped uncompromisingly in the bud."[64] In a state police informer's report of a KPÖ meeting in the early 1960s, Schütte-Lihotzky was quoted as urging those present "to never rest until the last 'war criminal,' the last 'neo-Nazi,' the last 'SS man' in Austria and Germany has been rendered harmless."[65] Later she addressed the Nazi era primarily by writing texts about the subject, a practice she explained in 1963 as follows: "More than half of our current population is so young that they have never consciously experienced Fascism themselves. So, we must impart to our progeny a broad and deep knowledge, a knowledge about cause and effect before and during the Nazi era."[66] In the 1980s, she finally published the widely read book about her time in the Resistance that was mentioned at the outset of this essay. A short time later, in 1988, she created headlines again when she refused to have Federal President Kurt Waldheim award her the Austrian Decoration for Science and Art because of his Nazi past.[67]

In the last two decades of her life, Schütte-Lihotzky repeatedly presented herself as a "warning contemporary witness." "I feel deeply that our youth, in particular, should know as much as possible about this matter—that precisely in Austria, an unimaginably courageous Resistance fight was continuously waged at great sacrifice throughout all seven years of Nazi rule," she declared in April 1989 at an event in Vienna.[68] She watched the rise of the right-wing populist Freedom Party of Austria (FPÖ) in this period with great concern. This was also why she joined four other persecuted victims of the Nazi period to file a lawsuit in 1995 against the leader of the FPÖ, Jörg Haider, after he dismissively referred to the Nazi extermination camps as "prison camps."[69]

63 Margarete Schütte-Lihotzky, "Ehrenamtliche, nicht berufliche Tätigkeiten nach 1945," UAUAK, NL MSL, Lebenslauf.

64 Grete Schütte-Lihotzky, "Keine Stimme für Nazi," extract from *Stimme der Frau* (October 9, 1971), UAUAK, NL MSL, TXT/497.

65 "Planungen des Weltkommunismus," June 11, 1961, DÖW, Vienna, no. 50120/Gc5, state police informer reports of KPÖ events, January 4, 1961 to April 9, 1962.

66 Österreichische Delegation, Ansprache am Frauenweltkongreß, Moskau 1963, gehalten von Frau Schütte-Lihotzky, Vorsitzende des Bundes Demokratischer Frauen Österreichs (manuscript), Zentrales Parteiarchiv der KPÖ, Wien, Nachlass Schütte-Lihotzky, sheet 2.

67 "Architektin Margarete Schütte-Lihotzky lehnt Ehrenzeichen ab," *Die Presse* (February 16, 1986).

68 Margarete Schütte-Lihotzky, presentation manuscript, [April 1927], UAUAK, NL MSL, TXT/426–65.

69 "'Ein Hohn für alle Opfer der Nazis.' Fünf NS-Opfer klagen Haider wegen 'Straflager'-Aussage," *Wiener Zeitung* (July 14, 1995).

It should also be noted that Schütte-Lihotzky's political activities are characterized by a great openness toward other movements and by a willingness to work together in nonpartisan alliances. By contrast, she tended to be rigid and traditionalist within the party, even putting the party above personal relationships when in doubt. An incident in the fall of 1956 illustrates this behavior. At the time, she went on a five-week study tour of China. Afterward, she reported to the KPÖ about her trip. In this context, she also reported on the professional and political backgrounds of her traveling companions with "the straightforwardness so typical of Schütte-Lihotzky," as Karin Zogmayer noted. In addition, she conjectured what these people might say about China after their return and whether they could possibly be won over to the Communist Party. "In these characterizations, Schütte-Lihotzky is writing about people with whom she was on friendly terms throughout an extensive journey," Zogmayer noted with bemusement, and rightfully so.[70] The fact that the architect subsequently went to the KPÖ and reported what was confided to her in personal conversations does indeed reveal a dubious understanding of the party.

Meanwhile, a document from late summer 1968 illustrates Schütte Lihotzky's attitude toward reform movements in Communism. It pertained to a declaration issued by members of the editorial advisory board of *Tagebuch* (Diary), the theoretical journal of the KPÖ. They criticized the violent suppression of the Prague Spring by troops of the Warsaw Pact countries and condemned their invasion of Czechoslovakia as an "outrageous breach of faith and of the law" and as a "diktat" and "extortion."[71] In fact, these events soon led to a deep crisis within the KPÖ. It culminated in 1969/70 in the expulsion of Ernst Fischer and Franz Marek, two prominent representatives of a reform movement that would later be called Eurocommunism. By the end of 1971, one-third of the KPÖ members had left the party. But when the *Tagebuch* declaration appeared, the fronts had not yet hardened to such a degree. On the contrary, the KPÖ leadership had also initially condemned the Soviet incursion—and "for the first time in its history [...] voiced open criticism of the CPSU and other parties in the Socialist countries."[72]

70 Karin Zogmayer, "Vorwort der Herausgeberin," in Margarete Schütte-Lihotzky, *Millionenstädte Chinas. Bilder- und Reisetagebuch einer Architektin (1958). Mit einem Nachwort von Albert Speer*, ed. Karin Zogmayer (Vienna: Springer, 2007), 11–27, here 26.

71 "Zur Okkupation der CSSR. Eine Erklärung" [with handwritten notes by Margarete Schütte-Lihotzky], September 2, 1968, UAUAK, NL MSL, TXT/381–410.

72 Manfred Mugrauer, "Von der Verurteilung zur 'bitteren Notwendigkeit.' Die KPÖ, der 'Prager Frühling' und die Militärintervention in Prag," *Mitteilungen der Alfred Klahr Gesellschaft* 15, no. 2 (2008): 1–9, here 3.

However, Schütte-Lihotzky already had a diverging opinion at this point—and expressed it by adding a large number of handwritten comments to the declaration. For instance, she commented on one passage with the words "Smear campaign!" At another place in the text she wrote the question: "And the true enemies of Socialism? They didn't just suddenly disappear, did they?" In one section the signatories declared their support of the critical statements the Central Committee of the KPÖ had issued on the invasion. Her comment was a terse "no." And at the bottom of the document she wrote: "This is certainly not a serious analysis[,] but rather a purely propagandistic critique!" The entire text was "dictated by hatred of the SU [Soviet Union]."[73]

73 "Zur Okkupation der CSSR" (as note 71).

"Traditionally Close Bond" with the Soviet Union

Where did this attitude originate, this uncritical trust in the party and in the Soviet Union? Was Schütte-Lihotzky in fact a "professed Stalinist," as the Frankfurt CDU would later call her? To answer this question, we must revisit the double exclusion that the architect had experienced: first she was persecuted by the National Socialists and then she was shunned after the war in her native city while fellow travelers of the Nazi regime were treated leniently. This experience of marginalization—or a "second exile"—elicited in her, as in many comrades in the 1950s, a circle-up-the-wagons mentality, "a retreat into the sect-like milieu of the KPÖ." Moreover, it could be observed at the time that many KPÖ members increasingly exalted the Soviet Union as the "better counter-world" in relation to Western capitalism. Moscow was seen by them as "a guarantee of the realization of and a bastion for [their] own Communist utopia."[74]

74 Kroll, *Intellektuelle*, 320, 636, and 638.

These same patterns emerged later on, too, in the debate on the crushing of the Prague Spring. Although most party intellectuals condemned the Soviet action at the time, Schütte-Lihotzky was by no means alone in her diverging opinion. Mugrauer notes "that owing to the traditionally close bond that the rank-and-file party members had with the Soviet Union, they tended to view critical statements on problems in the Socialist countries as 'anti-Soviet' and therefore gave only half-hearted support to the Central

Committee's condemnation of the incursion or rejected it in general."[75]

75 Mugrauer, "Verurteilung," 3.

This "traditionally close bond" with the USSR was in fact also a strong motive in the political stance that Schütte-Lihotzky took. It was undoubtedly based in part on the architect's biographical experiences. Of primary importance in this context is her stay in the Soviet Union in the 1930s, which she always remembered in a positive light. But even on later visits, she was enthusiastic about the country. For example, in a travel diary in 1958 she noted: "I am looking out my hotel window on the ninth floor early in the morning. The view is fantastic. To the left [is] a high-rise [...] and to the right, way in the back, [are] the Lenin Hills crowned by Moscow University, the landmark of the new Moscow, which gazes down into all parts of the city and [is] at the same time a landmark of the state in which knowledge and education and training form the basis of everything in life, [the state] in which the people's ideal is to learn, learn, and learn some more in order to create a better and happier life for people in the future."[76]

76 Moscow travel diary from July 17 to August 13, 1958, UAUAK, NL MSL, TXT/381–410, sheet 4.

Another factor for her deep bond with the Communist movement was quite simply material in nature. After all, Schütte-Lihotzky's exclusion from her profession was by no means a "typical professional ban," as she herself asserted.[77] The architect was not as dependent on employment in the civil service or on contracts from government institutions as those affected by the *Radikalenerlass* in the Federal Republic of Germany. Since she was a specialist in social housing construction and children's facilities, the City of Vienna's attitude toward her naturally did result in the loss of an important potential client. But Schütte-Lihotzky was nonetheless able to continue her career as an architect. She now built increasingly for private clients—namely, primarily for the KPÖ, which was said to be the "richest party in Europe" thanks to financial support from the GDR.[78] For instance, Schütte-Lihotzky and her colleague Fritz Weber planned a building in 1948 for Kärntner Volksverlag, a publishing house in Klagenfurt. A few years later, she was part of a four-person team of architects who built a printing and publishing building for Globus-Verlag, the publishing house of the

77 Schütte-Lihotzky, "Berufsverbote" (as note 37), sheets 4–5.

78 See Baier, *Jahrhundert*, 209–21.

KPÖ. This publishing house also had her design a bookstore and plan the rebuild of a workers' bookstore.[79]

79 Christine Zwingl, "'Den Frieden auf der Welt, wo er nicht herrsche, endlich aufzubauen….' Das 'zweite' Leben einer Architektin," in *Spuren in Wien*, 105–18, especially 113.

In addition, she traveled repeatedly to countries with "actually existing Socialism," where she did primarily conceptual work. Right after the war she spent some time in Bulgaria, where she founded and directed a department for children's facilities at the municipal building authority in Sofia. In 1956, she gave a lecture at the Beijing Institute of Technology during the above study tour and in 1963, she spent three months working for the Cuban Education Ministry in Havana and finally, in 1966, six months at the Bauakademie (Building Academy) in East Berlin.

So, Schütte-Lihotzky's attitude toward Communism was shaped not only by the negative experience of being excluded. On the contrary, it was rooted in a variety of positive experiences the architect had had in the Communist movement and in the Soviet Union. The movement provided her with professional contracts and political offices. In addition, the central thesis from Danzer's study should be noted—namely, "that social relationships played a major role in […] lifelong affiliation [with the Communist Party]."[80] This was also true of Schütte-Lihotzky. She had close personal ties with numerous Communists in Austria and abroad. Examples worth noting here would be the actors from the Resistance and her prison time, foreign Communist architects such as Kurt Liebknecht, and above all, the two most important men in her life: her ex-husband Wilhelm Schütte and her life partner after him, Hans Wetzler. Both were also members of the KPÖ.

80 Danzer, *Vertrauen*, 19.

The Bottom Line

After the demise of Real Socialism, the KPÖ fell into a severe crisis, as did most Communist parties in Western and Central Europe. Robbed of their financial support from the GDR, they had to dramatically reduce their party apparatuses. Most members left the party in the years that followed, including former party leaders. But Margarete Schütte-Lihotzky stayed on.

Yet at this point, she began to reflect critically on the history of Communism. This was something reported by her longtime friend, Ingeborg Rapoport, who herself remained a committed Communist up to her death. It was not until after 1990 that Schütte-Lihotzky began talking with her and her husband about the "political difficulties" in the Soviet Union in the 1930s:

> She refrained for a long time from talking to us about these awful things. She maintained iron discipline toward the party and did not want to make the matter public. Later she told us that in the end, she had had a grim time in the Soviet Union and that many comrades that she knew had disappeared—without her knowing where they had gone.[81]

Various manuscripts from the estate also verify that Schütte-Lihotzky was taking a critical look at Stalinism at this point. She admitted that Stalin had constructed "Socialism using utterly barbaric methods."[82] In March 1990, in other words just a few months after the Berlin Wall fell, she noted the following: "Dictatorial Socialism is dead—long live democratic Socialism!"[83]

In light of her comments, the term "committed Stalinist" is certainly exaggerated as a characterization of her political self-image and of little use in a scholarly context. Above all, it falls short of capturing the architect's multifaceted motivation for being politically engaged. She viewed herself as a fighter for a better world and wanted to end hunger, misery, and war. She wanted to improve the situation of women and stand up against Fascism. To do so, she accepted the professional disadvantages, was marginalized, and almost paid for her activism with her life. Occasionally, she followed a different path than other intellectuals in her age group: she was late in coming to Communism and did not move to the GDR later on. But she did not differ in at least one respect: she exalted and glorified the Soviet Union until its collapse. Her unconditional will to overcome capitalism with all its injustices allowed her to overlook exploitation, suffering, and repression in a system that was supposedly Socialist.

81 Author's interview with Ingeborg Rapoport in Berlin on November 15, 2015.

82 "Stalinismus" manuscript, UAUAK, NL MSL, Erinnerungen SU.

83 "Gedankengerüst am 1.III.1990" (manuscript), UAUAK, NL MSL, Erinnerungen SU II, Perestroika.

Margarete Schütte-Lihotzky's Fight against the Nazi Regime

Elisabeth Boeckl-Klamper

On January 22, 1941, one day before her planned return to Istanbul, Margarete Schütte-Lihotzky was arrested at Café Victoria am Schottentor (first district of Vienna, Schottengasse 10) by officers from the Gestapo headquarters in Vienna. Arrested with her was the leading functionary of the Communist Party of Austria (KPÖ), Erwin Puschmann, whom she only knew at the time by his code name "Gerber."

After her first interrogation at the Gestapo headquarters at Morzinplatz, she already had the terrible suspicion that her and Puschmann's arrest was largely due to the activity of a police informer who had been someone all members of the Communist Resistance group had blindly trusted. The Gestapo officers not only knew she had come to Vienna from Istanbul as a courier for the KPÖ Executive Committee abroad, but they were also aware that she had lived in Moscow for years and was a Communist.

This essay will attempt to trace Margarete Schütte-Lihotzky's personal journey, from being a daughter from "a good family" to being a committed Communist willing to fight and make sacrifices within the Austrian Resistance against the National Socialist regime.

"In Terms of Convictions, I Already Felt Attracted to the Communists Back Then"[1]

Margarete Schütte-Lihotzky grew up in a respectable middle-class family steeped in the traditions of the Austrian monar-

1 Margarete Schütte-Lihotzky, "Von Istanbul nach Wien" (unpublished manuscript), Documentation Centre of Austrian Resistance (DÖW), Vienna, Bibliothek Nr. 10159, p. 3.

chy. Her father was a civil servant, and her grandfather was the mayor of Chernivtsi. Her path to becoming a Communist and anti-Nazi Resistance fighter already began taking shape during her architectural studies. Inspired by her teacher Oskar Strnad and moved by the miserable living conditions prevailing among the working class, she began grappling with social issues. However, she quickly realized that social housing and better living conditions alone could not change the situation of workers in a lasting way. This could only be done through a radical change in sociopolitical conditions. In 1923, she became a member of the Social Democratic Workers' Party (SDAP) because she believed at the time that "the things being done there will lead to Socialism."[2]

2 Margarete Schütte-Lihotzky, *Erinnerungen aus dem Widerstand 1938–1945*, ed. Chup Friemert (Hamburg: Konkret Literatur Verlag, 1985), 24.

In 1925 she accepted Ernst May's offer to work with him as part of the New Frankfurt project he had initiated. In her memoirs, she expressed the amazement she still felt all those years later about the apolitical attitude of her Frankfurt colleagues, who, for instance, did not take part in the International Workers' Day celebrations on May 1.[3] The project in Frankfurt came to an end in the late 1920s because of the global economic crisis. Margarete Schütte-Lihotzky and Wilhelm Schütte, her husband since 1927, then joined the architectural staff around Ernst May in 1930 to help design and build schools and children's facilities in the Soviet Union.[4] Schütte-Lihotzky, a member of neither the KPÖ nor the Communist Party of the Soviet Union (CPSU) at the time, was deeply impressed by the tasks given to her and by life in the Soviet Union. This country had seen its society undergo a radical transformation since the October Revolution and had a great appeal, also for European intellectuals. What was happening there seemed to signal the emergence of a societal alternative to the Western world, which had been so shaken by economic and political crises. Even Stefan Zweig, who traveled to the Soviet Union in 1928 to do a book tour, was impressed by the "impulsive cordiality" of the people and their willingness to put up with deprivations and austerities "for the sake of a higher mission."[5]

3 Margarete Schütte-Lihotzky, *Warum ich Architektin wurde*, ed. Karin Zogmayer (Salzburg: Residenz, 2004), 118–19.

4 See Thomas Flierl's essay in this volume.

5 Stefan Zweig, *The World of Yesterday. An Autobiography* (New York: Viking Press, 1943), 335.

Margarete Schütte-Lihotzky was actively involved in many political discussions in the Soviet Union. However, they mostly took place within the circle of foreign specialists and skilled craftsmen simply due to the existing language barriers. She would later write: "In terms of convictions, I already felt attracted to the Communists back then."[6] This feeling was almost a logical consequence of those discussions, as were the ties she cultivated with KPÖ members. For instance, she had met, among others, Hermann Köhler, who had been a member of the Central Committee of the KPÖ since 1934 and one of the Austrian delegates to the Seventh World Congress of the Communist International (Comintern) in 1935. In a retrospective report from 1941 to Comintern General Secretary Georgi Dimitrov, Köhler described her as a "capable and talented individual, very enthusiastic and positive toward the Soviet Union."[7]

Schütte-Lihotzky remained true to her convictions even when nearly all members of the May Group successively returned to Western Europe from 1933 onward due to increasing differences with the Soviet authorities and the first major show trials were conducted in Moscow in August 1936[8] and January 1937. She and her husband did not leave the Soviet Union until August 1937, a few days after the secret Order No. 00439 issued by the People's Commissariat of Internal Affairs (NKVD) had come into force on July 25, 1937. It ordered "repressive measures to be taken against German citizens suspected of espionage against the USSR." However, Stalin penned a handwritten note on the draft of the order that read as follows: "All Germans in our armament plants, paramilitary and chemical factories, and on construction sites in all territories must be arrested." This note would end up carrying more weight than the actual wording of the order.[9] Following an expansion of the "German Operation," it targeted both Soviet citizens of German heritage and German and Austrian specialists and skilled craftsmen as well as German and Austrian émigrés, including members of the KPÖ and the Communist Party of Germany (KPD).

In contrast to Margarete Schütte-Lihotzky, Wilhelm Schütte appears to have sensed the risk of them being arrested.[10] This can be concluded, inter alia, from Hermann Köhler's report to Dimitrov mentioned above. In it Köhler stated:

> In 1937 he [the reference is to Wilhelm] wanted to leave. [...] She [the reference is to Margarete] did not want to

6 Schütte-Lihotzky, "Von Istanbul nach Wien," 3.

7 Report by Hermann Köhler to Georgi Dimitrov, August 19, 1941, Russian State Archive of Socio-political History (RGASPI), Moscow, f. 495, op. 73, d. 116, copies at DÖW: 35 200/005.

8 As early as the first show trial, political "deviationists" were equated with "Gestapo agents," which led to a wave of suspicion toward Germans and also Austrians. See Barry McLoughlin and Josef Vogl, *"... Ein Paragraf wird sich finden." Gedenkbuch der österreichischen Stalin-Opfer (bis 1945)* (Vienna: Dokumentationsarchiv des österreichischen Widerstands, 2013), 26.

9 Ibid., 43.

10 See Thomas Flierl, "Mit einem Karton voller Briefe auf Zeitreise," in *"Mach den Weg um Prinkipo, meine Gedanken werden Dich dabei begleiten!" Der Gefängnis-Briefwechsel 1941–1945*, Margarete Schütte-Lihotzky and Wilhelm Schütte, ed. Thomas Flierl (Berlin: Lukas Verlag, 2021), 409–576, here 424–28.

leave but given the difficulties faced by foreigners here, she agreed to leave with him.[11]

In her memoirs, Schütte-Lihotzky said the reason they left the Soviet Union was that both of their passports would soon expire and that the German embassy in Moscow would only extend them for entry into Germany. This would have precluded them from entering any other country. A return to Germany was out of the question for the Schüttes because by that time both of them had already resolved to fight the Nazi regime through all possible means. Since they were convinced that the anti-Nazi Resistance fight could be waged better and more effectively from abroad, they intended to join emigrated Resistance fighters in France or England.

After arriving in England, Margarete Schütte-Lihotzky and Wilhelm Schütte quickly realized there were almost no work opportunities for them there. They therefore accepted Bruno Taut's offer to work at the Academy of Fine Arts in Istanbul. They traveled to Turkey via Paris, where they established their first personal contacts with KPD and KPÖ émigrés. The *Anschluss* (annexation of Austria by Nazi Germany) had occurred in the meantime. In August 1938 they arrived in Istanbul, which would become a key hub of anti-Nazi Resistance in the years to follow.

11 Report by Hermann Köhler to Georgi Dimitrov, August 19, 1941.

The Resistance Efforts of Austrian Communists

Extensive arrests started immediately after Austria was forcibly annexed by Hitler's Germany. Nonetheless, the KPÖ, which had been operating as an underground political party since 1933,[12] succeeded in becoming the most active force within the Resistance movement against the Nazi regime. In keeping with the Volksfront (Popular Front) strategy of the Communist International since 1934, the KPÖ adopted emphatic Austrian patriotism as the basic approach to its Resistance fight. The most important weapons in the fight against the Nazi regime were flyers, leaflets, and magazines, which were produced and disseminated at great risk.[13]

The KPÖ Executive Committee abroad handled the political approach and organization of the Communist Resistance fight in Austria, modeling it closely on the political directives issued by the Comintern. The committee was

12 The KPÖ had been banned on May 26, 1933 by emergency decree of the authoritarian government under Engelbert Dollfuss during a wave of arrests following banned demonstrations on International Workers' Day on May 1.

13 See Wolfgang Neugebauer, *Der österreichische Widerstand 1938–1945*, revised and expanded new edition (Vienna: Edition Steinbauer, 2015), 91–96.

based in Paris from 1938 until the war broke out and then moved to Moscow. To maintain contact between the committee in Moscow and the Resistance activists in Austria, "foreign bases" run by "foreign emissaries" of the KPÖ were set up in Slovakia, Turkey, and Switzerland as well as Hungary, Croatia, and Sweden. The committee sent couriers and instructors to Austria via these bases. Their task was to take the political directives and the training and propaganda materials produced by the committee to the activists in Austria and to convey the activists' reports on the political situation and the Resistance activities in Austria back to the committee in Moscow.[14]

A key foreign base for the KPÖ was set up in Istanbul and was run by the architect Herbert Eichholzer[15] and the Styrian entrepreneur Herbert Feuerlöscher.[16] Besides preparing acts of sabotage in case of a German invasion, the activists in this group combated Nazi propaganda mostly with illegal flyer propaganda and whispering campaigns.[17] Herbert Eichholzer called on Margarete Schütte-Lihotzky to work in the KPÖ group soon after her arrival in Istanbul once he had received verification of her political trustworthiness from the Austrian Communists in Paris.[18] Within the group, discussions about Marxism and the Soviet Union were the order of the day, as were practical briefings about clandestine activities in Austria. Later on in Vienna, Schütte-Lihotzky closely followed the instructions from these briefings, for example "that someone doing illegal work may have contact with only two people, that you should use obscuration as much as possible, that you may not go from your apartment to an 'appointment' without first taking a circuitous route through desolate parks or streets to make sure you are not being followed."[19]

Already in the spring of 1939, Schütte-Lihotzky suggested to Herbert Eichholzer that he send her to Austria since the "personal bond between the domestic Resistance efforts and the Executive Committee abroad [...] was constantly needed. I would be especially suitable, I think, as a non-émigré and a non-Jew."[20]

Schütte-Lihotzky had to be patient, though, because Herbert Eichholzer returned to Austria first in mid-March 1940 after having assured the German authorities he would

14 See, inter alia, Hans Schafranek, "Wiener Gestapo-Spitzel im Umfeld sowjetischer Funk- und Fallschirmagenten und als Mitbegründer der 4. illegalen Inlandsleitung der KPÖ (1942)," *Zeitgeschichte* 40, no. 6 (2013): 323–37.

15 Herbert Eichholzer had been working at Clemens Holzmeister's Istanbul office since November 1938. See Antje Senarclens de Grancy's essay in this volume.

16 Herbert Feuerlöscher, who fled Austria in 1938, came from an entrepreneurial family with Jewish roots that ran a "mechanical pulp and paper factory" in Prenning, Styria. From 1933 on, Herbert Eichholzer spent many weekends in Prenning at the invitation of the Feuerlöscher family.

17 See Peter Pirker, *Subversion deutscher Herrschaft. Der britische Kriegsgeheimdienst SOE und Österreich* (Göttingen: V&R Unipress, 2012), 139–44.

18 Report by Hermann Köhler to Georgi Dimitrov, August 19, 1941.

19 Schütte-Lihotzky, "Von Istanbul nach Wien," 19.

20 Ibid., 7.

behave loyally toward the state in the future. The KPÖ Executive Committee abroad had ordered him, inter alia, to reorganize the KPÖ in Styria following the arrest of its leading functionaries and to set up a procedure for carrying out illegal border crossings to Zagreb. This was intended to serve as a new connection between the individual Communist Party groups in Austria and the KPÖ Executive Committee abroad in Moscow.

At the end of 1940, Margarete Schütte-Lihotzky finally received the order from Herbert Feuerlöscher to travel to Austria as a KPÖ courier—she had become a party member in 1939. She would not be advised of her exact task until she arrived in Zagreb—namely, by "Bobby," who ran the KPÖ foreign base in that city. "Bobby" was the code name used by Julius Kornweitz (fig. 1), one of the most important foreign cadres of the KPÖ, who coordinated contact among the "foreign emissaries" in Sweden, Switzerland, Slovakia, Turkey, and Hungary.[21]

On December 24, 1940, Margarete Schütte-Lihotzky departed Istanbul by train. Officially, she was visiting her sister in Vienna, who was not aware of her clandestine activities. Several days later, she met up in Zagreb with Kornweitz, whom she knew only by his code name at the time. She found out from him that besides conveying several messages relating more to organizational matters, her task was to persuade the leading KPÖ functionary Erwin Puschmann of the necessity of leaving Vienna as quickly as possible to avoid unnecessarily endangering himself and others.[22] In July 1940, Puschmann (fig. 2) went from Bratislava, where he had set up a foreign base for the KPÖ, to Vienna to iron out the ideological disputes and differences within the various Communist Party groups there. These resulted not least from the Hitler–Stalin Pact that forced Communists to walk the tightrope of supporting the pact while propagating the overthrow of the Nazi regime. During his stay in Vienna, Puschmann frequently contacted the foreign base of the KPÖ in Prague, which, in turn, was in constant contact with the KPÖ Executive Committee abroad in Moscow. His closest colleague "Ossi," a long-standing member of the KPÖ, acted as courier in this context.[23]

21 After the Wehrmacht had attacked Greece and Yugoslavia with a total of 680,000 soldiers on April 6, 1941, Kornweitz was able to continue his work in Croatia for another six months. In the fall of 1941, he returned from Croatia to Vienna in order to reorganize the illegal Communist Party leadership, which had been crushed several times. Kornweitz was arrested by the Gestapo on April 25, 1942. Since he was Jewish, he was not put on trial but sent to Mauthausen concentration camp as a "prisoner in protective custody," where he was murdered in 1944.

22 Schütte-Lihotzky, "Von Istanbul nach Wien," 20.

23 See verdict of the People's Court against Erwin Puschmann, Margarete Schütte-Lihotzky et al., Bundesarchiv (BArch) Berlin, R 3017/24835. The author would like to thank Manfred Mugrauer for providing copies of the judgment.

Fig. 1. Julius Kornweitz (code name "Bobby"), identification photo at the Gestapo.

The meeting between Kornweitz and Schütte-Lihotzky took place in the apartment of Franz Öhler, the former owner of the Kastner & Öhler department store, who had fled to Croatia in 1938 because he was Jewish. Öhler was not a Communist but did make his apartment available for illegal meetings.[24]

24 Franz Öhler was arrested after the invasion of the Germans and died in Buchenwald concentration camp on May 4, 1945.

Kornweitz eventually gave Schütte-Lihotzky the coded address of her first contact person in Vienna. To decode the address, she needed the book *Gari Holer* by Hugo Bernatzik. Since it was not available in Zagreb, Schütte-Lihotzky wrote the title on a cigarette paper, which she hid in her ear during her trip to Vienna.

Once in Vienna, she obtained the book, decoded the address, and got in touch with her first contact person. Then a further contact person named "Sonja" arranged her first meeting with Puschmann on January 2, 1941. Margarete Schütte-Lihotzky and Erwin Puschmann met a total of five times between January 2 and 22, 1941.[25] Puschmann's closest colleague "Ossi" was present at three of those meetings and "Sonja" was also present at one of them. Schütte-Lihotzky met twice with just "Ossi," whom she did not find very likable, which was also how she felt about "Sonja." She asked Puschmann why "Ossi" could frequently travel abroad without the Gestapo becoming suspicious. Puschmann explained that "Ossi" was a bookseller, which he said was a perfect front

25 See verdict of the People's Court against Erwin Puschmann, Margarete Schütte-Lihotzky et al., BArch Berlin, R 3017/24835.

that also predestined "Ossi" to arrange his (Puschmann's) planned illegal border crossing to Slovakia. Most of the meetings took place in Café Victoria am Schottentor and one in the apartment of a married couple named Konopicky.[26] Schütte-Lihotzky had already said she would pass on to the KPÖ Executive Committee abroad in Moscow information about the setup of the KPÖ, the production of flyers, and the prevailing attitudes within the Austrian population. Puschmann therefore took her to Anton and Therese Konopicky's apartment, where she sat for hours trying to commit to memory the content of all the documents Puschmann presented to her so she could relate this information from memory in Zagreb or Istanbul later on. She also intended to smuggle a book out of Vienna, which had documents hidden in its covers, and give it to Julius Kornweitz in Zagreb.

26 Therese and Anton Konopicky were also arrested in January 1941 for supporting the KPÖ—they had housed Erwin Puschmann and made their apartment available to him for meetings with other Communist Party functionaries. Therese Konopicky was charged with "making preparations for high treason" on October 29, 1942. She died of pulmonary tuberculosis at the Regional Court of Vienna on April 10, 1943. On June 2, 1943, Anton Konopicky was sentenced to six years in prison for "making preparations for high treason." He was presumably killed during the massacre at Stein prison on April 6, 1945 and was declared dead in 1947.

Fig. 2. Erwin Puschmann (code name "Gerber"), n.p., n.d. [before 1941].

Arrest, Interrogations, Conviction

Margarete Schütte-Lihotzky's departure from Vienna was scheduled for January 23, 1941. Puschmann was to travel a few days later to Moscow via Slovakia, with his border crossing being arranged by "Ossi." On January 21, Schütte-Lihotzky gave "Ossi" the book *Gari Gari*[27] at a meeting also attended by Puschmann. Hidden within its covers were training letters and various reports, for instance a remembered record of a discussion conducted by Communist functionaries in Vienna. On January 22, Margarete Schütte-Lihotzky and Erwin Puschmann were arrested (fig. 3). They were taken together in a car to the Gestapo at nearby Morzinplatz. There they were interrogated separately by officials from *Referat II A 1*, a subunit responsible for the prosecution of Communists. An official accused Schütte-Lihotzky outright of having worked as a courier for the KPÖ Executive Committee abroad. Within the first half hour, she was shown an organizational chart of the KPÖ, which contained the names and even the code names of about 300 members of the illegal KPÖ. Schütte-Lihotzky not only quickly realized that "the Gestapo was already familiar with our entire organization at that time" but also "that the Gestapo could have never arrived at those results through mere observation."[28] During her first night in the police prison on Rossauer Lände (ninth district of Vienna), where the Gestapo's prisoners were placed, she began to suspect that she had been betrayed by a Gestapo informer:

27 Interestingly, the book was written by Hugo Adolf Bernatzik, an Austrian ethnologist and founder of Applied Ethnology. Bernatzik also worked as a passive political informer for the Nazi counter-intelligence agency from 1944. From April 1944 on, he was listed as a "*Zubringer, Völkerkundler*" (regular informer, ethnologist) in Bereich III C 1, a subunit whose task was to counter enemy espionage in the ministries and state offices.

28 Report by M. Schütte, September 22, 1945, DÖW, no. 6188.

29 Ibid.

30 Schütte-Lihotzky, "Von Istanbul nach Wien," 54–55.

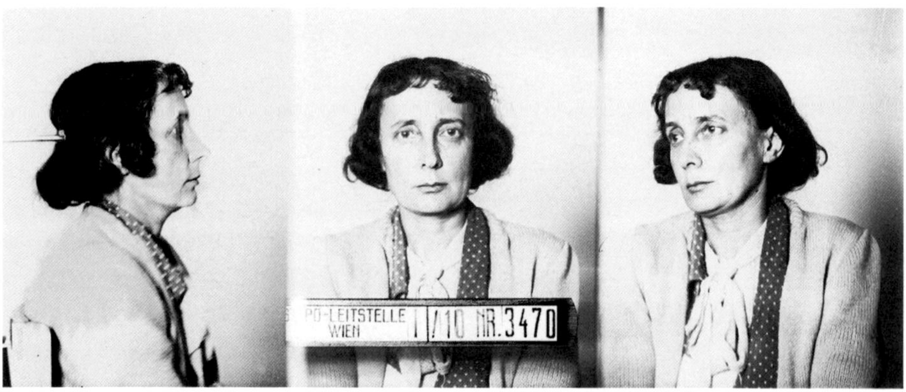

Fig. 3. Margarete Schütte-Lihotzky, identification photo at the Gestapo headquarters, Vienna, 1941.

> And the idea flashed through my head: "Ossi!" Horrified, I refused to accept this idea the way one initially refuses to accept something awful, because it was clear to me what dreadful consequences it would have to have for our party if my suspicion were confirmed. That first night, I also reproached myself for rashly suspecting a comrade of a terrible crime.[29]

Schütte-Lihotzky's suspicion was borne out when the Gestapo officer asked her about her husband's relations with the British intelligence service during the interrogation. She had told Puschmann at a meeting where "Ossi" was also present that in Istanbul her husband had been called to the German consulate and accused of being in contact with the British intelligence service. Wilhelm Schütte denied this accusation vehemently at the time. In her memoirs, Margarete Schütte-Lihotzky herself was still refuting that her husband had ties to the British intelligence service.[30] In actual fact, however, both Wilhelm Schütte and Herbert Feuerlöscher were among the more than one hundred German-speaking émigrés who offered their services to the British—namely, to the Special Operations Executive (SOE)—at the end of 1940 to conduct anti-German activities.[31]

Convinced that Puschmann was above suspicion, Schütte-Lihotzky soon concluded that "Ossi" was a Gestapo informer, and that the Gestapo had therefore been apprised of her every move. In fact both "Ossi," whose real name was Kurt Koppel, and "Sonja," whose real name was Grete Kahane, had been recruited as informers by Lambert Leutgeb, who headed up the intelligence department at the Gestapo headquarters in Vienna from 1940 to 1944. The use of informers was one of the Gestapo's most important weapons for uncovering Resistance groups.[32] It should not be overlooked, however, that about "two-thirds of the informers for the Gestapo headquarters in Vienna for whom there is biographical information were conducting this activity for their clients involuntarily, at least initially."[33] Kahane, born June 10, 1917, had already belonged to the Young Communist League (KJV) before 1938[34] and Koppel, born April 18, 1915, had also already been a member of the KPÖ before 1938.[35] The actual circumstances that led them to becoming informers are

31 See Pirker, *Subversion deutscher Herrschaft*, 139–44. The Special Operations Executive was a British special intelligence unit during World War II, which was founded in mid-July 1940 by Prime Minister Winston Churchill with the aim of waging subversive war. Also see Thomas Flierl, "Mit einem Karton voller Briefe auf Zeitreise," 526–39.

32 Elisabeth Boeckl-Klamper, Thomas Mang, and Wolfgang Neugebauer, *Gestapo-Leitstelle Wien 1938–1945* (Vienna: Edition Steinbauer, 2018), 187.

33 Hans Schafranek, "Drei Gestapo-Spitzel und ein eifriger Kriminalbeamter. Die Infiltration und Zerschlagung des KJV-Baumgarten (1940) und der Bezirksleitung Wien-Leopoldstadt (1940/41) durch V-Leute der Gestapo," in *DÖW-Jahrbuch 2009*, ed. Dokumentationsarchiv des österreichischen Widerstandes (Vienna: Dokumentationsarchiv des österreichischen Widerstandes, 2009), 250–77, here 274.

34 Proceedings before the Regional Court of Vienna as a People's Court against Kurt Koppel, Wiener Stadt- und Landesarchiv, Vg 5 Vr 966/49, copies at DÖW (19827).

35 Ibid.

unknown. What is known is that Kahane was classified under the Nuremberg Race Laws as a Jewish *Mischling* (a person of mixed Jewish and Aryan heritage) and had already been arrested by the Gestapo in 1938. Koppel, who was deemed a Jew under those same laws, had presumably already returned to Vienna from Paris in 1938 with help from the Gestapo. Since Koppel was close to Puschmann, he was aware of all interconnections and happenings within the Communist groupings, so the arrest of Schütte-Lihotzky and Puschmann marked the beginning of a huge wave of arrests, of which Herbert Eichholzer, among others, subsequently fell victim. Of the 1,507 people who were arrested for Communist activity in 1941 by the Gestapo headquarters in Vienna alone, about 700 to 800 were arrested in direct or indirect connection with the work of the two informers Koppel and Kahane.[36]

36 Hans Schafranek, "Wiener Gestapo-Spitzel," 324.

Since Schütte-Lihotzky had no contact at all with any other political prisoners in the police prison, she was initially unable to share her suspicion with anyone else. She adjusted her statements to the Gestapo in the sense that she talked mainly about "Ossi," whom she described as a "good comrade." It was not until she was transferred to the district prison on Schiffamtsgasse that she was able to establish contact with prisoners who were fellow Communists. Using "finger-talk," she "spoke" to her comrades who had cell windows on the opposite side of the prison courtyard or communicated in the evening through the evacuated toilet pipes.

Many of her comrades, such as Puschmann's wife Hella and Therese Konopicky, were initially incredulous that "Ossi" and "Sonja," who were also in a relationship, were Gestapo informers. At the end of 1941 while still in custody awaiting trial, Margarete Schütte-Lihotzky had her suspicion substantiated by Poldi Kovarik, a young prisoner who belonged to the Young Communist League. Kovarik, who had also been arrested because of Kahane and Koppel's activity as informers, now related that the sentence "Ossi is a traitor" was etched onto the bottom of the water pitchers at the police prison on Rossauer Lände. Thanks to this message, the prisoners were able to adjust their statements to the Gestapo in such a way that "Ossi" would be incriminated.[37]

37 Report by M. Schütte.

Schütte-Lihotzky did not see Puschmann again until

September 1942, when the two of them appeared before the Volksgerichtshof (People's Court). She had not been tortured in the course of her interrogations by the Gestapo officers, but Puschmann had been ravaged by the tortures he underwent. On September 22, 1942, she was sentenced to 15 years' imprisonment "for making preparations for high treason," whereas he was sentenced to death. Margarete Schütte-Lihotzky did her prison time at Aichach Prison in Bavaria until she was freed on April 29, 1945; Erwin Puschmann was guillotined on January 7, 1943 at the Regional Court of Vienna.

Epilogue

As early as September 1945, Schütte-Lihotzky wrote a report about her activities in the Resistance and the terrible acts of the Gestapo informers Grete Kahane and Kurt Koppel. She first learned their real names after the Nazi regime was crushed. Her report was an important piece of the puzzle in the criminal prosecution of the Gestapo officers involved in her arrest and of the two informers. Grete Kahane is believed to have died in 1950 in Yugoslavian custody, whereas Koppel managed to go underground and was therefore never held accountable.[38] Lambert Leutgeb, the Gestapo officer responsible for the network of informers, was sentenced to 10 years of hard time by a Yugoslavian military court in November 1948 but was deported to Austria after just four years. When he was questioned in 1958 as a witness in a trial against another Gestapo officer, he gave his profession as "chef in the Hohensalzburg castle restaurant."[39]

In retrospect, the question arises whether the Resistance fighters were aware of how dangerous their activities were, especially since the repeated assertion of "the embattled anti-Nazi Austrians" by the Communist Austrians in exile remained largely a chimera.

All her life, Schütte-Lihotzky responded with indignation when asked why she had taken such a big risk. For her, this step was the logical consequence of the two questions she had already asked herself in Moscow:

> What do we have to do to be able to live again in our native land with a clear conscience after the fall? What do we have to do to help bring about Hitler's fall?[40]

38 Grete Kahane was arrested soon after the end of the war and extradited to Yugoslavia on February 26, 1947 at the instigation of the Soviet occupying power since she had also betrayed Yugoslav partisans. According to her death certificate, she died of nephritis during her imprisonment. The certificate, issued in accordance with the death registration book of the National Committee of Belgrade's III raion, is dated April 8, 1950 but the exact date of her death is missing. See Hans Schafranek, *Widerstand und Verrat. Gestapospitzel im antifaschistischen Untergrund 1938–1945* (Vienna: Czernin, 2017), and also proceedings before the Regional Court of Vienna as a People's Court against Grete Kahane, Wiener Stadt- und Landesarchiv, Vg 9b Vr 373/55, copies at DÖW (51790).

39 Boeckl-Klamper, Mang, and Neugebauer, *Gestapo-Leitstelle*, 451.

40 Schütte-Lihotzky, "Von Istanbul nach Wien," 7–8.

From Anti-Fascist Consensus to Anti-Communist Hegemony. The Marginalization of the Communist Party of Austria at the Onset of the Cold War

Manfred Mugrauer

In the scholarly literature and public discourse concerning Margarete Schütte-Lihotzky, one undisputed finding is that her public contracts in the postwar era remained scanty for one reason: her membership in the Communist Party of Austria (KPÖ) and her long-standing position as president of the KPÖ-affiliated League of Democratic Women of Austria (Bund demokratischer Frauen Österreichs, BDFÖ) (fig. 1).[1] Schütte-Lihotzky herself said that she had virtually had a "professional ban" imposed on her due to the anti-Communist-driven marginalization occurring after 1945, also beyond the Austrian State Treaty in 1955. She linked the ban explicitly to the policies of the Vienna Socialist Party of Austria (SPÖ).[2]

1 By way of example: Otto Kapfinger, "Ich muß ja lachen," *Die Presse, Spectrum* (January 18, 1997): IV; Irene Nierhaus, "Techniken des Sozialen. Der Lebensweg der Architektin Margarete Schütte-Lihotzky," *Der Standard, Album spezial* (January 24, 1997): 2; Elisabeth Holzinger, "Widerstand in Zeiten des Terrors," in Margarete Schütte-Lihotzky, *Erinne-*

rungen aus dem Widerstand. Das kämpferische Leben einer Architektin 1938–1945 (Vienna: Promedia, 2014), 7–20, here 17. Also see Marcel Bois's essay in this volume.

2 Margarete Schütte-Lihotzky, *Erinnerungen aus dem Widerstand 1938–1945*, ed. Chup Friemert (Hamburg: Konkret Literatur Verlag, 1985), 40; "Aus einer besseren Welt zu scheiden …," *Mensch & Büro* 2 (2000): 16–21, here 21.

3 Example: "Berufsverbot in Österreich. Wie eine Expertin für Sozialbauten von der Gemeinde Wien kaltgestellt wurde," *Volksstimme* (December 19, 1976): 11.

As a senate councillor later confided to her, the boycott by the Stadtbauamt (central building authority in Vienna) resulted directly from a resolution by the SPÖ Executive Committee.[3]

This essay will trace the development of the KPÖ from a responsible party of good standing to an outsider within the Austrian party system. Anti-Communism is interpreted here as the integrating ideology during the reconstruction period. In terms of ideological history, the anti-Communist consensus continued the old traditions of anti-Slavic resentments, which were transferred directly to the KPÖ because of its close ties to the Soviet occupying power. Finally, the essay will explore what degree of latitude the KPÖ had in breaking through the anti-Communist constellation in the postwar era.

The KPÖ as Bogeyman

The isolation and marginalization of the KPÖ was a dominant and fundamental feature of Austria's development after World War II. Within a matter of years, the party went from being one of the founding parties of the Second Republic to being a bogeyman for the majority of the Austrian population. The main explanations for this turn of events were the international situation and the specific way in which existing geopolitical factors shaped the development of domestic politics. The transition of the Allies from the anti-Hitler coalition to the politics of the Cold War cemented the shifts in the political landscape in Austria too, a country occupied by four foreign powers at the time. One domestic political effect of this confrontation of systems was that the KPÖ was pushed into isolation. The course was set toward Western orientation, the restoration of capitalism, and anti-Communism. Domestic anti-Communism that was motivated by foreign policy and directed against the Socialist camp was turned against the Communist parties but in no other Western European countries with such vehemence as in West Germany and Austria. Austria became a Western bridgehead and a champion in the effort to contain Communism (fig. 2).

The marginalization of the KPÖ began even before the Cold War started to unfold; the party was on the defensive from the very outset. Although the KPÖ participated in the provisional Renner government as an equal partner of the

Fig. 1. First Austrian Women's Congress on February 24/25, 1951 in the Dreher Park in Vienna; *standing in the middle*, Margarete Schütte-Lihotzky, who was elected President of the League of Democratic Women; *to her left*, Hella Altmann-Postranecky.

Austrian People's Party (ÖVP) and the Socialist Party of Austria (SPÖ) from April 1945 on, the domestic political developments in 1945 already showed that its political influence was being suppressed. From the summer of 1945 on, it was evident that a "silent" ÖVP–SPÖ coalition sought to reduce what it viewed as the disproportionately large influence of the KPÖ. The majority of the SPÖ leadership would not agree to a "united front" or unity of action with the KPÖ, thereby eliminating the basis for the KPÖ's goal of Austria becoming a People's Republic.[4]

The suppression of the KPÖ can be seen at many levels: first on the national level, where in 1947/48 the Communist parties were pushed out of the ruling governments throughout Western Europe in the course of the Marshall Plan. For instance, in November 1947 after criticizing the currency reform, the KPÖ also left the national unity government formed by Leopold Figl. Attacks against positions held by the KPÖ

4 Manfred Mugrauer, *Die Politik der KPÖ in der Provisorischen Regierung Renner* (Innsbruck: StudienVerlag, 2006).

were launched at the local level in the provisional municipal committees and in the civil service, especially in the bureaucracy of the ministries and the Vienna police headquarters, where the KPÖ had considerable influence due to the specific situation in 1945.[5] Attacks also occurred in the factories and trade unions, where most of the Communist trade union secretaries were fired. After the 1950 *Oktoberstreik* (October strike), all but a handful of the Communist trade union secretaries were also expelled from the Austrian Trade Union Federation (ÖGB).[6] Other venues for the anti-Communist campaign included, inter alia, the KZ-Verband (National Association of Austrian Resistance Fighters and Victims of Fascism), the sports clubs, and the IKG (Israeliti-

5 Manfred Mugrauer, "Die KPÖ im Staatsapparat," *Mitteilungen der Alfred Klahr Gesellschaft* 23, no. 4 (2016): 1–18.

6 Peter Autengruber and Manfred Mugrauer, *Oktoberstreik. Die Realität hinter den Legenden über die Streikbewegung im Herbst 1950. Sanktionen gegen Streikende und ihre Rücknahme* (Vienna: ÖGB, 2016).

Fig. 2. "So that this is not your fate—vote for the Austrian People's Party," ÖVP poster for the National Council elections in 1949.

sche Kultusgemeinde, Jewish Community of Vienna). The KZ-Verband was organized as a non-partisan organization until 1948 but was then dissolved by Interior Minister Oskar Helmer because he felt it was being inordinately influenced by the Communists. In the sports clubs, about one-third of the presidents in office were Communists and nearly all of them were replaced by the early 1950s. The IKG was led by Communists until 1948. The list of KPÖ candidates won the majority that year but the other lists joined forces to prevent a Communist president.[7]

Similar examples can be cited in cultural, scholarly, and scientific realms. The actors at Neues Theater in der Scala, which was initiated by the KPÖ in 1948, received no engagements at other theaters or on the radio, even after the Austrian State Treaty was signed in 1955. There were also blacklists containing the names of artists suspected of being Communists.[8] In the anti-Communist climate of the postwar era, Communist scholars and scientists such as the musicologist Georg Knepler, the philosopher Walter Hollitscher, the biochemist Samuel "Mitja" Rapoport, and the historian Leo Stern found no opportunities to have an impact on scholarly and scientific life in Austria. All four of them emigrated between 1949 and 1951 to the GDR, where they launched university careers and worked in top positions. The same is true of the Austrian Communist and composer Hanns Eisler, who had applied unsuccessfully for a professorship in Vienna. The professional ban imposed on Margarete Schütte-Lihotzky by the public authorities must also be seen in this context.

The intellectual atmosphere and political culture of the country was negatively affected by the fact that the anti-Communism directed against the KPÖ did not stop at the party itself but also extended to sympathizers of the KPÖ, both actual and alleged. For instance, peace movement activists, the left-wing Socialists, and creative artists associated with the KPÖ were ghettoized. Hegemonic anti-Communism became a disciplinary instrument, which cast an air of general suspicion over any anticapitalist stance and dismissed it as Communist. In the anti-Communist climate of the postwar era, intellectuals participating in Austrian Peace

7 Manfred Mugrauer, "Die Jüdische Gemeinde als Politikfeld der KPÖ (1945–1955)," in *Genosse. Jude. Wir wollten nur das Paradies auf Erden*, ed. Gabriele Kohlbauer-Fritz and Sabine Bergler (Vienna: Amalthea Signum, 2017), 210–23, here 217.

8 Oliver Rathkolb, "Die Entwicklung der US-Besatzungskulturpolitik zum Instrument des Kalten Krieges," in *Kontinuität und Bruch. 1938 – 1945 – 1955. Beiträge zur österreichischen Kultur- und Wissenschaftsgeschichte*, ed. Friedrich Stadler (Vienna: LIT, 1988), 35–50, here 40–41.

Council campaigns or willing to cooperate with the KPÖ in the scope of the BDFÖ (League of Democratic Women of Austria) were discredited as a fifth column, as crypto-Communists, or as fellow travelers.

The Reconstruction Myth

The Communist parties played a major role in the range of political views in most Western European countries, whereas the anti-Communism in West Germany and Austria became not merely the predominant stance of the political elite but also the determining element of public opinion in general and a state ideology of sorts. Thus, it provided not only a means of dealing with the KPÖ as a political rival but was also a central component of the political culture in Austria after 1945. The anti-Fascist consensus in 1945 soon gave way to an anti-Communist consensus. The much-cited "*Geist der Lagerstrasse*" (spirit of the camp road)—that is, the solidarity that formed among the concentration camp prisoners from different parties during their incarceration—was replaced by an anti-Communist defensive. On the one hand, this shift kept the Communists from actively shaping the Second Republic; on the other, it slowed down efforts to grapple with the Nazi past. Former Nazi Party members were reintegrated into Austrian society. The Austrian-American historian Kurt Tweraser put the situation in a nutshell: "From 1947 onward, the motto of Austrian domestic politics was this: integrate the right, marginalize the left."[9] From 1948/49 onward at the latest, the hegemony of anti-Communism supplanted the efforts to come to terms with National Socialism, bringing denazification to a virtual standstill. Commenting on this aspect, Peter Huemer wrote as follows in the preface of a new edition of Schütte-Lihotzky's Resistance memoirs: "*Blutrichter* (hanging judges) of National Socialism, people with the filthiest hands, were able to continue their careers in Austria after 1945. No one threw them out, but the Resistance fighter against Hitler, who had narrowly escaped death, she was boycotted even though she was also a great authority in her field."[10]

Austrian anti-Communism took on its specific form as an ideology of reconstruction. It became the minimal

9 Kurt Tweraser, *US-Militärregierung für Oberösterreich, Bd. 1. Sicherheitspolitische Aspekte der amerikanischen Besatzung in Oberösterreich-Süd 1945–1950* (Linz: Oberösterreichisches Landesarchiv, 1995), 411.

10 Peter Huemer, foreword to *Erinnerungen aus dem Widerstand. Das kämpferische Leben einer Architektin 1938–1945*, by Margarete Schütte-Lihotzky (Vienna: Promedia, 1994), 9–14, here 13.

consensus between ÖVP and SPÖ, the integrating ideology in the reconstruction era, which culminated in the Social Partnership. The main purpose of this instrumental form of anti-Communism was to safeguard the restoration of capitalism. According to the analysis of the economic historian Fritz Weber, the leadership of the SPÖ and the Austrian Trade Union Federation (ÖGB) utilized anti-Communism "as a purposefully rational political weapon to push through their coalition and Social Partnership policies."[11] It became "the ideology of the masses in the Second Republic [...], [and] was cleverly exploited to *discredit any viewpoint favoring measures to change society*."[12] The key element in this functionalization of domestic politics was the putsch myth, whereby any protest movements and labor disputes influenced by the KPÖ were alleged to be revolt and revolution. Criticism of the one-sided Western orientation, the Marshall Plan, or the system for the wage-price agreements was stigmatized from the outset as Communist, thereby precluding any objective debate. This line of argumentation peaked during the *Oktoberstreik* in 1950, when the KPÖ and the striking workers faced the anti-Communist propaganda of the government, the union, the parties, and the media.

11 Fritz Weber, *Der kalte Krieg in der SPÖ. Koalitionswächter, Pragmatiker und Revolutionäre Sozialisten 1945–1950* (Vienna: Verlag für Gesellschaftskritik, 1986), 130.

12 Ibid., 2 [italics in the original].

Oliver Rathkolb pointed out the substantial significance of anti-Communism in the collective memory of the Second Republic, calling it "a repressed component of the Austrian identity." It had "a much more important unifying function among the elite and in the social discourse after 1945 than, say, the myth of the camp road."[13] Along with the victim myth (Austria as the first victim of National Socialism), the reconstruction myth also began to totter. However, in the mass media and in the speeches of politicians, the history of the postwar era is still interpreted even today as a Social Partnership success story and a successful effort to stave off the Communist threat. Although the KPÖ posed no real threat as a five-percent party, ÖVP and SPÖ styled themselves as saviors of Austria for averting the imminent transformation of the country into a Communist dictatorship. In the National Council elections in 1949, the ÖVP put up a total of 26 anti-KPÖ posters, whose slogans incited fear by raising the specter of a People's Republic. For instance, one poster with

13 Oliver Rathkolb, *Die paradoxe Republik. Österreich 1945 bis 2015* (Vienna: Paul Zsolnay, 2015), 33 and 35.

the slogan “Recognize the danger!” featured an octopus extending its tentacles from the Soviet Union across all of Europe (fig. 3). Another slogan, “You will become a slave to the collective farms!,” warned merchants and tradespeople that their stores and workshops were ostensibly threatened with nationalization and urged them to vote for the ÖVP.

Anti-Communism did weld together the ÖVP–SPÖ coalition, and both parties virtually outdid one other in disassociating themselves from the KPÖ. Nonetheless, in the election campaign they accused each other of making a secret deal with the Communists and of paving the way for a People’s Republic. The KPÖ never advanced beyond its small party status, and Austria becoming a People’s Republic had ceased to be a domestic political option by the November elections of 1945 at the latest. Moreover, anti-Communism was a unifying element between the Social Democratic and the bourgeois camps in Austria. Despite all that, it was a recurring propaganda motif of ÖVP and SPÖ into the 1960s to call the other ruling partner a backer and an aider and abettor of the KPÖ in its bid for power.

Fig. 3. “Recognize the danger! Vote for the Austrian People’s Party,” ÖVP poster for the National Council elections in 1949.

The Ideological History of Anti-Communism

In terms of ideological history, anti-Communism and anti-Sovietism were able to build on nationalistic and racist prejudices against *slawische Untermenschen* (Slavs as subhuman creatures), which reached far back into Austrian history. "Danger from the East," a phantasm summoned well into the 20th century, was generally and fundamentally based on an "abstract primeval fear of the 'barbarian' peoples from the East, whose invasions threatened the West time and time again."[14] Austria's conception of itself as a bulwark against the East can be traced back to the wars fought between the Ottoman Empire and the Hapsburg Monarchy and was reinforced during World War I. As Ingrid Fraberger and Dieter Stiefel noted: "Anti-Communism provided a new label for the old national conflicts from the time of the Monarchy."[15] In the interwar years, a non-partisan anti-Bolshevism emerged and was supported mainly by the bourgeoisie and the rural population but also by the Social Democrats. While the bourgeois-conservative camp turned its fear of revolution and its traditional anti-Socialism into anti-Communism, Social Democratic Austromarxism sought to distance itself from the Soviet path of development.

Fascist ideology, which was directed against "Jewish Bolshevism," could tap into Russophobia and into fears arising in the First Republic about the spread of Bolshevism. The racial fanaticism that the Nazis directed against the Russians proved to have the most powerful effect and continued to be bound up with anti-Communism even after 1945—in contrast to the anti-Semitic components of that fanaticism. For instance, in late 1946, KPÖ Provincial Councillor Laurenz Genner in Lower Austria leveled a criticism concerning the "infamous anti-Russian smear campaign," noting that "many a tenet of Goebbels's propaganda against the Soviet Union" still haunted the minds of Austrians. So, he concluded, the campaign was not solely attributable to the effects of the occupation.[16] The situation was further exacerbated by the anti-Communist Cold War propaganda coming from the West. In sum, Austrian anti-Communism and anti-Sovietism in the immediate postwar era were products of the anti-Slavic and anti-Bolshevist tradition, Fascist

14 Günter Bischof, "Österreich – ein 'geheimer Verbündeter' des Westens? Wirtschafts- und sicherheitspolitische Fragen der Integration aus der Sicht der USA," in *Österreich und die europäische Integration 1945–1993. Aspekte einer wechselvollen Entwicklung*, ed. Michael Gehler and Rolf Steininger (Vienna: Böhlau, 1993), 425–50, here 427.

15 Ingrid Fraberger and Dieter Stiefel, "'Enemy Images': The Meaning of 'Anti-Communism' and its Importance for the Political and Economic Reconstruction in Austria after 1945," in *The Marshall Plan in Austria* (vol. 8 of *Contemporary Austrian Studies*), ed. Günter Bischof, Anton Pelinka, and Dieter Stiefel (New Brunswick: Transaction, 2000), 56–97, here 63.

16 Stenographisches Protokoll, 1. Sitzung der II. Session der IV. Wahlperiode des Landtages von Niederösterreich, November 12, 1946, p. 25.

hate propaganda, and also Cold War polarization. The anti-Russian stereotypes nurtured by Nazi propaganda were also highly effective because the populace felt them "substantiated" by the assaults and other acts of violence by members of the Red Army, which were "reframed as the 'general behavior' of the Red Army.'"[17] Ela Hornung and Margit Sturm outlined the fears the Austrian population had of the "Russians" as follows: "The picture of Bolshevists, Slavs as uncivilized subhuman creatures who descend robbing, murdering, plundering, and raping found its continuation in a highly emotional anti-Communism, a conditioning reinforced by the global political polarization during the Cold War."[18]

In actual practice, the Soviet occupying power did take positive measures, such as quickly setting up democratic structures and a civilian administration and extending financial aid and spontaneous food aid. However, in the face of the assaults and the economic "pillaging" of the country these good deeds receded into the background in the minds of the public or disappeared altogether. Down to the present day, what dominates in the mass consciousness is a negative image of the Soviet occupiers that is shaped by pillages and rapes.

Even after 1945, anti-Soviet sentiment was largely bound up with the anti-Slavic sentiment rooted in Austria. Jacques Hannak, a journalist for *Arbeiter-Zeitung*, wrote that it was "the Socialists' responsibility to serve as the dam [to hold back] the despotic foreign national aspirations of Communism, a very thankless responsibility in the present day yet an absolutely crucial and truly glorious one for the future state of Western civilization and culture."[19] Quotations such as these prove that the SPÖ also employed the conservative occidental ideology espoused by the ÖVP and the Catholic Church as an instrument against the KPÖ. ÖVP and SPÖ were in lockstep in their resentment of the "Asian" character of Bolshevism. This stereotype of the uncivilized East and defense against Asian barbarianism was expressed most clearly in a term the Social Democrats coined: "Usiaten" (Usians). It alluded to the factories in Austria under Soviet management (USIA) and was part of the everyday vocabulary of the *Arbeiter-Zeitung* into the 1960s.[20]

17 Oliver Rathkolb, "Besatzungspolitik und Besatzungserleben in Ostösterreich vom April bis August 1945," in *Österreich 1945. Ein Ende und viele Anfänge*, ed. Manfried Rauchensteiner and Wolfgang Etschmann (Graz: Styria, 1997), 185–206, here 198–99 and 202.

18 Ela Hornung and Margit Sturm, "Stadtleben. Alltag in Wien 1945 bis 1955," in *Österreich 1945–1995. Gesellschaft, Politik, Kultur*, ed. Reinhard Sieder, Heinz Steinert, and Emmerich Tálos (Vienna: Verlag zur Gesellschaftskritik, 1995), 54–67, here 54.

19 Jacques Hannak, *Vier Jahre Zweite Republik. Ein Rechenschaftsbericht der Sozialistischen Partei* (Vienna: Verlag der Wiener Volksbuchhandlung, 1949), 12–13.

20 By way of example: "Der Aufmarsch der Usiaten," *Arbeiter-Zeitung* (October 5, 1950): 2; "Die Betriebsratswahlen," *Arbeiter-Zeitung* (November 3, 1951): 3; "Keine Zusammenarbeit mit Usiaten," *Arbeiter-Zeitung* (April 13, 1962): 2.

No-Win Situation

For the KPÖ, the anti-Soviet and anti-Communist propaganda was a practical political burden and difficult for the party to influence. There was little the KPÖ could do to counter it. Anti-Communism influenced all its policy fields, becoming a nearly insurmountable hurdle. It is the crucial reason why the KPÖ had only an outsider's role in the political system of the Second Republic. A vivid example of this is the socio-economic policy of the KPÖ in the years 1947 to 1950, a period of fierce social conflicts during which the KPÖ raised its oppositional profile with strikes and demonstrations. But in most cases, all it took to dampen the Social Democratic or non-partisan workers' willingness to fight was the mere accusation that a partial strike or a demand for higher wages was a Communist action. "Because the Communists were 'against it,' all of Austria was 'for it,'" wrote Jacques Hannak in an article about the third wage-price agreement concluded in May 1949,[21] thereby—involuntarily—encapsulating the no-win situation the KPÖ faced. At the end of 1949, KPÖ Secretary-General Friedl Fürnberg reported within the party on a conference of the Union of Private Sector Employees, where a KPÖ comrade made a motion for a 10-percent wage increase and was met with thunderous applause. Then the secretary of the Austrian Trade Union Federation noted that the woman making the motion was a Communist, whereupon the proposal was rejected by an overwhelming majority.[22]

These kinds of examples prove that it was nearly impossible for the KPÖ to break out of anti-Communist isolation through its own efforts. The party's scope of action was so limited by anti-Communism that alternative paths of development were largely ruled out. This is also true of the central problem of the KPÖ in the postwar era: its tight bonds with the Soviet Union. In the course of the Cold War, the party was no longer viewed as a partner in reconstructing democracy but rather as an extension of the Soviet Union acting on its behalf. Given the pro-Soviet policies of the KPÖ, the party's political opponents succeeded in branding it an anti-Austrian party, a "Russian party," despite the KPÖ's emphasis on Austrian patriotism. For instance, Karl Waldbrunner had this to say at the SPÖ party conference in November 1947:

21 Hannak, *Vier Jahre Zweite Republik*, 107.

22 ZPA der KPÖ, Protokoll des 4. ZK-Plenums der KPÖ am 11./12.11.1949, Beilage 23: Friedl Fürnberg, p. 1–2.

"Anyone who represents the interests of foreign powers the way the Communists are doing today has forfeited the right to be called an Austrian party."[23] A paradoxical situation arose: the political player that had put the restoration of Austria's independence at the forefront in its Resistance against Nazi Fascism and had paid a heavy death toll in the process was now being defamed as the henchman of a foreign power.

23 *Protokoll des dritten Parteitages der SPÖ, Wien, 23.–26.10.1947*, ed. Parteivorstand der Sozialistischen Partei Österreichs (Vienna: Vorwärts, 1947), 199.

The two major parties—SPÖ and ÖVP—and the Western powers sought to exploit existing anti-Communism and anti-Soviet resentments and turn them against the KPÖ. Anti-Sovietism and anti-Communism, "Russians," and Communism were identical in the minds of the Austrian public, which meant that anti-Soviet biases were seamlessly transferred to the KPÖ. The KPÖ became "an enclave perceived as alien, an 'out-group,' a foreign element viewed as hostile."[24] The process was facilitated by the unconditional identification of the KPÖ with the Soviet Union. The party was largely uncritical of negative events arising from Soviet practices as an occupying power in Austria: assaults by members of the Red Army on the civilian population, the dismantling of industry, and the confiscation of property. The same held true for undesirable developments and crimes in the Socialist countries. The KPÖ trivialized, ignored, or legitimized problems faced by the People's Republics, even going so far as to defend state terror. So, the exclusion of the Communists from actively shaping the Second Republic was coupled with an act of self-exclusion on their part.

24 Anton Pelinka, "Auseinandersetzung mit dem Kommunismus," in *Österreich. Die Zweite Republik, Bd. 1*, ed. Erika Weinzierl and Kurt Skalnik (Graz: Styria, 1972), 169–201, here 183.

The KPÖ had limited latitude in breaking out of this constellation. If the party had publicly distanced itself from the Soviet assaults in Austria and condemned the crimes being perpetrated in the Socialist countries, its credibility would undoubtedly have increased, not least among Social Democratic workers. If the party had adopted a more independent strategy toward Soviet politics, its possibilities within the Austrian labor movement would certainly have expanded. Those who were dissatisfied with the policies of the Figl–Schärf government and the social burdens they entailed would have had an easier time switching to the KPÖ. However, the party's complete identification with the

Soviet Union kept many people from putting their faith in the KPÖ.

That said, one must question the thesis of the political scientist Anton Pelinka that a "break with the Soviet Union" and "an anticipated, consistent Eurocommunism" could have saved the KPÖ "from the fate of total ghettoization."[25] A "break" with the Soviet Union was basically not an option for the KPÖ, especially since no European Communist party took that step in those years. After fierce criticism from the Information Bureau of the Communist and Workers' Parties (Cominform), the Communist Party of Yugoslavia (later League of Communists of Yugoslavia) embarked on an independent path in 1948, which resulted a year later in its expulsion from the global Communist movement. At the founding conference of the Cominform in Szklarska Poręba in September 1947, the Soviet representative Andrej Shdanov had sharply criticized the Communist parties of France and Italy for doing what he described as overemphasizing their independence from Moscow.[26] This sharpness of tone shows just what tight reins the Soviets kept on the movement. A break between the KPÖ and the Soviet Union would have done little to make the party's position in domestic politics easier. In fact, a split of this kind "would have completely pulled the rug from under the work of the Communist Party."[27] By the same token, the massive financial support the KPÖ received from the Soviet Union during the decade-long occupation should not be ignored. What Georg Fülberth said about the Communist Party of Germany (KPD) in the postwar era applies equally to the KPÖ: "There was no possibility [for the KPD] to distance itself from Soviet politics without forsaking itself [...]. In the polarization of the Cold War, subtler positions would hardly have had better prospects than the unconditional loyalty of the KPD to the Soviet Union."[28]

It is also doubtful that a more autonomous KPÖ would have substantially diminished the anti-Communist hysteria during the Cold War. Even if the KPÖ had been critical of Moscow, it would still have been forced into isolation and marginalized at the end of 1947. After all, the anti-Communist propaganda had less to do with the actual internal state and substantive orientation of the party and much more to do

25 Anton Pelinka, "Zur Gründung der Zweiten Republik. Neue Ergebnisse trotz personeller und struktureller Kontinuität," in *Wien 1945 – davor/danach*, ed. Liesbeth Waechter-Böhm (Vienna: Christian Brandstätter, 1985), 21–22, here 22.

26 Grant M. Adibekov, *Das Kominform und Stalins Neuordnung Europas* (Frankfurt am Main: Peter Lang, 2002), 92 and 94.

27 Hans Hautmann, "Die KPÖ in den 1960er bis 1990er Jahren," in *90 Jahre KPÖ. Studien zur Geschichte der Kommunistischen Partei Österreichs*, ed. Manfred Mugrauer (Vienna: Alfred Klahr Gesellschaft, 2009), 53–59, here 55.

28 Georg Fülberth, *KPD und DKP 1945–1990. Zwei kommunistische Parteien in der vierten Periode kapitalistischer Entwicklung* (Heilbronn: Distel, 1990), 41.

with political and ideological exigencies. Without wanting to trivialize the escalations on both sides after the founding of Cominform and the verbal radicalism of the KPÖ toward the SPÖ leadership, one can assume that even if the KPÖ had been "Eurocommunist" the SPÖ would still not have formed a "united front" with it in order to change the direction of domestic politics. Moreover, one can rest assured that the *Oktoberstreik* in 1950 would have been classified as an attempted Communist putsch even if the KPÖ had already broken with the Soviet Union in the preceding years. Even if the KPÖ had not been seen as an unconditionally loyal henchman of the Soviet Union, the Congress of the Peoples for Peace held in Vienna in December 1952 would still have been subjected to a silent boycott, and the Peace Movement would still have been decried as a Communist "camouflage organization." And even if the KPÖ had acted more critically toward the Soviet Union, Margarete Schütte-Lihotzky would probably still not have received more public contracts from the City of Vienna in the postwar era.

Anti-Communism saw its function transformed in the decades to follow. The constellation of the 1950s and 1960s was weakened, especially by the 1968 protests. As a result, Schütte-Lihotzky was rediscovered by architectural historians in the 1980s and 1990s and showered with honors and awards. It should not be forgotten that it was Schütte-Lihotzky's long life that allowed her to experience the public recognition she so deserved. Anti-Communist Cold War rhetoric has still not been completely overcome. That is clear not least from the campaign that the Christian Democratic Union (CDU) launched in Frankfurt am Main in 2000, when a discussion arose about naming a public traffic area in the city after Margarete Schütte-Lihotzky. The anti-Communist biases mobilized at the time ("professed Stalinist," "follower of an inhuman ideology") differed little from those with which Schütte-Lihotzky had already been confronted in the 1940s and 1950s.[29] Ultimately the CDU did not succeed in preventing a park in Siedlung Praunheim, a housing development in Frankfurt, from being named after her. This honor highlights an important difference from the anti-Communist hegemony of the 1950s.

29 See Marcel Bois's essay in this volume.

On the Order of Cooking Spoons. Margarete Schütte-Lihotzky and Women's Politics within the Communist Party of Austria after 1945—A Case Study

Karin Schneider

Not only was Margarete Schütte-Lihotzky a member of the Communist Party of Austria (KPÖ) during her time in the Resistance against National Socialism, but she remained in the party to her dying day, a total of more than 60 years, despite all the upheavals in society and within the party.[1] From 1948 to 1968, she served as president of the League of Democratic Women of Austria (Bund demokratischer Frauen Österreichs, BDFÖ; also referred to below as the "League"), an organization affiliated with the KPÖ. For her, this clear-cut political commitment resulted in marginalization and professional disadvantages due to prevailing anti-Communist sentiment.[2] Although she was able to work as an architect, she received virtually no contracts from the City of Vienna, a major client of the day. She viewed this situation as akin to a professional ban.[3] In addition, anti-

1 See Marcel Bois's essay in this volume.

2 Oliver Rathkolb, "Die Entwicklung der US-Besatzungskulturpolitik zum Instrument des Kalten Krieges," in *Kontinuität und Bruch. 1938 – 1945 – 1955. Beiträge zur österreichischen Kultur- und Wissenschaftsgeschichte*, ed. Friedrich Stadler (Münster: LIT, 2004), 35–50, here 41–43; also see Manfred Mugrauer's essay in this publication.

Fascist Resistance fighters generally fell into disrepute in postwar Austrian society, being viewed as "traitors to the Fatherland," at least from the late 1940s on.[4]

Margarete Schütte-Lihotzky was therefore excluded from the public arena for decades, not only professionally but also in a broader social and cultural sense. Between 1953 and 1985 she did not take part in a single exhibition and did not appear in the media again until the 1970s.[5] Under these circumstances, she moved closer to the KPÖ during the postwar era and intensified her political engagement there. As the president of the BDFÖ and as an activist in the peace movement and in anti-Fascist efforts, she gave speeches at demonstrations and served as a delegate at international conferences and meetings.[6]

Depicting the political Margarete Schütte-Lihotzky and her party-related work poses difficulties, which themselves express the various logics of marginalization under which this work unfolded and are also reflected in the gaps in the research conducted thus far. So, neither architectural historiography nor biographical research on Margarete Schütte-Lihotzky focuses on her engagement in the KPÖ and the BDFÖ. Marcel Bois points out that although Schütte-Lihotzky's political activities may have been mentioned in scholarly studies or biographical summaries, they have not yet been subjected to the same systematic analysis and interpretation as her architectural work. In his essay, he undertakes the first-ever attempt "to analyze Schütte-Lihotzky's lifelong political engagement and to put it in a historical context."[7] Bois's diagnosis of a research gap also applies to historiographies by and about the KPÖ. Apart from isolated articles, these writings do not specifically explore Schütte-Lihotzky's own work and generally deal very little with the work of women in the party or their activities on women's politics, including policymaking on women's issues.[8] One common difficulty in grasping the actual individual directions of Schütte-Lihotzky's political activities in substantive terms arises from the fact that party functionaries tend to operate not as individual personalities but rather within and in the name of party structures and ideologies, which they may help to shape yet to which they also con-

3 Susanne Sohn, "Eine außergewöhnliche Frau. Zum 90. Geburtstag von Margarete Schütte-Lihotzky," in *Frauen der KPÖ. Gespräche und Portraits*, ed. Frauenreferat der KPÖ, Maria Lautischer-Grubauer, and Susanne Sohn (Vienna: Globus, 1989), 53–55, here 53; for a critical and analytical perspective, see Bois's essay.

4 See Bois's essay.

5 Ibid.

6 Ibid.

7 Ibid.

8 Vera Schwarz, *Meine roten Großmütter. Politische Aktivität aus der KPÖ ausgetretener/ausgeschlossener Frauen* (Frankfurt am Main: Peter Lang, 2010), 60. In her master's thesis, Vera Schwarz aims to close this research gap in two respects by focusing on women who were excluded from or left the KPÖ in the party crisis around 1968. Margarete Schütte-Lihotzky is thus not part of her sample.

sciously adapt themselves. Therefore, the task must be to reach a deeper understanding of Margarete Schütte-Lihotzky's political and ideological field of activity as a female Communist within the organizations and to subject it to critical analysis. As regards her work as BDFÖ president, this would entail fathoming out images of women and gender constructions at play within the League. This could be done, for example, by examining the existing sources—journals, programs—for evidence of these constructions, in both the texts and the illustrations. An image and text analysis of this kind could entail linking the image and text with the political developments on gender orders of the time to find out what policy ideas female Communists had to offer in the postwar era. Since such an extensive project exceeds the scope of the present essay, I will broach this research perspective using a single source as a case study—namely, a 1952 BDFÖ brochure entitled *Von Frau zu Frau* (From woman to woman), which I will examine here in a manner informed by discourse analysis. To the extent secondary literature allows, I will start by contextualizing this source in a brief description of the structures of Communist women's politics in the postwar era and their ideological directions.

Communist Women's Politics in the Postwar Era

At the first KPÖ women's conference in April 1946, Margarete Schütte-Lihotzky was elected to the Central Women's Committee of the KPÖ.[9] Two months later, the League of Democratic Women of Austria (BDFÖ) was founded at the Musikverein in Vienna as a non-partisan and interdenominational organization for women.[10] It brought together a variety of women, some prominent and most from the middle and upper classes.[11] Several of them worked in a bourgeois setting, such as the first head of the newly reinstated postwar version of the National Council of Women—Austria, Henriette Hainisch;[12] others, such as the Resistance fighters Anna Grün and Margarete Schütte-Lihotzky, had close ties to the KPÖ.[13]

In 1948, the BDFÖ acceded to the Women's International Democratic Federation (WIDF), founded in Paris in 1945. It was a broad alliance of different women's organizations from "the leftist spectrum [...], which opposed gender-

9 Zentrales Frauenkomitee der KPÖ (ed.), *Frauen sprechen! Die erste österreichische Frauenkonferenz der Kommunistischen Partei Österreichs im April 1946* (Vienna: Stern-Verlag, 1946).

10 Heidi Niederkofler, *Mehrheit verpflichtet: Frauenorganisationen der politischen Parteien in Österreich in der Nachkriegszeit* (Vienna: Löcker, 2009), 47–48.

11 Niederkofler, *Mehrheit*, 48–49; Manfred Mugrauer, "Hella Altmann-Postranecky (1903–1995). Funktionärin der ArbeiterInnenbewegung und erste Frau in einer österreichischen Regierung," in *Forschungen zu Vertreibung und Holocaust. Jahrbuch 2018*, ed. Dokumentationsarchiv des österreichischen Widerstandes (Vienna: Dokumentationsarchiv des österreichischen Widerstandes, 2018), 267–306, here 293.

12 Niederkofler, *Mehrheit*, 48.

13 Irma Schwager, "Kommunistische Frauenpolitik in der Nachkriegszeit," presentation at the Alfred Klahr Gesellschaft symposium *Befreiung und Wiederaufbau – Die KPÖ als Regierungspartei* on April 16, 2005 in Vienna, accessed May 7, 2022, http://www.klahrgesellschaft.at/Mitteilungen/Schwager_2_05.html.

specific, class-specific, colonial, and ethnic or 'racist' inequalities."[14] The WIDF was also originally conceived as nonpartisan and had initially tried to position itself as supporting "the peaceful coexistence of systems and the anti-Fascist consensus."[15] But it, too, was compelled by the Cold War to adopt a polar view of the world. By the time of its second congress in Budapest in 1948, the vast majority of non-Communist members were already gone, and the organization's policies took on a "decidedly pro-Soviet" bent. At the same time, the WIDF itself became the target of anti-Communist politics. It was forced out of its headquarters in Paris and subsequently moved them to East Berlin.[16]

By 1948, the WIDF was already clearly positioned politically. After the BDFÖ acceded to it, "the bourgeois women left [the BDFÖ], because they considered it to be under excessive Communist influence."[17] At the same time, the KPÖ and the BDFÖ grew closer together. Mugrauer points out that the League had not developed any activities in the period after its founding and therefore talks about the KPÖ reactivating it "with an altered understanding of its politics and organization."[18] In 1949, at the 14th Party Congress of the KPÖ, the internal party structures dealing with women's issues up to that point were eliminated, and the established KPÖ women's groups were integrated into the BDFÖ, a move that met with criticism from several of the female comrades.[19] Thanks to the support of the KPÖ, the BDFÖ was able to expand its scope of activities massively and extend them beyond Vienna. In 1949, the BDFÖ held its first congress, where Ida Flöckinger, Margarete Schütte-Lihotzky, and Lina Loos were elected as co-presidents.[20] Although its staff and its magazine *Stimme der Frau* were funded by the KPÖ, the BDFÖ acted as an independent and non-partisan association. This approach was only partially successful, also because Social Democratic women resented cooperating with their Communist counterparts in the BDFÖ. Even when short-term alliances were involved—for instance, for staging joint women's conferences—the watchword of the women in the Socialist Party of Austria (today's Social Democratic Party of Austria; both abbreviated SPÖ) was "Competition, not cooperation."[21]

14 Francisco de Haan, "Hoffnungen auf eine bessere Welt: Die frühen Jahre der Internationalen Demokratischen Frauenföderation (IDFF/WIDF) (1945–1950)," *Feministische Studien* 2 (2009): 241–57, here 241.

15 Ibid.

16 Ibid.

17 Schwager, "Kommunistische Frauenpolitik," n.p.; Niederkofler, *Mehrheit*, 49.

18 Mugrauer, "Altmann-Postranecky," 293.

19 Niederkofler, *Mehrheit*, 60.

20 Ibid., 59.

21 Maria Mesner, "Mit dem Strom und gegen den Wind: Frauentag in den Nachkriegsjahren," in *Frauentag! Erfindung und Karriere einer Tradition*, ed. Heidi Niederkofler et al. (Vienna: Löcker, 2011), 140–71, here 154.

One of Margarete Schütte-Lihotzky's major tasks as BDFÖ president was to call for demonstrations on International Women's Day and to appear at them as a speaker.[22] Until 1955, these rallies had a general motto each year. In 1946 it was "Peace and liberty. Rebuilding democracy." The next year the KPÖ women called for "an independent, democratic, progressive Austria!" A focus of the BDFÖ in general and thus also of women's demands in the late 1940s and early 1950s was a political commitment to peace, which was often combined with an appeal to "women as mothers."[23] Women's Day in 1948 featured the fight "against war" and "for the child."[24]

22 Ibid.

23 Mugrauer, "Altmann-Postranecky," 296; Mesner, "Strom und Wind," 158.

24 Mesner, "Strom und Wind," 158.

Women as Responsible for "Family Happiness"

In 1956, the BDFÖ conducted a survey about the wishes and demands of Austrian women. It summarized these "urgent problems of life" the following year in an "Emergency Program." Women want peace, the program said, and to that end, it is important to protect Austrian neutrality; the government must promote understanding among the major powers and oppose the Cold War. Women want a healthy and happy family because that is the foundation of the state. They want adequate protection for mother and child. Society must also afford women special protection because they bear life. Further demands raised time and again in this brochure and throughout the postwar era are these: equal pay for equal work, protection of motherhood, and modern laws on marriage and the family. One essential demand connected to Communist women's policy in the First Republic was the call to reform Paragraph 144, under which abortion was a punishable offense.[25] In contrast to its stance in the First Republic, however, the KPÖ in the postwar era did not demand that this paragraph be abolished, but rather amended to allow abortion on the basis of social indications.[26]

Generally speaking, one topos of KPÖ/BDFÖ women's politics in the postwar decades that is well-substantiated by the sources was to appeal to women specifically as mothers and to deduce their commitment to a policy of peace, in particular, from this role, "thus asserting a substantial connectedness between women/mothers and peace" (fig. 1).[27] As progressive as the Communists' demands at the time were

25 Bund Demokratischer Frauen Österreichs (ed.), *Was wir fordern. Sofortprogramm des Bundes Demokratischer Frauen Österreichs* (Vienna: Bund Demokratischer Frauen Österreichs, 1957).

26 Mugrauer, "Altmann-Postranecky," 299.

27 Ibid., 298.

in terms of labor law (equal pay for all) and family policy (equality of father and mother within the family), the party was nonetheless unable to continue the more radical social policy concepts it had espoused in the early 1920s, such as the socialization of the household.[28] Most articles about the "household" appearing at the time in the KPÖ magazine for working women *Die Arbeiterin* describe the private sphere as an exclusively reactionary negative foil to the potentially revolutionary industrial world of work.[29] By contrast, the household and the living space were key fields of action in the 1950s for *Stimme der Frau* in addressing women directly about how they themselves could better meet basic needs in their own personal lives.

Stimme der Frau repeatedly featured articles by "Arch. G. Schütte-Lihotzky" that tried to convey to readers architectural knowledge about the design of the living space and the kitchen that would enable women, even in cramped living conditions, to maintain a semblance of privacy, simplify housework, and live as a "*Kleinfamilie*" (nuclear fam-

28 Karin Schneider, "Verborgene Feminismen. Denk- und Utopieangebote der österreichischen Arbeiterinnenbewegung der Ersten Republik unter Fokus auf die KPDÖ" (master's thesis, University of Vienna, 2004).

29 Ibid.

Fig. 1. Margarete Schütte-Lihotzky (*center*) at the Congress of the Austrian Woman in Vienna, March 26 to 28, 1954; *on her left*, Maria Subik; *far right*, Irma Schwager.

ily).[30] From the perspective of social history, the new understanding of housework and home life in the KPÖ propaganda concerning women's politics should be described as complex and not simply as reactionary. As the economic upswing set in, the model of the bourgeois nuclear family became an attainable life vision for the vast majority of the population. The Social Democrats had already been proposing it for the working class in the 1920s. In terms of social history, this model can be viewed as an innovation, yet on a discursive level it was simultaneously based on reactionary images of women of the kind propagated in Fascism and National Socialism.[31]

Neither in the First Republic nor in the postwar era did the female Communists broach the relationship between the genders as a subject to be understood politically as a societal contradiction. This did not change until the late 1970s following discussions and debates with, by, and within the new women's movement.[32] Paradoxically, however, references to a political understanding of this kind are more likely to be found in writings by Margarete Schütte-Lihotzky—despite her rather conservative image of women—than in the radical dismissals of the private sphere by female KPÖ authors in the early 1920s. For instance, Schütte-Lihotzky wrote as follows in her 1953 article "Planen und Bauen, Euch Frauen geht es an" (Planning and building—these things matter to you women):

> It is so very important for all aspects of our life—that things are built and how they are built—so important for our work in the household, factory, office [...] so important for overall happiness in our families and in our lives! And practically everything is important for us women—starting with overall regional planning to urban planning, from housing construction to apartment appointments, to furniture and even to the way we can store our cooking spoon in the kitchen, all these things are interdependent.[33]

Women are made implicitly and, later in the text, explicitly responsible for the kitchen, cooking spoons, and family happiness and are addressed in the scope of these responsibilities as important agents in building the state. Besides

30 See, for example, Grete Schütte-Lihotzky, "Hubers bekommen ein Kind," *Stimme der Frau* 51 (December 17, 1949), University Archive of the University of Applied Arts Vienna, Nachlass Margarete Schütte-Lihotzky (UAUAK, NL MSL), TXT/295; the quotation marks around "*Kleinfamilie*" (nuclear family) relate to the construction of a particular life model along a father-mother-child(ren) schema. For the nuclear family to live together successfully, the generations and genders must be separated into different living areas, at least according to Margarete Schütte-Lihotzky's writings.

31 Mesner, "Strom und Wind," 164.

32 Mugrauer, "Altmann-Postranecky," 297.

33 Grete Schütte-Lihotzky, "Planen und Bauen. Euch Frauen geht es an," *Stimme der Frau* 6 (February 7, 1953), UAUAK, NL MSL, TXT/297. Also see Christine Zwingl's essay in this volume.

conservatively equating women with mothers and housewives, this text also lays out the perspective of seeing private life as political and of recognizing the order that is imposed on cooking spoons as a field of political action.

Von Frau zu Frau: A Case Study in Analysis

In 1952 the BDFÖ published a brochure entitled *Von Frau zu Frau* (From woman to woman).[34] Under the heading "For the Protection of Mother and Child," we see on page four a photo of a small child (probably a girl) standing in a gloomy narrow street looking lost. In the background are another male-connoted, adult-appearing figure and an older child, likely a girl judging from her hairstyle. Laundry is drying on clotheslines hung across the street; everything seems miserable and dreary (fig. 2).

In the lower lefthand corner on the same page is a photo of a young person with the attributes of a boy: billed cap, striped shirt, x-back suspenders, hands on his hips. He is standing in front of a comic book rack. The caption for the

34 Bund Demokratischer Frauen Österreichs and Rosl Grossmann Breuer (eds.), *Von Frau zu Frau* (Vienna: Bund Demokratischer Frauen Österreichs, 1952). All quotations from a primary source cited below refer to this brochure. The page numbers are given in the text.

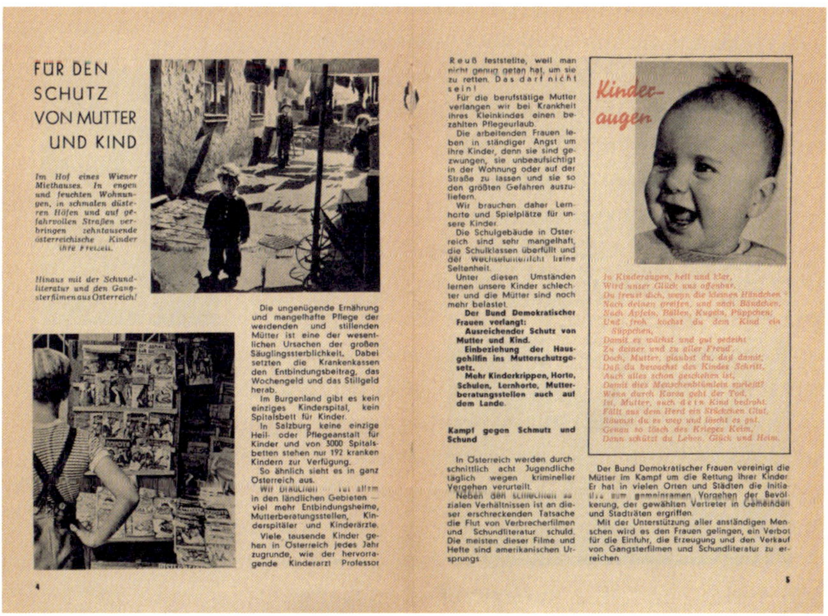

FÜR DEN SCHUTZ VON MUTTER UND KIND

Im Hof eines Wiener Miethauses. In engen und feuchten Wohnungen, in schmalen düsteren Höfen und auf gefahrvollen Straßen verbringen zehntausende österreichische Kinder ihre Freizeit.

Hinaus mit der Schundliteratur und den Gangsterfilmen aus Österreich!

Die ungenügende Ernährung und mangelhafte Pflege der werdenden und stillenden Mütter ist eine der wesentlichen Ursachen der großen Säuglingssterblichkeit. Dabei setzten die Krankenkassen den Entbindungsbeitrag, das Wochengeld und das Stillgeld herab.

Im Burgenland gibt es kein einziges Kinderspital, kein Spitalsbett für Kinder.

In Salzburg keine einzige Heil- oder Pflegeanstalt für Kinder und von 3000 Spitalsbetten stehen nur 192 kranken Kindern zur Verfügung.

So ähnlich sieht es in ganz Österreich aus.

Wir brauchen — vor allem in den ländlichen Gebieten — viel mehr Entbindungsheime, Mutterberatungsstellen, Kinderspitäler und Kinderärzte.

Viele tausende Kinder gehen in Österreich jedes Jahr zugrunde, wie der hervorragende Kinderarzt Professor Reuß feststellte, weil man nicht genug getan hat, um sie zu retten. Das darf nicht sein!

Für die berufstätige Mutter verlangen wir bei Krankheit ihres Kleinkindes einen bezahlten Pflegeurlaub.

Die arbeitenden Frauen leben in ständiger Angst um ihre Kinder, denn sie sind gezwungen, sie unbeaufsichtigt in der Wohnung oder auf der Straße zu lassen und sie so den größten Gefahren auszuliefern.

Wir brauchen daher Lernhorte und Spielplätze für unsere Kinder.

Die Schulgebäude in Österreich sind sehr mangelhaft, die Schulklassen überfüllt und der Wechselunterricht keine Seltenheit.

Unter diesen Umständen lernen unsere Kinder schlechter und die Mütter sind noch mehr belastet.

Der Bund Demokratischer Frauen verlangt:

Ausreichender Schutz von Mutter und Kind.

Einbeziehung der Hausgehilfin ins Mutterschutzgesetz.

Mehr Kinderkrippen, Horte, Schulen, Lernhorte, Mutterberatungsstellen auch auf dem Lande.

Kampf gegen Schmutz und Schund

In Österreich werden durchschnittlich acht Jugendliche täglich wegen krimineller Vergehen verurteilt.

Neben den schlechten sozialen Verhältnissen ist an dieser erschreckenden Tatsache die Flut von Verbrecherfilmen und Schundliteratur schuld. Die meisten dieser Filme und Hefte sind amerikanischen Ursprungs.

Kinderaugen

In Kinderaugen, hell und klar,
Wird unser Glück uns offenbar.
Du freust dich, wenn die kleinen Händchen
Nach deinen greifen, und nach Bändchen,
Nach Äpfeln, Bällen, Kugeln, Püppchen;
Und froh kochst du dem Kind ein Süppchen,
Damit es wächst und gut gedeiht
Zu deiner und zu aller Freud'.
Doch, Mutter, glaubst du, daß damit,
Daß du bewachst des Kindes Schritt,
Auch alles schon geschehen ist,
Damit dies Menschenblümlein sprießt?
Wenn durch Korea geht der Tod,
Ist, Mutter, auch dein Kind bedroht.
Fällt aus dem Herd ein Stückchen Glut,
Räumst du es weg und löschst es gut.
Genau so lösch des Krieges Keim,
Dann schützt du Leben, Glück und Heim.

Der Bund Demokratischer Frauen vereinigt die Mütter im Kampf um die Rettung ihrer Kinder. Er hat in vielen Orten und Städten die Initiative zum gemeinsamen Vorgehen der Bevölkerung, der gewählten Vertreter in Gemeinden und Stadträten ergriffen.

Mit der Unterstützung aller anständigen Menschen wird es den Frauen gelingen, ein Verbot für die Einfuhr, die Erzeugung und den Verkauf von Gangsterfilmen und Schundliteratur zu erreichen.

4

5

Fig. 2. *Von Frau zu Frau*, ed. Rosl Grossmann-Breuer and Bund Demokratischer Frauen Österreichs (Vienna: Bund Demokratischer Frauen Österreichs, 1952), 4 and 5.

first photo reads: "In the courtyard of a tenement in Vienna. Tens of thousands of Austrian children spend their leisure time in cramped, damp apartments, in narrow, dreary courtyards, and on streets full of danger." The caption for the second photo reads: "Get the trashy literature and gangster movies out of Austria." The body of the text deals with the destitution of mothers and children, the high level of child mortality, the lack of childcare facilities, health care for mothers and children, too few facilities for children of working mothers, and overcrowded classrooms. At the end of the article is a summary of the demands: "Adequate protection for mother and child. Inclusion of the servant girl in maternity protection law. More nursery schools, after-school care centers, schools, after-school learning centers, advice centers for mothers, also in rural areas."

Then comes the following phrase, also in boldface implying that it could be one of the demands but set off from the rest of the text and therefore more likely to be the heading of the next article: "Fight against Filth and Trash." The article reports that "in Austria, an average of eight young people a day [are convicted] of a criminal offense." "Besides bad social conditions" it is noted that the "deluge of crime movies and trashy literature" is to be blamed for this situation. Now it is clear how the boy in front of the comic book rack fits in and what he is supposed to be protected against. On a semantic level, the "filth" in the neighborhood in the first picture goes hand in hand with the "filth and trash" in movies and literature and with the need for "protection" from both. The text goes on to say that "most of these movies and comic books originate in America" and that the "League of Democratic Women of Austria (BDFÖ) [...] unites the mothers in the fight to save their children." Actually, the collaboration between the Communists and other groups such as the Catholic Youth was amazingly effective in the massive, aggressive, and successful campaign against "filth and trash" in the early 1950s.[35]

On page five opposite the first two photos is a further photo of a child, the portrait of a decidedly happy and well-fed baby. Underneath the photo is a poem addressed to mothers. It describes a child's sweet eyes and hands and the

35 Edith Blaschitz, Der *"Kampf gegen Schmutz und Schund." Film, Gesellschaft und die Konstruktion nationaler Identität in Österreich (1946–1970)* (Vienna: LIT, 2014), 102.

DIE ENTWÜRDIGTE FRAU

Es gibt Länder, in denen alles käuflich ist — auch die Ehre und [illegible] an, die Filme, die aus den USA zu uns herüberkommen. Wie zeigen sie die Frau? Als bloßes Lustobjekt des Mannes, als „Vamp", der es versteht, sich um Höchstpreise zu verkaufen, als Wesen, dessen einziger Wert im „Sex-Appeal" liegt, in seiner Fähigkeit, die Männer anzuziehen.

Das sehen wir im Film. Und wir erleben es auch in der Praxis. Die österreichischen Zeitungen sind voll mit Berichten über Prostitution Minderjähriger, über die Invasion von „Amigirls" in den Garnisonstädten, in der Zunahme von Sexualverbrechen und Überfällen. Es gibt Städte in unserem Land, wie z. B. Salzburg, wo sich eine Frau am Abend nicht mehr allein auf die Straße traut.

Boogi-Woogi, Hollywood und Prostitution von halben Kindern — bewahrt unser Land vor diesem Gift.

8

In der Sowjetunion, in den Ländern der Volksdemokratie ist der alte Traum der Frau, gleichberechtigt und frei zu sein, verwirklicht. Es gibt dort kein Arbeitslosenelend, Frau und Mann erhalten für gleiche Arbeit gleichen Lohn, die Frau hat jede Aufstiegsmöglichkeit, kein Beruf ist ihr verschlossen, es gibt weibliche Bürgermeister, Richter, Minister, und ihre Zahl nimmt immer mehr zu. Die Frau hat sich einen Ehrenplatz erkämpft.

[illegible] sondern auch für die Kinder. In Kindergärten und -horten sind die Kinder gut aufgehoben, auch wenn die Mutter arbeiten geht. Solche Kindergärten gibt es auch in den Dörfern. In den Ferien werden die Kinder auf Kosten des Staates auf Erholung geschickt. Auch für sie hat ein neues, schöneres Leben begonnen.

Für dieses 27stöckige Hochhaus auf dem Smolenskplatz in Moskau haben die fünf Architektinnen die Pläne gezeichnet und an der Ausgestaltung führend mitgearbeitet

Die befreite Frau

9

Fig. 3. *Von Frau zu Frau*, ed. Rosl Grossmann-Breuer and Bund Demokratischer Frauen Österreichs (Vienna: Bund Demokratischer Frauen Österreichs, 1952), 8 and 9.

joy the mother derives from taking care of and protecting her child. The poem ends as follows: "If death spreads across Korea, Mother, *your* child is also threatened." With this sentence, mothers are once again called upon to combine their concern about their own children with a concern about the world—specifically, with the dangers of war, which, like the danger from violence-inducing gangster movies, emanate from the USA.

This projection of all threats in the world onto the United States and its popular culture is expressed even more drastically on page eight, where it is linked directly to the construction of images of women. At the top right is a cartoon rendition of a woman, with the depiction of her body ending just above her thighs. She is wearing a tight-fitting bodysuit that makes her appear almost naked and emphasizes her ample breasts. Her arms are quite muscular, and she holds a pistol in each hand, aiming them in two different directions at points outside the picture. She is looking out of the picture to the right, in the opposite direction to the potential line of fire (fig. 3). Across the lower left is the word "suspense." The article suggests that it is a movie poster or perhaps a poster for a special event. Next to it is the following explanation in capital letters: "The Degraded Woman." The accompanying text offers the following explanation: "There are countries where everything is for sale—even the honor and dignity of women. Take a look at them, the movies coming to us from the USA. How do they depict women? As mere sexual objects of men, as vamps who are adept at selling themselves to the highest bidder, as creatures whose only value lies in their sex appeal, in their ability to attract men." The photo under the first column of text contains clippings of three newspaper headlines: "Schoolgirl Secretly a Prostitute," "The Moral Morass at US Headquarters Endangers Our Youth," and "Americans Seduce Minors." And then in boldface: "Boogie-woogie, Hollywood, and prostitution of individuals who are practically still children—protect our country from this poison."

This text is highly irritating, not only because equating popular culture with prostitution and crime in this way would hardly be associated with a leftist position today. It is also interesting that today's phantasms of "the Other" and the menace are constructed according to the exact same pattern. Women are always the ones whose physical integrity is at stake and who must be protected from being sexually assaulted by "the Other." These "Others" manipulate their own women too and endanger "our own culture" with their false notions of femininity. Associations with today's anti-Muslim racism are obvious, but also the differences. Whereas in this example from the early 1950s, the exposure of the female body in public is the reference point for the oppression and exploitation of women, in the case of today's anti-Muslim discourse it is the covering of the female body. Communist ill feelings in 1952 were directed against the strong influences of an occupying power's popular culture[36] while right-wing politics today target a small and precarious group of refugees and resident Muslim men and women.

The "filth and trash" debate lost significance in the late 1960s. In the context of the new women's movement, left-

36 Kaspar Maase, *BRAVO Amerika. Erkundungen zur Jugendkultur der Bundesrepublik in den fünfziger Jahren* (Hamburg: Junius, 1992); Rathkolb, "US-Besatzungskulturpolitik," 46–47.

ist feminists and Communists had another, more pointed repertoire of reflections to criticize "women as sexual objects of men" than to refer to their "honor and dignity." Nonetheless, impulsive anti-Americanism[37] and resentment toward certain forms of popular or youth culture associated with America remained a variation of leftist everyday thought. Anti-Americanism of the kind clearly expressed in the text analyzed above, in particular, and in the "filth and trash" debate in general, implies the idea that a "harmful" popular culture from the USA, as the imagined outside world, was fed as "poison" into "our" individual and social body, which we construe to be unified and "pure." These types of constructions also contain anti-Semitic constructions of meaning in a subtle form. "Poison" and the idea of "invisible penetration" and "contamination" were well-known anti-Semitic metaphors being spread before and during the Nazi era. These metaphors did not simply disappear after World War II; they became components of political vocabulary.[38]

The image of "The Degraded Woman" is juxtaposed with a different depiction of women on the opposite page (page nine). It is a photo of five women all bent over work documents with the heading "The Liberated Woman." Their hair is cut short or tied back; all of them are wearing garments with virtually closed collars. Above this photo is another one showing a very modern-looking skyscraper. The caption: "The five female architects drew up the plans for this 27-floor skyscraper on Smolensk Square in Moscow and played lead roles in designing it." The women reading this article find out that the Soviet Union had already met the demands for equality and the alleviation of child poverty described in the initial sections of the brochure.

In loose association with the "female architects" as prototypes of "The Liberated Woman," Margarete Schütte-Lihotzky appears on the last page of the brochure. Underneath the heading "Women at the Helm of the League of Democratic Women," she is quoted as follows:

> [...] We must set aside everything that is divisive in order to stand up together for our families, for our children. After all, what is the use of the individual being a good housewife, a good educator and worker?

37 On basic theoretical instruments for critiquing the anti-Americanism of the left, see Moishe Postone, "Geschichte und Ohnmacht. Massenmobilisierung und aktuelle Formen des Antikapitalismus," in *Deutschland, die Linke und der Holocaust. Politische Interventionen* (Freiburg: ça ira, 2005), 195–212; on the National Socialist topos of the "cultureless" American and the deeper roots of anti-Americanism in Austria, see Rathkolb, "US-Besatzungskulturpolitik," 38–39.

38 Alexander Bein refers to the "comparison of the stock exchange with a poisonous tree," which "became common parlance among anti-Semites," and to the image of the "*Volkskörper*" (national body), which had been a commonplace concept since the 19th century and took on an increasingly real biological meaning when there was talk that the "poisons of Bolshevism, capitalism, and intellectualism sought to penetrate and destroy it." Alexander Bein, "'Der jüdische Parasit.' Bemerkungen zur Semantik der Judenfrage," *Vierteljahrshefte für Zeitgeschichte* 2 (1965): 121–40, here 121. While the Communists of the 1950s also pointed out other "poisons," they did utilize the metaphorical images of a "healthy national body" and "penetrating poison."

> Things happen over her head that make a mockery of her industriousness, that ruin her efforts. I am thinking now primarily about the horrible danger of a new war. Every woman wants peace. Today, countless women from all countries and continents are already employing all means available to them to preserve peace [...].

The contradictory situation in which Communist women's politics were conducted in the postwar era becomes plain here. On the one hand, the female Communists sought to set aside everything that was divisive, unlike their Social Democratic counterparts. They did so primarily by supporting the BDFÖ, which was conceived as non-partisan. On the other hand, they were caught up in the dichotomies of the Cold War and therefore often stood for views that were divisive, at least from the standpoint of potential allies. The construction of images of women served as one of the foils with which the dualism of the Cold War was spelled out: the chaste, group-oriented, working, thinking "Liberated Woman" from the Soviet Union versus the sexualized, individualized, fictional vamp/"Degraded Woman" as emblematic of the USA.

Regardless of whether the above quote really is from Margarete Schütte-Lihotzky and whether she was aware of the exact context of this brochure, her partisan political work in the postwar era is tied up in precisely these contradictory scenarios, which shaped her and which she generally helped to shape. The next step needed at this juncture would be to investigate such contradictory, sometimes even unsettling images of women and their significance to society, also with respect to the decades of Communist women's politics to follow, and to examine the relationship between them and other contemporary sources. Research of this kind is required to arrive at a more comprehensive understanding of Schütte-Lihotzky's scope of action as a significant figure in Communist women's politics in Austria.

Conclusion

The attempt to describe Margarete Schütte-Lihotzky's political work as an active member of the KPÖ and a central functionary of the KPÖ-affiliated League of Democratic Women of Austria entails several difficulties and contradictions. The framing of the task itself points to research gaps both in biographical and architectural historiography concerning Schütte-Lihotzky and in the historiography of the Communist movement in Austria. This general historiography of the KPÖ has hardly touched on questions relating to the politics of women and gender and to the work of female functionaries. The most recent well-developed papers aimed at closing these research gaps in both directions were presented in 2018 by two scholars: Marcel Bois describes Margarete Schütte-Lihotzky as a "Communist intellectual" in his critical and analytical essay and puts her in a contemporary historical context, while Manfred Mugrauer traces the paradigms of KPÖ and BDFÖ women's politics in the postwar era in critical and precise terms in his essay on Hella Altmann-Postranecky. From the perspective of feminist research, Heidi Niederkofler's paper from 2009 provides information on the early history of the BDFÖ and on its relationship with the KPÖ. A history of the BDFÖ for the entire period in which Schütte-Lihotzky served as president has yet to be written.

Another challenge arises from the fact that the actions of a female Communist functionary are determined by how she relates to the party structures and their ideologies. To present a critical and analytical (and not merely descriptive) account of Schütte-Lihotzky's engagement in (women's) politics after 1945, one must put into bolder relief the given structures in each case, but also the KPÖ's production of ideas and images. As regards the BDFÖ, this means exploring one major question: Which image of women and which ideas about gender orders did the Communists, male and female, bring into circulation and how did these ideas fit into the context of their time? The sources on Communist women's politics required for understanding Margarete Schütte-Lihotzky's political scope of action must be critically analyzed. However, this does not mean measuring the thoughts of female Communists at the time against today's standards, but rather taking seriously their effects on later horizons of leftist feminist action. The very way in which Schütte-Lihotzky herself also appealed directly to women in several of her pragmatic articles in *Stimme der Frau* can be read as creating a discursive arena of image politics for negotiating constructions of national identities, as can the images and slogans with which women were addressed in the BDFÖ propaganda materials while she was president. This holds true in particular for the postwar era, when the dualisms of the Cold War developed in an interplay with national self-construction and reconstruction ideology. During this period, women's tasks and responsibilities as well as the relative distribution of the spheres pertaining to public and private life, to family and work, were also being reconfigured and newly negotiated.

The female Communists posited figures of thought that linked being a woman with being a mother and being a peace advocate, but they also appealed to women as mothers to fight the infiltration of a popular culture of "filth and trash" from America. Both factors contributed to these negotiation processes insofar as they established paradigms for new avenues of leftist and anti-hegemonic thinking. In general, it turns out that in the prevailing conservative climate accompanied by an economic upswing, female Communists, too, circulated role models that were more conservative and traditional as regards notions of gender orders instead of returning to their more radical positions from the (early) 1920s, which were critical of the bourgeois model of family and home life. In texts that Schütte-Lihotzky published in *Stimme der Frau*, women are responsible for the private sphere; home life, the household, and children are described as intrinsically important politically and are not disparaged. Paradoxically, these ideas tend to be more in tune with the slogan of the new women's movement, "the personal is political," than with the KPÖ writings on women's politics in the 1920s with their dismissals of the private sphere.

Images of and appeals to women in the postwar era serve as a foil to the marginalization logics of the Cold War as expressed in a blanket anti-Americanism, which was also permeated with elements of anti-Semitic tropes. In terms of realpolitik, the female Communists, especially Schütte-Lihotzky, attempted to sidestep the prevailing polarities by entering into non-partisan alliances. Thus, several contradictions can be described in the fields in which Margarete

Schütte-Lihotzky was politically active and which she helped to shape as a functionary, at least until the advent of the new women's movement in the 1970s.

Kindergartens and Kitchens: Reflection and Reception

Margarete Schütte-Lihotzky's "House for Children." Pedagogical Reflections

Sebastian Engelmann

Besides the famous Frankfurt Kitchen, Margarete Schütte-Lihotzky is probably best known for her "buildings for children."[1] Her pavilion system for kindergartens is often mentioned in this regard and was implemented in numerous places.[2] However, there have been no attempts to examine the works of Schütte-Lihotzky with respect to their implicit pedagogical mechanisms, let alone classify them in the larger context of the history of pedagogical ideas. In this essay, I will seek to close this research gap by taking a closer look at children's facilities—of course only to conclude by again drawing attention to the desideratum and pointing out possible reference points for follow-up projects on educational history and theory.

The thesis I will attempt to make plausible in this essay is that the work of Schütte-Lihotzky offers such reference points in abundance. To prove this, I will first examine Schütte-Lihotzky's concept of the child, and her understanding of education based on the kindergarten she planned at Kapaunplatz in Vienna (1950–52).[3] In the process, I will avail myself directly and indirectly of the treasure trove of educational theory, the ideas of Jean-Jacques Rousseau, Friedrich Wilhelm Fröbel, the philanthropinists, a number of progressive educators, and not least, critical pedagogy.

1 An in-depth examination of planning sketches and the construction of buildings for children is provided by Christoph Freyer in this volume.

2 On this and on the transfer of ideas from the Asian region, see Helen Young Chang's essay in this volume and also Elija Horn, *Indien als Erzieher. Orientalismus in der deutschen Reformpädagogik und Jugendbewegung 1918–1933* (Bad Heilbrunn: Klinkhardt, 2018); on the internationality of progressive educational thinking, see Steffi Koslowski, *Die New Era der New Education Fellowship. Ihr Beitrag zur Internationalität der Reformpädagogik im 20. Jahrhundert* (Bad Heilbrunn: Klinkhardt, 2013).

I loosely follow the definition of *Allgemeine Pädagogik* (General Pedagogy) formulated by Markus Rieger-Ladich: General Pedagogy deals with fundamental theoretical issues, taps knowledge from other disciplines, and also imparts that knowledge within its own discipline.[4] Thus, I interpret Schütte-Lihotzky's architecture as being design *for* and *with* education. My assumption here is that one can discern pedagogical processes in architecture and any type of designed structures if one is guided by the understanding of pedagogy "as intentional control of learning processes throughout the history of humankind."[5] For some time now, spatial arrangements have been debated in this field, sometimes in a theoretically ambitious way, sometimes in a highly expressive way based on the materials used.[6] In each case, it can be said that space also became the subject of analysis in education, at the latest with the spatial turn proclaimed by the social and cultural sciences but certainly even earlier.[7] Thus, the place where educators work is itself conjectured as a condition and important influencing factor of pedagogical action, indeed re-construed as a means of bringing about pedagogical effects.

In the case of Schütte-Lihotzky, her buildings for children, also referred to as kindergartens, are especially deserving of pedagogical attention. They serve as organizational and material expressions of a large-scale project of progressive education. With the term "progressive education," I do not just mean the "great" canonical theories of, say, Maria Montessori or Rudolf Steiner.[8] Instead, I understand progressive education, following Ralf Koerrenz, as a type of pedagogical action "which critically addresses a *Schon-Jetzt*, a state that already exists now, and attempts to bring about a difference toward a *Noch-Nicht*, a state that does not yet exist, by influencing those being educated. This happens through reforms that largely manifest themselves in changes to pedagogical structures and practices."[9]

The critical analysis of a state that already exists now and of a change with the clear Utopian goal of working toward a state that does not yet exist is already exemplified in the pedagogical theories of Jean-Jacques Rousseau, which have been referred to as "progressive education before

3 My reflections are based on a 2017 project by students at TU Wien, whose videos are available online, accessed August 23, 2022, https://kindergartenamkapaunplatz.wordpress.com/die-architektin/.

4 Markus Rieger-Ladich, "Allgemeine Pädagogik," in *Lexikon der Pädagogik. Hundert Grundbegriffe*, ed. Stefan Jordan and Marnie Schlüter (Ditzingen: Reclam, 2015), 23–25.

5 Sebastian Engelmann, "A. H. Niemeyers Blick auf die Pädagogik des 18. Jahrhunderts – Heterogenität, Normativität, Differenz," in *Reformpädagogik als Projekt der Moderne. August Hermann Niemeyer und das pädagogische 18. Jahrhundert*, ed. Ralf Koerrenz (Paderborn: Ferdinand Schöningh, 2018), 49–72, here 49.

6 See Daniel Burghardt, *Homo spatialis. Eine pädagogische Anthropologie des Raums* (Weinheim: Beltz Juventa, 2014); Martin Viehhauser, *Reformierung des Menschen durch Stadtraumgestaltung. Eine Studie zur moralerzieherischen Strategie in Städtebau und Architektur um 1000* (Weilerswist: Velbrück Wissenschaft, 2017).

7 Of course, space had already been a topic in education previously. From an anthropological per-

[historical] progressive education."[10] This progressive educational attitude is expressed with particular power in the manifold reflections on the education of young children undertaken by Friedrich Wilhelm Fröbel, the German doyen of early childhood education. I will present all these potential connecting lines in this essay. To start with, I will take a closer look at Fröbel's concept of the child and the consequences of that concept for education. In a next step, I will turn to the pedagogical significance of space as an aspect that both excludes and enables education. In a final step, I will focus on the spatial arrangement itself and, in conclusion, point to further questions that still remain unanswered.

Children as Small Plants—Between a Wild Garden and an Orderly Greenhouse

A passage from a work by Friedrich Wilhelm Fröbel (1782–1852) appears on the wall of the entry hall to the kindergarten on Kapaunplatz in Vienna designed by Margarete Schütte-Lihotzky. The gist of Fröbel's words is that there is no more wonderful activity than the education of children.[11] In Fröbel's eyes, children were more precious than anything else. If we do not simply accept this statement unquestioningly, it leads us to this question: How exactly are children imagined? After all, a notion of who it is that faces educators as they educate, teach, and train is a substantial factor in determining their actual practices. With Fröbel, the question of which concept of the child guides action is easy to answer. He formulated the basis and task of education as follows: "Education consists in leading man, as a thinking, intelligent being, growing into self-consciousness, to a pure and unsullied, conscious and free representation of the inner law of Divine Unity, and in teaching him ways and means thereto."[12]

For Fröbel, the human being, even when small, is a being that becomes conscious of himself or herself. This being thinks and experiences, is driven by an inner law. He or she can achieve self-determination and awareness if supported by others. All these factors play a not insignificant part in the reasons given for the pedagogical practices in Fröbel's kindergartens. The concept of the child shapes how the child is treated. Fröbel explicated his assumptions about

spective, it attracted the attention of Otto Friedrich Bollnow, for example, and is examined in his study *Mensch und Raum* (Stuttgart: Kohlhammer, 1963) on the basis of its atmosphere too.

8 Sebastian Engelmann, "Alles wie gehabt? Zur Konstruktion von Klassikern und Geschichte(n) der Pädagogik," in *Erinnern, Umschreiben, Vergessen. Die Stiftung des disziplinären Gedächtnisses als soziale Praxis*, ed. Markus Rieger-Ladich, Anne Rohstock, and Karin Amos (Weilerswist: Velbrück Wissenschaft, 2019), 65–93.

9 Sebastian Engelmann and Mathias Dehne, "Pädagogisierung der Zeit als Antwort auf die Sündhaftigkeit der Welt – Landerziehungsheime nach Hermann Lietz," in *Lernen zwischen Zeit und Ewigkeit. Pädagogische Praxis und Transzendenz*, ed. Alexander Maier et al. (Bad Heilbrunn: Klinkhardt, 2018), 130–48, here 133.

10 Eva Matthes and Sylvia Schütze, "Reformpädagogik vor der Reformpädagogik," in *Handbuch Bildungsreform und Reformpädagogik*, ed. Heiner Barz (Wiesbaden: Springer, 2017), 31–41.

11 The precise wording is: "It is not possible to gain from anything higher joy, higher enjoyment, than we do from the guidance

of our children, from living with and for our children," from Friedrich Fröbel, *The Education of Man*, translated from the German and annotated by W. N. Hailmann (New York: D. Appleton, 1887), 87.

12 Ibid., 3.

13 See Ralf Koerrenz, *Reformpädagogik. Eine Einführung* (Paderborn: Ferdinand Schöningh, 2014), 42.

14 Jean-Jacques Rousseau, *Emile or Education*, translated by Barbara Foxley MA (London: J. M. Dent & Sons, 1911), 5.

15 The idea of "naturalness" was justifiably deconstructed in the course of feminist, poststructuralist, and posthumanist theoretical work.

16 Rousseau, *Emile*, 5.

17 Klaus Mollenhauer, *Vergessene Zusammenhänge. Über Kultur und Erziehung* (Weinheim: Juventa, 1983).

human beings. In other pedagogies, these assumptions are often handed down only implicitly; they exist nonetheless.[13]

If one explores the references on which Friedrich Fröbel draws in his works, one finds another anthropological foundation that I consider relevant: Jean-Jacques Rousseau's bildungsroman *Emile or on Education*, originally published in 1762. This text by the well-known author of writings on social theory begins with a sentence that would become significant for the entire further history of education: "God makes all things good; man meddles with them and they become evil."[14] In this sense, children are "good" at birth; they are, by nature, "pure" beings.[15] It is only societal influences that allow negative factors to arise and drive human development in the wrong direction. In his *Emile*, Rousseau criticizes the court norms in 18th century France. In this educational Utopia, he advocates a negative, protective education, which keeps societal influences away from the pupils yet otherwise leaves them a large measure of freedom. Of course, this freedom is a "walled-in" freedom, which enables only selected aspects to enter while in turn excluding others, a point I will return to later.

The metaphors Rousseau uses in his text make for an interesting aspect of his reflections. He starts *Emile* with the story of a tree bent by external influences. Nature "would be like a sapling chance sown in the midst of the highway, bent hither and thither and soon crushed by the passers-by."[16] One must think of the nature of a child as analogous to the bent tree. Without harmful influences, like the court values and norms criticized by Rousseau, the child would develop according to his or her nature as the anthropological constant, like a plant that is let to grow untouched yet protected.

Equating children with plants is not unusual for 18th century pedagogy. This approach can be seen in numerous paintings, which, in the words of Klaus Mollenhauer, are representations of social conditions.[17] For instance, the well-known painting *The Hülsenbeck Children* by Philipp Otto Runge can be interpreted as representing a developmental process that is intended to be construed pedagogically (fig 1).

The children in Runge's painting are eye-level with the viewer; this can be interpreted to mean that the children are imagined as equal to the viewer. The deliberate choice of perspective can be seen as an expression of a general turn toward the acceptance of children as a norm of pedagogical action.[18] Also of interest is that the youngest of the Hülsenbeck children is sitting quite immobile in a handcart. The toddler is grasping a sunflower but is being pulled by the older children toward the house, a developmental process away from nature and toward culture. It is no surprise that Runge links plants and children in precisely this way. Kristin Heinze notes that greenhouse cultivation was on the rise in the second half of the 18th century. As a metaphor, the greenhouse "is associated in a negative connotation with the idea that the unnatural heat from the greenhouse forces the maturation process and that forced plants are deemed to be of less value, and is meant to underscore the potential danger of education that forms [the pupil] prematurely."[19]

18 See Markus Rieger-Ladich and Julia Janzcyk, "'Vom Kinde aus.' Kleine Fallstudie zum pädagogischen Denkstil," in *Mythen – Irrtümer – Unwahrheiten. Essays über das 'Valsche' in der Pädagogik*, ed. Hans-Ulrich Grunder (Bad Heilbrunn: Klinkhardt, 2017), 121–25.

19 Kristin Heinze, "Das 'Treibhaus' als Metapher für eine widernatürliche Erziehung im Kontext der sich im 18. Jahrhundert herausbildenden Pädagogik als Wissenschaft," in *Wissenschaftsgeschichte als Begriffsgeschichte. Terminologische Umbrüche im Entstehungsprozess der modernen Wissenschaften*, ed. Michael Eggers and Matthias Rothe (Bielefeld: Transcript, 2009), 107–31, here 107.

Fig. 1. Philipp Otto Runge, *The Hülsenbeck Children*, 1805/06, oil on canvas.

This negative connotation is congruous with the ideas of Rousseau, who has his tutor develop the pupil's powers in moderation, always in line with the pupil's nature as the anthropological constant. As a metaphor, the greenhouse is diametrically opposed to this natural course of development. Instead of plants developing with the support of environmental factors, what we have with the greenhouse is an artificial space that virtually forces plants to grow.

In the dichotomous depiction of education that controls in the metaphorical greenhouse versus education that is aimed at the individual's autonomy in and through nature, there emerges a further difference, which is relevant to the analysis of buildings for children: the difference between a pedagogy of control and a pedagogy of autonomy.

Pedagogy of Control and Pedagogy of Autonomy—Spatially Interwoven

The philosopher Anton Hügli distinguishes between the pedagogy of control and the pedagogy of autonomy. The former seeks to "control in the more precise meaning of the word as used in cybernetics and automata theory: A controls B if and only if A can elicit in B any state it wishes to elicit in relation to the states B is capable of assuming in the first place."[20] The pedagogy of control attempts to control and render usable all factors influencing the system in order to achieve the educational intentions. According to Hügli, this endeavor is doomed to failure; the world is too complex and too many different factors influence human learning. For Hügli, the opposite of the pedagogy of control is the pedagogy of autonomy. But even this variety of educational thought and action aimed at the autonomy of the pupils faces the problem of having to give impetus to autonomy.

20 Anton Hügli, *Philosophie und Pädagogik* (Darmstadt: Wissenschaftliche Buchgesellschaft, 1999), 92.

The element connecting the pedagogical models discerned by Hügli is the creation of a teaching–learning arrangement. Educational settings such as these are always structured intentionally. They enable things but at the same time also exclude things in order to ensure that teaching and learning are done in the intended way. Whether it is the philanthropinia—independent pedagogical provinces with fixed rules and clear educational intentions—or large-

Fig. 2. An inside view of the kindergarten on Kapaunplatz, Vienna, around 1952, planning: Margarete Schütte-Lihotzky.

scale literary projects such as *Utopia* by Thomas More or *The Republic* by Plato, all these spatial arrangements exclude selected elements and integrate other elements. In this case, Klaus Mollenhauer talks about presentation and representation. The world is presented in any case; adults live unreflected lives, thereby presenting young people with different dispositions that are available for them to acquire. For Mollenhauer, the presentation of conditions and relationships is an ineluctable act of exerting influence: "If we live with children, we must lead *our* lives with them; there is no way around it; we cannot erase ourselves as social living beings, cannot pretend to be dead or impartial."[21] However, this presentation can be interrupted and supplemented by representation. Representation assumes that adults intentionally choose between different acquirable objects and thus reduce the totality of possibilities in the teaching–

21 Mollenhauer, *Vergessene Zusammenhänge*, 20.

Fig. 3. An inside view of the kindergarten on Kapaunplatz, Vienna, around 1952, planning: Margarete Schütte-Lihotzky.

learning arrangement. They limit the totality of possibilities, but thereby open up the possibility for children to acquire individual dispositions efficiently.

In connection with Rousseau and Fröbel, the kindergarten must be understood as a space that allows and reinforces selected influences deemed beneficial to children. This feature is reflected in its design. In Schütte-Lihotzky's kindergarten on Kapaunplatz, many details make this clear. Be it the unblocked view into the garden through the windows that extend all the way to the floor or the possibility of playing freely in the outdoor area, these elements are not randomly arranged. They represent occasions for learning that are intentionally constructed by the architect and designer. The same holds true for the layout of rooms in the kindergarten on Kapaunplatz. Despite the division into individual groups, the children can gather together in a large hall to experience community and to have celebrations. In the kindergarten on Kapaunplatz, the intent is to show the children that becoming acquainted with nature and interacting with other children are both part of normal life. The furniture is scaled to the physical size of the children, helping them to make sensible use of the setting that is oriented to their norm (figs. 2 and 3).

At first glance, this appears to be very free and unconstrained. On closer inspection, the arrangement suggests another interpretation. The windows extending all the way to the floor create a high degree of visibility; the children are always visible to the educators. The children are allowed to "do what they want, always under the condition that they will only want to do what the teacher wants them to do. And how does an educator reach this goal? By yielding control over this setting to the children but always making sure that the setting leads the children to the place where the educator would like them to be. In other words, [the educator exerting] indirect influence over the controlled setting is meant to bring about the same effect as the doer applying the direct method vainly attempts to achieve."[22]

22 Hügli, *Philosophie und Pädagogik*, 54.

The example of the window reveals how the pedagogy of control is spatially interwoven with the pedagogy of autonomy. On the one hand, the windows open a view to the outdoors, into the open area outside the interior. On the other hand, the windows are used to keep an eye on the children at all times and to watch them at play. Are they also playing correctly? Are they doing something undesirable? Is an intervention necessary? The windows create visibility and basically have a restrictive effect. If we take this perspective, the children's seemingly unsupervised and free activity in the kindergarten is already determined by the construction of the setting. It is certainly conceivable that play opportunities may be put to different purposes or appropriated for specific purposes. Quiet corners and possibly "unseen" locations are also conceivable in the structure of a kindergarten. However, even the most liberated pedagogical setting complies with a norm. In the case of Margarete Schütte-Lihotzky, in particular, one can assume from her own political background that her architecture aims to encourage a special form of rationality and at the same time a specific form of individuality in community with others. It is not accidental that the kindergarten is fitted with the hall for community play mentioned above or that the groups in the kindergarten are assigned their own section corresponding in size and furnishings with that assigned to each of the other groups. The spatial arrangement is meant to encourage community and equality in community with others; that would be my summary.

Margarete Schütte-Lihotzky and Pedagogy—An Open Question

This imagined tour through the rooms of the kindergarten at Kapaunplatz was aimed at revealing the architectural and educational mechanisms at play and has shown that spatial arrangements can always be understood as pedagogical projects. Schütte-Lihotzky's buildings for children are by no means exceptions to this rule. The intentionally designed setting transports ideas about what is intended to be shown, about how the setting is to be dealt with, and finally also about which human beings are to grow and develop within this setting. This look at this selected project of Schütte-Lihotzky is informed by educational theory but really must be supplemented by further considerations relating primarily to the history of education. Did Margarete Schütte-Lihotzky have any associations with the many thinkers and practitioners in the progressive education network and if so, what did she think of them? Beyond being integrated in networks of architects and designers, Schütte-Lihotzky was evidently also in contact with educators. Her design considerations were supplemented by and grounded in her readings of pedagogical works.[23] This thesis is worth pursuing and is substantiated by the fact that Schütte-Lihotzky made explicit reference to Maria Montessori. The question remains: *Which* aspects of Montessori's work did she incorporate in her own work?

23 I would like to thank Christoph Freyer for pointing out this connection.

A closer examination of the scattered statements she made may reveal which pedagogical ideas flowed into Schütte-Lihotzky's buildings. Her time in the Soviet Union, which continues to be a major gap in the research on Schütte-

Lihotzky,[24] also suggests that the architect may have come into contact with the influential ideas of Lev Vigotsky or Pavel P. Blonskij. Finally, Schütte-Lihotzky undoubtedly always viewed her architectural planning for children as a contribution to reforming society, be it for Germany in the late 1920s, for the Soviet Union between 1930 and 1937, for Kemalist Turkey from 1938 to 1940, or lastly for postwar Austria. As indicated above, Schütte-Lihotzky's work truly is a rich source for pedagogy as well. A further examination of her work would not only be a gain for architectural history but would also serve to present a more differentiated history of pedagogical thought and enhance the complexity of that history.

24 See Thomas Flierl's essay in this volume.

Margarete Schütte-Lihotzky's Buildings for Children

Christoph Freyer

> The kindergartens [...] are the link between home life and work life in the school; they gradually guide the child out of the family setting and into the public, into the community and bring enrichment to the child's life, enrichment to which we architects also want to contribute in our own way.[1]

This essay on Margarete Schütte-Lihotzky's buildings for children is devoted entirely to her kindergartens. I will first give a brief overview of the historical development of this institution to outline its genesis up to Schütte-Lihotzky's own planning work and then present "houses for children," as the architect called them, from various creative periods of her life. I will focus on her kindergartens with a central hall, a standard type that Schütte-Lihotzky developed and that was a recurrent theme in her oeuvre. Drawing on selected examples, I will point out the significance of this specific design in her work.

A brief overview of the development of early childhood educational institutions shows that the first kindergartens were actually schools for preschool age children, known then and still today in parts of the United Kingdom as "infant schools." One early example is the infant school that Robert Owens opened in New Lanark, Scotland in 1816. This model was modified just a few years later in England by Samuel Wilderspin (1823[2]), who developed not only an educational method but also a school type, which would spread from England to the rest of the world. Josef Ritter von Wertheimer,

1 Margarete Schütte-Lihotzky, "Neue Kinderhäuser in der DDR" (typescript, around 1954), 7, University Archive of the University of Applied Arts Vienna, Nachlass Margarete Schütte-Lihotzky (UAUAK, NL MSL), PRNR 189/2/TXT. Friedrich Fröbel coined the term "kindergarten" in 1840 when he changed the name of his "play and activity" institute to "kindergarten." This word is now used across the globe but with different meanings and connotations. In this text, it is used in the German/Austrian/Swiss sense of a separate early childhood educational institution, usually for children age three to six.

2 I have chosen here the date of the first edition of his seminal work, of which he published several revised editions: Samuel Wilderspin, *On the Importance of Educating the Infant Children of the Poor; Showing How Three*

a philanthropist based in Vienna, became acquainted with the Wilderspin system on a trip to England. He was so enthusiastic about this system's ideas on early childhood education that he translated Wilderspin's seminal book on infant schools into German, rearranging the contents and publishing his German version of it in 1826.[3] Inspired by Josef Wertheimer and Samuel Wilderspin, the Hungarian countess Theresia Brunsvik von Korompa founded Hungary's first *Kleinkinderbewahranstalt* (akin to a day nursery focused on providing young children with a safe and healthy environment) just two years later, in 1828, in Budapest. It was called "angel garden" and is known to posterity thanks to, inter alia, an 1830 report that referred to it as a "model school for young children."[4] That same year, Josef Wertheimer joined with the pastor Johann Lindner to open Vienna's first kindergarten, naming it "Institute for Preschool-Age Children." Additional schools of this type were founded that same year, also at the initiative of Empress Maria Karolina Augusta, making Vienna one of the early centers of kindergarten education.[5] It was not until 10 years later, in 1840, that Friedrich Fröbel's "kindergarten" first came into being in Bad Blankenburg in Thuringia, but there was not yet a specific architecture to go with it.[6]

The Architecture of Early Kindergartens

Architecturally, the early kindergartens tended to be based on schools of the time, as indicated by a description of an infant school modeled on Samuel Wilderspin's ideas. The children sat along the walls and in a gallery and were instructed by the teacher and what were referred to as monitors (older children). In terms of the features of the building itself, Wilderspin recommended glare-free rooms flooded with light and fitted with windows placed high enough so that children were not affected by drafts and also not distracted by outdoor activity. For health reasons, he recommended a separate cloakroom area for wet clothing and considered a schoolyard with a playground and rotary swings to be essential.[7]

In 1898, to mark the 50th anniversary of Emperor Franz Joseph's accession to the throne, the Viennese architect Albert

Hundred Children, from Eighteen Months to Seven Years of Age; May Be Managed by One Master and Mistress: Containing Also an Account of the Spitalfields Infant School (London: Goyder, 1823).

3 Samuel Wilderspin, *Ueber die frühzeitige Erziehung der Kinder und die englischen Klein-Kinder-Schulen: oder Bemerkungen über die Wichtigkeit, die kleinen Kinder der Armen im Alter von anderthalb bis sieben Jahren zu erziehen; nebst einer Darstellung der Spitalfielder Klein-Kinder-Schule und des daselbst eingeführten Erziehungs-systems*. Freely translated from English, based on the third, greatly expanded and revised edition, and supplied with notes and additions, by Joseph Wertheimer (Vienna: Gerold, 1826).

4 Prof. Dr. Rump in Gran, "Besuch der Kleinkinder-Musterschule und der weiblichen Arbeitsschule zu Ofen," *Oesterreichisches Bürgerblatt für Verstand, Herz und gute Laune* (August 30, 1830).

5 Amelie Köhler, "Die ersten Kinderbewahranstalten in Oesterreich," *Reichspost* (November 7, 1926): 18.

6 Also see Sebastian Engelmann's essay in this volume.

7 The rotary swing consisted of a pole with a

wire hoop at the top to which ropes were attached. The hoop pivoted, allowing the ropes to move freely around the pole.

Pecha was commissioned by the Association of Kindergartens and Nursery Schools in Vienna to design a model kindergarten, which was also presented at the Vienna Jubilee Trade Exhibition.[8] Besides an entry hall, access throughout the building was provided by a central corridor. There were a cloakroom and two group rooms on one side of it and a playroom and ancillary spaces on the other side. The toilets were centrally located; the large schoolyard had covered verandas on both sides, and the upper story contained the apartment for the educators.

8 Albert Pecha, "Der Musterkindergarten," *Der Architekt* 4 (1898): 24, plate 48.

A building from 1910 by Adolf Stöckl, an architect at the Vienna Stadtbauamt (central building authority of the city), can be cited as representative of typical plans drawn up just a few years later. The multistory kindergarten on Bunsengasse in Vienna's 21st district has several activity rooms on both floors as well as a playroom and a veranda. The staircase leads to the central cloakrooms, through which the playroom and activity rooms can be accessed. The overall impression of the layout and the exterior not only resembles a school building of the time, but Max Fiebiger, the director of the Stadtbauamt, also emphasized that "the principles and style of architecture for municipal school buildings are fully applied [...] in the construction of municipal kindergarten buildings."[9]

9 Max Fiebiger, "Schulen und Kindergärten der Stadt Wien," *Zeitschrift des Österreichischen Ingenieur- und Architektenvereins, Sonderabdruck* 31/32 (1915): 11.

Quantum Leap in the 1920s

One must preface any examination of Margarete Schütte-Lihotzky's kindergartens with an opinion she voiced time and time again: "The misery of working women who are unable to arrange for their preschool-age children to be under the supervision of trained educators during working hours is well known. The solution to this problem cannot be to reduce the number of working women; it can only be to build a great many children's facilities."[10]

10 Margarete Schütte-Lihotzky, *Warum ich Architektin wurde*, ed. Karin Zogmayer (Salzburg: Residenz, 2004), 170.

The architect turned her attention to kindergarten construction relatively early on. While working in the typification department in Frankfurt, a post she received in 1926 from Ernst May, she and Eugen Kaufmann designed a single-group Montessori kindergarten in 1928 for a municipal housing development in Frankfurt-Ginnheim. A year later, in 1929, she drew up a program for kindergartens[11] and planned

11 Margarete Schütte-Lihotzky, "Programm für einen Kindergarten," UAUAK, NL MSL, PRNR 80/13/TXT.

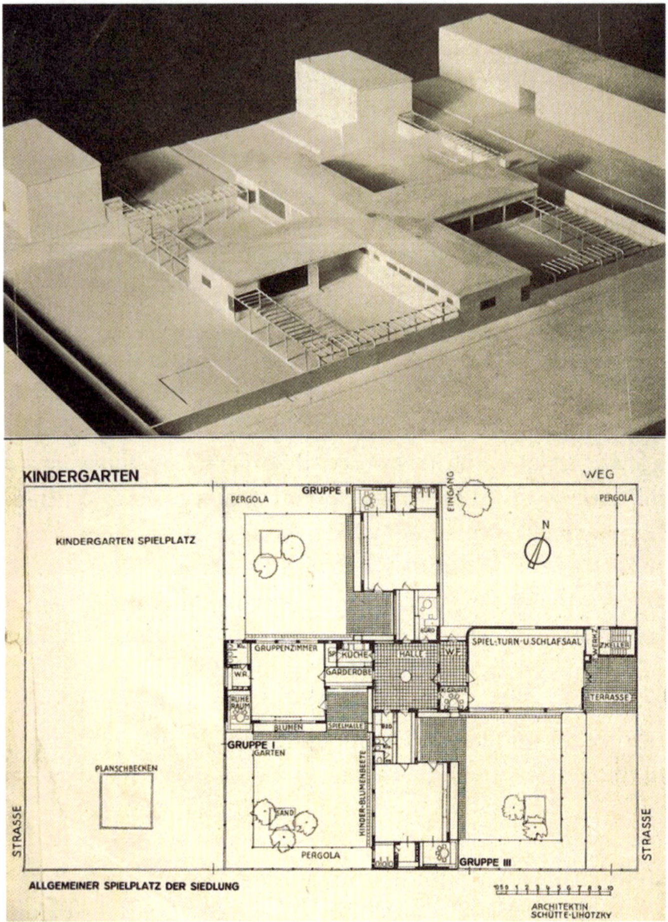

Fig. 1. Margarete Schütte-Lihotzky, Frankfurt-Praunheim kindergarten, 1929, photo of the model and floor plan.

a completely new type of kindergarten in pavilion style for Siedlung Praunheim, a municipal housing development in Frankfurt-Praunheim (fig. 1). This kindergarten for 100 children, like the one in Frankfurt-Ginnheim, was never actually built, but it did form the basis for later planning and the architect returned to it time and again. Her estate, now in the University Archive of the University of Applied Arts Vienna, contains a documentation of this forward-looking design, which definitely deserves to be called a quantum leap in the history of kindergarten development.

According to the documentation, Margarete Schütte-Lihotzky was planning pavilions for three groups as well as a gymnastics room. “Each group is assigned its own part of the building with its own garden.”[12] The advantage of the pavilions is that they enable as close a connection as possible between outdoors and indoors, and each group has a strong affinity to its own room. This style of architecture was advocated at the time by progressive educators and public health specialists.

Inspired by the idea of keeping distances short and wasting minimal space, this design was the first kindergarten with a central hall. The pavilions are arranged in the shape of a cross around a central room, “from which all rooms not intended for the individual groups [...] are directly accessible.”[13] This arrangement enables the architect to avoid long expensive corridors, and the money saved can be invested in a useful space, the central hallway.

Further innovations in Schütte-Lihotzky’s kindergartens included playgrounds divided by group, large windows with low parapets to allow the children to look outdoors, and planting beds in front of the windows. These elements are not all “inventions” of Margarete Schütte-Lihotzky, but rather were ideas “in the air” at the time. Her time working in Frankfurt coincided with the construction in Vienna of Franz Schuster’s[14] “Haus der Kinder” (children’s house) on Rudolfsplatz (1929), much admired by her, and Franz Singer and Friedl Dicker’s Montessori kindergarten in the Goethehof, a municipal housing complex (1929/30). Both facilities have elements that can also be found in Schütte-Lihotzky’s designs. The large windows extend to just above the floor; in Praunheim and in Vienna, the parapet height was designed to be just 60 cm. The windowsills are deep enough that plants can be placed on them or they can be put to other uses. The group rooms have alcoves that can serve other purposes—say, as a place of retreat for children or a work area (e.g., sink for washing dishes). These modern concepts were devised by Schütte-Lihotzky but also by other architects in close collaboration with educators and physicians.

In Vienna, the Montessori educator Lili Roubiczek took the lead. She had been heavily involved in co-designing the

12 Margarete Schütte-Lihotzky, “Beschreibung zum Projekt eines Kindergartens für die Siedlung Praunheim,” Frankfurt am Main (typescript, 1929), p. 1, UAUAK, NL MSL, PRNR 80/11/TXT.

13 Ibid.

14 Franz Schuster worked in Ernst May’s team in Frankfurt at the same time as Margarete Schütte-Lihotzky.

spatial program for Franz Schuster's "Haus der Kinder" and wrote the following about this particular kindergarten: "We are trying to create a children's house—in other words, a building in which all furniture and utensils are scaled to the children [...]." The windows were conceived in accordance with Schütte-Lihotzky's design: "In a children's house, it is a matter of course to make the windowsills low enough so the children are also able to look out the windows. The windows in the hall are designed so that the sill is 60 cm above the floor (the height of a children's table)."[15]

15 Franz Schuster and Lili E. Roubiczek, "Haus der Kinder (Entwurf), Vorwort" (typescript), pp. 13–14, accessed April 20, 2023, www.eichelberger.at/?p=658.

Parallel to the accelerated housing construction in the late 1920s, other cities also built modern kindergartens—for instance, the one Hans Hofmann and Adolf Kellermüller completed in Zurich-Wiedikon in 1932 (fig. 2). It is considered to be the first pavilion-style kindergarten in Switzerland and resulted from a competition in 1928. As in Frankfurt and Vienna, each pavilion has its own sanitary facilities and its own exit into the garden. The large, glazed area opens the group rooms in Zurich to the garden to an even greater extent than in the designs of Schuster and Schütte-Lihotzky. What was unique to Schütte-Lihotzky's plans was that a portion of the garden was assigned to each group for its own use.

Fig. 2. Hans Hofmann and Adolf Kellermüller, inside view of the Zurich-Wiedikon kindergarten, 1932.

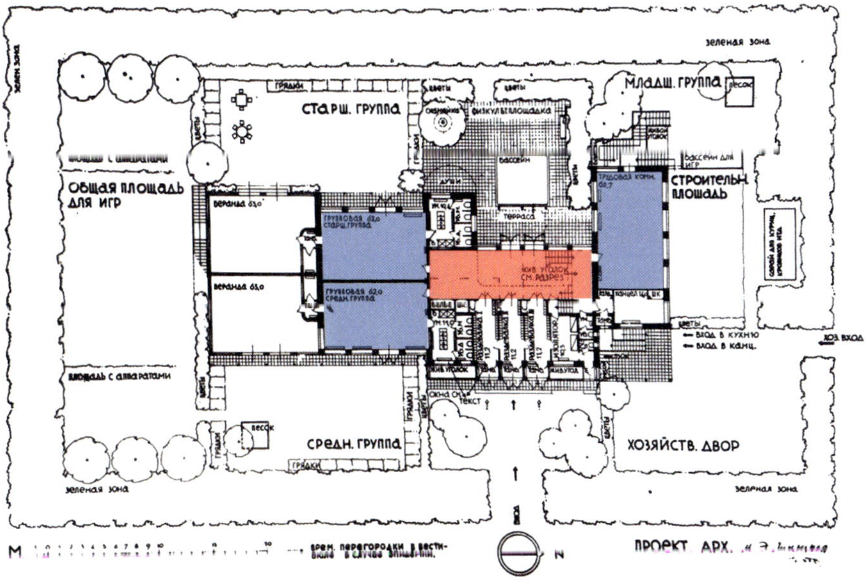

Fig. 3. Margarete Schütte-Lihotzky, kindergarten type for the Soviet Union—floor plan with central hall (red) and group rooms (blue), 1933, adapted by Christoph Freyer.

A further element that makes these three buildings forward-looking examples is the central arrangement of cloakrooms, washrooms, and toilets. Along with a garden area, each group room also had its own infrastructure.

The 1930s—the Soviet Union

Margarete Schütte-Lihotzky was one of the architects in Frankfurt who accompanied Ernst May to the Soviet Union in 1930 to help build new cities there. Besides housing, schools, and furniture, she also planned kindergartens again as the head of the children's facilities department within the May Group and made rapid progress on developing the model that she conceived in Frankfurt. However, she opted for a more compact style of architecture rather than pavilions, a decision she justified by citing the climatic conditions in the Soviet Union: the pavilion-style complexes would cool down too much in the Russian winters. Nonetheless, she sought to implement the basic idea of a central hall that she had developed in Frankfurt and also to make the corridors as short as possible (fig. 3). As with her design in Frankfurt, this spatial concept was aimed at keeping the construction costs as low as possible by using minimum space.

These 1933 designs for standard types of kindergartens can be viewed as precursors to the modular system concept that the architect would be working on for decades to come.[16] To this end, she designed standardized, prefabricated modules, which could be combined to create different variations.

16 See *Margarete Schütte-Lihotzky, Soziale Architektur. Zeitzeugin eines Jahrhunderts*, exhibition catalog, MAK—Austrian Museum of Applied Arts, Vienna, ed. Peter Noever (Vienna: Böhlau, 1993), 151–52.

The 1950s—Vienna

It was not until 1950 to 1952 that a kindergarten designed by Margarete Schütte-Lihotzky was built in her hometown. This was the 150th kindergarten to be erected by the City of Vienna and was named after the educator Friedrich Fröbel. This educational facility on Kapaunplatz was built in pavilion style, which was already common, especially in Vienna. However, it had no central hall, a feature Margarete Schütte-Lihotzky had designed in the 1920s for the first time and had repeatedly advocated thereafter (fig. 4). It is striking that almost no other architects made efforts to include central halls in their designs in the 1950s either. The only exceptions are a 1953 project in which Schütte-Lihotzky converted a villa into a children's house for Glanzstoffwerke St. Pölten, a rayon production company, and a Viennese municipal kindergarten by Franz Schuster at the municipal housing development Am Schöpfwerk.[17] From many details of Margarete Schütte-Lihotzky's planning work for Vienna, one can discern type plans that she had already designed in Bulgaria in 1946 and that had a corridor layout—in other words, they dispensed with a central hall

The kindergarten on Kapaunplatz, located in Vienna's densely populated 20th district, is now protected as a historical monument. It showcases the architect's treasure trove of experience in kindergarten construction and incorporates nearly all of the fundamental principles that became part of her standard repertoire: windows with low parapets; a clearly visible connection to the outdoors; group rooms, each of which opens onto its own covered terrace through large glass doors; lines of sight extending across rooms to offer a good

17 See Christoph Freyer, "Margarete Schütte-Lihotzky und Franz Schuster – Kindergärten für Wien," lecture at the symposium *Bauen für Kinder ist Bauen für die Zukunft*, Margarete Schütte-Lihotzky Raum, Vienna, June 6, 2021.

18 See Manfred Berger, "Zur Geschichte des Kindergartens in Österreich. Brief an Friedrich Fröbel zum 175. Geburtstag des Kindergartens," on the nifbe—Niedersächsisches Institut für frühkindliche Bildung und Entwicklung website, accessed May 9, 2022, https://www.nifbe.de/component/themensammlung?view=item&id=561

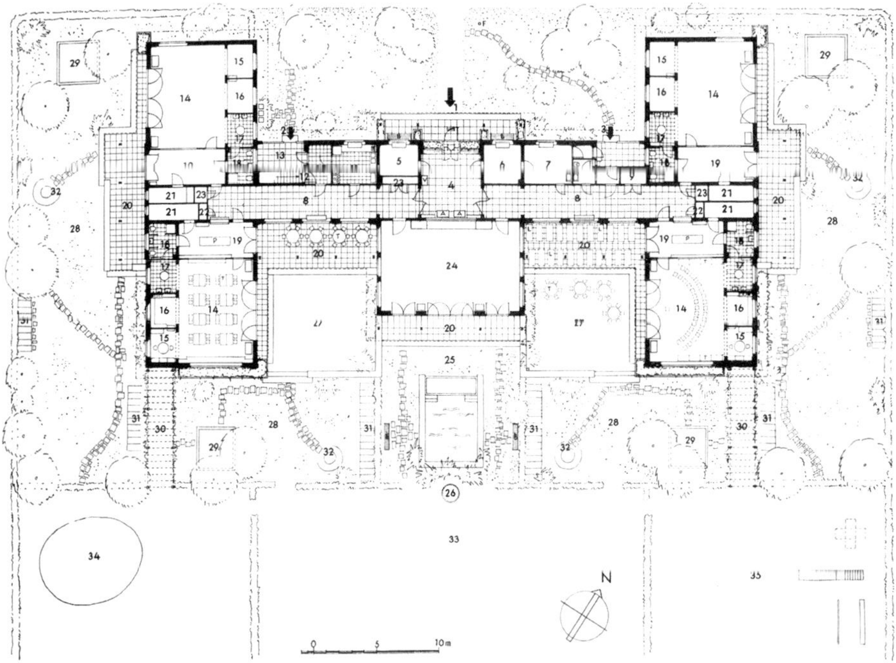

Fig. 4. Margarete Schütte-Lihotzky, kindergarten on Kapaunplatz, Vienna's 20th district (1950–52).

overview of the group; and, of course, effective cross-ventilation. In the group rooms, alcoves provide places of retreat for children, but certain alcoves can also serve as task stations where children can become active themselves, as educational and practical elements. The oft-peddled assertion that this feature was first implemented in the kindergarten on Kapaunplatz is by no means correct.[18] As indicated above, Margarete Schütte-Lihotzky already included alcoves of this kind in her plans for Siedlung Praunheim (see fig. 1). In 1929, she wrote the following on this subject in her manuscript "Das Kinderhaus in der Flachbausiedlung" (The children's house in settlements with low-rise buildings): "Adjacent to its own group room, each group has a small rest area in the form of an alcove, where individual children can retreat; there is also a washing alcove, which has a table, sink, and draining board for washing dishes, all of which are built-in for the children [...]."[19]

:brief-an-friedrich-froebel-zum-175-geburtstag-des-kindergartens&catid=37:paedagogik; Manfred Berger, "Recherchen zum Kindergarten in Österreich: Gestern – Heute – Morgen, 2005," in *Das Kita-Handbuch*, ed. Martin R. Textor and Antje Bostelmann, accessed May 9, 2022, https://www.kindergartenpaedagogik.de/1240.html.

19 Margarete Schütte-Lihotzky, "Das Kinderhaus in der Flachbausiedlung," Artikel 2 (manuscript, typescript, Frankfurt, 1929), p. 4, UAUAK, NL MSL, PRNR 80/14/TXT.

An ingenious color scheme was created to help the children at Kapaunplatz find their way around and to enhance their sense of well-being.[20] The individual color design for the individual groups was consistently carried out down to the last detail. The architect had already described the color schemes she favored when she wrote an article about exemplary foreign kindergartens in 1935 for the Russian journal *Arkhitektyra za rubezhom* (Architecture abroad).[21] In that article, she mentioned the color-based guidance system in the kindergarten in the Goethehof municipal housing complex in Vienna designed by Franz Singer and Friedl Dicker as well as the Zurich kindergarten building cited above, where each group was assigned its own colors for windows and doors. Schütte-Lihotzky went a step further at Kapaunplatz by linking not only the colors but also the children's tasks to their group symbol. For instance, the green group whose symbol was a fish were given the task of taking care of the aquariums.[22]

20 The color scheme was destroyed during renovation work while the architect was still alive.

21 Margarete Schütte-Lihotzky, "Kindergartenbau im Ausland," *Arkhitektura za rubezkom* 5 (1935): 7–20.

22 See Grete Schütte-Lihotzky, "Der Plan und der Bau," in *Der 150. Kindergarten der Stadt Wien "Friedrich Wilhelm Fröbel" XX, Kapaunplatz*, ed. Stadtbauamt der Stadt Wien (Vienna: Verlag für Jugend und Volk, 1952), 14.

German Democratic Republic—Typification and Rationalization

In 1954, Margarete Schütte-Lihotzky was commissioned to do a research project at the Bauakademie in Berlin. It entailed working out typification and rationalization proposals for kindergarten construction in the German Democratic Republic (GDR). In her study, she pointed out wasted space and the high costs it incurred.[23] As a positive comparison, she cited the kindergartens in Vienna in particular, which were internationally viewed as exemplary in the 1950s, and a Soviet construction manual.[24] She made the following comments on the matter:

> The types of floor plans shown here have been implemented multiple times abroad. Years of experience, especially from the Soviet Union, were utilized in the process. They show what a wonderful, fascinating, and rewarding task this area of construction offers to architects. For them, the problem of planning children's facilities in the GDR today no longer consists of the task of designing a lovely individual project or of building an attractive kindergarten here or there. Instead, it consists

23 Margarete Schütte-Lihotzky, "Kritische Stellungnahme zu den besichtigten Bauten und Plänen von Kinderanstalten" (typescript, Berlin, September 21, 1954), UAUAK, NL MSL, PRNR 189/4/TXT.

24 In her "Kritische Stellungnahme," Margarete Schütte-Lihotzky quotes several times from the following architect's manual: *Spravochnik arkhitektora* (Moscow: Izd-vo Akad. arkhitektury SSSR, 1946–60).

of laying the groundwork for building typical solutions to enable the creation of a large number of good children's facilities as quickly as possible containing as few doors or other scarce materials as possible and using as few qualified workers as possible.[25]

25 Margarete Schütte-Lihotzky, "Neue Kinderhäuser in der DDR" (typescript, around 1954), pp. 6–7, UAUAK, NL MSL, PRNR 189/2/TXT.

The 1960s—Kindergarten on Rinnböckstrasse

The architect took kindergarten construction another step forward in 1961/62, when she designed the kindergarten on Rinnböckstrasse in the 11th district for the City of Vienna. With this five-group kindergarten, she drew directly on her design for Frankfurt-Praunheim from 1929 (fig. 5). In Vienna, too, the pavilions for the 30-children groups complete with cloakrooms are also arranged in the shape of a cross around a central hall.

The fifth group intended for the youngest children, which Frankfurt did not include, is placed on the first upper

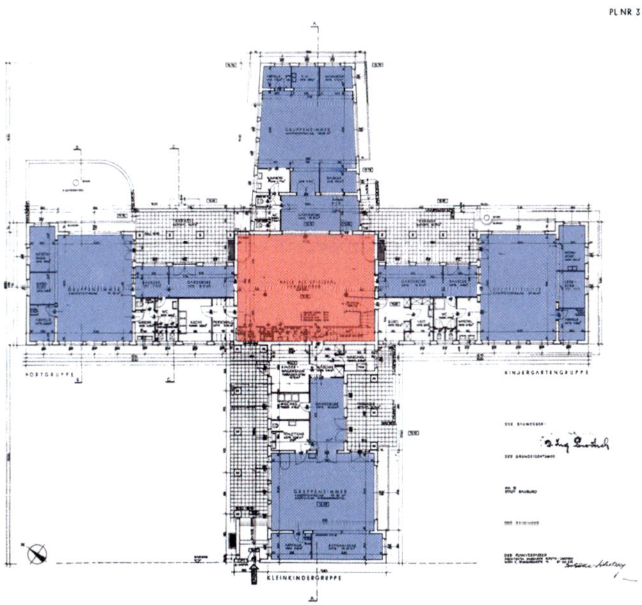

Fig. 5. Margarete Schütte-Lihotzky, kindergarten on Rinnböckstrasse, Vienna's 11th district, 1962, floor plan with central hall (red) and group rooms (blue), adapted by Christoph Freyer.

floor of the building and has a terrace right outside it. So, each group had its own exit to the outdoors. The kindergarten is closed off from the street by a wall, making it a quiet, self-enclosed spatial system. This feature has a parallel in traditional Chinese architecture, which is characterized primarily by the creation of a central courtyard and the separation of private and public space.[26] The individual parts of the building, already modular in design, would become significant several years later in her *Baukastenmodell* ("modular model").

26 Also see Helen Young Chang's essay in this volume.

The *Baukastenmodell*

In 1965, Margarete Schütte-Lihotzky presented a *Baukastenmodell* to the City of Vienna, which allowed kindergartens of various sizes to be assembled out of prefabricated wood or concrete components.[27] Only three different modules were required for this task:

1. one structure as a group pavilion,
2. one structure for ancillary spaces,
3. one structure as a connecting space (central hall), which could also serve as a playroom.

Using a supplementary statistical sheet, she showed that this system was substantially more efficient than the kindergartens already existing in Vienna. Thanks to the central hall, less space had to be built per child. Moreover, the construction costs could be reduced considerably with the prefabricated elements.

The photo of the model demonstrates how kindergartens with different numbers of groups can be built by joining together additional group modules opposite each other (fig. 6).[28] Margarete Schütte-Lihotzky divided the interior spaces by group function in the models, and to demonstrate the concept more clearly, ancillary spaces could also be combined differently as separate components. With the detailed design and the cruciform shape, she once again drew on her original idea from Frankfurt. According to her first description sheet, kindergartens could be built using this system to hold one to eight groups and still have uniform exposure to sunlight. As in the Frankfurt model, each group room on the ground floor had its own exit into the garden area assigned to it.

27 As early as 1963, she suggested a modular system that predated the Viennese modular model in her design theory for kindergartens developed for Cuba and the associated exposé. Margarete Schütte Lihotzky, "Entwurfslehre für Kinderanstalten" (typescript, around 1963), p. 4, UAUAK, NL MSL, PRNR 196/3/TXT, and Margarete Schütte-Lihotzky, "Exposée" (typescript, October 27, 1963), UAUAK, NL MSL, PRNR 196/1/TXT.

28 The model can be found in UAUAK, NL MSL, 198/69/Q.

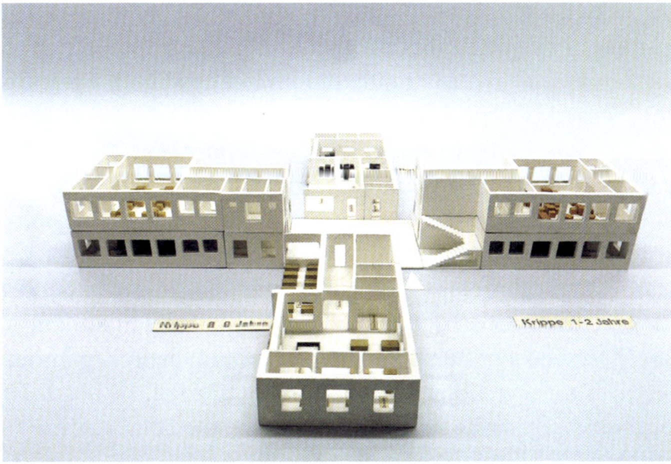

Fig. 6. Margarete Schütte-Lihotzky, modular system, 1965, configuration for six groups based on the model designed by the architect.

One year after presenting the model in Vienna, Schütte-Lihotzky was called to the Institute for Housing and Public Buildings (IWG) at the Bauakademie in Berlin, where she revised the plans for her modular system to meet the requirements in the GDR. This entailed changing the dimensions and the arrangement of the interior. But her system was turned down once again, despite the great interest shown at the time in rationalization and typification.[29] The plans would undergo further but only marginal changes in 1968 and 1974. She expanded the variations from 12 to 20 possible combinations. This system, based on Schütte-Lihotzky's nearly 40 years of experience in kindergarten construction, can be seen as the culmination of her work in rational kindergarten construction, but it was never implemented.

29 See Carla Aßmann's essay in this volume.

To backtrack a moment, the kindergarten on Rinnböckstrasse in Vienna was clearly not completed as a prefabricated building, but its spatial structure already largely corresponded to the modular model system. In subsequent development efforts, the City of Vienna designed several of its own prefabricated-component systems in the 1970s in order to build standard types of kindergartens.

The Bottom Line

Margarete Schütte-Lihotzky turned her attention early on to kindergarten construction based on a central hall, a feature that served two vital functions: economical access and community space. This type of construction is evident in the architect's work throughout her various creative periods, and she often propagated it in the widest variety of versions, something she also did with rational prefabricated construction. Margarete Schütte-Lihotzky was a recognized expert in kindergarten construction all her life. Apart from buildings, she designed children's furniture and also held numerous lectures on the subject in Austria and abroad. In 1947, she proposed creating a central institute for the construction of children's facilities in Austria to aid all architects in the planning of kindergartens. It never came into being. The projects that never got past the paper stage and those that were carried out—whether in Germany, the Soviet Union, Austria, Cuba, or the GDR—attest to her constant striving to arrive at the best possible solution and to her numerous attempts to share her knowledge.

The Frankfurt Kitchen as a Museum Object

Änne Söll

Margarete Schütte-Lihotzky's Frankfurt Kitchen was integrated into social housing projects from 1926 through 1930 and is one of the best-known examples of modern, functional design and interior decoration that are hygienic, standardized, and efficient. Like many other kitchen designs in the 1920s, it must be dubbed a "sociotechnical reform project."[1] The Frankfurt Kitchen was closely associated with the whole idea of a "modern" housewife and contributed to an understanding of cooking as a household task organized down to the last detail. Prior research shows that it was part of larger efforts to take the concepts of work process rationalization espoused in Taylorism and apply them to the domestic sphere.[2] The Frankfurt Kitchen is called a prototype for all modern built-in kitchens. It is the model for most kitchens in the 21st century and therefore continues to shape our image of housework, how it is performed, and who takes care of it.

The Frankfurt Kitchen has arrived as an exhibit in a variety of museum collections in the United States and in German-speaking countries, including the Museum of Modern Art in New York (MOMA),[3] the Minneapolis Institute of Art (MIA), the Museum für Angewandte Kunst and the Historisches Museum in Frankfurt, the Germanisches Nationalmuseum in Nuremberg, the Museum der Arbeit and the Museum für Kunst und Gewerbe (MK&G) in Hamburg, the Werkbundarchiv—Museum der Dinge (Werkbundarchiv) in Berlin, and the MAK—Austrian Museum of Applied Arts Vienna.[4] In its various stagings at these museums, the kitchen is presented as a prototype either for modern interior design

1 Marion von Osten, "Gespenstische Stille. Die arbeitslose Küche," in *Die Küche. Lebenswelt, Nutzung, Perspektiven*, ed. Klaus Spechtenhauser (Basel: Birkhäuser, 2006), 130–47, here 137.

2 Susan R. Henderson, "A Revolution in the Woman's Sphere: Grete Lihotzky and the Frankfurt Kitchen," in *Architecture and Feminism*, ed. Debra Coleman, Elizabeth Danze, and Carol Henderson (New York: Princeton Architectural Press, 1992), 221–53, here 245–46; Lore Kramer, "Rationalisierung des Haushaltes und Frauenfrage – Die Frankfurter Küche und zeitgenössische Kritik," in *Ernst May und das Neue Frankfurt 1925–1930*, exhibition catalog, Deutsches Architekturmuseum (DAM), Frankfurt am Main, ed. Heinrich Klotz (Berlin: Ernst & Sohn, 1986), 77–84, here 78–79; on the relationship of modernist architects to the "new woman," see Mark Peach, "'Der Architekt Denkt, Die

or for industrial design. Questions about the performance and equitable distribution of (unpaid) housework, which are closely tied to the genesis of the Frankfurt Kitchen, are only marginal topics or ignored altogether in most museum presentations. In museum displays where housework is addressed as a theme, the emphasis is on the ways in which housework has been rationalized or allegedly made easier. However, "to date 90 percent [of it] is left to women and outsourced worldwide to people, primarily women, with a migratory background."[5] Through its musealization and its integration into the history of modern design, the Frankfurt Kitchen as a museum exhibit, I will argue, has been decoupled from aspects of gender; in a word, it has been "degendered." When I use the concept "degendering" in this context, I am not referring to positive effects or utopian ideas connected to the vision of a gender-neutral environment or a gender-free world where the negative effects of heteronormative gender regimes have disappeared. Instead, I understand degendering here in its literal sense. I show, for example, how issues pertaining to the gender order and the gender-specific division of labor, which played a crucial role in the development of the Frankfurt Kitchen and also in later discussions surrounding it, were supplanted by the major formalistic narrative of modern design. As a result, the Frankfurt Kitchen as an exhibit can be historicized in museums and detached from gender issues (and issues related to the performance of housework). The only exception is the presentation of the kitchen at the MAK in Vienna.

So, in what ways is the Frankfurt Kitchen actually linked to gender issues? First, it is important to point out that it was designed by one of the first women to be trained as an architect at the Kunstgewerbeschule (School of Arts and Crafts; today's University of Applied Arts Vienna). As a young architect in Vienna, Schütte-Lihotzky already turned her attention to the ideas of standardization and rationalization, also with respect to interior design for social housing construction and for cooperative housing construction projects. In 1926 she moved to Frankfurt am Main, where she worked in the standardization and typification department at the Hochbauamt (central building authority in the city) under Ernst May,

Hausfrau Lenkt': German Modern Architecture and the Modern Woman," in *German Studies Review* 18, no. 3 (1995): 441–63; Peter Noever (ed.), *Die Frankfurter Küche von Margarete Schütte-Lihotzky, Die Frankfurter Küche aus der Sammlung des MAK – Österreichisches Museum für angewandte Kunst Wien* (Berlin: Ernst & Sohn, 1992); Gert Kuhn, *Wohnkultur und kommunale Wohnungspolitik in Frankfurt am Main 1880–1930. Auf dem Wege zu einer pluralen Gesellschaft der Individuen* (Bonn: Dietz, 1998), 142–76.

3 The Frankfurt Kitchen was on display at MoMA in the following exhibition: *Counter Space: Design and the Modern Kitchen*, exhibition catalog, Museum of Modern Art, New York, ed. Juliet Kinchin et al. (New York: Museum of Modern Art, 2011), 19–20.

4 Unfortunately, for reasons of space it is not possible to provide an exhaustive account here of all museum exhibitions featuring the Frankfurt Kitchen.

5 von Osten, "Gespenstische Stille," 134.

thereby becoming a participant in the social housing construction project known as New Frankfurt.[6] Typification and standardization were the key means there to reduce costs of construction and interior furnishings. Components produced in series and interior furnishings such as cupboards, closets, and especially kitchens were to be used to save space and money. In line with the ideas of the Werkbund and Bauhaus, the search for the ultimate form and the most expedient design in the New Frankfurt construction projects was also aimed at reducing class differences.[7] In the planning process, the design of the kitchen was viewed as the central design issue that influenced all the other architectural decisions.[8] The kitchen, clearly a female workplace, became the focal point of planning work.[9] However, standardization and rationalization in the kitchen did not mean that men would participate in housework. Cooking, dish washing, cleaning, and taking care of the children were indisputably women's matters in the 1920s. Rationalization was intended to save women time and effort, so they could, among other things, become gainfully employed (at most on a half-day basis). The Frankfurt Kitchen was a prime example of the strategy of "modernizing" housework in terms of design and architecture but by no means on a sociological level and with respect to the division of labor. Thus, owing to aspects of "architectural social engineering in modernism, the foundation of the gender-based division of labor in a 'breadwinner household' was not challenged but rather in a certain respect spatially institutionalized."[10]

The Modern Housewife's Kitchen

As Lore Kramer, Ingeborg Beer, and others have noted, the small Frankfurt Kitchen was no longer a live-in kitchen where the family could cook, eat, and spend time. Instead, it was designed as a space for a single housewife working alone. Before running water and electricity were generally accessible and central heating became common, the live-in kitchen was the only heatable room for workers' families because the cooking stove doubled as a source of heat. In developing the Frankfurt Kitchen, Schütte-Lihotzky availed herself of technical advances to create a place designed exclusively for

6 See Claudia Quiring's essay in this publication.

7 Renate Flagmeier, "Gebrauchsanweisung für eine Frankfurter Küche im Museum (der Dinge)," in *Die Frankfurter Küche. Eine museale Gebrauchsanweisung*, museum brochure (Berlin: Werkbundarchiv—Museum der Dinge, 2013), 9–19, here 11.

8 See, for example, Henderson, "A Revolution in the Woman's Sphere," 232.

9 On gender issues in the planning of the Frankfurt Kitchen, see Henderson, "A Revolution in the Woman's Sphere," 221–53; for a more general account of the gender question in the planning of social housing in Germany, see Ingeborg Beer, *Architektur für den Alltag. Vom sozialen und frauenorientierten Anspruch der Siedlungsarchitektur in den zwanziger Jahren* (Berlin: Schelzky & Jeep, 1994). Here, Beer compares the various kitchen designs in social housing projects in Berlin, Frankfurt, and Munich; see 120–34.

10 von Osten, "Gespenstische Stille," 138.

cooking. As a result, the living and eating areas were separated, an idea that met with opposition from the public and especially from housewives' associations.[11] Schütte-Lihotzky herself referred to the kitchen as a laboratory, indicating that cooking and other household chores were now to be viewed as activities that were to be taken seriously. Housekeeping became a category of labor that one could measure and optimize.[12] Cooking was now carried out in a separate, strictly "female" area of the home. Schütte-Lihotzky modeled her interior design accordingly, basing it on professional kitchens in dining cars on trains, where a large number of meals were produced in a confined, expediently equipped space.[13] The notion of an efficient, well-organized kitchen was geared to a modernist understanding of space, which Penny Sparke once aptly described as follows: "For the Modernist the interior was simply the space within buildings, [...] which, in order for daily life to take place, had to be 'equipped' albeit as minimally as possible."[14] Once a private area of housework, the kitchen thus also became a public place. As mentioned above, the establishment of cooking as a professionalized activity supported by modern interior design did not result in a change in the division of labor. Instead of transforming housework either into collective labor and thus turning it into a community task, as was the goal in the *Einküchenhäuser* (residential buildings with central kitchens),[15] or even redistributing housework, the Frankfurt Kitchen cemented the modern housewife's traditional role. Adelheid von Saldern describes the developments in the performance of housework as "progressive modernization without direct emancipation, especially for women."[16] As Marion von Osten concluded, housework has also not disappeared as a result of the attempts to rationalize it; instead of saving time, "new work steps keep getting created at the same time."[17]

Let us return to the Frankfurt Kitchen, its aesthetic, and its museum history. Susan Henderson impressively described its "gleaming metal surfaces, its high imageability, the specificity of its interlocking parts, its modular totality and its largesse of technical fittings."[18] According to Henderson, "the Frankfurt Kitchen epitomized the transformation of everyday life in the modern age. [...] Intricately coordinated

11 For an insight into contemporary reactions to the Frankfurt Kitchen, see Kramer, "Rationalisierung des Haushaltes und Frauenfrage," 77–84; Beer, *Architektur für den Alltag*, 123–25.

12 Schütte-Lihotzky conducted ergonomic studies on cooking and washing dishes by observing work processes in the kitchen, calculating the most efficient procedure, and adjusting her planning accordingly.

13 Grete Schütte-Lihotzky, "Der neuzeitliche Haushalt. Die Ausstellung bei der Frankfurter Frühjahrsmesse," *Der Baumeister* 7, supplement (July 1927); also see Grete Schütte-Lihotzky, "Rationalisierung im Haushalt," *Das Neue Frankfurt* 5 (April/June 1927): 120–23.

14 Penny Sparke, *The Modern Interior* (London: Reaktion Books, 2008), 130.

15 On the history of *Einküchenhäuser* (residential buildings with central kitchens), see Beer, *Architektur für den Alltag*, 103–4 and 153–55.

16 Adelheid von Saldern, "The Workers' Movement and Cultural Patterns on Urban Housing Estates and in Rural Settlements in Germany and Austria during the 1920s," *Social History* 15, no. 3 (1990): 333–54, here 346.

and tightly configured, the Frankfurt Kitchen was realization of the kitchen as machine."[19] More than a mere machine operated by a trained housewife, it was conceived aesthetically as a *Gesamtkunstwerk*, a total work of art, as a space envisioned to be a perfectly integrated whole and aimed at having both an aesthetic and a homey effect, of course without being overladen with decoration or "sentimental knickknacks." It was designed to bring order into labor-intensive processes through rationalization. Women working in this kitchen—as Renate Flagmeier argues and her point is crucial—had to subordinate themselves to this new order, adapt to it, and endeavor to be part of a vision of the "new life."[20]

The Frankfurt Kitchen Enters the Museum

Since most Frankfurt Kitchens in a museum context have been refurbished and are shown restored to their "original" —that is, unused state, the idea of newness and thus the promise of a "new life" are conveyed through design (figs. 1 and 2). Both MOMA in New York and the Germanisches Nationalmuseum in Nuremberg have restored their Frankfurt Kitchens to a state that is intended to look like an original utopian condition.[21] The kitchens have been cleaned and freshly painted, so they look brand new. One could say they seem ready to have visitors "move right in" during their brief time at the exhibit. The MOMA kitchen gives the impression of being an already inhabited room with cupboards holding an assortment of pitchers, plates, and glasses whereas most of the kitchens elsewhere remain empty. In the latter cases, the modernist ideal of an "almost empty, not overladen, dematerialized space"[22] is put to the forefront, as can be seen, for instance, at MIA in Minneapolis and the Germanisches Nationalmuseum in Nuremberg. One of the few Frankfurt Kitchens that was not restored to its unused, original condition and is thus shown in a non-renovated state can be seen at the Werkbundarchiv in Berlin (fig. 3). According to curator Renate Flagmeier, it was a conscious decision not to restore the kitchen because "the signs and traces of use should remain visible."[23] The non-restored state of the Werkbundarchiv kitchen also counteracts what Flagmeier correctly calls the "reduction [of the Frankfurt Kitchen] to a design

17 von Osten, "Gespenstische Stille," 138. According to von Osten, household technologies encourage the privatization of housework and counteract its redistribution. Housework has not been significantly reduced by technology; although it requires less physical effort, new tasks have been added for the housewife. Technology reinforces the traditional division of labor between couples and "confines women even more to their traditional role." As a result of its technologization, housework is regarded as "abolishable" and thus also as inferior. Unlike paid work, housework is still seen "not as an attractive social integration area for both genders, nor are the activities at home [...] viewed as activities that are actually productive for our society, even though they are vital in the truest sense. The desperate abolition of housework is to be read as the story of the contempt with which it is treated [...]." von Osten, "Gespenstische Stille," 139 and 144.

18 Henderson, "A Revolution in the Woman's Sphere," 235.

19 Ibid.

20 Flagmeier, "Gebrauchsanweisung," 15.

21 For a detailed description of the restoration of the Frankfurt Kitchen by the Germanisches

Figs. 1 and 2. Margarete Schütte-Lihotzky, Frankfurt Kitchen, Museum of Modern Art, New York (gift of Joan R. Brewster in memory of her husband George W. W. Brewster), and Margarete Schütte-Lihotzky, Frankfurt Kitchen, Germanisches Nationalmuseum, Nuremberg.

icon."[24] The presentation of the Frankfurt Kitchen in used condition makes the museum visitor aware of the kitchen's function and also shows that the materials have not fully stood the test of time. The chipped corners and peeling paint point to the lives lived in this room and not to the life of the designer who created it. This presentation is neither about the grand narrative of modernist design as a continual optimization and rationalization of forms nor about an attempt to convince visitors of the intrinsic "beauty" of the design. What is consistently emphasized here is the practical value of the kitchen, not its design value. Thus, the status of the Frankfurt Kitchen as a design icon is put up for discussion.

What is the relationship between the Frankfurt Kitchen, on the one hand, and the approach museums take in displaying it and its status as an exhibit, on the other? From the outset, it was conceived as a showpiece and, as Joachim Krausse notes, envisaged as a room intended both for practical use and for being displayed at contemporary exhibitions seeking to persuade housewives of the great benefits of the new kitchen design and new technologies.[25] As a room that was well lit, organized, and clean, the Frankfurt Kitchen was not meant to be hidden in the back of the home, as had been the case with most kitchens in the past. Instead, it was

Nationalmuseum, see Martin Meyer and Ursula Peters, "Die Frankfurter Küche aus der Römerstadt Siedlung," in *Anzeiger des Germanischen Nationalmuseums* (2006): 189–214.

22 Sparke, *The Modern Interior*, 152.

23 Flagmeier, "Gebrauchsanweisung," 16.

24 Ibid., 17.

25 See "Eine Architektur der Raum Zeit. Joachim Krausse im Gespräch mit Renate Flagmeier," in *Die Frankfurter Küche. Eine museale Gebrauchsanweisung*, 35–60, here 52. On exhibitions that aim to educate women about household management and promote the new kitchen design, see Beer, *Architektur für den Alltag*, 129–41.

conceived as a "shop window" for displaying the modern, (petit) bourgeois housewife in her modernized terrain, who, following the decline in the employment of domestic servants, had to perform the bulk of the housework herself.[26] With the development of the Frankfurt Kitchen, the bourgeois kitchen was no longer an invisible workroom peopled with domestic servants. Instead, it became a central location

26 For a summary of the "servant girl question," see von Osten, "Gespenstische Stille," 134–36.

Fig. 3. Margarete Schütte-Lihotzky, Frankfurt Kitchen, Werkbundarchiv—Museum der Dinge Berlin collection.

of a visible lifestyle where the housewife's activities were openly presented.[27] One could therefore argue that another reason the Frankfurt Kitchen is so well suited for display in a museum is that it fits superbly into the narrative of the development of a designed—that is, carefully fashioned—"lifestyle" in which cooking takes on an integral and prominent role.

27 Ibid., 139.

Let us return again to the Frankfurt Kitchen in a museum setting. What types of narratives are conveyed by these museum kitchens and what do they have to do with issues of gender, gender equality, and the redistribution and professionalization of housework? The Frankfurt Kitchen is incorporated in museum collections with such frequency because its "clean design" makes it an excellent example of modernity, and not necessarily because it was designed by a woman or because it symbolizes the rationalization of housework. In many collections, the Frankfurt Kitchen can be seen as a prime example of the radical change that took place in early 20th century architecture and interior design and fundamentally altered the lives of the inhabitants. This approach, in turn, fits into the canon of 20th century design history as depicted in most museums—namely, as a "natural development" toward modernist design. Modern design, so goes the inherent ideology, stands for efficiency and progress, promises a better life, and—mostly as an unspoken subtext—is generally created by men with clear visions of the future. The project of modernism is still a clearly male-connoted concept in most museums. Apart from the fact that its originator was a woman, the Frankfurt Kitchen meets all these criteria. Thus, it is integrated in the "grand narrative of modernism" and qualifies as a central showpiece in many museums of applied arts and design history. So, it also comes as no surprise that there are no direct references to gender topics in most museum presentations. Questions about the use of the kitchen or the distribution of housework are rarely posed proactively. One exception is a short promotional film from the late 1920s which is shown in direct proximity to the Frankfurt Kitchen displayed at the MK&G in Hamburg, at the Werkbundarchiv in Berlin, and at the MAK in Vienna. The film illustrates the use of the kitchen, thereby propagating

28 At the Historisches Museum in Frankfurt, for example, an information sheet at the entrance to the kitchen asks visitors to identify the steps involved in peeling and cooking potatoes. This sheet is primarily aimed at children but is also available to adults. Another such sheet

Fig. 4. Information panel about Margarete Schütte-Lihotzky, Frankfurt Kitchen, reconstruction, Vienna, 1989, MAK Design Lab.

points out to readers that the Frankfurt Kitchen was designed to relieve women of the burden of housework in order to facilitate their economic independence from men in the long term. There is no mention of the fact that the kitchen did not help to achieve this goal.

the usefulness of the new design by underscoring the more efficient work methods that the Frankfurt Kitchen allows, with the housewife naturally acting as protagonist. Hardly any of the installed information panels (with the exception of the MK&G in Hamburg) bring up the topic of gender. Most of the museums concentrate on the subject of rationalization[28] and dispense with didactic texts that could link the kitchen to problems surrounding the equitable distribution of housework. The MAK in Vienna is the only museum that addresses these problems. So, except for this presentation and the one at the Werkbundarchiv in Berlin, what we see is the staging of a progressive design icon. One topic is seldom raised: the fact that housework remained in women's hands even in the Frankfurt Kitchen and that the kitchen, contrary to its designer's objectives, was a restorative rather than a progressive invention with respect to gender roles.

The Frankfurt Kitchen as a Multilayered Exhibit

Let us turn to the two presentations that do not correspond to the standards described above. The Werkbundarchiv in Berlin attempts to broaden the context by showing not only the above promotional film but also excerpts from interviews with Schütte-Lihotzky and parts of a documentary that Joachim Krausse made about the Frankfurt Kitchen in 1985. These films are projected directly onto the kitchen, emphasizing its status as an article of daily use, as an actively used space that has definitely undergone major changes. Museum visitors can walk into the installation at the Werkbundarchiv, as is also the case at the Historisches Museum in Frankfurt. On entering the space at the Werkbundarchiv, visitors hear information from a voice coming over a loudspeaker explaining several key concepts associated with the development of the Frankfurt Kitchen, such as "rationalization," "timesaving," and "ergonomics." This approach ensures that even impatient visitors, the ones who neither read accompanying texts nor watch the film, leave with at least a rough idea of the objectives driving the development of the Frankfurt Kitchen. Unlike in Frankfurt, visitors to the Werkbundarchiv in Berlin can interact directly with the installation. For instance, they can sit on the swivel chair, open the drawers, and look into the sink. In doing so, they get an impression (albeit superficial) of how the kitchen was used and how people lived and worked in it—an experience visitors to almost all other museums are denied. This makes the Frankfurt Kitchen at the Werkbundarchiv the most accessible of all of the exhibited kitchens mentioned here, but gender issues are not directly referred to even in this museum presentation. The tangle of gender-structure modernization and simultaneous consolidation in which the Frankfurt

Kitchen originated and the role it assumed in that tangle is not rendered visible.

The only exception is the presentation of the Frankfurt Kitchen at the MAK in Vienna (fig. 4). There, it is part of a cultural historical exhibition on the topic of cooking and kitchens with the title: *And Now: The Feminist Point of View! Or: Housework = Women's Work*. The clenched fist to the left on the panel and the red-striped background signal to museum visitors that what they have before them is a special point of view, a challenge, and a provocation. Short essays and interviews on the topic can be viewed directly below the panel, the promotional film from 1926 is shown, and a stool bids visitors to linger for a while. They are invited to contemplate the equitable distribution of housework, with the Frankfurt Kitchen serving as an example.[29] The MAK presentation is the only attempt to address the hot-button issue of housework in connection with the Frankfurt Kitchen, an issue involving not only its gender coding but also the outsourcing of housework to migrant women. Although presented as the "feminist point of view" complete with clenched fist, the presentation runs the risk of housework being perceived as a problem for a category of women decried as radical rather than as a challenge for society as a whole with far-reaching consequences for everyone's day-to-day life.

29 An information panel also explains that the accusation that the Frankfurt Kitchen chained women to the stove even more than before was a heavy blow for Schütte-Lihotzky.

Despite their direct reference to the lived-in world, the museum presentations of the Frankfurt Kitchen—in sum and with the exception of the MAK—avoid issues concerning the distribution of housework and do not address the fact that this work continues to be associated with women. This degendering, as I called it at the outset, results from subsuming the Frankfurt Kitchen under the design history of modernism, for which gender issues generally still play no role in a museum context or only a subordinate role. However, as the examples of the presentations of the Frankfurt Kitchen in Berlin and Vienna show, exhibition strategies do exist for questioning the history of the modern design icon, for presenting a more complex picture of design history, and, among other things, for addressing the distribution of housework. This gives reason to hope that design history presented in museums in the future can also be a form of gender history and can reflect the scholarly work that has been conducted for years now in the fields of gender, architecture, and design. After all, the relationship between objects and gender issues is one of the "fundamental components of the cultural framework which holds together our sense of social identity."[30]

The Frankfurt Kitchen should therefore become an open, contradictory, and multilayered exhibit, as Anke te Heesen and Petra Lutz formulated it when describing the status of objects in a museum.[31] As my analysis of the presentations of the Frankfurt Kitchen has revealed, in order to anchor the gender discourse in museums, one must question ideologically shaped gestures of museological "showing"[32] and find new channels of communication. After all, museums deliver "very specific spaces of possibility or impossibility, in which identities, values, and norms are performatively tried out, negotiated, and rendered visible."[33] It is precisely an exhibit like the Frankfurt Kitchen, with its complex history of disputed modernization, distribution, and rationalization of unpaid housework, that is perfectly suited to becoming one of these "spaces of impossibility."

30 Pat Kirkham and Judy Attfield, introduction to *The Gendered Object*, ed. Pat Kirkham (Manchester: Manchester University Press, 1996), 1–11, here 1.

31 Anke te Heesen and Petra Lutz (eds.), introduction to *Dingwelten. Das Museum als Erkenntnisort* (Cologne: Böhlau, 2005), 11–24.

32 Daniela Döring and Jennifer John, "Einleitung. Museale Re-Visionen: Ansätze eines reflexiven Museums," *Frauen Kunst Wissenschaft* 58 (April 2015): 5–27, here 11.

33 Ibid., 11.

"Facadism." The Reception of the Frankfurt Kitchen and the Art Market

Marie-Theres Deutsch

The defeat of Germany and Austria in World War I and the revolutionary overthrow of their monarchies, the political and financial upheaval they faced following the harsh peace conditions imposed by the Allies, and finally the snowballing devaluation of their currencies and asset values led to severe social and economic crises in those two countries in the early 1920s. Sentiment in society fluctuated in tendency between revolutionary, reformist, and reactionary-conservative. From late 1923 on, the situation stabilized somewhat. The various political factions geared themselves to resolving their conflicts within a republican form of government. Over the next six years prosperity slowly began to grow, creating a climate for social and political experiments both in the Weimar Republic and in Red Vienna. The Bauhaus architects and designers closely associated with Socialism were given various opportunities to implement their radical ideas. Ernst May and his team were able to plan and build in Frankfurt am Main. There was a massive housing shortage, especially among the lower and lower middle classes, which were now impoverished by war and inflation. Major municipal housing developments forming large-scale settlements were seen as a way of alleviating this shortage.

May was not squeamish in these efforts. North of Frankfurt am Main lay the Castrum, an extensive Roman archaeological site. Back in 1827, the Association of History and Archeology had uncovered ancient finds in Frankfurt-Heddernheim, proving the existence of the Roman town of Nida. It was precisely at this site that Ernst May and his team built the Siedlung Römerstadt between 1927 and 1929. The plans showed no consideration toward archaeological traces from the past (fig. 1). During the construction of the 1,220 housing units, only excavation-pit archeology was possible; the official excavation commission had already been disbanded in 1925.

Pot hunting, private appropriation, and family excavation tourism were the unwanted results. A cynical and sarcastic mood prevailed among experts and in the general public, but did not bother the planning team around Ernst May. May's practical self-assertiveness is what made "Das Neue Frankfurt" (DNF, New Frankfurt) an exemplary brand name worldwide for its creative innovation, rational design, and use of modularity in construction. Parallel to construction, May and his team concentrated strategically on public relations and publicity work. They put the DNF brand into circulation as an idea and a reality by staging exhibitions, trade shows, and conferences. The monthly journal *DNF* helped in this endeavor, as did brochures, furniture and interior decoration catalogs, public readings, and not least, a film club.

Fig. 1. Postcard—"Gruß aus Heddernheim" (Greetings from Heddernheim)—satirizing excavation tourism.

For propaganda reasons, the May team gave women a significant part to play. With the introduction of universal suffrage in 1919, they had politically become formally emancipated. However, they were also appreciated for their role as consumers of household goods, the mass media, and film. An attempt was made to win them as allies in the transformation of housing traditions.

New Frankfurt still stands today as a symbol of revolutionary thought in publicly subsidized housing construction. Along with Bauhaus and the Weissenhofsiedlung in Stuttgart, DNF has been the central international concept for these efforts to the present day. One should not underestimate the extent to which postwar pathos and the Socialist-inspired ethos of the “New Human” also resonated in these ideas for reshaping public space and the private sphere. The concept revolved around redefining gender roles. In the domestic and family sphere, the “new woman” was to be given suitable new space for creativity. However, the “new woman” was reflected to only a limited extent in the new housing construction plans. She was given the task of “modernizing” the home and the kitchen. Besides assuming her traditional role as the family’s guardian, she was to be put in a position where she could organize more efficiently and work more purposefully. One question became critical: How could women be persuaded to support the ambitions of Neues Wohnen (New living), which were in part utopian and revolutionary, in part market-conform in terms of technology and practicality?

Diagrams show the sequence of steps the young architect Margarete Schütte-Lihotzky followed in designing her strictly standardized kitchen (fig. 2). 1.87×3.44 m = 6.43 m^2 had to suffice to meet the needs of the family in the shortest amount of time. The sliding door to the dining room was the essential connection to the family. The kitchen was not large enough for two people and was clearly defined as the woman’s realm.

Bruno Taut published his book *Die Neue Wohnung. Die Frau als Schöpferin* (The new dwelling. The woman as creator) in 1924. It contains a list of do’s and don’ts: he wrote that if the new woman wanted to be creative—that is, to be a creator—

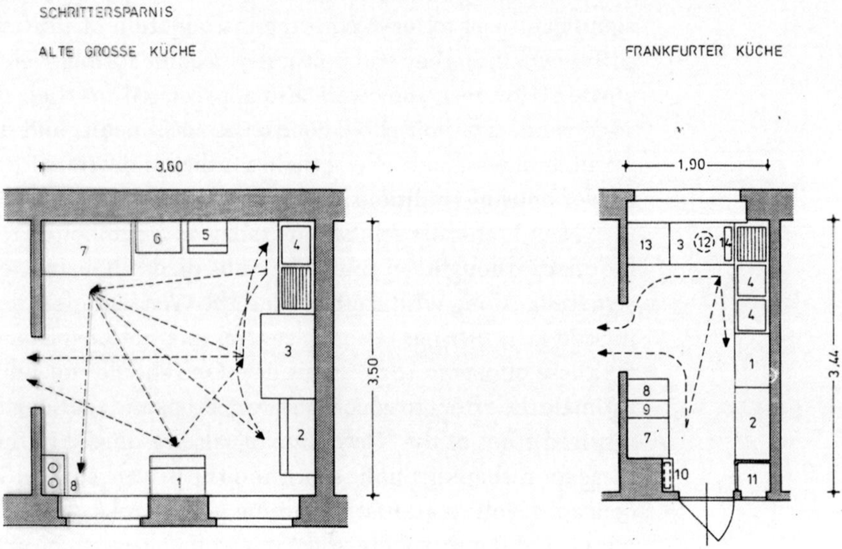

Fig. 2. Margarete Schütte-Lihotzky, Frankfurt Kitchen—studies of distances walked and how steps can be saved, 1927, print on film.

she should get rid of any and all odds and ends and knick-knacks. And on an even more fundamental level: she should cast off the "emotional ballast" instilled in her. His appeal speaking before representatives of housewives: "If everything—and I mean everything—not directly needed for life goes flying out of a dwelling, not only will her work become easier but new beauty will arise automatically." Taut turned to women because he needed them as allies—so they would actively long for the *Neues Heim* (The new home).[1] With a diktat of stylistic logic, he brushed away any notion that the future inhabitants might have already acquired furniture or become emotionally attached to "odds and ends" they had grown fond of. The totalitarianism of Soviet or Fascist provenience that arose in the 1920s found its aesthetic precursor here.[2]

1 Bruno Taut, *Die Neue Wohnung. Die Frau als Schöpferin*, 2nd ed. (Leipzig: Klinkhardt & Biermann, 1924), 31.

2 See Walter Gropius, "Die soziologischen Grundlagen der Minimalwohnung," in *CIAM. Internationale Kongresse für Neues Bauen. Dokumente 1928–1939*, ed. Martin Steinmann (Basel: Birkhäuser, 1979), 56–59.

The New Household

Erna Meyer's book *Der neue Haushalt* (The new household) was the standard work for rational housework reform. It was first published in 1926, and 38 (!) editions of it had appeared by 1929. The picture on the cover of the book shows a mother ironing in "her" room, the kitchen (fig. 3). The open cupboard doors demonstrate the impeccable orderliness with which kitchenware is stored. Her young daughter peeks in but remains at the door—as if she had no business in this room. The mother half turns toward the child, sensibly holding up the

Fig. 3. Dr. Erna Meyer, *Der neue Haushalt* (Stuttgart: Franck, 1926).

iron in the process to avoid singeing the item she is ironing. The expression on her face is clear: best to stay out, my child. I have work to do here; you have to occupy yourself in other ways. The illustration indicates at a glance how the functionalist work kitchen effectively shuts out social aspects of life.

The kitchen designed by Margarete Schütte-Lihotzky and installed about 10,000 times in New Frankfurt became the epitome of new, modern household management and famously entered the annals of architectural and design history. But the picture in actual practice was different. The settlements along with their kitchens soon became a subject of criticism. The kitchen was fixed in place on a concrete base and attached to the wall with steel anchors, so it was neither adaptable nor expandable. In other words it was part of the building and therefore not mobile—it had to be acquired or rented along with the home. It was not an eat-in kitchen. The family was shut out of the kitchen, and the housewife was separated from the family. Social life took place elsewhere.

This letter describes the mood in the first settlements into which people moved:

> It may have come to your attention, esteemed Mr. Mayor, that the houses have an extraordinarily large number of shortcomings because of various attempts to implement a new mode of construction. To list all of them would be a treatise in itself; we are conducting separate negotiations with the Bauamt (central building authority in Frankfurt) about these matters. However, we do not want to leave unmentioned that renowned construction experts say that in addition to the constructional defects, poor-quality construction materials have been used, and work that the site office would have to have rejected as useless has been accepted. So, the situation transpired that had to transpire. The inhabitants believed they would be able to lead a contented, modest life in a new home but until now there is probably not a soul in the settlement who is enjoying life. Repairs began the moment people moved into the houses and have not ended since then. In all probability, they will never end; new reports of structural damage arrive daily. The funds spent for repairs in the Praunheim Settle-

> ment speak for themselves, conveying a clearer message than words ever could. This situation is not changed even by the Bauamt's opinion that the damage the city must cover would have to have been completed by now *in general*. The facts prove the contrary [...].[3]

A half century later, Margarete Schütte-Lihotzky was less than enthusiastic looking back:

> As far as I recall, May came up with the name "Frankfurt Kitchen" and used it in a propagandistic way. Just as he always emphasized in word and image that the *Frankfurt Kitchen* was made by a woman for women. It fed into the notions among the bourgeoisie and petite bourgeoisie at the time that women essentially work in the home at the kitchen stove. That is why a woman architect would know best what is important for cooking. This message was effective propaganda at the time. But, to be quite honest, I never ran a household, never cooked, and never had any cooking experience prior to creating the Frankfurt Kitchen. Looking back on my life, I must say that I consider myself a systematic person in professional matters and that I naturally always began *every* assigned project task in a systematic way.[4]

3 Excerpt from a letter from the Siedler-Verein Frankfurt am Main, Praunheim e.V. dated July 24, 1933, quoted in *Wem gehört die Welt. Kunst und Gesellschaft in der Weimarer Republik*, exhibition catalog (Berlin: Neue Gesellschaft für bildende Kunst, 1977), 150.

4 Margarete Schütte-Lihotzky, *Warum ich Architektin wurde*, ed. Karin Zogmayer (Salzburg: Residenz, 2004), 149–50.

Reception

Until 1995, the cooperatives strictly prohibited the tenants of the rental properties from repairing or even altering their kitchens themselves. Nonetheless, the kitchens were decorated over the years and the sliding doors so crucial for the planners were sealed shut. In the kitchens, the tenants placed a refrigerator or dishwasher in front of the sealed sliding door and converted the dining room to their *Gute Stube* (parlor) with a living room suite and a TV. It should also be mentioned that the prefabricated furniture in the *Frankfurter Register* could be viewed as precursors to the IKEA culture. They could be modified and expanded where budgets allowed and as the years passed. Lower sections, mountable parts, intermediate cabinets—each individual component fit as a module on top of or next to another one.

From the mid-1990s on, the cooperatives no longer maintained the kitchens; the tenants were allowed to do repairs themselves or to expand and replace the kitchen. Many kitchens landed on the curb. Collectors were roaming the streets of New Frankfurt at the time, and the kitchens gradually began appearing at auction houses as a consequence. Astoundingly high prices were paid, prices that far exceeded the estimated value. The kitchen became the focus of attention for collectors and museums. In this context, one can observe five different categories of users and collectors of the Frankfurt Kitchen:

1. "Original residents" with original kitchens

There are still a handful of "original residents" or their direct descendants whose dwellings contain the originally installed kitchens, often "prettified" by them.

2. Experts and enthusiasts

Another category consists of fans of New Frankfurt, including architects and artists who purchased the houses from the 1920s in recent decades and restored the buildings and interiors to their original state. In the various municipal housing developments, corresponding circles of friends formed. One example is Damaschkeanger in Praunheim, where four architect friends live in five houses extending not even one hundred meters along the street.

The objective is often to acquire two adjacent houses and combine them to accommodate a four-person family (fig. 4). The existing kitchens are opened up to the dining area by installing large pass-throughs or passages.

3. Vintage marketers and auction houses

After 1995, when the cooperatives stopped repairing and watching over the kitchens and allowed them to be removed, one could find the kitchens on the curb as bulky waste for pickup on the one hand or on the other hand, they were sought out and collected by the Gesellschaft für Kunst und Denkmalpflege, a society of art and historic preservation in Stuttgart.

From 2004 on, the prices obtained in major auction houses exploded, setting Frankfurt vintage collectors off on searches, removals, and pickups of kitchens from the curbs. The crowning moment came with the 2010 sale of a kitchen to MoMA, the Museum of Modern Art in New York. The kitchen had finally become a design icon.

Fig. 4. Kitchen in Damaschkeanger, Praunheim, Frankfurt am Main, 2018.

4. Organizers of cooking events

Collectors and artists set up the Frankfurt Kitchen in large rooms, thereby releasing it from its actual functional idea (fig. 5). They offer cooking and dining with the slogan: "[...] working at a studio functions sort of like a family [...]"—social life through communal experiences.

Furniture components with the original paint peeling off—"as found"—create a seemingly homogeneous whole when placed next to each other and thereby cynically assert a claim to authenticity.

5. The kitchen as a design object

Once removed, the kitchen cabinets are released from their function, become estranged as design elements, and find themselves in living rooms or dining rooms again. Because of their modular design and strictly proportional specifications, the robust craftsmanship of their connections, and the material on hand, upper or lower cabinets can be added and combined without any difficulty. Totally released from their social function, they become individualized objects; with or without homogenizing coats of paint, they become collector's items (fig. 6). If only cabinet doors can be found, these "precious" parts are combined to create kitchen objects; the three-dimensional design icon is literally flattened to the point of "facadism."

The Frankfurt Kitchen was criticized primarily for its immobility, which prevented tenants from supplementing it with their own furniture. The planner's attempt to change modern humans and their family structures can be viewed as

Fig. 5. Frank Landau—Office & Warehouse, Frankfurt am Main, 2018.

Fig. 6. Living space in Tobias Rehberger's house, Frankfurt am Main, 2018.

a failure. Is it not an ironic turn of events that 90 years later the immobile kitchens are disassembled and serve collectors and marketers as single components akin to children's blocks? Is this the late revenge of the Socialist-tinged, one-size-fits-all approach of the original planners?

The Frankfurt Kitchen—Reflections in Contemporary Art Projects

Tobias Rehberger is featured worldwide in exhibitions and at art fairs, for instance at Art Basel in 2017. This Frankfurt artist has repeatedly used local memorabilia as part of his artistic work (fig. 7). One of these items is the legendary Frankfurt Kitchen, which he fashioned as a fully functional (!) kitchen on a 1:1 scale out of glazed yet porous porcelain for an installation entitled *Performance of Two Lonely Objects That Have a Lot in Common* (2014–17). The artist envisaged it being acquired for less than EUR 200,000, not by a museum but ideally by a private collector, and then integrated into an existing kitchen. The porous surface would end up with spots, scratches, and other signs of wear through daily use—

Fig. 7. Tobias Rehberger, *Performance of Two Lonely Objects That Have a Lot in Common*, 2014–17, Art Basel.

in other words, through performance, as suggested in the title of the installation.[5] With this work, Rehberger questioned the reception of the Frankfurt Kitchen in a museum context, where touching, let alone using, exhibited items is generally impossible. Yet at the same time, he created a hybrid, a hermaphrodite, from a severely overtaxed piece of utilitarian furniture and an artwork made of highly sensitive, vulnerable material.

5 See Christiane Oelrich, "XXL-Kunst auf der Art Basel" (June 13, 2017), accessed May 11, 2022, https://www.fnp.de/kultur/xxl-kunst-basel-10456320.html.

The curator Nicolaus Schafhausen invited the British artist Liam Gillick to create an installation for the German Pavilion at the Biennale 2009 in Venice. Like so many of his predecessors, Gillick made his main theme the pavilion itself, a building redesigned by the Nazis. What did he contrast it with? The Frankfurt Kitchen, as an important marker of applied modernism in industrial modernism (fig. 8). However, he used pinewood riddled with knotholes as his material, thereby referencing Scandinavian build-it-yourself furniture.

In this juxtaposition, the kitchen became a topic that was highly charged ideologically. Is Gillick's Frankfurt Kitchen, tweaked to an IKEA design, a valid response to the ideas of an architectural modernism that was enthusiastic about the mass industrial elements of Taylorism and Fordism yet wanted to use the capitalist rationality of those theories to

Fig. 8. Liam Gillick, *How Are You Going to Behave? A Kitchen Cat Speaks*, German Pavilion at the 53rd Venice Biennale, 2009.

bring about truly social or even Socialist housing construction? For Gillick, the Frankfurt Kitchen is an "emancipatory model of domestic activity." Yet he ignores the misogynous aspects of a design that banished the woman to the kitchen stove and arranged the family's dwelling according to standardized criteria.

What became of this modernism enthused about the idea of mass happiness? To Gillick, the Frankfurt Kitchen is a charming, select design object. It is the pure antithesis of the ideas of the Bauhaus avant-garde as it meanders through and counterbalances the temple-like building hierarchy of the German Pavilion—incidentally, just like the emancipated woman of the present is the opposite of the woman's role in New Frankfurt embodied in the Frankfurt Kitchen.

Appendix

Margarete Schütte-Lihotzky—Biography

1897 Margarete Lihotzky was born in Vienna on January 23, 1897 to a middle-class family with an interest in art and music. Her father was a civil servant, and his family originally came from Chernivtsi. Her mother had northern German roots and was related to the well-known art historian Wilhelm Bode.

1897–1915 Margarete Lihotzky grew up in Vienna's fifth district with her sister Adele, who was four years older. After attending a *Bürgerschule* (primary and vocational school), she took private lessons in painting and attended the Graphische Lehr- und Versuchsanstalt (Graphic Teaching and Research Institute) from 1913 to 1915.

1915–19 Studied at the Kunstgewerbeschule (School of Arts and Crafts; today's University of Applied Arts Vienna). She soon decided to pursue architectural studies under Oskar Strnad. Another important teacher for her was Heinrich Tessenow (building construction). In 1917, she won the Max Mauthner Prize for "A live-in kitchen in the outer suburbs." Strnad sent her into the workers' districts to do research. Based on what she learned there, she aspired from then on to approach every planning task with a deep sense of social responsibility. In 1918, practical experience at Strnad's firm; designs for theater projects and for buildings in *Siedlungen* (settlements)—that is, municipal housing developments.

1919–20 She graduated with top grades in 1919 and received the Lobmeyr Prize that same year for her design of a "Cultural Palace." Practical experience at Robert Oerley's architecture firm, then opened an office of her own as an independent architect in the Hofburg winter palace in Vienna. At the end of 1919, she accompanied Viennese children to Rotterdam, where they were sent to convalesce. There she gave art lessons and worked for Melchior & D. A. Vermeer Jr., a local architectural firm. After returning in the summer of 1920, she produced her own designs of buildings for municipal housing developments.

1921–22 From 1921 on, Lihotzky worked for the First Non-Profit Settlement Cooperative for Austrian War Invalids; she also worked with Adolf Loos at the building office for Siedlung Friedensstadt by Lainzer Tiergarten. Became acquainted with Ernst May during his stay in Vienna to conduct research. May arranged for the publication of Lihotzky's first article, "Einiges über die Einrichtung österreichischer Häuser unter besonderer Berücksichtigung der Siedlungsbauten" (A thing or two about the construction of Austrian houses with special account taken of settlement buildings) in *Schlesisches Heim* (1921). From that point forward, she published regularly and held lectures, initially about the optimization of living in small spaces. Worked at Ernst Egli's firm. From 1922 on, worked for the Austrian Settlement and Allotment Garden Association (ÖVSK), where she became acquainted with Otto Neurath, among others. Turned her attention to the rationalization of house-keeping; Lihotzky exhibited a model cooking-niche and scullery built on a scale of 1:1 at the fourth Viennese Allotment Garden, Settlement, and Housing Exhibition at Vienna City Hall and was awarded the bronze medal of the City of Vienna.

1923–25 At the fifth Viennese Allotment Garden, Settlement, and Housing Exhibition, she displayed several types of *Kernhäuser* (core-houses) as models on a scale of 1:1; she received the silver medal of the City of Vienna for her type 7 core-house featuring multipurpose "built-in furniture." In 1924, she was one of eight architects who planned 70 apartments in the Winarskyhof, a *Gemeindebau* (municipal housing complex). She fell ill with tuberculosis, which had killed her father and mother in 1923 and 1924 respectively. While convalescing at the sanatorium in Grimmenstein, she designed a "Tuberculosis Sanatorium," which was featured at the *Hygiene Exhibition* in Vienna in the spring of 1925. Following her release from the sanatorium, she developed "prefabricated furniture to fit the installation space." Impressed by the accomplishments of Red Vienna, Margarete Lihotzky joined the Social Democratic Workers' Party of German Austria (SDAP) in 1924.

1926–28 Appointed to the Hochbauamt Frankfurt (central building authority of the city) by Ernst May to work in the typification department, where she focused on housing construction and the rationalization of housekeeping. From the spring of 1926 to 1930, Lihotzky lectured regularly and published numerous writings on this subject. Designed housing, including standard-type row houses for the Praunheim Settlement. In the fall of 1926, the first standard-type kitchens were put in the Bruchfeldstrasse, Praunheim, and Ginnheim settlements—a total of about 10,000 of these kitchens were installed. The exhibition *Die neue Wohnung und ihr Innenausbau* (The new apartment and its interior finishings) in March and April of 1928 was instrumental in making her kitchen design known to the public.

In the spring of 1927, she married the architect Wilhelm Schütte (1900–68), who was working at the Hochbauamt in the school construction department; the couple moved into a studio apartment. Schütte-Lihotzky supervised the construction of the prefabricated building that the Hochbauamt presented at the Werkbund exhibition in Stuttgart, where her standard-type kitchen was also on display. She was given building assignments related primarily to women; she exhibited, among other things, an "Apartment for a working woman" in Essen in 1927 and in Munich in 1928, and gave lectures on the subject. From 1928 on, she planned school/training kitchens and kindergartens for the Ginnheim and Praunheim settlements. The global economic crisis that broke out in the late 1920s prevented any of the kindergartens from ever being built.

While in Frankfurt, Schütte-Lihotzky cultivated close ties with individuals at the Frankfurt Institute for Social Research. In 1927, she left the SDAP following the Palace of Justice fire in Vienna by sending "a pathetic letter to the party leadership."

1929–30 Ernst May organized the second International Congress of Modern Architecture (CIAM) in Frankfurt on a theme expressed in the name of the accompanying exhibition: *Die Wohnung am Existenzminimum* (The dwelling for minimal existence). Schütte-Lihotzky and her husband were jointly involved in the exhibition and a related project. Due to the economic crisis and a new regulation against double earners (i.e., hiring both members of a married couple), she lost her job and subsequently entered a number of competitions with her husband.

1930–33 At Josef Frank's invitation, she planned two single-family homes dimensioned six by six by six meters for the Werkbundsiedlung in Vienna (1930–32).

In October 1930, Schütte-Lihotzky and her husband went to Moscow with a group of German-speaking architects around Ernst May to bring their expertise to bear in building new cities in the Soviet Union. She headed up the group for children's facilities, planned individual but also standard-type projects for nursery schools, kindergartens, and clubs, and conducted corresponding courses. In 1933 she was featured at the World's Fair in Chicago. In Moscow, she worked for the Central Institute for the Protection of the Health of Children and Adolescents from 1933 on.

1934–36 The Schüttes traveled to Japan, where they visited their friend Bruno Taut. A lecture tour took Margarete Schütte-Lihotzky through China, where she produced guidelines for kindergarten construction for the Chinese Education Ministry. Once back in Moscow, she worked for the Academy of Architecture and designed children's furniture in collaboration with physicians and educators. She and Wilhelm Schütte produced plans for schools in Makiivka in 1935. In 1936/37, she worked on typification projects for children's facilities and standard-type furniture for various People's Commissariats.

1937 In August 1937 the Schüttes left the Soviet Union: the political climate had deteriorated dramatically. They traveled to France via Odessa, Istanbul, Athens, and Trieste. In Paris they found short-term work and stayed there for a year. Many émigrés were living in the city, and she established her first contacts with Resistance fighters. It was there that she very likely first met Hans Wetzler (1905–83), who would later become her life partner.

1938–40 The Schüttes traveled to London in April of 1938 but were unable to gain a professional foothold there. They therefore accepted Bruno Taut's invitation to join him in Istanbul to work at the Academy of Fine Arts for the Turkish Education Ministry. Schütte-Lihotzky designed village schools, among other things, and countless numbers of them were then built by the villagers themselves. In 1939 she and her husband became members of the Communist Party of Austria (KPÖ), where they met the architect Herbert Eichholzer, who was forming an Austrian Resistance group in Turkey.

1940–45 In December 1940, Schütte-Lihotzky traveled to Vienna, where she was supposed to establish contacts between the Austrian Resistance and supporters abroad. An act of betrayal led to her being arrested shortly before her intended return, and she narrowly escaped execution. The People's Court of Berlin sentenced her to 15 years' imprisonment at a women's prison in Aichach, Bavaria.

1945 Aichach Prison was liberated in April by American troops. Schütte-Lihotzky wanted to help build the young Austrian republic, but it took her months to return to Vienna. Her tuberculosis flared up again, and she convalesced at the tuberculosis sanatorium in Hochzirl, Tirol. Once back in Vienna, she worked on creating a central building institute for children's facilities.

1946–48 Her husband was unable to leave Turkey immediately, so Schütte-Lihotzky traveled to meet him part way. She waited for him in Sofia, where in 1946 she set up a department for children's facilities within the central building authority of the city and planned several kindergartens and nursery schools. The Schüttes arrived in Vienna on New Year's Day, 1947.

Schütte-Lihotzky designed the exhibition architecture for *Wien baut auf* (Vienna builds) in 1947 and for *Wien 1848* (Vienna 1848) in 1948. She participated in the CIAM Congresses in Zurich and the English town of Bridgwater, where the decision was made to establish an Austrian CIAM delegation. Schütte-Lihotzky became the president of the League of Democratic Women of Austria (BDFÖ) and was involved as a delegate in the Women's International Democratic Federation (WIDF).

1948–67 She designed memorials for Resistance fighters (1948–53) with her husband, from whom she separated in 1951, and also with Fritz Weber. Another joint project with her husband involved buildings for the KPÖ and clients closely affiliated with it, including Kärntner Volksverlag (1948–50), the printing and publishing building for Globus Verlag (1953–56), and decorations for a number of festivals (1950–59).

Schütte-Lihotzky participated in the CIAM Congress in Bergamo in 1949, spoke on "Buildings for Children" at the CIAM Congress in Vienna in 1951, and exhibited with the Austrian CIAM Group in Vienna in 1953. She took many trips, including a study tour to China; her book manuscript *Millionenstädte Chinas* (Chinese cities with over a million inhabitants) was published posthumously in 2007.

With the advent of the Cold War, the Communist Schütte-Lihotzky received almost no contracts anymore from the City of Vienna; the only exceptions were two residential buildings, one on Barthgasse (with Wilhelm Schütte, 1949/50) and the other on Schüttelstrasse (1952–56). The City of Vienna called on her only twice as an international expert in buildings for children; two kindergartens were built: one on Kapaunplatz according to her design (1950–52) and the other on Rinnböckstrasse (1961–63) in the pavilion style that she had developed. Her modular system (*Baukastensystem*) for kindergartens that she developed from 1964 to 1968 was never implemented although she proposed its use numerous times.

Her expertise was valued elsewhere. In 1961 and in 1963 she was in Cuba, where she created a design theory for children's facilities for the Education Ministry. In 1966 she worked at the Bauakademie (Building Academy) in East Berlin and wrote a research report on children's facilities in the German Democratic Republic (GDR). She paid regular visits to East Berlin, where her life partner Hans Wetzler had lived since 1963.

1967–75 She planned her new apartment on Franzensgasse over the course of two years (1967–69). She was able to move in after a stay at the tuberculosis sanatorium in Schwarzach. In 1975 she worked on a four-story residential building featuring ground-floor apartments with gardens and upper-floor apartments with terraces. At the same time she began to pen her memoirs after being urged to do so from many quarters.

1975–99 Schütte-Lihotzky was "rediscovered" from the mid-1970s on. She received numerous honors and awards, among them the City of Vienna Prize for Architecture (1980), honorary memberships in universities (University of Applied Arts Vienna in 1987, University of Fine Arts Hamburg in 1991), honorary doctorates (Technical University of Graz in 1989, Technical University of Munich in 1992, Technical University of Vienna in 1994), and the award from the IKEA Foundation Amsterdam in 1989. The Republic of Austria honored her with the Austrian Decoration for Science and Art (1992) and the Grand Decoration of Honor in Gold with Star for Services to the Republic of Austria (1997). In 1997 a square was named in her honor in Radstadt, a town in the Austrian province of Salzburg where Schütte-Lihotzky spent her summers for decades.

1985 saw the publication of her Resistance memoirs *Erinnerungen aus dem Widerstand. Das kämpferische Leben einer Architektin 1938–1945* (new editions in 1995 and 2014). Schütte-Lihotzky now appeared repeatedly as a "warning witness of the times." She followed the rise of the right-wing Freedom Party of Austria (FPÖ) with concern. In 1995 she and four other people persecuted during the Nazi era sued the party's chairman Jörg Haider for statements he had made that trivialized the Nazi concentration camps.

Schütte-Lihotzky's architectural work found its way into numerous exhibitions, including *Women Architects in Austria, 1900–1987* (Vienna; United States). One highlight was the exhibition on her entire oeuvre as an architect: *Margarete Schütte-Lihotzky. Soziale Architektur. Zeitzeugin eines Jahrhunderts* (Margarete Schütte Lihotzky. Social Architecture. Contemporary Witness of a Century) at the MAK in Vienna in 1993 (modified in Milan, 1996). She was frequently asked to give lectures, also outside Austria.

2000 Margarete Schütte-Lihotzky died in Vienna on January 18, 2000, just days before her 103rd birthday. Parts of her memoirs were published posthumously under the title *Warum ich Architektin wurde* (Why I became an architect) (2004; new edition: 2019).

She bequeathed her estate to the Archive of the University of Applied Arts Vienna, her alma mater. It is available there and in the online database at any time for research. Current information can also be obtained through the Margarete Schütte-Lihotzky Network: https://kunstsammlungundarchiv.at/universitaetsarchiv/margarete-schuette-lihotzky-netzwerk/.

In the autumn of 2022, the Margarete Schütte-Lihotzky Center was opened in her apartment in Franzensgasse. The Margarete Schütte-Lihotzky Club has been offering an ambitious program of events there since its founding back in 2013: https://www.schuette-lihotzky.at/de/.

Selected Bibliography

This bibliography provides a brief overview of Margarete Schütte-Lihotzky's own book publications, documentation of her life and work, and short biographical texts and works of secondary literature that deal more specifically with the architect's biography.

Schütte-Lihotzky, Margarete. *Erinnerungen aus dem Widerstand*. Edited by Chup Friemert. Hamburg: Konkret Literatur Verlag, 1985.

Schütte-Lihotzky, Margarete. *Erinnerungen aus dem Widerstand. Das kämpferische Leben einer Architektin von 1938–1945*. Edited by Irene Nierhaus. Vienna: Promedia, 1994 (new editions published in 1998 and 2014).

Schütte-Lihotzky, Margarete. *Warum ich Architektin wurde*. Edited by Karin Zogmayer. Salzburg: Residenz, 2004 (new edition—Vienna: Residenz, 2019).

Schütte-Lihotzky, Margarete. *Millionenstädte Chinas. Bilder- und Reisetagebuch einer Architektin (1958). Mit einem Nachwort von Albert Speer*. Edited by Karin Zogmayer. Vienna: Springer, 2007.

Schütte-Lihotzky, Margarete. "Passages from *Why I Became an Architect*." Selected and translated by Juliet Kinchin. *West 86th* 18, no. 1 (2011): 86–96.

Schütte-Lihotzky, Margarete, and Wilhelm Schütte, *"Mach den Weg um Prinkipo, meine Gedanken werden Dich dabei begleiten!" Der Gefängnis-Briefwechsel 1941–1945*. Edited by Thomas Flierl. Berlin: Lukas Verlag, 2021.

Akcan, Esra. "Civilizing Housewives versus Participatory Users: Margarete Schütte-Lihotzky in the Employ of the Turkish Nation State." In *Cold War Kitchen. Americanization, Technology, and European Users*, edited by Ruth Oldenziel and Karin Zachmann, 185–208. Cambridge, MA: MIT Press, 2009.

Baldessarini, Sonia Ricon. "Margarete Schütte-Lihotzky. Bauen und Leben mit sozialer Verantwortung." In *Wie Frauen bauen. Architektinnen von Julia Morgan bis Zaha Hadid*, 64–80. Berlin: Aviva, 2001.

Bois, Marcel. "Margarete Schütte-Lihotzky und das Frankfurter Institut für Sozialforschung." *maybrief* 049 (June 2018): 16–17.

Bois, Marcel. "Soziale Beziehungen und kommunistische Netzwerke. Annäherungen an Hans Wetzler (1905–1983)." In *Margarete Schütte-Lihotzky. Architektur. Politik. Geschlecht. Neue Perspektiven auf Leben und Werk*, edited by Marcel Bois and Bernadette Reinhold, 224–36. Basel: Birkhäuser, 2019.

Bois, Marcel. "Frau in der Mannschaft. Die beruflichen Netzwerke der Architektin Margarete Schütte-Lihotzky." In *Feministische Theorie nur mit feministischer Solidarität. Texte für Gisela Notz*, edited by Redaktionskollektiv aus dem Gesprächskreis Geschichte der Rosa-Luxemburg-Stiftung, 97–104. Neu-Ulm: AG SPAK, 2022.

Bois, Marcel. "Soziale Architektur und sozialistische Politik. Margarete Schütte-Lihotzky als Akteurin des Neuen Frankfurt." In *Die Politik in der Kultur und den Medien der Weimarer Republik*, edited by Andreas Braune and Tim Niendorf, 247–62. Stuttgart: Franz Steiner Verlag, 2022.

Flierl, Thomas, and Claudia Quiring. "Schütte-Lihotzky, Margarete (auch Grete)." In *Akteure des Neuen Frankfurt. Biografien aus Architektur, Politik und Kultur*, edited by Evelyn Brockhoff et al., 177–79. Frankfurt am Main: Societäts-Verlag, 2016.

Friedl, Edith. *Nie erlag ich seiner Persönlichkeit ... Margarete Schütte-Lihotzky und Adolf Loos. Ein sozial- und kulturgeschichtlicher Vergleich.* Vienna: Milena, 2005.

Henderson, Susan R. "Revolution in the Women's Sphere: Grete Lihotzky and the Frankfurt Kitchen." In *Architecture and Feminism*, edited by Debra Coleman, Elizabeth Danze, and Carol Henderson, 221–53. New York: Princeton Architectural Press, 1996.

Heßler, Martina. "The Frankfurt Kitchen: The Model of Modernity and the 'Madness' of Traditional Users, 1926 to 1933." In *Cold War Kitchen: Americanization, Technology, and European Users*, edited by Ruth Oldenziel and Karin Zachmann, 163–84. Cambridge, MA: MIT Press, 2009.

Hochhäusl, Sophie. "'Dear Comrade,' or Exile in a Communist World: Resistance, Feminism, and Urbanism in Margarete Schütte-Lihotzky's Work in China (1934/1956)." *ABE Journal 16* (2019). https://journals.openedition.org/abe/7169.

Hochhäusl, Sophie. "Spatial Histories of Dissidence: Imagination, Memory, and Resistance in Istanbul, Vienna, and Santiago de Chile, 1938–1945." *ARQ* 105 (2020): 40–61.

Horncastle, Mona. *Margarete Schütte-Lihotzky. Architektin. Widerstandskämpferin. Aktivistin.* Vienna: Molden, 2019.

Kihnç, Kivanç. "Homemaker or Professional? Girls' Schools Designed by Ernst Egli and Margarete Schütte-Lihotzky in Ankara, 1930–1938." *New Perspectives on Turkey* 48 (2013): 101–28.

Köster, Magdalene. "'Ich bin eine alte Systematikerin.' Margarete Schütte-Lihotzky, Architektin." In *"Sei mutig und hab Spaß dabei." Acht Künstlerinnen und ihre Lebensgeschichte*, edited by Magdalene Köster and Susanne Härtel, 155–88. Weinheim: Beltz & Gelberg, 1998.

Maasberg, Ute, and Regina Prinz. "Margarete Schütte-Lihotzky – 'Ich bin ein schrecklich systematischer Mensch.'" In *Die Neuen kommen! Weibliche Avantgarde in der Architektur der zwanziger Jahre*, 61–67. Hamburg: Junius, 2004.

Nierhaus, Irene. "Nicht zuschütten. A Personal Remembrance of Margarete Schütte-Lihotzky." In *Women Architects and Politics. Intersections between Gender, Power Structures and Architecture in the Long 20th Century*, edited by Mary Pepchinski and Christina Budde, 21–27. Bielefeld: Transcript, 2022.

Noever, Peter, ed. *Margarete Schütte-Lihotzky. Soziale Architektur. Zeitzeugin eines Jahrhunderts.* Exhibition catalog, MAK—Austrian Museum of Applied Arts, Vienna. Vienna: Böhlau, 1993 (second edition published in 1996).

Nosiska, Dorothea. "Zum Sexus in der Architektur der Moderne: Annäherungen an Margarete Schütte-Lihotzky." In *Eros und Sexus*, edited by Daniel Sollberger, Hans-Peter Kapfhammer, Erik Boehlke, and Thomas Stompe, 190–205. Berlin: Frank & Timme, 2015.

ÖGFA and Ute Waditschatka, ed. *Wilhelm Schütte. Architekt. Frankfurt, Moskau, Istanbul, Wien.* Zurich: Park Books, 2019.

Ottillinger, Eva B. "Die Architektin Margarete Schütte-Lihotzky." *maybrief* 044 (September 2016): 11–13.

Scheffler, Tanja. "Margarete Schütte-Lihotzky. Küche, Kinder, Kommunismus." In *Frau Architekt. Seit mehr als 100 Jahren: Frauen im Architekturberuf*, edited by Mary Pepchinski, Christina Budde, Wolfgang Voigt, and Peter Cachola Schmal, 122–29. Tübingen: Wasmuth, 2017.

Werkner, Patrick, ed. *Ich bin keine Küche. Gegenwartsgeschichten aus dem Nachlass von Margarete Schütte-Lihotzky*. Vienna: University of Applied Arts Vienna, 2008.

Zieher, Anita. *Auf Frauen bauen. Architektur aus weiblicher Sicht. Mit einem Beitrag von Ulla Schreiber und einem Gespräch mit Margarete Schütte-Lihotzky*. Salzburg: Anton Pustet, 1999.

Zwilling, Jutta. "'Ich würde es genossen haben, ein Haus für einen reichen Mann zu entwerfen.' Margarete Schütte-Lihotzky: Architektin – Widerstandskämpferin – Kommunistin." In *Frankfurter Frauengeschichte(n)*, edited by Evelyn Brockhoff and Ursula Kern, 190–205. Frankfurt am Main: Societäts-Verlag, 2017.

Zwingl, Christine. "Grete Lihotzky, Architektin in Wien, 1921–1926." In *Die Revolutionierung des Alltags. Zur intellektuellen Kultur von Frauen im Wien der Zwischenkriegszeit*, edited by Doris Ingrisch, Ilse Korotin, and Charlotte Zwiauer, 243–51. Frankfurt am Main: Lang, 2004.

Zwingl, Christine. "Die Spülküche von Margarete Lihotzky." In *Das Rote Wien. Ideen, Debatten, Praxis*, edited by Werner Michael Schwarz, Georg Spitaler, and Elke Wikidal, 184–87. Basel: Birkhäuser, 2019.

Zwingl, Christine, ed. *Margarete Schütte-Lihotzky. Spuren in Wien*. Vienna: Promedia, 2021.

Index

Abbreviations

BArch Bundesarchiv (German Federal Archives)

BDFÖ Bund demokratischer Frauen Österreichs (League of Democratic Women of Austria)

BGBl. Bundesgesetzblatt (Federal Law Gazette)

CDU Christlich Demokratische Union Deutschlands (Christian Democratic Union of Germany)

CIAM Congrès internationaux d'architecture moderne (International Congresses of Modern Architecture)

CPSU Communist Party of the Soviet Union

DAM Deutsches Architekturmuseum (German Architecture Museum), Frankfurt am Main

DÖW Dokumentationsarchiv des österreichischen Widerstandes (Documentation Centre of Austrian Resistance), Vienna

FPÖ Freiheitliche Partei Österreichs (Freedom Party of Austria)

GDR German Democratic Republic

GESIBA Gemeinwirtschaftliche Siedlungs- und Baustoffanstalt (Cooperative Settlement and Building Material Association)

IAWA International Archive of Women in Architecture, Virginia Tech, Blacksburg, Virginia

ISG Institut für Stadtgeschichte Frankfurt (Institute for the History of Frankfurt)

KPD Kommunistische Partei Deutschlands (Communist Party of Germany)

KPÖ Kommunistische Partei Österreichs (Communist Party of Austria)

MAK Museum für angewandte Kunst (Austrian Museum of Applied Arts), Vienna

MK&G Museum für Kunst und Gewerbe, Hamburg

MoMA Museum of Modern Art, New York

NL MSL Nachlass Margarete Schütte-Lihotzky (Margarete Schütte-Lihotzky's estate)

NL MSL, WS Nachlass Wilhelm Schütte (Wilhelm Schütte's estate)

ÖGFA Österreichische Gesellschaft für Architektur (Austrian Society of Architecture), Vienna

ÖNB Österreichische Nationalbibliothek (Austrian National Library), Vienna

ORF Österreichischer Rundfunk (Austrian Broadcasting Corporation)

ÖStA/AdR Österreichisches Staatsarchiv/Archiv der Republik (Austrian State Archives/Archive of the Republic), Vienna

ÖVP Österreichische Volkspartei (Austrian People's Party)

ÖVSK Österreichischer Verband für Siedlungs- und Kleingartenwesen (Austrian Settlement and Allotment Garden Association)

RGASPI Rossijskij gosudarstvennyj arkhiv social'no-politicheskoj istorii (Russian State Archive of Sociopolitical History), Moscow

SDAP Sozialdemokratische Arbeiterpartei (Social Democratic Workers' Party)

SPÖ Sozialistische Partei Österreichs/Sozialdemokratische Partei Österreichs (Socialist Party of Austria/Social Democratic Party of Austria)

TH Technische Hochschule (technical university/college)

TU Technische Universität (technical university)

UAUAK Universitätsarchiv der Universität für angewandte Kunst Wien (University Archive of the University of Applied Arts Vienna)

UIA Union Internationale des Architectes (International Union of Architects)

USPD Unabhängige Sozialdemokratische Partei Deutschlands (Independent Social Democratic Party of Germany)

WIDF Women's International Democratic Federation

WStLA Wiener Stadt- und Landesarchiv (Municipal and Provincial Archives of Vienna)

ZPA KPÖ Zentrales Parteiarchiv der KPÖ (Central Party Archives of the Communist Party of Austria), Vienna

Image Credits

Kinchin
UAUAK MSL NL XXX, photo: Bernadette Reinhold, 2018

Bois and Reinhold
UAUAK, NL MSL, 50/29/FW

Zogmayer
UAUAK, NL MSL, F/528

Zwingl
UAUAK, NL MSL, 197/TXT

Plakolm-Forsthuber
Fig. 1: ÖStA/AdR, HBbBuT BMfHuW Titel ZivTech S-Z 9343, Schütte-Lihotzky Margarethe, GZl. 220.091-I/1-48
Fig. 2: UAUAK, 9394/1
Fig. 3: Ran Shechori, *Dora Gad. The Israeli Presence in Interior Design* (Tel Aviv: Architecture of Israel, 1997), 166
Fig. 4: Private collection

Reinhold
Figs. 1 and 3: Margherita Spiluttini Fotoarchiv, Architekturzentrum Wien
Fig. 2: Robert Rotifer and Lelo Brossmann, from the video "Rotifer—The Frankfurt Kitchen" (Wohnzimmer Records, 2008)

Eisterer
Fig. 1: UAUAK, NL MSL, TXT/2
Fig. 2: Horst Zecha, Geschichteverein, Siedlung Friedensstadt
Fig. 3: UAUAK, NL MSL, PRNR 24/1, photo: Robert Newald
Fig. 4: Verband der Kleingärtner Österreichs
Fig. 5: UAUAK, NL MSL, PRNR 34/11, photo: Robert Newald

Quiring
Fig. 1: UAUAK, NL MSL, F/93
Fig. 2: ISG/Hermann Collischon
Fig. 3: UAUAK, NL MSL, 50/5A/TXT
Fig. 4: UAUAK, NL MSL, F/91

Flierl
Fig. 1: Shchusev Museum, Moscow
Fig. 2: From Evgenija Konyševa and Mark Meerovič, *Linkes Ufer, rechtes Ufer. Ernst May und die Planungsgeschichte von Magnitogorsk (1930–1933)*, ed. Thomas Flierl (Berlin: Theater der Zeit, 2014), 70.
Fig. 3: UAUAK, NL MSL, PRNR 116/7/FW
Fig. 4: UAUAK, NL MSL, PRNR 118/7/FW
Fig. 5: UAUAK, NL MSL, PRNR 119/1
Fig. 6: UAUAK, NL MSL, PRNR 121/23

Dogramaci
Fig. 1: UAUAK, NL MSL, PRNR 134/2, repro photo: Robert Newald
Fig. 2: UAUAK, NL MSL, PRNR 136/2
Fig. 3: UAUAK, NL MSL, PRNR 136/15
Fig. 4: Courtesy of the artist and Burosarigedik
Fig. 5: UAUAK, NL MSL, PRNR 135/19 FW

Platzer
Fig. 1: UAUAK, NL MSL, PRNR 152/6/FW, photo: City of Vienna press office, photo service
Fig. 2: UAUAK, NL MSL, TXT/382
Fig. 3: UAUAK, NL MSL, PRNR 190, source: WStLA

Chang
Fig. 1: UAUAK, NL MSL, F/CH/268
Fig. 2: UAUAK, NL MSL, F/CH/327
Fig. 3: UAUAK, NL MSL, TXT/287/A (Margarete Schütte-Lihotzky, Beijing, Peking, separatum—"Casa Bella" manuscript)
Fig. 4: UAUAK, NL MSL, PRNR 195/5, photo: Robert Newald
Fig. 5a: UAUAK, NL MSL, F/CH/36
Fig. 5b: UAUAK, NL MSL, PRNR 195/63A/FW

Aßmann
Fig. 1: BArch Berlin, DH 2/3055: daycare centers, weekly care homes for children
Fig. 2: ÖNB Wien / Chmel 6979
Fig. 3: Photo: Carla Assmann

Sandner
Fig. 1: Josef Böhmer/Verein für Geschichte der ArbeiterInnenbewegung Wien
Fig. 2: UAUAK NL MSL, TXT/280/9

Senarclens de Grancy
Figs. 1 and 3: Archive of TU Graz
Fig. 2: *Stimme der Frau*, 1961

Baum
Fig. 1: UAUAK, NL MSL, F/97
Fig. 2: UAUAK, NL MSL, F/164
Fig. 3: ÖGFA, photo: Karin Mack

Bois
Fig. 1: UAUAK MSL NL, F-186, photo: Oscar Horowitz
Fig. 2: UAUAK MSL NL, F-187, photo: Oscar Horowitz
Fig. 3: UAUAK MSL NL, Q/164/1/3/F

Boeckl-Klamper
Figs. 1 and 2: DÖW, photo 1065 and 49
Fig. 3: Bildarchiv der KPÖ

Mugrauer
Fig. 1. UAUAK, NL MSL, F/169
Figs. 2 and 3: Private collection

Schneider
Fig. 1: Bildarchiv der KPÖ
Figs. 2 and 3: Archiv der KPÖ

Engelmann
Fig. 1: Kunsthalle Hamburg
Fig. 2: UAUAK, NL MSL, 172/87/FW
Fig. 3: From *Der 150. Kindergarten der Stadt Wien "Friedrich Wilhelm Fröbel," XX, Kapaunplatz*, ed. Stadtbauamt der Stadt Wien (Vienna: Verlag für Jugend und Volk, 1952), 61

Freyer
Fig. 1: UAUAK, NL MSL, 80/10/TXT
Fig. 2: From *Arkhitektura za rubezkom* 5 (1935): 15
Figs. 3 and 5: From *Margarete Schütte-Lihotzky. Soziale Architektur. Zeitzeugin eines Jahrhunderts*, exhibition catalog, MAK—Austrian Museum of Applied Arts, Vienna, ed. Peter Noever (Vienna: Böhlau, 1993), 152 and 225
Fig. 4: From *Der 150. Kindergarten der Stadt Wien "Friedrich Wilhelm Fröbel" XX, Kapaunplatz*, ed. Stadtbauamt der Stadt Wien (Vienna: Verlag für Jugend und Volk, 1952), 17
Fig. 6: UAUAK, NL MSL, 198/69/O, photo: Christoph Freyer

Söll
Fig. 1: © 2018 Digital image, The Museum of Modern Art, New York/ Scala, Florence
Fig. 2: Germanisches Nationalmuseum, Nuremberg, photo: M. Runge
Fig. 3: Werkbundarchiv—Museum der Dinge Berlin collection
Fig. 4: © MAK—Austrian Museum of Applied Arts Vienna, Contemporary Art, Kristina Wissik

Deutsch
Fig. 1: Private collection
Fig. 2: UAUAK, NL MSL, 50/43
Fig. 3: Private collection
Figs. 4 and 6: Photo: Laura Gerlach
Fig. 5: Photo: Marie-Theres Deutsch
Fig. 7: Tobias Rehberger, courtesy of the artist and Galerie Urs Meile, Beijing-Lucerne
Fig. 8: Guggenheim Bilbao collection, donated by the artist with the generous support of Casey Kaplan Gallery, New York and Esther Schipper, Berlin

Carla Aßmann. Cultural studies at the European University Viadrina in Frankfurt an der Oder and metropolitan studies at the Technische Universität Berlin. Ongoing dissertation project on large-scale residential settlements in the 1960s as part of the Leibniz Graduate School program "Disappointment in the 20th Century," funded by the Ludwig-Maximilians-Universität München and the Leibniz Institute for Contemporary History (IfZ). 2016–19 on the research staff for *Konfliktfeld autogerechte Stadt* (Automotive city as a source of conflict), a lighthouse project of the Historical Research Center at the Leibniz Institute for Research on Society and Space (IRS) in Erkner, Germany. Her main research fields are the history of cities and urbanization, and postwar modernism in East and West. Has worked for the Left Party (Die Linke) in Berlin since 2019.

David Baum. Studied architecture at the Technical University of Vienna, the University of Applied Arts Vienna, and the University of Art and Design Linz. Has worked for many years at the Architekturzentrum Wien (Az W) in the library, archive/collection, and Achleitner Archive. Member of FEA–Forum experimentelle Architektur. Currently pursuing a PhD project on Wilhelm Schütte at Ghent University and the University of Applied Arts Vienna and doing archival work at the studio of the Austrian architect Adolf Krischanitz.

His publications include "Wilhelm Schütte und die Ära des Reformschulbaus im Neuen Frankfurt (1925–1930)" and "Wilhelm Schütte als Vermittler und Architekt im Nachkriegs-Wien (1947–1960)" in *Wilhelm Schütte. Architekt. Frankfurt – Moskau – Istanbul – Wien*, ed. ÖGFA and Ute Waditschatka (Zurich: Park Books, 2019).

Elisabeth Boeckl-Klamper. Studied history and German philology and holds a doctorate from the University of Vienna; since 1991, has served on the research staff of the Documentation Centre of Austrian Resistance (DÖW) while also working as a researcher and curator for numerous exhibitions, for instance for the Jewish Museum of the City of Vienna.

Author of many scholarly publications, among others in collaboration with Thomas Mang and Wolfgang Neugebauer, *Gestapo-Leitstelle Wien 1938–1945* (Vienna: Edition Steinbauer, 2018).

Marcel Bois. Studied history, sociology, and art history at the universities of Constance and Hamburg. Earned a PhD in modern and contemporary history at the Technische Universität Berlin. 2015–2018 lecturer at the Ruhr-Universität Bochum. He carried out a project on Margarete Schütte-Lihotzky's biography on a research grant from the Gerda Henkel Foundation and then conducted research on behalf of the Education and Science Workers' Union (GEW). He has worked at the Research Center for Contemporary History in Hamburg (FZH) since 2020.

His publications in English include "A Transnational Friendship in the Age of Extremes: Leon Trotsky and the Pfemferts," *Twentieth Century Communism. A Journal of International History* 10 (2016), 9–29; "Opposing Hitler and Stalin: Left Wing Communists After Expulsion from the KPD," in *Weimar Communism as Mass Movement. 1918–1933*, ed. Ralf Hoffrogge and Norman LaPorte (London: Lawrence & Wishart, 2017), 150–69; "'The Art!—That's One Thing! When It's There.' On the History of the Arbeitsrat für Kunst in the Early Weimar Republic," *Bauhaus Imaginista* (January 2019), https://www.bauhaus-imaginista.org/articles/3207/the-art-that-s-one-thing-when-it-s-there; "'March Separately, But Strike Together!' The Communist Party's United-Front Policy in the Weimar Republic," *Historical Materialism* 28, no. 3 (2020), 138–65.

Helen Young Chang. Writer and translator based in Pittsburgh, Pennsylvania. She is currently working on a literary biography of Margarete Schütte-Lihotzky. Her essays and reviews have appeared in *frieze, ARTnews,* and the *Wall Street Journal*, among others. Her work has been recognized with the Milena Jesenka Fellowship, Arthur F. Burns Fellowship, Margarete Schütte-Lihotzky Stipend, and the 2017 Austrian Art Critics Award. She studied literature at Duke University in North Carolina and cultural anthropology at Columbia University in New York.

Marie-Theres Deutsch. Studied architecture at the Trier University of Applied Sciences and the University of Applied Sciences Wiesbaden (today's RheinMain University of Applied Sciences); postgraduate studies in architecture at the Städelschule in Frankfurt am Main; started an architectural firm while also serving as a guest professor at universities in Detmold, Kassel, and Siegen. In 2013, one of her designs was on the shortlist for the "Nike für Fügung" (Nike for integration), an architecture prize awarded by the Association of German Architects (BDA).

A sampling of her exhibitions: *Bauen heute*, Deutsches Architekturmuseum (DAM), Frankfurt am Main; *Design Heute*, DAM/Tokyo Laforet Museum Harajuk; *Museumsarchitektur in Frankfurt 1980–1990*, DAM/Art and Exhibition Hall of the Federal Republic of Germany, Bonn; *Maßstabssprung*, DAM; *Das Neue Frankfurt 2018: Wohnen für Alle*, DAM; "*Frau Architekt*," DAM (contributed a film); *Große Häuser, Kleine Häuser*, DAM.

Burcu Dogramaci. Studied art history and German language and literature at the University of Hamburg. Received her doctorate in 2000 and habilitated in 2007 in Hamburg. Habilitation thesis on the works of German-speaking architects, sculptors, and art historians in Turkey. Has been a professor of art history at Ludwig-Maximilians-Universität München since 2009. In 2016, received an ERC Consolidator Grant for the project "METROMOD" focusing on six metropolitan destinations for refugee European artists (https://metromod.net). Co-director of the Käte Hamburger Research Centre "Dis:connectivity in Processes of Globalisation" (globaldisconnect.org/kate-hamburger-kolleg) since 2021.

Her publications include *Kulturtransfer und nationale Identität. Deutschsprachige Architekten, Stadtplaner und Bildhauer in der Türkei nach 1927* (Berlin: Gebr. Mann, 2008); *Fotografieren und Forschen. Wissenschaftliche Expeditionen mit der Kamera im türkischen Exil nach 1933* (Marburg: Jonas, 2013); *Urban Exile. Theories, Methods, Research Practices*, co-edited with Ekaterina Aygün et al. (Bristol: Intellect, 2023, Open Access).

S. E. Eisterer. Assistant professor of history and the theory of architecture at Princeton University, New Jersey. Studied architecture at the Academy of Fine Arts, Vienna, and history and the theory of urbanism at Cornell University, New York. S. E. is completing two book projects: the interdisciplinary history and translation project *Memories of the Resistance: Margarete Schütte-Lihotzky and the Architecture of Collective Dissidence* and the book *Housing Cooperative: Architecture, Politics, and Upheaval in Vienna, 1894–1934*.

S. E.'s work has been supported by the Radcliffe Institute for Advanced Study at Harvard University, the United States Holocaust Memorial Museum, the Humboldt Foundation, the Princeton-Mellon Initiative, and the Mellon Initiative at the University of Pennsylvania as well as the Margarete Schütte-Lihotzky Project Grant from the Austrian Federal Chancellery, among other awards. Her work has appeared in *Architectural Histories, Architecture Beyond Europe, Log, Platform, Aggregate,* and *ARQ*

Ediciones, among other publications. In 2022, her co-edited volume with Erin Sassin *States of Emergency: Architecture, Urbanism, and the First World War* was published by Leuven University Press and Cornell University Press.

Sebastian Engelmann. Studied social sciences, English language and literature, education, and applied ethics at the universities of Oldenburg and Jena and received his doctorate from the University of Jena. Post-doctoral research in the General Education Department at the University of Tübingen; since 2021 assistant professor of the history and theory of pedagogical thought and action at Karlsruhe University of Education.

His publications include *Pädagogik der Sozialen Freiheit. Eine Einführung in das Denken Minna Spechts* (Paderborn: Ferdinand Schöningh, 2018); *Sozialismus & Pädagogik. Verhältnisbestimmungen und Entwürfe*, in collaboration with Robert Pfützner (Bielefeld: Transcript, 2018); *Lebensformen des Demokratischen. Pädagogische Impulse* (Weinheim: Beltz Juventa, 2021).

Thomas Flierl. Studied philosophy and aesthetics at Humboldt-Universität zu Berlin and received his doctorate there in 1985. He worked in the cultural sphere and politics and has been a freelance architectural historian and journalist since 2006; member of the advisory board of the Ernst-May-Gesellschaft Frankfurt am Main and at the Bauhaus Institute for History and Theory of Architecture and Planning in Weimar; lectureships at the Bauhaus-Universität in Weimar and at Freie Universität Berlin; guest professor at the University of Constance. Member of the Academy of Arts in Berlin since 2021.

His publications include *Standardstädte. Ernst May in der Sowjetunion 1930–1933. Texte und Dokumente* (Berlin: Suhrkamp, 2012); editor of the series *Gegenstand und Raum* (all published by Theater der Zeit in Berlin), including the following volumes: Evgenija Konyševa and Mark Meerovič, *Linkes Ufer, rechtes Ufer. Ernst May und die Planungsgeschichte von Magnitogorsk (1930–1933)*, 2013; *Von Adenauer zu Stalin. Die Tätigkeit des Kölner Stadtplaners Kurt Meyer in Moskau und der Einfluss des traditionellen deutschen Städtebaus in der Sowjetunion um 1935*, in collaboration with Harald Bodenschatz, 2016. Also of note is *Hannes Meyer und das Bauhaus. Im Streit der Deutungen*, co-edited with Philipp Oswalt (Leipzig: Spector, 2018). Most recent work: Margarete Schütte-Lihotzky and Wilhelm Schütte, *"Mach den Weg um Prinkipo, meine Gedanken werden Dich dabei begleiten!" Der Gefängnis-Briefwechsel 1941–1945*, ed. Thomas Flierl (Berlin: Lukas Verlag, 2021).

Christoph Freyer. Studied art history at the University of Vienna. Has been working at the Wien Museum since 2019. Dissertation project on the architectural development of kindergartens in Vienna and taking inventories of the estates of Raimund Abraham, Günther Domenig, and Karl Schwanzer. Curator for the exhibition *Architekt Raimund Abraham. Back Home*, Schloss Bruck Lienz; was involved in the projects *Arch 4579. Entwicklung einer Bewertungsmethodik der Architektur von 1945 bis 1979, Schutzzonenmodell Basisinventarisierung,* and *Hofprojekt*; took inventories for the municipal housing complexes in Vienna (*Gemeindebauten*); and worked on *Architektenlexikon Wien 1770–1945*.

His publications include "Die Kinderfreibäder Wiens – über den Verlust eines vielfach unbeachteten Baujuwels," *Kunstgeschichte aktuell, Mitteilungen des Verbandes Österreichischer Kunsthistorikerinnen und Kunsthistoriker* 26, no. 2 (2009); "Kindgerichtete Architektur im Roten Wien," in *Das Rote Wien. 1919 bis 1934.*

Ideas. Debatten. Praxis, publication on the occasion of the centenary of Red Vienna at Wien Museum MUSA, ed. Werner Michael Schwarz, Georg Spitaler, and Elke Wikidal (Basel: Birkhäuser, 2019); "'Die Gartenstadt für Kinder' – Zur Idee eines Kinderheimes am Stadtrand von Wien," *Eselsohren* 3, nos. 1 and 2 (2020).

Juliet Kinchin. Independent design historian and former curator of modern design at the Museum of Modern Art (MoMA), New York. Has held faculty positions at the University of Glasgow (as the founding director of postgraduate studies in decorative arts and design history), The Glasgow School of Art, and the Bard Graduate Center, New York as well as curatorial positions at the Victoria and Albert Museum (V&A), London and in Glasgow museums and art galleries. During her MoMA tenure she featured Schütte-Lihotzky in her exhibitions and related catalogues for *Counter Space: Design and the Modern Kitchen* (2010) and *Century of the Child: Growing by Design* (2012), and acquired a Frankfurt kitchen for the permanent collection.

Manfred Mugrauer. Studied political science and history at the University of Vienna and Humboldt-Universität zu Berlin. Works at the Documentation Centre of Austrian Resistance (DÖW) and is the scientific secretary of the Alfred Klahr Gesellschaft, Vienna.

Publications on political history and cultural policy of the Communist Party of Austria, including *Die Politik der KPÖ in der Provisorischen Regierung Renner* (Innsbruck: StudienVerlag, 2006); *Die Politik der KPÖ 1945–1955. Von der Regierungsbank in die innenpolitische Isolation* (Göttingen: V&R Unipress, 2020).

Sabine Plakolm-Forsthuber. Studied art history and Italian at the University of Vienna and at the Università per Stranieri, Perugia; received her doctorate from the University of Vienna in 1986 and habilitated at the Technical University of Vienna in 2000. Instructor at the Institute of History of Art, Building Archeology, and Restoration at the Technical University of Vienna and at the University of Vienna.

Her research and publications focus mainly on Austrian art and architecture from the 19th to the 21st century, especially exhibition architecture, 20th century Austrian women artists and architects, the architecture of 15th and 16th century Italian convents, contemporary school construction in Austria, the architecture in Steinhof, and National Socialist art.

Monika Platzer. Head of collection and curator at the Architekturzentrum Wien (Az W). Studied art history and holds a doctorate from the University of Vienna. Her research focuses on the history of 20th century Austrian architecture and cultural history. International curatorial and research activity at leading institutions such as the Canadian Centre for Architecture (CCA) and the Getty Research Institute (GRI).

Her exhibitions include: *Shaping the Great City. Modern Architecture in Central Europe, 1890–1937*, Kunstforum, CCA, GRI exhibition and associated catalog (1999); *a_show. Austrian Architecture in the 20th and 21st Centuries*, Az W permanent exhibition on Austrian architecture (2004–21) and the associated catalog (2006; second enlarged edition 2016); *Kinetismus. Wien entdeckt die Avantgarde* [Kineticism: Vienna Discovers the Avant-Garde], Wien Museum, Az W exhibition and catalog (2006); *Lessons from Bernard Rudofsky. Life as a Voyage*, Az W, CAA exhibition and catalog (2007); *"Vienna. The Pearl of the Reich." Planning for Hitler*, Az W exhibition and associated catalog (2015); *Cold War and Architecture. The Competing Forces that Reshaped Austria after 1945*, Az W exhibition and associated catalog (2019/20); *Hot Questions—Cold Storage*, Az W permanent exhibition (since 2022) and associated catalog (2023).

Has taught at the University of Vienna and the Technical University of Vienna; editor of *icamprint* (2004–20), the journal for members of the International Confederation of Architectural Museums; in 2014 she was a visiting scholar at the Center for European Studies, Harvard University, USA. Her current research focuses on the history of transnational architectural history.

Claudia Quiring. Studied art history, history, and ethnology at the University of Münster and received her doctorate there in 2003. Taught at the University of Bielefeld and was an interim professor for architectural theory at OWL University of Applied Sciences and Arts. Curator of exhibitions on, among other topics, Fritz Högor, Ernst May, and Walter Müller-Wulckow's *Blaue Bücher*. Project manager for *"Akteure des Neuen Frankfurt."* Member of the advisory board of the Ernst-May-Gesellschaft. Since 2016, custodian for architectural history and urban development at Stadtmuseum Dresden with the 2019 exhibition *Dresdner Moderne 1919–1933*.

Her publications include *Ernst May (1886–1970)*, co-edited with Wolfgang Voigt et al. (New York: Prestel, 2011); "Evropeĭskie arkhitektory v SSSR. Žizn' každyj den'" (European architects in the USSR. Everyday life) with Evgeniia Konysheva, in *Sbornik materialov meždunarodnoj naučnoj konferencii pamjati S.O. Chan-Magomedova* (Moscow: NIITIAG RAASN, 2012) [Academic Research Institute for the Theory and History of Architecture and Urban Planning (NIITAG RASN): Materials on the conference in memory of S.O. Khan-Magomedov from January 18 to 20, 2012 in Moscow]; *Akteure des Neuen Frankfurt. Biografien aus Architektur, Politik und Kultur*, co-edited with Evelyn Brockhoff et al. (Frankfurt am Main: Societäts-Verlag, 2016).

Bernadette Reinhold. Studied art history, history, and philosophy and holds a doctorate from the University of Vienna; from 1991 on, freelance researcher at the Federal Monuments Authority Austria (BDA) in Vienna and 1997–2008 on the Commission for Provenance Research; 2000–5 on the board of the Austrian Society for Architecture (ÖGFA); 2005–8 involved in the FWF Austrian Science Fund research project about the Hofburg in Vienna at the Austrian Academy of Sciences; since 2011, co-organizer of the research network Österreichische Architektur 19. und 20. Jahrhundert; since 2008, director of the Oskar Kokoschka Center and senior scientist at the superordinate Collection and Archive at the University of Applied Arts Vienna. Research projects, publications, and teaching on architecture and urban planning from the 19th century to the present, modern art, and cultural policy in Austria from 1900 on, all accompanied repeatedly by exhibitions. Current research project *Angewandte as a Special Case. The University of Applied Arts Vienna during Austrofascism, National Socialism, and the Postwar Era;* latest publication: *Oskar Kokoschka und Österreich. Facetten einer politischen Biografie* (Vienna: Böhlau, 2022).

Günther Sandner. A senior research fellow at the Institute Vienna Circle of the University of Vienna; teaches at the University of Vienna and at the Social Academy of the Vienna Chamber of Labor. As part of an FWF Austrian Science Fund research project he heads up (P 31500), he and Christopher Burke are writing the history of Isotype (International System of Typographic Picture Education). The book he co-edited with Boris Ginner, *Emanzipatorische Bildung. Wege aus der sozialen Ungleichheit*, won the Bruno Kreisky Prize in 2021. His publications include *Otto Neurath. Eine politische Biographie* (Vienna: Zsolnay, 2014) and *Weltsprache ohne Worte. Rudolf Modley, Margaret Mead und das Glyphs-Projekt* (Vienna: Turia + Kant, 2022).

Karin Schneider. Studied history in Vienna, directs art education at the museums of the City of Linz, at Lentos, and at Nordico City Museum as well as the EU project MemAct! (2020–22); conducts research and publishes writings on participative action research in policies regarding museums, education, and history.

Her publications include "Historische Bezüge von frauen- und genderpolitischen Positionen im Austromarxismus" in *Otto Bauer und der Austromarxismus. "Integraler Sozialismus" und die heutige Linke*, ed. Walter Baier, Lisbeth Trallori, and Derek Weber (Berlin: Dietz Verlag, 2008); *Partizipative Aktionsforschung mit Kindern und Jugendlichen. Von Schulsprachen, Liebesorten und anderen Forschungsdingen*, co-written with Veronika Wöhrer, Doris Arztmann, and Teresa Wintersteller (Wiesbaden: Springer, 2016); *Das Museum verlernen? Kolonialität und Vermittlung in ethnologischen Museen*, co-edited with Stephanie Endtner and Nora Landkammer (Vienna: Zaglossus, 2021).

Antje Senarclens de Grancy. Architectural historian and associate professor at the Institute of Architectural Theory, Art History, and Cultural Sciences, Graz University of Technology. Academic studies in art history, history, and anthropology in Graz, Vienna, and Paris. Publications exploring architecture, politics and society in the 19th and 20th century, the history of the relationship between (refugee) camps and modern architecture, modernist reform movements (Werkbund, Heimatschutz), and canonization processes within the history of architecture, among others: *Keine Würfelwelt. Architekturpositionen einer "bodenständigen" Moderne. Graz 1918–1938* (Graz: HDA, 2007); *Architektur. Vergessen. Jüdische Architekten in Graz*, co-edited with Heidrun Zettelbauer (Vienna: Böhlau, 2010); "Different Housing Spaces—Space, Function, and Use of Barrack Huts in World War I Refugee Camps," in *Reflections on Camps—Space, Agency, Materiality*, co-edited with Heidrun Zettelbauer, *Zeitgeschichte* 45, no. 4 (2018) (Göttingen: V&R Unipress, 2019).

Änne Söll. Studied art history and English at Middlesex University London, Goethe University Frankfurt, and Rutgers University in New Jersey. Researcher at the universities of Dortmund and Potsdam, full professor of modern art history, visual cultural and gender studies at Ruhr Universität Bochum since 2016.

Her publications include *Der Neue Mann? Männerporträts von Otto Dix, Christian Schad und Anton Räderscheidt* (Paderborn: Fink, 2016); "Vom Stilraum zum periodroom. Wie Amerika in den Besitz europäischer Kulturgeschichte kam und sich selbst seinen eigenen Stil gab," in *Stil als (geistiges) Eigentum*, ed. Julian Blunk and Tanja Michalsky (Munich: Hirmer, 2018); *Revisiting the Past in Museums and at Historic Sites*, ed. Anca I. Lasc, Andrew McClellan, and Änne Soll (London: Routledge, 2022).

Karin Zogmayer. Studied German philology and philosophy at the University of Vienna and at Humboldt-Universität zu Berlin. Dissertation, lectures, and publications on the work of Elias Canetti. Examined and cataloged edition-relevant texts from the estate of Margarete Schütte-Lihotzky at the University Archive of the University of Applied Arts Vienna. Proposed events and exhibitions on Margarete Schütte-Lihotzky and assisted with the content involved.

Editor of Margarete Schütte-Lihotzky, *Warum ich Architektin wurde* (Salzburg: Residenz, 2004; new edition in 2019); Margarete Schütte-Lihotzky, *Millionenstädte*

Chinas. Bilder- und Reisetagebuch einer Architektin (1958) (Vienna: Springer, 2007).

Christine Zwingl. Studied architecture at the Technical University of Vienna, awarded a degree in 1985. Member of the Schütte-Lihotzky research group since 1986, processed her archive. This work resulted in a research anthology entitled *Das Werk der Architektin Margarete Schütte-Lihotzky*, funded by the Austrian Science Fund (FWF); project manager. Devised the scholarly concept and design of the 1993 exhibition on Schütte-Lihotzky's architectural oeuvre at MAK—Austrian Museum of Applied Arts, Vienna. An independent architect since 1994, taught at HTL Mödling in the civil engineering and building construction department (2000–14), lecturer at the Institute of Architectural Theory at the Technical University of Vienna, BKA grant for Margarete Schütte-Lihotzky project. Since 2014 director of the Margarete Schütte-Lihotzky Room, Vienna's third district, which was moved to her former apartment on Franzengasse in the fifth district in 2021. The Margarete Schütte-Lihotzky Center was opened at this same site in 2022.

Her publications include, among others: *Margarete Schütte-Lihotzky. Soziale Architektur. Zeitzeugin eines Jahrhunderts*, exhibition catalog, MAK, Vienna, ed. Peter Noever (Vienna: Böhlau, 1993) (she was an author in the 2nd edition in 1996); *Margarete Schütte-Lihotzky – Spuren in Wien*, ed. Christine Zwingl (Vienna: Promedia, 2021).

Thanks to all authors and also to:
Gerald Bast, Judith Burger, Claude and Nelio Dierig, Paulus M. Dreibholz, Nathalie Feitsch, Svea Gruber, Kirsten Heinsohn, Silvia Herkt, Lea Herzl, Katharina Holas, Beate Huber, Luzie Lahtinen-Stransky, Milan Mentz, Stefan Mörchen, Maike Raap, Anja Seipenbusch-Hufschmied, Dorothea and Michael Stransky, Mark Wilch, Olga Wukounig, Belinda Zauner, Gerd Zillner, Philomena and Zeno Zillner

Imprint

Editors
Marcel Bois, Research Centre of Contemporary History in Hamburg (FZH)
Bernadette Reinhold, Oskar Kokoschka Center & Collection and Archive, University of Applied Arts Vienna

Printed with the financial support of the National Fund of the Republic of Austria for Victims of National Socialism, A-Vienna

This book is the updated and slightly revised English-language edition of a volume published in 2019 following the international conference *Architecture. Politics. Gender. New Perspectives on the Life and Work of Margarete Schütte-Lihotzky*, which was held at the University of Applied Arts Vienna on October 9 and 10, 2018.

Project Management "Edition Angewandte" on behalf of the University of Applied Arts Vienna: Olga Wukounig, A-Vienna

Content and Production Editor on behalf of the Publisher: Katharina Holas, A-Vienna

Translation from German into English
Mark Wilch, A-Vienna

Proofreading/Copyediting
Belinda Zauner, A-Baden bei Wien

Design
Atelier Dreibholz, Paulus M. Dreibholz and Lea Herzl, A-Vienna

Printing
Holzhausen, the book-printing brand of Gerin Druck GmbH, A-Wolkersdorf

Paper
Munken Lynx 100 gsm and 240 gsm

Library of Congress Control Number: 2022948106

Bibliographic information published by the German National Library
The German National Library lists this publication in the Deutsche Nationalbibliografie; detailed bibliographic data are available on the Internet at http://dnb.dnb.de.

ISSN 1866-248X
ISBN 978-3-0356-2699-5
e-ISBN (PDF) 978-3-0356-2702-2
German print
ISBN 978-3-0356-1959-1

987654321 www.birkhauser.com

Cover image
Margarete Schütte-Lihotzky, 1935, photo: Franz Pfemfert, University of Applied Arts Vienna, Collection and Archive, F/136

FSC
www.fsc.org
MIX
Papier aus verantwortungsvollen Quellen
FSC® C108696